International Development Policies: Structure and Analysis

International Development Policies: Structure and Analysis

Elina Stevens

MURPHY & MOORE
www.murphy-moorepublishing.com

www.murphy-moorepublishing.com

MURPHY & MOORE

Cataloging-in-publication Data

International development policies : structure and analysis / Elina Stevens.
p. cm.
Includes bibliographical references and index.
ISBN 978-1-63987-711-9
1. Law and economic development. 2. Economic development--International cooperation. 3. Economic assistance--International cooperation. 4. International economic relations. 5. International organization. 6. International law. I. Stevens, Elina.
K3820 .I58 2023
343.07--dc23

Murphy & Moore Publishing
1 Rockefeller Plaza,
New York City,
NY 10020, USA

ISBN 978-1-63987-711-9

Contents

Preface

Development policies refer to plans or actions designed to encourage economic and social development. International development policies aim to achieve primary education, promote gender equality and empower women, reduce mortality, improve maternal health, and combat HIV/AIDS, malaria and other diseases at the international level. They also integrate the principles of sustainable development into country policies and programs to ensure environment sustainability. These policies address the special needs of the least developed countries (LDCs), land-locked developing countries (LLDCs), and small island developing states (SIDSs). Analysis of development policies is based on two types of methodologies which include qualitative research and quantitative research. Qualitative analysis includes case studies and interviews whereas quantitative analysis is based on survey research, statistical analysis, and model building. This book presents the structure and analysis of international development policies in the most comprehensible and easy to understand language. It will serve as a valuable source of reference for scholars and policy makers.

This book unites the global concepts and researches in an organized manner for a comprehensive understanding of the subject. It is a ripe text for all researchers, students, scientists or anyone else who is interested in acquiring a better knowledge of this dynamic field.

I extend my sincere thanks to the contributors for such eloquent research chapters. Finally, I thank my family for being a source of support and help.

Elina Stevens

1

Modeling and Evaluation of Policy Impact and Processes

Ousmane Badiane, Christian Henning, and Eva Krampe

In 2003, African leaders endorsed the Comprehensive Africa Agriculture Development Programme (CAADP) as the action plan for putting agriculture back on Africa's development agenda. A critical challenge for all policymakers wrestling with economic development and poverty reduction in Africa—as well as everywhere else in the world—is how to assess which programs and policies actually work. A corollary to this challenge is to identify, among the programs that do work, those that provide the best value for money (OECD 2004). A key approach of CAADP is the promotion of evidence-based policies, where it has been fully recognized that policy impact evaluation is an important prerequisite for evidence-based policy processes. In the literature, quantitative policy impact evaluation is considered a key method for generating scientific knowledge on which policies actually work best in a country. However, the incorporation of this knowledge into the political decisionmaking process is a non-trivial process. Hence, beyond generating knowledge, incorporating it into the political process is another prerequisite of an effective evidence-based policy process. In this regard, it is widely expected that active stakeholder participation will not only increase politicians' incentives to select the most efficient policies, but also increase the capacity of policy learning inherent in a political system (see e.g. Ball 1995). The principles of review, accountability, and inclusivity, which are core principles of CAADP, reflect the belief that participatory policy processes at the continental, regional, and

---

O. Badiane (✉)
International Food Policy Research Institute, Washington, DC, USA
e-mail: obadiane@cgiar.org

C. Henning
Department of Agricultural Economics, University of Kiel, Kiel, Germany

E. Krampe
European Investment Bank, Luxembourg, Luxembourg

national levels lead to improved coordination, mutual learning, and the adoption of best practices, which together should result in improved policy planning and execution, better growth, and poverty reduction outcomes.

Linking economic analysis to policy formulation and outcome is a very complex and tedious process. The problem is not just one of applying rigorous economic theory to high-quality data in order to tackle relevant questions. This is difficult enough but may still be the easiest part. A greater challenge is for the knowledge and insights generated from policy research and analysis to find their way into the decisionmaking process. And even when it does, science-based evidence forms only one part, and often not the most important part, of the understanding that influences the decisionmaking process, where imperfect political competition often induces biased incentives for politicians, impeding the implementation of available best-practice politics.

Contained in the present volume are a selection of tools and methodologies that can help to tackle the complexities in the analysis of policy processes and outcomes under the implementation of the CAADP agenda. The contributions go beyond the innovative methods and tools applied for quantitative policy impact analyses by international organizations like the Organisation for Economic Co-operation and Development (OECD), the World Bank or the European Union, as they also to examine the process behind the choice of policies and the factors that determine the likelihood of their adoption and implementation. It is the product of a workshop organized by the University of Kiel (CAU), the *International Food Policy Research* Institute (IFPRI) and the *Poverty Reduction, Equity, and Growth* Network (PEGNet) of the Kiel Institute of World Economy in 2011. The workshop brought together scholars working in the field of policy modeling and evaluation at the microeconomic and macroeconomic level or in the field of quantitative modeling of policy processes.

The various contributions in these proceedings are not targeted only to experts and interdisciplinary scholars working on empirical or theoretical research using quantitative policy modeling and evaluation techniques. They are also intended for technical experts, including policymakers and analysts from stakeholder organizations, who are involved in formulating and implementing policies to reduce poverty and to increase economic and social well-being in African countries.

In order to facilitate discussion on the recently developed evaluation methodologies and their applicability in the context of CAADP and its evaluation mechanisms, we first develop a general assessment framework. This framework incorporates guidelines and principles not only for economic policy impact evaluation, but also for methodological approaches and tools assessing policy processes quantitatively.

1 A General Framework for Policy and Policy Process Evaluation

1.1 The Basic Setup

At an abstract level, impact evaluation of a given policy instrument, say 'γ', includes two different aspects. First, it is necessary to assess the technical transformation of policy γ into relevant policy outcomes z. This transformation is captured by the technical transformation function $T(z, \gamma)$, which links specific outcomes to the policy in question. Second, different policy outcomes have to be evaluated from the viewpoint of society. Formally, welfare analysis is a tool that provides for an adequate evaluation criterion, i.e., an index function $EC(z)$. $EC(z)$ transforms each state of the world z into an index number, and by doing so allows for a consistent ordering of states. For example, $EC(z1) > EC(z2)$ implies that state $z1$ is preferred to state $z2$. Accordingly, if we were to know both functions, EC and T, evaluation would be a purely technical task. For a set of available policies $\gamma \in A$, where A is the set of all feasible policies a society can choose from, the policy with the maximal evaluation value EC would be implemented:

$$E(\gamma) = \text{Max}\{EC(z)|T(z, \gamma) = 0\} \tag{1}$$

In reality, however, an empirical specification of both the welfare function EC and the technical transformation function T is extremely complex and difficult. Conventional policy impact analyses that focus on identifying the technical transformation function usually assume a welfare function as exogenously given. The main argument for this assumption is that a comprehensive modeling of the decisionmakers' evaluation of his or her preferred outcome and of the political decisionmaking processes cannot be attained with the research approaches at hand. A corollary to this argument is that research can at best focus on the technical relationship (T) between alternative policies and outcomes, thereby offering evidence-based guidance for decisionmaking.

Even when assuming an exogenously given welfare function ($EC(\gamma)$), policy impact evaluation still remains a quite complex undertaking, because it is by no means straightforward to specify the technical transformation function. This results from many different reasons. First, policy outcomes are often formulated in terms of abstract, higher level policy objectives, e.g., equal quality of life conditions in rural and urban regions. These objectives need to be transformed into a set of measurable policy outcome indicators, which then can be systematically related to policy programs. Second, the relationship between policy programs and lower level policy objectives, as well as the relationship between the latter and higher level objectives, all reflect the behavior of people and thus require a theory of human behavior. Therefore, a quantitative specification and assessment of the technical relationship between inputs of a policy program and their effects on higher level policy objectives remains a tricky business. More importantly, disentangling the effects of a specific policy program becomes more challenging when many policy programs are implemented simultaneously.

1.2 Policy Impact Evaluation

The framework includes three major components, which are discussed in the subsequent sections. They include policy evaluation criteria, intervention logic, and evaluation methods.

1.2.1 Policy Evaluation Criteria

Clear and relevant evaluation criteria should be the starting point of developing adequate evaluation tools. Five such evaluation criteria can be distinguished (European Commission 2004):

- Relevance: What are the general needs, problems, and issues, both short and long term, that are being targeted under the policy programs? Given the identified needs, a hierarchy of general, intermediate, and specific program objectives can be derived, where objectives at a lower-level function as inputs to achieve objectives at the next higher level.
- Effectiveness: To what extent does a policy program deliver results or outputs that correspond to program objectives? Effectiveness is a technical relationship between program objectives and program results.
- Efficiency: To what extent are program objectives achieved at the lowest costs? Efficiency is a technical relationship between program inputs and program results.
- Utility: To what extent does a policy program contribute to the identified needs?
- Sustainability: To what extent does the utility of a program last after the program has been terminated?

1.2.2 Intervention Logic

Any evaluation of policy programs is based on intervention logic, or the systematic derivation of the hierarchy of measurable objectives relating a policy program, all the way from specific, operational objectives to more abstract, general policy objectives. The intervention logic, as a central evaluation tool, thus corresponds to a set of hypothetical cause-and-effect linkages that describe how an intervention is expected to attain its global objectives.

To this end, an intervention can be systematically subdivided into specific elements that are related to each other at specific stages of the project, as demonstrated in Fig. 1.

In general, we can distinguish program implementation and program effects. Any policy program starts with its implementation; for example, financial inputs or administrative capacities are used to realize specific outputs. In an investment program, for example, the inputs might correspond to a specific amount of financial resources that are spent to subsidize investment projects on farms. The output of

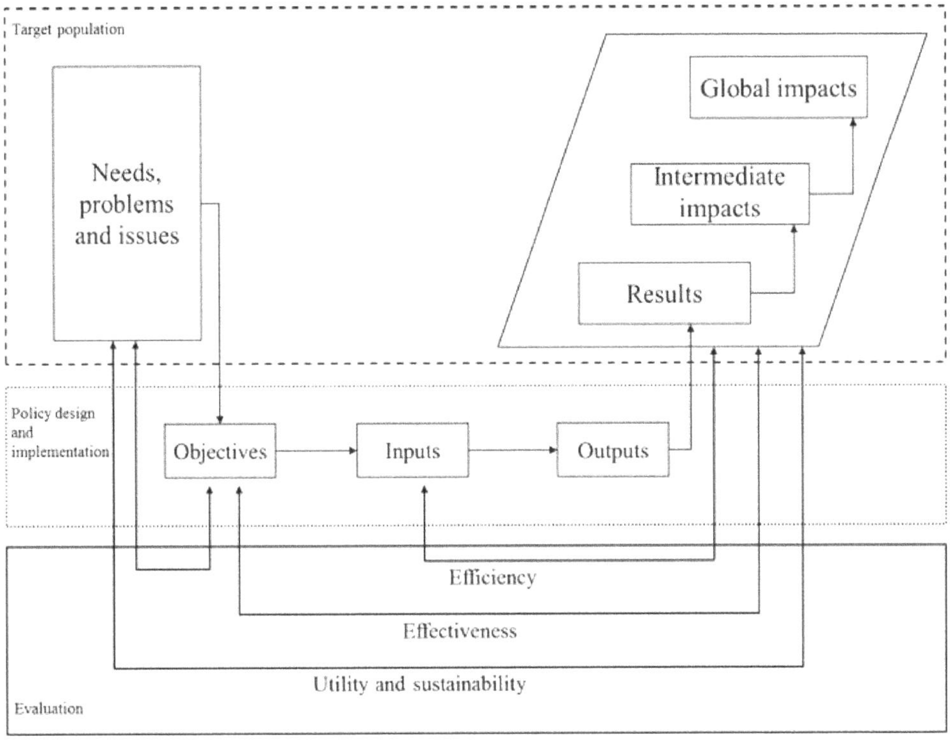

Fig. 1 Schematic presentation of a policy impact evaluation framework. Source: Authors, based on European Commission (2004)

this investment project corresponds to the number and type of investment programs that are actually subsidized. Depending on the applied implementation procedure, the number and type of investment projects might differ. In particular, if farms are heterogeneous, the type of farms that will be subsidized under a program might differ according to applied implementation procedures.

The outputs of a project generate effects, which can be further subdivided into results (short-term effects that occur at the level of direct target groups) and impacts (medium- and long-term effects). Medium-term impacts involve effects on both direct and indirect beneficiaries/recipients of assistance, while long-term effects correspond to the global impacts of a policy program. Moreover, the global impact of a policy program is related to the general needs, problems, and issues identified at a higher policy level, where the program's utility is defined as its contribution to identified needs (see Fig. 1).

1.2.3 Evaluation Methods

Any intervention logic for policy programs is based on theory. Two different evaluation approaches can be distinguished: (1) qualitative and (2) quantitative models. Qualitative models, for example the logical framework matrix, simply provide a qualitative description of the intervention logic. Quantitative impact evaluation is based on a quantitative specification of relevant cause-and-effect linkages. Quantitative evaluation models can be further subdivided into model based, and econometric policy evaluation approaches.

Model-Based Policy Evaluation

The common approach in economics for specifying an intervention logic of policy programs is to apply a theoretical model. Different approaches are available for model-based policy evaluation, ranging from simple incidence analysis, to more advanced micro and macro behavioral models, to complex micro-macro linkages models. These approaches differ regarding the set of agents and actions they consider, as well as the assumed coordination mechanism of individual actions. The complexity increases with the number of agents and the level of behavioral response that models explicitly take into account.

Simple Incidence Analysis

Simple incidence analysis ignores any behavioral response of involved actors. For example, an ex ante evaluation of a planned tax reform or a planned investment subsidization project may be based on a simple arithmetic representation of the incidence of a tax or subsidy, without simulating any policy response of involved agents (Bourguignon et al. 2002). However, policies often have important price or income effects, which in turn induce changes of agents' behavior, such as changes in supply, consumption, or labor demand behavior. A behavioral model is needed in this case.

Micro-simulation Partial Equilibrium Models

In contrast to incidence models, behavioral models take the policy responses of involved actors explicitly into account. However, there exist different types of behavioral models that differ regarding the level of response they take into account. Micro-simulation models take only the direct policy response of involved actors into account. Basically, these models are partial equilibrium models that neglect the indirect effects of policy programs resulting from agents' interaction at the macro level. The structure of these models can be described as follows:

$$x_i = F(\xi, \varphi_i, \gamma) \tag{2}$$

$$z = G(x_i, \xi, \varphi_i, \gamma) \tag{3}$$

where x_i denotes the vector of relevant behavioral variables of an individual agent i, φ and ξ denote the general and agent-specific exogenous variables, respectively, that determine individual behavior, γ is the evaluated policy, and z is the policy outcome.

For a policy evaluation, the behavioral Eq. (2) has to be estimated based on survey data. Given the specified Eqs. (2 and 3), the impact of different policies can be simulated. The relevant agents are, for example, all households or firms in a specific region. Often census data is used to provide information on their individual characteristics. The response of all relevant agents can be estimated using Eq. (3), given this information. The behavioral function $F()$ is either specified as a reduced form or an explicit functional form is derived from the underlying microeconomic optimization problem.[1] All micro-simulation models neglect the interaction of individual agents. Micro-simulation models are not adequate tools for policy evaluation if behavioral response at the micro level crucially depends on interactions among actors at the macro level.

Macro or General Equilibrium Models

General equilibrium models are designed to include policy effects at the macro level (Bourguignon et al. 2002). The most simple general equilibrium models are linear models, e.g., regional input-output models or social accounting matrices (SAMs). More advanced (nonlinear) general equilibrium models are standard computable general equilibrium (CGE) approaches. With the CGE approach, policy-induced behavioral responses at the micro level are explicitly transmitted onto the overall economy via induced price changes at the macro level. However, the explicit inclusion of macro-level effects comes at a cost. Standard CGE models are highly aggregated, assuming only a small number of representative economic agents (firms and households). Theoretically, CGE models could be more disaggregated into a large number of heterogeneous firms and households, but they become difficult to solve with the computer capacities usually available. Moreover, the empirical estimation of functional parameters of the CGE model is also a major problem due to very limited adequate data. Thus, although CGE models can be linked with a micro-accounting model, if relevant policy evaluation criteria include distributional effects, aggregated CGE models are less appropriate tools for an adequate policy evaluation (see Chapter "Sequential Macro-Micro Modelling with Behavioral Microsimulations" in this volume).

[1] A very interesting nonparametric approach applies propensity score matching techniques, originally developed as an advanced ex post evaluation technique, to simulate policy effects at the micro level (Todd and Wolpin 2006). An advantage of a nonparametric estimation strategy, when compared to parametric approaches, follows from the fact that the former are less demanding regarding data requirements and do not require any specific functional form assumptions (Todd and Wolpin 2006). However, in many cases nonparametric approaches are not applicable to ex ante policy evaluation, but stronger modeling assumptions, e.g., functional form assumption, have to be made.

Micro-Macro Linked Models

In order to deal with computational capabilities and empirical complexity issues, some authors suggest micro-macro linked models, which combine micro-simulation models and macro general equilibrium models (Robilliard et al. 2001). A full integration of micro and macro models is hard to achieve, although technically possible (Bourguignon et al. 2008). Therefore, often a sequential approach is applied where first macro models are solved and central variables of the macro model are then incorporated into corresponding micro models (Robilliard et al. 2001). Standard CGE models assume that interactions among individual agents are coordinated through perfect markets. In reality, transaction costs as well as market power imply imperfect competition and thereby perfect markets rarely exist. Of course, the standard CGE approach can be extended to include market imperfection due to transaction costs or market power. But these extended approaches are technically more demanding and therefore have been rarely applied for policy evaluation. More feasible alternatives include a linked or sequential micro-macro model, in which different micro-behavioral models can be combined with macro equilibrium models. Linked micro models include farm-household models incorporating non-market activities or nonlinear transaction costs (Singh et al. 1986).

1.3 Econometric Policy Evaluation

A general problem of model-based policy evaluation is that models are often quite complex, and an empirical specification of the model is often impossible due to limited data. Central causal relationships assumed by a model cannot easily be verified or tested empirically. Hence, it is necessary to develop methods that are able to provide empirical evidence suitable for guiding policy. This is not an easy task, because it refers to causal inferences that require special research methods that are not always easy to communicate due to their technical complexity.

This section surveys econometric methods that the economics profession has used increasingly over the past decade to estimate causal effects of policies. A causal linkage can be specified as a simple binary relationship between program participation and a relevant performance variable, e.g., the impact of participation in a training program on farm profit or employment. The most straightforward way to measure the policy impact in this context would be to compare the performance of a program participant with the counterfactual performance of the participant without participation. A major challenge of this approach is to simultaneously observe both performances, assuming participation and the counterfactual performance. The different methods applied in this area are designed to distinguish accidental association from causation. They provide empirical strategies to identify the causal impact of different reforms on any kind of policy outcomes.

The best approach to identifying program impact on a given performance variable is to conduct field experiments, i.e., to undertake a random selection of the units of interest into participating (treatment) and non-participating (control) groups in a policy program. Based on a comparison of the average performance of the randomly selected treatment and control groups, the impact of the policy program can be statistically evaluated. While experimental approaches can be applied for ex post and ex ante policy evaluation, a huge drawback of this approach is that it is extremely expensive and, for many policies, it is impossible to design sophisticated field experiments allowing a quantitative evaluation. In this case, other econometric procedures based on observational data are available that allow one to identify the true impact of a policy program assuming a non-random selection of treatment and non-treatment groups. These econometric approaches can be subdivided into non-parametric and parametric approaches. An increasingly popular non-parametric approach to policy evaluation is matching on observable factors, especially propensity score matching (PSM) (Caliendo and Hujer 2006). Matching and other econometric methods that build on the idea of controlling for observable factors have clear limitations. The policy impact is very often determined by factors that are unobserved by the researcher. This implies that PSM delivers biased results or that policy impact is heterogeneous across participants. In order to get around these problems, alternative methods have been developed. They are used to emulate experimental settings using observational data, i.e., 'natural' experiments, such as the instrumental-variable approach and the regression-discontinuity approach, or panel-data-based methods that aim to account for endogeneity.

A general cutback of all statistical models, however, is the fact that they are limited to causal inferences, i.e., empirical testing on the question of whether a given policy program achieved its intended outcome or not. In general, they are not alone suitable to elucidate the question of why or how a policy program works. Therefore, the best approach to policy evaluation is to combine model-based and econometric methods as complementary approaches, where econometric techniques are applied to identify causal relations between specific policy programs (γ) and central economic factors (θ), and model-based techniques to analyze the impact of a change in these economic factors on central outcome indicators (z). The transformation function $T(z, \gamma)$ is separated into two parts: (i) a policy impact function $\theta = PI(\gamma)$ describing the relationship between policy interventions and the economic factors θ, and (ii) a policy outcome function $PO(z, \theta)$ describing the linkages between the economic factor θ and policy outcomes z. Econometric methods are more suitable for tackling the policy impact function, whereas economic models do a better job of tracking the policy outcome function.

1.4 Modeling and Evaluation of Policy Processes

Many countries around the globe continue to apply suboptimal policies despite available scientific knowledge demonstrating the existence of policy instruments that would lead to more desirable overall economic and social outcomes. For example, there is evidence that many developing countries that still largely depend on agriculture, especially in Africa, underinvest in this sector. They especially spend too little budget on, e.g., agricultural research and extension which are areas of public investment with high returns in terms of growth and poverty reduction (Fan and Rao 2003).

Thus, evidence-based policy formulation includes, beyond the generation of scientific knowledge, the effective incorporation of this knowledge into the political decisionmaking process. The latter is by nature complex and dynamic, involves multiple actors (individuals and organizations), and is defined by local political, social (cultural and belief systems) and institutional realities (bureaucratic structures and capacities). Essentially, the policy process corresponds to an aggregation of the heterogeneous preferences of different stakeholder groups into a common policy decision. In representative democracies, preference aggregation is subdivided into two steps. First, heterogeneous voter preferences are transformed into the corresponding preferences of a subset of political representatives via democratic elections. A central property of democratic elections is their representativeness, i.e., the correspondence between the distribution of preferences among elected representatives with the distribution of preferences among the voting population. Second, the heterogeneous preferences of political representatives are aggregated into a final political decision via legislative voting procedures.

The above process can be modeled as follows: Let a society comprise of n_I different groups, where $I = 1, \ldots, n_I$ denotes the index of stakeholder groups. Further, let $U_I(z)$ denote the utility function of an individual group member $i \in I$, and w_I denotes the population share of group I. Then, an ideal policy process can be defined as a process that results in a policy choice γ^*:

$$\gamma^{ideal} = \arg\max_{\gamma} \sum_{I} w_I U_I(z) \quad s.t. \quad T(z, \gamma) = 0 \tag{4}$$

where $T(z, \gamma)$ is the political technology, that is, the subset of all policy outcomes z that can be optimally achieved by available policies γ, given existing political knowledge.

Differences between observed and ideal policy choices result from two different sources. First, a biased aggregation of society preferences, i.e., real policy processes, results in different political weights of groups when compared to the ideal democratic process. At a theoretical level, existing political economy models highlight this bias as a main cause of persisting inefficient policies. Biased political weights correspond to biased incentives of elected politicians, and result from asymmetric lobbying activities (Grossman 1994) or biased voter behavior (Bardhan and Mookherjee 2002). More recently, Persson and Tabellini (2000) highlight the role of formal constitutional rules as determinants of politicians' incentives to misrepresent society interests and choose inefficient policies.

Beyond biases resulting from the aggregation of society preferences, a second source of biased policy is that the true political technology is not fully known by the relevant political actors. Understanding the complex relationship between policy instruments and induced policy outcomes is difficult. As a result, political actors use simple mental models to understand how policies translate into outcomes. We call these simple mental models policy beliefs. Based on their policy beliefs, political actors derive their individual preferences with respect to policies. Similarly, some authors have recently highlighted the role of biased voter beliefs as a main determinant of inefficient policy choices (Beilhartz and Gersbach 2004; Bischoff and Siemers 2011; Caplan 2007). In particular, the work by Caplan (2007) has been highly recognized in public choice literature, as he has collected an impressive amount of evidence showing persistently biased voter beliefs. Based on his empirical findings, Caplan (2007) draws the rather pessimistic conclusion that democratic mechanisms of preference aggregation naturally lead to the choice of inefficient policies.

In this context, two key underlying premises that define the framework of evaluating policy processes are adopted here. The first premise is that biased voter beliefs imply biased voter behavior and hence a biased aggregation of preferences. The second premise is that politicians and lobbyists do not fully understand the complex relationship between political instruments and desired policy outcomes. Hence, beyond biased incentives, lack of political knowledge becomes another important cause of policy failure.

The evaluation of policy processes can be based on the comparison between actual, implemented policy choice γ^{actual} and the ideal policy choice γ^{ideal}: $\|\gamma^{actual} - \gamma^{ideal}\|$. $\|\|$ is the Euclidian distance. That is, the evaluation of policy processes should be able to identify political performance gaps as defined above. Policy diagnosis should also allow for the separation of identified performance gaps into incentive-induced and knowledge-based gaps. Finally, a comprehensive evaluation of policy processes should provide the possibility of developing a political therapy, i.e., the derivation of a strategy to reduce identified performance gaps. The latter in particular calls for model-based evaluation methodologies.

Our methodology is derived from the model described in Fig. 2.

Schematically, a dynamic policy process includes a sequence of political decisionmaking based on actors' policy beliefs, the transformation of the selected policy into outcomes via induced policy responses in the economic system, the translation of economic and political outcomes into political support via elections and lobbying and policy learning, i.e., the updating of policy beliefs (see Fig. 2). Policy learning occurs via two mechanisms. First, based on observed outcomes, political actors engage in observational policy learning, i.e., they update their policy beliefs by comparing observed outcomes with the policy outcomes they expected based on their initial policy beliefs. Individual observations, however, are noisy and hence individual observational learning is limited. Accordingly, political actors engage in communication learning, i.e., they update their policy beliefs based on political beliefs communicated by other actors. Within policy processes, communication learning occurs via political mass communications, i.e., the formation of a public opinion, as well as via exclusive political communication within a political elite comprising of relevant politicians and stakeholder organizations. Interestingly, the social organization of political communication processes has a significant

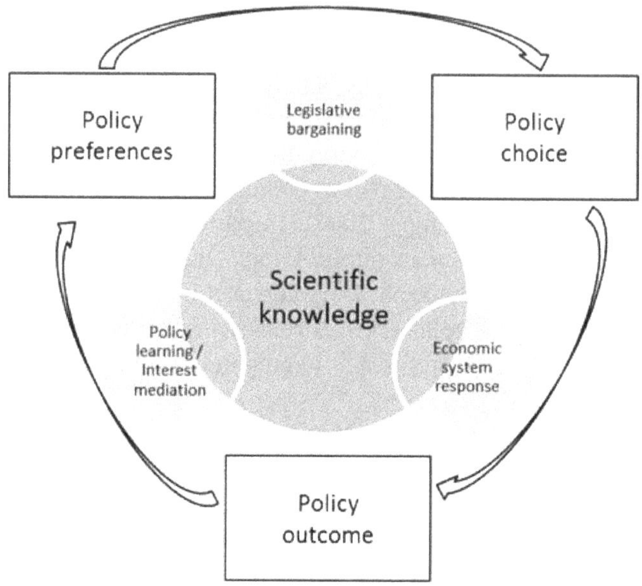

Fig. 2 Schematic representation of a policy process. Source: Authors

impact on the speed of policy learning. In particular, the structure of a communication network has a significant impact on its capacity to aggregate decentralized information within a political elite. Moreover, network structure also determines the influence of individual organizations on the policy beliefs of relevant politicians and hence the direction of the bias of political decisionmaking.

Few studies have explicitly mapped out the above processes in explaining the poor past performance of policy reforms and investment strategies, particularly in the agricultural sector. Most have offered narratives based on historical accounts, pointing to the strong role of powerful personalities, vested interests, corruption, and external pressures, in influencing policy outcomes (Clay and Schaffer 1984; Juma and Clark 1995; Keeley and Scoones 2003; Young 2005).

The challenge of analyzing participatory and evidence-based policy processes empirically is to develop an applicable model framework that allows for quantitative modeling of political decisionmaking and policy-learning processes, including the endogenous formation of a legislator's political preferences and policy beliefs. In this context, four components of a political process framework can be distinguished (see Fig. 2): (i) the derivation of politicians' incentives from electoral competition and lobbying, i.e., modeling voter behavior and interest group activities; (ii) modeling legislative bargaining, i.e., the derivation of a collective policy decision by a set of heterogeneous legislators based on constitutional rules; (iii) economic modeling of policy impacts, i.e., the transformation of policies into outcomes; and (iv) modeling of policy learning, i.e., the formation and updating of policy beliefs via observational and communication learning. The existing evaluation literature focuses only on the third component, although the other three components represent aspects of the policy process that play a key role in explaining why some nations succeed while others fail in adopting efficient and effective policies.

The current volume assembles different contributions, which together provide a comprehensive set of innovative quantitative approaches that can be used to model these various aspects of the policy process. In particular, Chapter "Modeling and Evaluation of Political Processes: A New Quantitative Approach" presents an evolutionary computable general political economy equilibrium (eCGPE) model, combining all four components listed above as an integrated quantitative approach to model and evaluate real policy processes.

2 Contributions to This Volume

Following this overview of methodological approaches to quantitative policy evaluations, the twelve contributions to these proceedings can be subdivided into two parts: I. Theory and application of quantitative policy impact evaluation models, and II. Theory and application of quantitative approaches to model and evaluate policy processes.

Part I is subdivided into three sections: 1. Macroeconomic Models, 2. Micro-Econometric Models and 3. Micro-Macro Linked Models. As an opener to Sect. 1, O. Badiane, S. Odjo and F. Wouterse present their results for CAADP-reform strategies and the long-term outlook for growth and poverty reduction of Economic Community of West African States (ECOWAS) member countries (Chapter "Comparative Analysis of Strategies and Long Term Outlook for Growth and Poverty Reduction among ECOWAS Member Countries"). They use a recursive dynamic CGE model linked with a micro accounting model, transforming economic macro shocks into individual household income changes for their analysis. The second contribution of the section is by M. Wiebelt, K. Pauw, J.M. Matovu, E. Twinmukye and T. Benson. They provide a comprehensive analysis of the different policy options to use oil revenues in Uganda (Chapter "How to Spend Uganda's Expected Oil Revenues? A CGE Analysis of the Agricultural and Poverty Impacts of Spending Options"). As their analysis focuses on the implication on poverty, a recursive dynamic CGE model is linked with a micro accounting model transferring average income changes of representative households generated in the CGE model into a corresponding change of individual household income at the micro level.

Econometric evaluation techniques are applied and discussed by S. Benin et al. in Chapter "Impact of the National Agricultural Advisory Services (NAADS) Program of Uganda: Considering Different Levels of Likely Contamination with the Treatment". In particular, they develop and apply innovative matching approaches to assess the impact of an agricultural advisory services program in Uganda based on observational data.

Furthermore, Sect. 2 contains two innovative micro-macro-linked approaches. In Chapter "Modeling Agricultural Growth and Nutrition Linkages: Lessons from Tanzania and Malawi", K. Pauw applies a CGE model that is sequentially linked with a microeconomic nutrition demand model to analyze the impact of different growth strategies on income growth and nutrition in Tanzania and Malawi. J. Lay derives and applies a macroeconomic CGE model that is sequentially linked with a reduced form model of households' occupational choices on formal and informal labor markets (Chapter "Sequential Macro-Micro Modelling with Behavioral Microsimulations"). The micro model explicitly includes household's fixed effects to include unobserved heterogeneity among households into the structural labor market model. The approach is used to empirically analyze poverty and the distributional implications of Doha round scenarios in Brazil and poverty and the distributional implications of the Bolivian gas shock.

Part II focuses on innovative quantitative models to evaluate evidence-based and participatory policy processes under CAADP. In particular, an eCGPE approach is theoretically derived and empirically applied to the CAADP reform process in Malawi. It is demonstrated how political performance and incentive gaps can be identified and quantitatively calculated using an eCGPE. This part opens with the presentation of the complete eCGPE framework by C. Henning (Chapter "Modeling and Evaluation of Political Processes: A New Quantitative Approach"). In particular, the theories used to develop an eCGPE, which includes an economic, a legislative decisionmaking, an interest mediation, and a political belief formation module, are explained. The other contributions of the section present findings from the empirical application of the framework to Malawi's policy process.

Chapters "A Network Based Approach to Evaluate Participatory Policy Processes: An Application to CAADP in Malawi" and "The Formation of Elite Communication Networks in Malawi: A Bayesian Econometric Approach" focus on the findings from the political belief formation module. Applying social network theory and methods, they analyze collective political belief formation of governmental and non-governmental actors through communication learning in networks. C. Henning and E. Krampe (Chapter "A Network Based Approach to Evaluate Participatory Policy Processes: An Application to CAADP in Malawi") also develop an evaluation framework for participatory policy processes based on the political belief formation module. C. Aßmann, E. Krampe and C. Henning (Chapter "The Formation of Elite Communication Networks in Malawi: A Bayesian Econometric Approach") test some theoretical hypotheses on the determinants of communication ties among key national stakeholder organizations, donors and central political actors. They apply an adaptation of the Bayesian estimation scheme for binary probit models, which can deal with missing values inevitably occurring within survey data.

L. Seide, C. Henning, and S. Petri (Chapter "Voter Behavior and Government Performance in Malawi: An Application of a Probabilistic Voting Model") present an analysis of voter behavior and its impact on governmental accountability and capture. They derive the implications of voter behavior on governmental accountability and capture using probabilistic voting theory.

The final chapter of Part II is by C. Henning, J. Hedtrich, L. Sene, and E. Krampe. They use the eCGPE model to provide a comprehensive analysis of the economic impacts of policy options and knowledge and political incentive gaps in Malawi (Chapter "Whither participation? Evaluating Participatory Policy Processes Using the CGPE Approach: The Case of CAADP in Malawi").

The book closes with two chapters summarizing the central practical policy implications of the presented scientific work. In particular, M. Johnson discusses how quantitative policy monitoring and evaluation systems can be translated into political action based on the empirical example of the strategic analysis and knowledge support system (SAKSS) implemented within CAADP (Chapter "Strategic Analysis and Knowledge Support Systems (SAKSS): Translating Evidence into Action"). In Chapter "Lessons Learned and Future Challenges", C. Henning and O. Badiane present lessons learned for practical policy implementations by highlighting the book's main findings in the areas of economic modeling of growth-poverty and policy-growth linkages, as well as political economy modeling of participatory policy processes. Beyond presenting innovative methodological approaches, the empirical studies in this book also shed light on the role of voters, stakeholders, and donors in participatory policy processes, and provide convincing evidence that beyond constitutional rules, policy beliefs and policy network structures are important determinants of government performance. The chapter also highlights the future outlook and challenges to the modeling and evaluation of policies and political processes.

References

Ball, R. 1995. Interest groups, influence and welfare. *Economics and Politics* 7 (2): 119–146.

Bardhan, P., and D. Mookherjee. 2002. *Relative capture of local and central governments: An essay in the political economy of decentralization*. Working Paper C99-109. Hong Kong: Center of International and Development Economics Research.

Beilhartz, H.-J., and H. Gersbach. 2004. *General equilibirium effects and voting into a crisis*. Center for Economic and Policy Research (CEPR) Discussion Paper 4454.

Bischoff, I., and L.-H. Siemers. 2011. Biased beliefs and retrospective voting: Why democracies choose mediocre policies. *Public Choice* 156 (1–2): 163–180.

Bourguignon, F., L. P. da Silva, and N. Stern. 2002. *Evaluating the poverty impact of economic policies: Some analytical challenges*. Mimeo. Washington, DC: The World Bank.

Bourguignon, F., C. Diaz-Bonilla, and H. Lofgren. 2008. *Aid, service delivery, and the millennium development goals in an economy-wide framework*. Policy Research Working Paper 4683. Washington, DC: The World Bank.

Caliendo, M., and R. Hujer. 2006. The microeconometric estimation of treatment effects – An overview. *Journal of the German Statistical Society/Allgemeines Statistisches Archiv* 90 (1): 197–212.

Caplan, B. 2007. *The myth of the rational voter – Why democracies choose bad politics*. Princeton: Princeton University Press.

Clay, E., and B. Schaffer. 1984. *Room for Manoeuvre; An exploration of public policy in agricultural and rural development*. London: Heineman Educational Books.

European Commission. 2004. *Evaluating EU activities? A practical guide for the commission services*. Luxembourg: Office for Official Publications of the European Communities.

Fan, S., and N. Rao. 2003. *Public spending in developing countries: Trends, determination and impact*. EPTD Discussion Paper 99. Washington, DC: International Food Policy Research Institute.

Grossman, J.B. 1994. Evaluating social policies: Principles and U.S. experience. *The World Bank Research Observer* 9 (2): 159–180.

Juma, C., and N. Clark. 1995. Policy research in sub-Saharan Africa: An exploration. *Public Administration and Development* 15 (2): 121–137.

Keeley, J., and I. Scoones. 2003. *Understanding environmental policy processes: Cases from Africa.* London: Earthscan.

OECD (Organisation for Economic Co-operation and Development). 2004. *Analysis of the 2003 CAP Reform.* Number 16. 2003. Paris: OECD.

Persson, T., and G. Tabellini. 2000. *Political economics – Explaining economic policy.* Cambridge: MIT Press.

Robilliard, A.-S., F. Bourguignon, and S. Robinson. 2001. *Crisis and income distribution: A micro-macro model for indonesia.* Mimeo. Washington, DC: The World Bank.

Singh, I., L. Squire, and J. Strauss. 1986. *Agricultural household models. Extensions, applications, and policy.* Baltimore: The Johns Hopkins University Press.

Todd, P. E., and K. I. Wolpin. 2006. *Ex-ante evaluation of social programs.* Penn Institute for Economic Research Working Paper 06-022. Philadelphia: University of Pennsylvania. http://ssrn.com/abstract=931393.

Young, J. 2005. Research, policy and practice: Why developing countries are different. *Journal of International Development* 17: 727–734.

Ousmane Badiane is the Director for Africa at the International Food Policy Research Institute (IFPRI), based in Washington, DC. He oversees the Institute's regional offices for West and Central Africa, in Dakar, Senegal, and Eastern and Southern Africa, in Addis Ababa, Ethiopia. He received a Master's Degree and PhD in agricultural economics from the University of Kiel in Germany. His awards include being selected as a 2015 Yara Prize Laureate, a Doctoral Degree Honoris Causa from the University of KwaZulu Natal in South Africa and induction as Distinguished Fellow of the African Association of Agricultural Economics.

Christian Henning is professor and chair of agricultural economics, University of Kiel (Germany). He studied economics, agricultural economics, sociology, political science and mathematics. He earned a PhD in economics, in agricultural economics and in political science. His main areas of specialization are applied political economy and applied economic modelling of agricultural policies. To date he has published five books and various articles in refereed journals including PLoS ONE, American Journal of Agricultural Economics, European Review of Agricultural Economics, Journal of Public Policy, Journal of Mathematical Sociology and Journal of Theoretical Politics.

Eva Krampe is an agricultural sector expert at the European Investment Bank. She studied agricultural economics and earned a PhD in agricultural economics at the University of Kiel (Germany). Her main areas of specialization are Agricultural Policies in the European Union and Sub-Saharan Africa, Applied Political Economy, Agriculture Value Chain Finance, and Economic Analysis of Agricultural Investment Projects.

Part I
Perspectives on Economic Policies and their Modeling

2

Techniques for Poverty Reduction and Growth: A Comparative Study

Ousmane Badiane, Sunday P. Odjo, and Fleur Wouterse

1 Introduction

The Common Agricultural Policy of ECOWAS (ECOWAP) was adopted in January 2005, following a close consultation among member states and regional professional organizations. The adoption came <2 years after the launch of the Comprehensive Africa Agriculture Development Program (CAADP) under the New Partnership for Africa's Development (NEPAD), an initiative of the African Union. In March 2005, ECOWAS organized, in Bamako, Mali, the Regional Implementation Planning Meeting for CAADP in West Africa. The meeting reviewed the objectives, targets, and principles of CAADP and their alignment with ECOWAP, and confirmed the latter as the political as well as institutional framework for the implementation of the former in the West Africa region. In May 2005, ECOWAS and the NEPAD Secretariat developed a joint ECOWAP/CAADP action plan for the period 2005–2010 for the development of the agricultural sector.

In adopting CAADP, African governments had, amongst others, set for their countries a collective goal of achieving a 6% agricultural growth rate as a key strategy toward achieving the Millennium Development Goal of reducing poverty to 50% of its 1990 level by 2015. They had also opted for a partnership framework to mobilize the required funding to achieve the above growth rate, including the allocation by national governments of a budget share of at least 10% to the agricultural sector. Finally, CAADP also reflects an option for evidence and outcome based planning and implementation in support of an inclusive sectoral review and dialogue process, in line with the broader NEPAD peer review and accountability principle. A key element of ECOWAP/CAADP is, therefore, to

O. Badiane (✉) • S.P. Odjo • F. Wouterse
International Food Policy Research Institute, Washington, DC, USA
e-mail: o.badiane@cgiar.org

support and add value to the efforts of individual member states, where necessary, to ensure that they meet the above growth, budgetary, and poverty reduction targets and align with the above principles.

An important part of the planning work carried out by the technical teams in individual member states consisted of reviewing past, current, and emerging country efforts against the above objectives. This includes:

1. Examining the recent growth performance of the agricultural sector, as well as future growth and poverty outcomes based on observed trends;
2. Determining how such outcomes compare with the targets established for the sector under the ECOWAP/CAADP agenda and how they compare with the Millennium Development Goal to halve the proportion of people living on less than a dollar a day (MDG1);
3. Measuring the prospects of meeting these targets and analyzing the implications for future sector growth and poverty-reduction strategies;
4. Estimating the long term funding needs to accelerate agricultural growth and achieve the poverty MDG.

The embracing of ECOWAP/CAADP as the centerpiece of poverty-reduction strategies by member states also implies that agriculture and its individual subsectors must play a primary role as leading sources of pro-poor growth at the national and rural levels. Successful implementation of the agenda at the country level should therefore be guided by a good understanding of the impact of sector wide growth and growth within individual agricultural subsectors on income and poverty levels among different categories of rural households and across geographic zones.

To facilitate implementation of ECOWAP/CAADP, the ECOWAS Commission established a task force and mobilized the necessary technical expertise and funding for the preparation of regional and national agricultural investment programs, including US$9 million of its own funds. The technical preparation of the National Agricultural Investment Plans (NAIPs) was coordinated by the ministries in charge of integration, led by the ministries in charge of agriculture, and carried out by a team of national and regional experts, with assistance from the International Food Policy Research Institute (IFPRI) and the Regional Strategic Analysis and Knowledge Support System (ReSAKSS), established at the International Institute of Tropical Agriculture (IITA).

The current report summarizes the content of the NAIPs as well as the findings of the technical analysis that has guided their formulation. It is organized around the four main questions that constitute the focus of the analytical work to guide country level planning processes. These questions deal with the key sources of agricultural growth and related impact on poverty levels; the extent to which individual countries are on track to meet the CAADP growth and budgetary targets; the required growth rates and expenditure levels to achieve alternative growth and poverty reduction outcomes; and finally the degree of realism of proposed country investment plans to achieve the CAADP growth and budget targets.

1.1 What Are the Key Sources of Agricultural Growth and Poverty Reduction in ECOWAS Countries?

Figures 1 and 2 show the recent growth and poverty reduction performance among ECOWAS countries compared to other African countries. Figure 1 categorizes countries in four groups based on the rates of agricultural growth and poverty reduction at the start of the new millennium. Countries that perform better overall with higher rates of growth (>6%) and relatively lower rates of poverty (<40%) would occupy the North-West quadrant. The opposite holds for countries in the South-East quadrant. On the whole, the ECOWAS region seems to perform better in terms of recent growth but shows relatively higher average rates of poverty. Between 1999 and 2005, the agricultural sector in the region grew by 5.0% a year, well above the African average of 3.3%. However, the average poverty rate in the region (50.2%) for the same period is higher than the African average (45.6%). As a result, only two ECOWAS countries, Cape Verde and The Gambia, are found in the North-West corner of Fig. 1. In contrast, a majority of its member countries, eight in all, are assembled in the South-East corner. Figure 2 presents a separate distribution of ECOWAS countries with respect to both past agricultural growth and poverty outcomes: 54% of countries are in group IV, with growth rates that are below 6% and poverty rates that exceed 40%.

A recursive dynamic version of the standard IFPRI Lofgren-Harris-Robinson CGE model coupled with a micro-simulation module is used to simulate future agricultural growth and its impact on poverty levels in individual ECOWAS

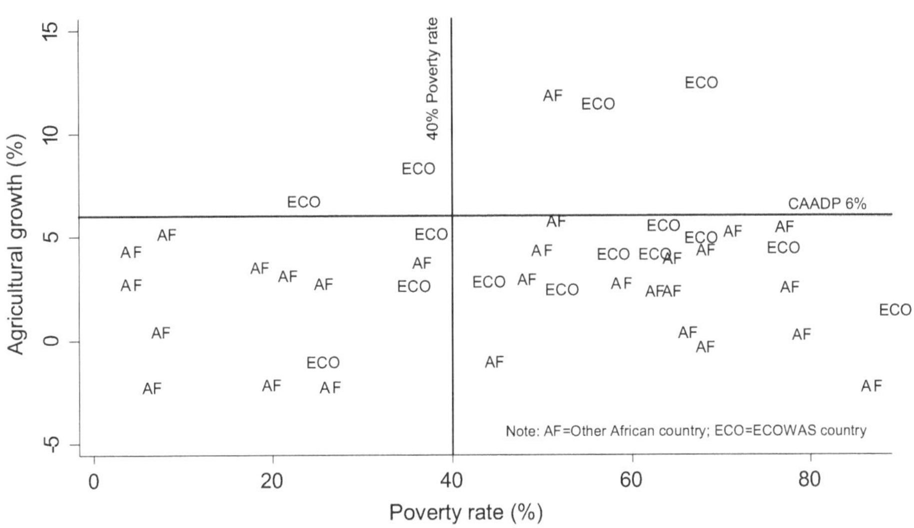

Fig. 1 Position of ECOWAS with respect to CAADP growth and poverty targets (1999–2005). Source: World Development Indicators (2008). Notes: AF indicates a non-ECOWAS African country and ECO an ECOWAS member country

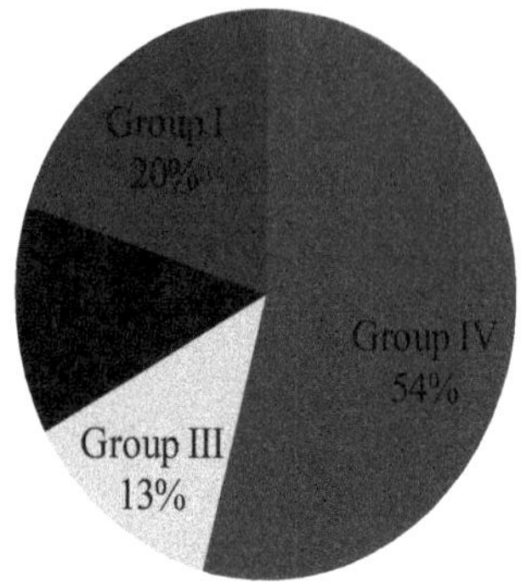

Fig. 2 Distribution of ECOWAS countries with respect to CAADP growth and poverty targets (1999–2005). Source: World Development Indicators (2008). Note: Group I countries have growth rates <6% and poverty rates <40%; group II countries have growth rates >6% but poverty rates <40%; group III countries have growth rates >6% and poverty rates >40%; and group IV countries have <6% growth rates and poverty rates >40%

member countries.[1] Due to lack of sufficient data, instead of the CGE model a simplified model was used for The Gambia and Liberia. Table 1 summarizes the results of the simulation for 13 ECOWAS member countries. The first two columns compare the simulated reductions in poverty rates resulting from an additional 1% point increase in the agricultural and non-agricultural rates of growth through to 2015. Although the simulations are run separately for each sector, the prices, activity levels, and factor incomes in the other sectors also change. Hence, the observed decline in poverty rates resulting from growth in one of the sectors in reality also reflects the effect of changes in the remaining sectors. Given that the latter changes emanate from the intersectoral multiplier effects induced by growth in the sector under consideration, we attribute the entire reduction in poverty to that sector. The figures in the Table represent the sectoral shares in the combined decline in poverty rates. The contribution of agricultural growth is consistently higher but diverges considerably across countries: from 10–20% higher in Benin, Ghana, and Senegal to nearly three times higher in Cape Verde, Côte d'Ivoire, Nigeria, and Togo. For most other countries, the contribution of agriculture is at least 50% higher compared to other sectors.

The importance of accelerated agricultural growth for poverty reduction in individual countries is demonstrated by the figures in the last two columns. They indicate the contribution by 2015 of an additional 1% point increase in the rate of agricultural growth to farm incomes and poverty reduction in various ECOWAS countries. Accelerating the rate of agricultural growth as indicated above would raise agricultural GDP (value added) by amounts ranging from US$21 million in the Gambia to as much as nearly $400 million in Mali. The corresponding reduction in the national poverty rates is shown in the last column and hovers around 10% for

[1]See Löfgren et al. (2002) for description and Löfgren (2001) and Thurlow (2004) for other applications of the model.

Table 1 Agricultural growth and poverty reduction in ECOWAS countries

	Sectoral contribution to poverty reduction resulting from an additional 1% point of sectoral growth by 2015		Growth and poverty impact of an additional 1% point agricultural growth by 2015	
	Due to Agricultural growth	Due to Non-agricultural growth	Increase in Agricultural Value Added (US$ million)	Reduction in national poverty rate (%)
Benin	52.5	47.5	270.9	−10.7
Burkina Faso	60.0	40.0	215.6	−10.3
Cape Verde	72.0	28.0	27.5	−25.9
Gambia	66.7	33.3	20.8	−11.1
Ghana	54.0	46.0	296.2	−2.9
Guinea	59.2	40.8	57.0	−10.0
Côte d'Ivoire	73.0	27.0	498.5	−6.5
Liberia	69.6	30.4	53.0	−11.9
Mali	65.2	34.8	389.5	−6.7
Niger	60.0	40.0	253.0	−6.5
Nigeria	75.0	25.0	NA	NA
Senegal	56.6	43.4	132.0	−12.6
Togo	75.0	25.0	231.0	−9.8

Source: Model simulation results for ECOWAS countries. Figures for Nigeria and Ghana are from Diao et al. (2010) and Breisinger et al. (2008), respectively

most countries. It is highest for Cape Verde, Senegal, and Liberia and lowest for Ghana, where it amounts to <3%.

Although accelerated growth of the agricultural sector as a whole may be the most promising strategy currently available to ECOWAS countries for poverty reduction, such a strategy must also recognize that agricultural sub-sectors do not contribute to the same extent to growth and poverty reduction. The importance of the contribution to growth of each subsector is determined by its initial share in income and employment and its potential for future growth. For each country, the impact on growth and poverty reduction resulting from an incremental 1% point increase in the rate of growth by 2015 in individual subsectors was simulated. The leading sectors in terms of poverty reduction impact are listed in Table 2. For most countries, the food staples subsector has the greatest potential to contribute to increases in farm incomes and poverty reduction. Livestock also emerges as a strategic subsector, in particular among Sahelian countries. The main message from Table 2 should not be to identify winners but rather to highlight the relative contribution of various subsectors. Given limited growth potential and the geographic as well as demographic implications of growth in individual subsectors, the best strategy would be to marry such concerns with the priority ranking to harness the contribution of a broad range of subsectors. In fact, results from the same simulations show that isolated strategies exclusively targeting a commodity or a subsector would be less effective for poverty reduction than a comprehensive strategy aiming for largely diversified agricultural and non-agricultural growth.

Table 2 Strategic agricultural subsectors for agricultural growth and poverty reduction

Benin	Food crops (maize, roots and tubers)[a]
Burkina Faso	Cattle and sorghum/millet
Cape Verde	Food crops
Côte d'Ivoire	Yam, cassava and plantains
The Gambia	Cereals (millet/sorghum)[a] and livestock
Ghana	Root crops and fisheries
Guinea	Rice
Guinea Bissau	Food crops and fisheries
Liberia	Food crops
Mali	Food crops (rice; millet/sorghum)[a]
Niger	Livestock
Nigeria	Cassava, Rice
Senegal	Livestock and food crops (millet/sorghum; rice)[a]
Sierra Leone	Cassava, rice
Togo	Food crops

Source: Model simulation results for ECOWAS countries. Figures for Nigeria and Ghana are from Diao et al. (2010) and Breisinger et al. (2008), respectively

[a]Country SAMs do not usually disaggregate the food sector. The subsectors in parentheses are added here only for the purpose of illustrating the leading food commodities in the respective countries

1.2 Are ECOWAS Countries on Track to Meeting CAADP's Growth and Poverty Reduction Targets by 2015?

Under current trends or business-as-usual (BAU), agricultural growth among ECOWAS countries is projected to stabilize at around 4–5% by 2015, as indicated in the first column of Table 3.[2] Although these rates are high by historical standards for most countries, they are less than the 6% targeted under CAADP. Mali and Nigeria are the only countries with expected rates of growth that are close to that target. It can also be seen from the figures in the third column that the projected rates of growth under current trends would not allow any county, except Cape Verde and Ghana, to achieve the MDG1 target of halving poverty by 2015. Senegal and Sierra Leone and, to a lesser extent, Burkina would come close. In three countries, Benin, Côte d'Ivoire and Liberia, the rate of poverty in 2015 is expected to be, respectively, 18%, 37% and 24% higher in 2015 compared to 1990. The problem in these countries is that poverty has continued to rise after 1990 in the face of severe economic contraction in the first and prolonged civil wars in the other two countries. The decline in poverty resulting from projected agricultural growth under current trends would not be sufficient to offset the increase in the poverty rate by 2015.

[2]Current trends describes the period leading up to the signing of the CAADP compact, which for most countries refers to the first decade of the 2000s.

Table 3 Long term growth and poverty outcomes under alternative scenarios (%)

Country	Agricultural growth rate by 2015 under BAU/current trends	Agricultural growth rate by 2015 under pre-CAADP strategies	Poverty reduction by 2015 under current trends	Poverty reduction by 2015 under pre-CAADP strategies	Poverty reduction by 2015 under CAADP 6% growth target
Benin	5.1	14.3	17.7	−55.9	9.4
Burkina Faso	5.1	5.3	−40.0	−44.1	−50.5
Cape Verde	2.6	5.0	−61.0	−75	−78.0
Gambia	3.7	3.8	−9.8	−10.4	−11.3
Ghana	4.2	7.5	−50.1	−54	−66.0
Guinea	3.0	3.2	−25.9	−28.2	−42.2
Côte d'Ivoire	2.5	2.6	37.0	35.3	10.0
Liberia	5.0	4.0[a]	24.3	24.2	22.6
Mali	5.5	8.5	−11.0	−29	−14.1
Niger	4.4	6.2	−6.5	−17.4	−16.6
Nigeria	5.7	9.5	−10.0	−30.0[b]	[c]
Senegal	4.1	NA	−43.8	NA	−49.7
Sierra Leone	4.2	NA	−42.5	NA	−47.6
Togo	4.7	5.0	−17.2	−19.4	−26.4

Source: Model simulation results for ECOWAS countries. Figures for Nigeria and Ghana are from Diao et al. (2010) and Breisinger et al. (2008), respectively
NA Not applicable
Notes: [a] The rate of growth is projected to decline as the country transitions out of the immediate post-war recovery period (current trends scenario). [b] The target year chosen by Nigeria is 2017. [c]There were no separate simulations of this scenario, given that the country was already growing at 5.7% under the current trends scenario

Prior to embracing CAADP, many countries had on-the-shelf strategies that pre-date the signing of the Compact and were at difference stages of readiness for implementation. The implied growth rates under these strategies, assuming that they could be successfully implemented and their declared targets achieved, are listed in the second column of the Table. The rates are universally higher than projected rates under current trends. The only exception is Liberia, for which the scenario under current trends refers to the post-conflict period. For the region as a whole, the average rate of growth for the agricultural sector would increase from under 5% under status quo to slightly more than 6%, thus meeting the CAADP growth target. However, for several of the countries, such as Benin, Nigeria, and Mali, the implied growth rates are significantly higher than would be expected based on recent performance, hence suggesting a problem of realism of declared investment and growth targets under these strategies. The implied rate of growth is high for Ghana as well, relative to historical records, but is less challenging in absolute terms than the rates for the other three countries. Nevertheless, the projected rates of growth for the majority of countries would still fall well short of the CAADP target of 6%.

With respect to the goal of poverty reduction, Benin would be the only country to join Ghana and Cape Verde in halving poverty rates below the 1990 levels under the present scenario, as shown in column 4. It is, however, clearly unrealistic to expect Benin's agricultural sector to nearly triple its pre-CAADP rate of growth to 14.3% a year by 2015. Strategies for all other countries would imply changes in poverty levels that are significantly below the MDG1 target. And for the two post-conflict countries, Liberia and Côte d'Ivoire, poverty rates would still be considerably higher than their 1990 levels: by nearly 25% and 35%, respectively. In contrast, the adoption and successful implementation of strategies and programs that would enable all ECOWAS member countries to achieve the 6% CAADP growth target would lead to substantial reduction in poverty rates across the region, although less than half of the countries would be expected to reach MDG1 by 2015 (fifth column). The challenge in realizing the poverty MDG by 2015 is made difficult for Benin, Côte d'Ivoire, and Liberia because poverty rates in these countries have continued to rise after 1990 and have not stabilized or started to decline before the end of that decade. In the case of Liberia, the poverty rate jumped from 61% in 1990 to 84% in 2007. Under continuation of growth trends during the period leading up to the signing of the CAADP compact, with a rate of 5%, as shown in the first column, the rate of poverty by 2015 would have fallen by <10% points to 76%, still close to 25% above the 1990 level. Because the rate of growth under current trends is already close to the CAADP target and projected to even decline slightly under implementation of pre-CAADP strategies, the rate of poverty in Liberia is significantly higher than the 1990 level in all of these scenarios.

In Côte d'Ivoire, the rate of poverty rose by 50% from 32% in 1993 to 49% in 2008. The achievable reduction in poverty under the BAU scenario or the implementation of pre-CAADP strategies is <5% points for that country. Realization of the CAADP growth targets would have merely brought poverty levels close to their levels of the early 1990s. The increase in poverty during the 1990s was less considerable for Benin. Poverty level estimates in that country rose from slightly more than 25% in 1990 to 36% in 2006. Under the BAU scenario, poverty levels would fall to 30% by 2015, corresponding to a decline of about 18% compared to the 1990 level.

1.3 How Fast Should ECOWAS Countries Grow to Achieve the Poverty MDG? How Much Would They Have to Spend?

In order to achieve the goal of halving poverty by 2015, many countries would have to reach double digit rates of growth in the agricultural sector: between around 12% and 15% for Benin, Mali, The Gambia, Niger and Côte d'Ivoire, and as much as 26% for Liberia, as shown in the first column of Table 4. A history of civil war explains the very serious situation in the latter country. These extremely high growth rates indicate that it will be impossible for these countries to achieve the

Table 4 Long term agricultural growth and funding requirements

Country	Required agricultural growth rate to achieve the poverty MDG target by 2015 (%)	Required agricultural growth rate to achieve the poverty MDG target by 2020 (%)	Required agricultural funding growth rate to achieve the poverty MDG target by 2015 (%)	Required agricultural funding growth rate to achieve the poverty MDG target by 2020 (%)	Required agricultural funding growth rate to achieve CAADP 6% target rate by 2015 (%)
Benin	13.1	9.1	22.8	13.9	7.9
Burkina Faso	7.1	5.9	11.6	9.0	9.1
Cape Verde	–	–	–	–	11.2
Gambia	14.4	8.6[a]	99.3	59.3[a]	19.6
Ghana	–	–	–	–	21.7
Guinea	10.3	7.5	33.5	26.5	12.3
Côte d'Ivoire	14.8	9.0	62.2	25.1	27.0
Liberia	26.1	14.6[a]	117.7	65.7[a]	27.0
Mali	12.5	8.1	45.8	13.7	8.2
Niger	11.9	9.0	25.1	18.2	26.5
Nigeria	–	9.5[a]	–	23.8[a]	4.7[b]
Senegal	–	6.8[c]	–	10.0[c]	7.6
Sierra Leone	–	–	–	–	10.0
Togo	9.6	6.9	74.2	43.1	35.4

Source: Model simulation results for ECOWAS countries

Notes: Not applicable as these countries are already on track under current trends to achieving the poverty MDG by 2015 (Cape Verde and Ghana) or scenarios were otherwise not relevant or feasible

[a]Projection years are 2017 for Nigeria and 2025 for The Gambia and Liberia

[b]For Nigeria, this is the required agricultural spending growth rate to sustain current growth trends, which at 5.7% is nearly identical to the CAADP target of 6%

[c]For Senegal, the numbers shown correspond to the required agricultural growth rate and funding growth rate to achieve the government's objective of the reducing poverty rate to 17% by 2020

poverty reduction goal by 2015. Some could, however, do so by 2020, namely Benin, Côte d'Ivoire, Mali and Niger, although all would require growth rates of around 9%, which by historical standards are still high (Table 3, second column). For The Gambia and Liberia, the poverty MDG could not be achieved by 2020 but could be reached by 2025, if they were to realize agricultural growth rates of nearly 9% and 15%, respectively. While it is true that post-conflict countries can sometimes grow rapidly during the recovery phase, whether Liberia would be able to sustain such a high growth rate over a long time is questionable.

The extent of the challenge for many countries in achieving the poverty MDG or the CAADP growth target is also illustrated by the required rise in public funding for the agricultural sector. As shown in the third column of Table 4, the required funding growth rate to achieve the poverty MDG by 2015 is prohibitively high for most countries. The required annual rate of increase in public expenditure remains still extremely high, even if the target date for achieving MDG1 is moved to 2020. For six of the eleven countries for which estimates are available, funding for the agricultural sector would have to rise by around 20% or more annually. The remaining countries would still have to expand funding for the sector by double digit rates or close to that in the case of Burkina Faso. Realization of the MDG poverty target by ECOWAS member countries is therefore not only a question of physically achievable agricultural growth but also a question of financial resource mobilization capacity.

The significance of the financial resources constraint is illustrated by the increase in funding required for achieving the CAADP target of 6% growth through to 2015. Although the increase in funding may be feasible for several of the countries, it is still quite challenging and would nonetheless not be sufficient to allow any of the countries to realize the poverty MDG, as can be seen from the last columns of Tables 3 and 4. The only exception would be Burkina Faso. A look at current levels of sectoral funding sheds light on the feasibility of the pace of funding increase that is called for under the various scenarios. Figure 3 below presents the share of agricultural sector funding for the various countries in the latest year for which the information is available. Several countries such as Benin, Côte d'Ivoire, Nigeria, Sierra Leone and Togo are currently allocating the lowest share of country budgets to agriculture. The scope of raising the level of agricultural funding should, a priori, be greater in these countries. For instance, achieving the CAADP growth target by 2015 or MDG1 by 2020 in Benin or Mali would call for annual rates of growth in agricultural funding of around 8% and 14%, respectively. Starting from agricultural sector budget shares in the range of 9–10%, there may be some room to achieve such increases in sectoral spending. The scope for expanding agricultural sector spending is greater in the case of Nigeria, which spends currently only about 3% of

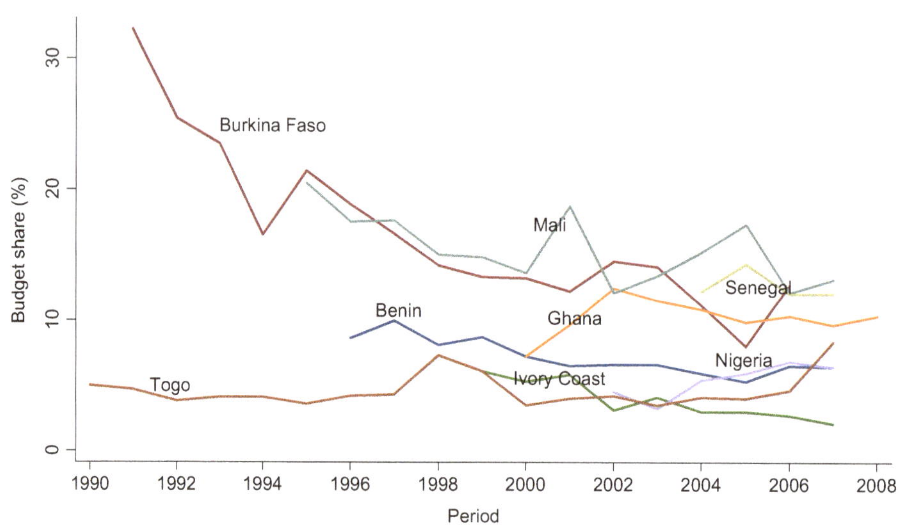

Fig. 3 Trends in pre-compact agricultural sector budget shares (%). Source: Based on agricultural budget data survey across West Africa countries

Table 5 Public expenditure allocation to agriculture and efficiency

	Agricultural sector budget share at time of compact signing (%)[a]	Estimated expenditure elasticity of agricultural growth
Benin	8.6	0.26
Burkina Faso	21.2	0.24
Cape Verde	1.3	0.11
Gambia	6.6	0.15
Ghana	4.9	0.15
Guinea	13.7	0.25
Côte d'Ivoire	3	0.25
Liberia	6	0.22
Mali	9.7	0.25
Niger	22.3	0.53
Nigeria	3.4	0.39
Senegal	19.2	0.48
Sierra Leone	2.8	0.24
Togo	3.2	0.11

Source: Budget shares are from respective country CAADP Roundtable Brochures No. 4 (http://www.resakss.org); elasticities are based on model simulation results for ECOWAS countries. The average elasticity estimate for Africa by Fan et al. (2008) as a whole is 0.31

[a]Current refers to the latest year for which data is available at time of compact signing

its budget on agriculture. The required rate of increase of 24% of sectoral funding to achieve MDG1 by 2017 should be considered realistic and feasible.

The other challenge related to meeting the funding requirement of achieving the CAADP growth and MDG poverty targets is reflected in the numbers in the last column of Table 5. Out of 13 ECOWAS countries for which estimates are available, only three show an elasticity of agricultural growth with respect to public expenditure that is above the African average of 0.31 estimated by Fan et al. (2008). For many of these countries, therefore, achieving the CAADP growth target by 2015 or MDG1 within the next 10 years would require both an increase in the level and in the efficiency of agricultural sector funding. This is because these countries are already spending relatively high shares of their budgets on agriculture and also have historically recorded relatively lower levels of responsiveness of agricultural growth to public sector spending. Other countries have very little room to raise already very high shares of agricultural spending and thus would need to focus primarily on raising the efficiency of funding to the sector. Burkina Faso, for instance, would need to expand sectoral spending by <10% annually to meet the CAADP growth target and realize MDG1 by 2020 (Table 3). However, the country is already allocating more than 20% of its budget to agriculture (Table 5). On the other hand, the elasticity of agricultural growth with respect to public funding in that country is estimated at 0.24 or 20% below the average African estimate. Gambia, Liberia, and Togo, on the other hand, are currently spending much less on agriculture but require a significantly larger increase in agricultural spending (above 20%) to meet either the CAADP growth target or MDG1 by 2020. The three countries also have historically lower expenditure elasticities of growth compared to the African average, with estimates of 0.15, 0.22, and 0.11, respectively. Niger and Senegal are in a peculiar situation characterized by high sector spending shares and above-average public expenditure elasticities of growth but still needing to further increase sectoral funding, albeit moderately in the case of Senegal, to achieve the CAADP growth and MDG1 poverty targets.

The CAADP target of allocating at least 10% of national budgets to agriculture translates the conviction that achieving the growth target would require most countries to significantly raise the level of funding allocated to the sector. The figures in Table 5 show where individual ECOWAS member countries stand with respect to the budget target. Although the average agricultural sector budget share of 11% for ECOWAS as a whole is above the CAADP target, there is a wide variation across countries with shares ranging from about 3% in Sierra Leone to 22% in Niger.

Five of the 13 countries for which data is available, namely Burkina, Mali, Ghana, Niger and Senegal, have managed to allocate at least 10% of their budget to agriculture. The first two have had historically high levels of agricultural funding, which is primarily explained by heavy subsidies to the cotton sector. Senegal has recently considerably expanded funding for agriculture under a variety of presidential programs.

The funding levels do not only vary across counties, they have also been unstable over time. More noticeably, they have trended downwards for most countries during the decade and a half preceding the adoption of the CAADP expenditure target. The declining trend has continued in Ghana, Nigeria and Mali up until the time of compact signing, as shown by a comparison of shares in Table 5 and by considering the shares for the three countries at the end of the period shown in Fig. 3. In contrast, Senegal, Burkina, and to a lesser extent Benin have raised sector expenditures going into the CAADP roundtable and the signing of the compact. On the other hand, Togo went from a stable and rising trend in expenditure levels to a sharp drop by the time of the signing of the CAADP compact. The change in trends in the latter country can be explained by the political crisis and interruption of external funding for the sector for most of the 2000s. The continued decline in sectoral funding in Côte d'Ivoire in the period leading up to the signing of the compact can also be explained by the political crisis in that country and its impact on local fiscal resources and domestic services delivery institutions.

The likelihood of countries expanding and sustaining levels of agricultural sector funding is not only a function of political will but also of domestic fiscal capacities. Figure 4 presents domestic resources as a share of total agricultural spending. In most countries, the domestic share represents 60% or less of total agricultural sectoral spending over the nearly 20 year period covered by the data.

In order to achieve the CAADP budget target by relying only on domestic sources, most countries would have to nearly double their current share of domestic resources in total agricultural spending. The mobilization of external funding will therefore be a critical component of CAADP implementation among ECOWAS countries. This is particularly so for Niger and Burkina, which already allocate a

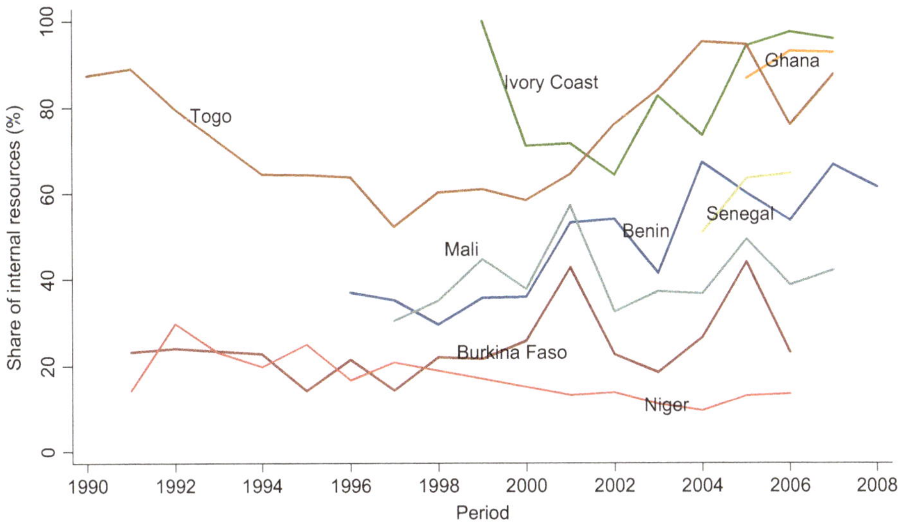

Fig. 4 Share of internal resources in agricultural spending (%). Source: Based on agricultural budget data survey across West Africa countries

significant share of overall funding to agriculture but rely on external sources for 80% or more of the funding for agriculture.

In addition to the level and efficiency of funding, the degree of actual budget execution has historically been the third dimension of the problem of effective financing of agricultural growth among African countries. As shown in Fig. 5, the average rate of disbursement of agricultural budgets is distinctly lower than the rate of overall budget execution, which for most countries is in the 80% range or lower. The exceptions are Burkina and Senegal, which show higher execution rates for agriculture, although it is to be noted that Burkina exhibits an extremely low rate of overall budget execution of <50%. High performers in terms of agricultural budget disbursement include Senegal, Nigeria and Ghana with execution rates exceeding 90%; lagging behind are Burkina, Côte d'Ivoire, and Togo. The key message from Fig. 5 is that efforts to increase agricultural funding under CAADP will have to address the constraints to effective budget execution, which appears to be a general problem and not specific to the agricultural sector.

1.4 How Consistent Are Agricultural Investment Priorities and Related Growth and Poverty Outcomes Among ECOWAS Countries?

The National Agricultural Investment Plans (NAIPs) are the next step in the CAADP implementation process after the agreement around key policy, budgetary, and partnership priorities during the roundtable. They define specific sub-sector objectives and identify specific activities to be funded. The main priority sectors

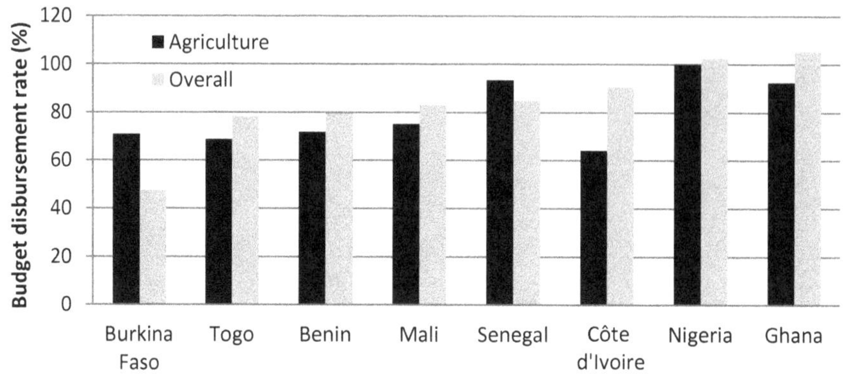

Fig. 5 Agricultural and overall budget disbursement rates (%; latest year). Source: Based on ReSAKSS survey of agricultural budget data across West Africa countries

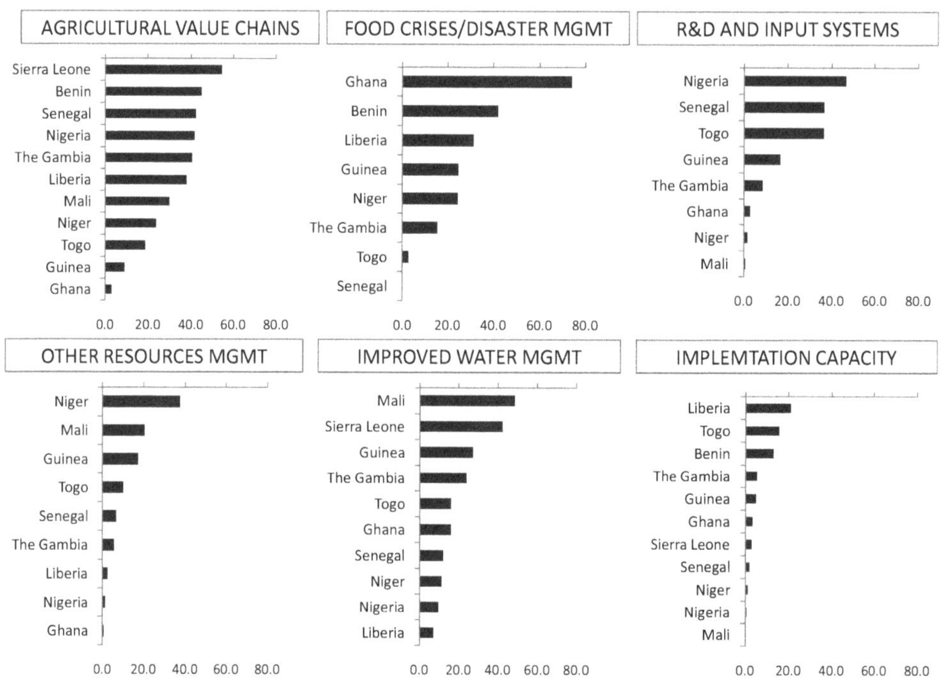

Fig. 6 Common priority areas in country investment plans. Source: Authors using information from various agriculture investment plans

that cut across individual countries are presented in Fig. 6. They cover the following: value chain development; food and other emergency crises and disaster management; research and development, including seeds systems; improved water and other resources management; as well as capacity building for successful implementation. The horizontal bars denote the percentage share of each of these sectors in the overall investment budgets of individual countries. The difference across countries reflects the diverging priorities accorded to individual investment areas by different countries. Although the differences most likely reflect different advances in specific areas by different countries, it is interesting to note the wide variations between countries. The overall level of planned investments is shown in the second column of Table 6. It is in the one billion US$ range for most countries, and double that amount or more for four countries. It is highest for Ghana and Nigeria, where planned investment levels exceed the US$5 billion mark. The smallest countries, Cape Verde and Gambia, have, as expected, the smallest levels of planned investments. In addition to defining priority investment areas and investment levels, country investment plans in many cases also specify a given rate of agricultural growth to be achieved. In others, they specify specific investment outcomes such as total areas of land under irrigation or specific crop yields that can be converted to corresponding changes in overall output and translated into sector growth rates.

Ideally, the design of the investment plans should be guided by the results from the analysis of alternative growth and poverty reduction options. The speed of planning and implementation was so high that the growth analysis and planning activities have overlapped, leading to an iterative rather than sequential process in integrating the two sets of activities. In all countries, however, a key step is a consistency analysis that takes place after the first version of the investment plan is completed. The consistency analysis assesses the extent to which investment levels as well as growth and poverty reduction outcomes that are being pursued in individual country investment plans are in line with the alternative long term growth, poverty reduction, and funding requirement scenarios, as well as historical expenditure levels discussed in the previous sections. In carrying out the analysis, proposed investment activities and related crop yields and/or target subsectoral growth rates are fed into the country CGE models to simulate the overall rate of agricultural growth and reduction in poverty levels that would result from individual country NAIPs. The results are then contrasted with the outcomes from the alternative long term scenarios. The comparisons can be as detailed as looking at differences in subsector growth rates and poverty outcomes among targeted geographic areas or demographic groups.[3]

For the current paper, we are considering consistency between target outcomes under investment plans and long term scenarios at the sectoral or national level. The results are summarized in Table 6 and Fig. 6. The Table compares the sectoral growth targets and associated expenditure levels under individual investment plans (first and second columns) with those of the closest long term growth scenario (third and fourth columns). The comparison suggests that in some cases there are significant discrepancies between proposed investment levels and simulated funding requirements for similar rates of growth. As shown by the ratios in the last column, the discrepancies are observed in both directions. For countries such as The Gambia, Mali, Nigeria, and Benin, the investment plans appear to be significantly underfunded in order to deliver the expected growth outcome. In contrast, suggested funding levels for the investment plans appear considerably higher than

[3]See IFPRI Discussion Paper No. 1019 by Badiane et al. (2010)

Table 6 NAIP costs versus long term funding benchmarks

	National Agricultural Investment Plans (NAIPs)		Comparable pre-compact growth scenario		
	Expected agricultural growth rate (%)	Cost (million USD)	Expected agricultural growth rate (%)	Cost (million USD)	Cost ratio
	[1]	[2]	[3]	[4]	[2]/[4]
Benin	14.3	884.1	14.3	1276.2	0.69
Cape Verde	6.9	96.4	6.0	51.6	1.87
Gambia	8.0	296.6	8.6	1065.8	0.28
Ghana	5.2	5479.5	6.9	3082.2	1.78
Guinea	10.3	1601.2	10.3	222.0	7.21
Liberia	9.9	947.7	9.4	149.5	6.34
Mali	8.8	727.2	8.5	5376.4	0.14
Niger	7.4	2457.0	6.4	2233.4	1.1
Nigeria	21.0	7535.4	9.5	28563.1	0.26
Senegal	9.7	2727.5	6.8	1771.1	1.54
Sierra Leone	7.0	388.0	7.1	100.6	3.86
Togo	6.8	947.2	6.7	989.3	0.96

Source: Respective country investment plans and CAADP Roundtable Brochures No 4 (http://www.resakss.org)

Note: The comparable growth scenarios for the different countries are summarized below: Benin (PSRSA), Cape Verde (ECOWAP/PDDAA), Gambia (MDG1 by 2025), Ghana [MIC (reaching Middle Income Country status by 2015)], Guinea (MDG1 by 2015), Liberia (MDG1 by 2025), Mali [SDDR (Schéma Directeur de Développement Rural)], Niger [SDR (Stratégie de Développement Rural)], Nigeria (Agricultural TFP growth driven by agricultural expenditure only), Senegal (Government's objective to reduce poverty rate to 17% by 2020), Sierra Leone [MDG1-2015 (while keeping non-agricultural sectors growing at current rates)], Togo (MDG1 by 2020)

required to meet the growth targets in the case of Sierra Leone, Liberia, and Guinea, and to a lesser extent for Cape Verde, Ghana, and Senegal. Only for Togo and Niger do the suggested funding levels appear to be consistent with projected long term growth outcomes.

The consistency analysis also assesses the degree of realism of pursued poverty reduction outcomes. It does so by comparing targeted poverty reduction levels under the investment plans with projected outcomes under continuation of pre-CAADP trends or business as usual (BAU). The results are plotted in Fig. 7. Benin, Nigeria, and Guinea exhibit the largest potential improvement from successful implementation of country investment plans. The first two however appear to have underfunded their investment plans and are thus less likely to achieve the expected poverty reduction outcome. Gambia and Mali are other countries with underfunded NAIPs, which may not achieve the expected improvement in poverty outcomes. Sierra Leone, Liberia, Guinea, Ghana, and Senegal all have seemingly overfunded NAIPs and should be in a position to realize the expected decline in poverty levels at a lower cost than budgeted under the current investment plans.

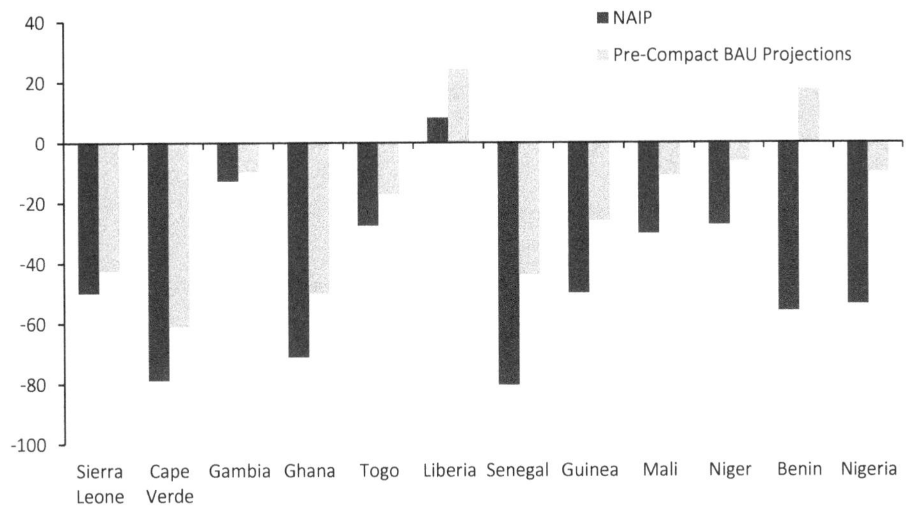

Fig. 7 Decline in poverty rates by 2015 under investment plans compared to pre-compact projections under BAU (%). Source: Authors' model simulation results for ECOWAS countries

2 Conclusion

Overall, there were no data to evaluate post-compact food security trends. It is vital that necessary arrangements are made to regularly update the baseline household survey information so as to facilitate tracking of poverty, food security and distributional impacts of the investment plans.

To ensure high return, investment commitments under the NAIPs must be supported by strong governance and monitored in a timely and transparent fashion. Therefore, it should be of high priority that countries improve policymaking by adopting an evidence-based approach. Such an approach should include review and dialogue mechanisms and knowledge support systems to facilitate benchmarking, mutual learning, and capacity strengthening, which would improve agricultural policy, program design, and implementation. The data available and the knowledge flow observed in the course of CAADP implementation suggests an urgent need to undertake institutional mapping of all actors involved in the policymaking process in the agricultural sector. This analysis should include data collection/gathering, policy analysis, and drafting of policy notes or policy dialogues. There is also a need for a full-fledged monitoring and evaluation framework for the agricultural sector with clear individual and institutional responsibilities. Such an M&E framework would need to include (i) data processing and policy analysis; (ii) policy dialogue and advocacy; and (iii) a monitoring and evaluation system.

ANNEX

Description of the Model Used to Simulate Long Term Growth and Poverty Reduction Outcomes

Model Specification and Calibration Data

We used a Dynamic single-country Computable General Equilibrium (DCGE) model for individual ECOWAS member countries for which a Social Accounting Matrix (SAM) was available.[4] The model is a recursive dynamic version of the standard IFPRI Lofgren-Harris-Robinson CGE model coupled with a micro-simulation module.[5] Annex provides a mathematical description of the model specifications. It is designed as a set of simultaneous linear and non-linear equations that represent the first order conditions of the profit and utility maximization behaviors of national economic agents, along with key macroeconomic constraints within a period. The model also specifies the process through which the values of some selected exogenous variables are updated to account for changes in population, labor and land supplies, capital accumulation, total factor productivity and government expenditures between successive periods. This kind of model is appropriate for the analysis of the impacts of alternative policy options on agricultural growth and poverty reduction outcomes as it explicitly takes into account the interactions between disaggregated agricultural and non-agricultural sectors and between the national economy and the rest of world while allowing to follow the distribution of income among factors and among households and other institutions.

In each activity of the national economy, production is carried out following a nested technology in which value-added quantity is a Constant Elasticity of Substitution (CES) function of primary factors, while aggregate intermediate input quantity is a Leontief function of specific intermediate inputs from different sectors, and overall activity output is a Leontief function of value-added and aggregate intermediate input quantities. Primary factors, including land, labor and capital, are fully employed within a period. Land and labor are mobile across activities while capital is activity-specific. Household groups receive income from factor remuneration proportionally to their shares of factor endowment. In addition, they may receive transfers from other household groups, the government and the rest of the world. They spend their income on direct taxes, transfers, and savings and for the consumption of different commodities according to Linear Expenditure System (LES) demand functions, which are derived from maximizing a Stone-Geary utility function. The model uses a Constant Elasticity of Transformation (CET) function to allocate domestic outputs between domestic sales and exports in shares that reflect the ratio of prices in domestic and foreign markets. Armington aggregation of

---

[4]For The Gambia, Guinea Bissau, Liberia and Sierra Leone for which a SAM was not available, a simplified model was used, instead of the CGE model.

[5]See Löfgren et al. (2002) for a detailed description of the static model version and Löfgren (2001) and Thurlow (2004) for dynamic applications of the model.

Table 7 Values of CES and CET elasticities

	Substitution between capital, labor and land	Substitution between imports and domestic sales	Transformation into exports and domestic sales
Agriculture	0.61	1.5	5.0
Industry	0.70	4.0	3.0
Services	0.80	2.5	1.2

Source: Based on elasticity estimates found in a broad literature review across developing countries by Annabi et al. (2006)

imports and domestic sales of domestic output determines the composite market supply that should meet the sum of demands for private consumption, government consumption, intermediate input, and investment. Government consumption demands of different commodities are exogenous while government savings adjusts to ensure the equality between government expenditures and revenues. Investment is savings-driven, with fixed marginal propensities to save, a fixed current account deficit and a flexible exchange rate.

The data used to calibrate the DCGE model for individual countries are largely derived from their respective SAMs using an income elasticity of 1.0 for household consumption demand and CES and CET elasticities as summarized in Table 7. As mentioned above, the model's dynamics are recursive, in the sense that the model is run as a repetitive static model while updating some exogenous variables between successive periods such as to replicate the economy's observed long term growth patterns. The rate of changes in population, land use, yields and government expenditures are projected from the series of data available on national accounts and agricultural statistical databases over the last decades. These rates are used to update some exogenous variables, including the LES supernumerary income, land and labor stocks, total factor productivity, and government consumption of the different commodities. In each period, the capital accumulation rate is endogenously determined from investment made during a preceding period and new capital is distributed between sectors proportionally to sectoral capital returns, taking into account a depreciation rate of 0.1.

This core DCGE model is linked to the microsimulation module in a top-down relationships (i.e., without feedback effects) through a transmission of changes in per capita household expenditures to the country's household survey data, where standard poverty and inequality measures are re-calculated given a defined poverty line.

Mathematical Model Description

The Tables 8 and 9 below describe the DCGE model utilized for the analysis of growth and poverty reduction scenarios for individual ECOWAS member countries. A comprehensive description of model specifications and closures is provided in Löfgren et al. (2002), Löfgren (2001) and Thurlow (2004).

Table 8 Model sets, parameters, and variables

Symbol	Explanation	Symbol	Explanation
Sets			
$a \in A$	Activities	$c \in CMR(\subset C)$	Regionally imported commodities
$a \in ALEO(\subset A)$	Activities with a Leontief function at the top of the technology nest	$c \in CMNR(\subset C)$	Non-regionally imported commodities
$c \in C$	Commodities	$c \in CT(\subset C)$	Transaction service commodities
$c \in CD(\subset C)$	Commodities with domestic sales of domestic output	$c \in CX(\subset C)$	Commodities with domestic production
$c \in CDN(\subset C)$	Commodities not in *CD*	$f \in F$	Factors
$c \in CD(\subset C)$	Exported commodities	$i \in INS$	Institutions (domestic and rest of world)
$c \in CEN(\subset C)$	Commodities not in *CE*	$i \in INSD(\subset INS)$	Domestic institutions
$c \in CM(\subset C)$	Aggregate imported commodities	$i \in INSDNG$ $(\subset INSD)$	Domestic non-government institutions
$c \in CMN(\subset C)$	Commodities not in *CM*	$h \in H(\subset INSDNG)$	Households
Parameters			
$cwts_c$	Weight of commodity c in the CPI	pwm_c	Import price (foreign currency)
$dwts_c$	Weight of commodity c in the producer price index	$pwmr_{cr}$	Import price by region (foreign currency)
ica_{ca}	Quantity of c as intermediate input per unit of activity a	$qdst_c$	Quantity of stock change
$icd_{cc'}$	Quantity of commodity c as trade input per unit of c' produced and sold domestically	$\overline{qg_c}$	Base-year quantity of government demand
$ice_{cc'}$	Quantity of commodity c as trade input per exported unit of c'	$\overline{qinv_c}$	Base-year quantity of private investment demand
$icer_{cc'r}$	Quantity of commodity c as trade input per exported unit of c' from region r	$shif_{if}$	Share for domestic institution i in income of factor f
$icm_{cc'}$	Quantity of commodity c as trade input per imported unit of c'	$shii_{ii'}$	Share of net income of i' to i (i' ∈ INSDNG'; i ∈ INSDNG)
$icmr_{cc'r}$	Quantity of commodity c as trade input per imported unit of c' from region r	ta_a	Tax rate for activity a
$inta_a$	Quantity of aggregate intermediate input per activity unit	$\overline{tins_i}$	Exogenous direct tax rate for domestic institution i

iva_a	Quantity of aggregate intermediate input per activity unit	$tins01_i$	0–1 parameter with 1 for institutions with potentially flexed direct tax rates
$\overline{mps_i}$	Base savings rate for domestic institution i	tm_c	Import tariff rate
$mps01_i$	0–1 parameter with 1 for institutions with potentially flexed direct tax rates	tmr_{cr}	Regional import tariff
pwe_c	Export price (foreign currency)	tq_c	Rate of sales tax
$pwer_{cr}$	Export price by region (foreign currency)	$trnsfr_{if}$	Transfer from factor f to institution i
Greek symbols			
α_a^a	Efficiency parameter in the CES activity function	δ_c^t	CET function share parameter
α_a^{va}	Efficiency parameter in the CES value-added function	δ_{fa}^{va}	CES value-added function share parameter for factor *f* in activity *a*
α_c^{ac}	Shift parameter for domestic commodity aggregation function	γ_{ch}^m	Subsistence consumption of marketed commodity c for household h
α_c^q	Armington function shift parameter	θ_{ac}	Yield of output c per unit of activity a
α_c^t	CET function shift parameter	ρ_a^a	CES production function exponent
α_c^m	Shift parameter in the CES regional import function	ρ_a^{va}	CES value-added function exponent
α_c^e	Shift parameter in the CES regional export function	ρ_c^{ac}	Domestic commodity aggregation function exponent
β^a	Capital sectoral mobility factor	ρ_c^q	Armington function exponent
β_{ch}^m	Marginal share of consumption spending on marketed commodity c for household h	ρ_c^t	CET function exponent
δ_a^a	CES activity function share parameter	ρ_c^m	Regional imports aggregation function exponent
δ_{ac}^{ac}	Share parameter for domestic commodity aggregation function	ρ_c^e	Regional exports aggregation function exponent
δ_c^q	Armington function share parameter	η_{fat}^a	Sector share of new capital
υ_f	Capital depreciation rate		
Exogenous variables			
$\overline{CPI}$	Consumer price index	$\overline{MPSADJ}$	Savings rate scaling factor (=0 for base)
$\overline{DTINS}$	Change in domestic institution tax share (=0 for base; exogenous variable)	$\overline{QFS_f}$	Quantity supplied of factor

(continued)

Table 8 (continued)

Symbol	Explanation	Symbol	Explanation
$\overline{FSAV}$	Foreign savings (FCU)	$\overline{TINSADJ}$	Direct tax scaling factor (=0 for base; exogenous variable)
$\overline{GADJ}$	Government consumption adjustment factor	$\overline{WFDIST_{fa}}$	Wage distortion factor for factor f in activity a
$\overline{IADJ}$	Investment adjustment factor		
Endogenous variables			
AWF_{ft}^{a}	Average capital rental rate in time period t	QF_{fa}	Quantity demanded of factor f from activity a
$DMPS$	Change in domestic institution savings rates (=0 for base; exogenous variable)	QG_c	Government consumption demand for commodity
DPI	Producer price index for domestically marketed output	QH_{ch}	Quantity consumed of commodity c by household h
EG	Government expenditures	QHA_{ach}	Quantity of household home consumption of commodity c from activity a for household h
EH_h	Consumption spending for household	$QINTA_a$	Quantity of aggregate intermediate input
EXR	Exchange rate (LCU per unit of FCU)	$QINT_{ca}$	Quantity of commodity c as intermediate input to activity a
$GOVSHR$	Government consumption share in nominal absorption	$QINV_c$	Quantity of investment demand for commodity
$GSAV$	Government savings	QM_c	Quantity of imports of commodity c
$INVSHR$	Investment share in nominal absorption	QMR_{cr}	Quantity of imports of commodity c by region r
MPS_i	Marginal propensity to save for domestic non-government institution (exogenous variable)	QER_{cr}	Quantity of exports of commodity c to region r
PA_a	Activity price (unit gross revenue)	QQ_c	Quantity of goods supplied to domestic market (composite supply)
PDD_c	Demand price for commodity produced and sold domestically	QT_c	Quantity of commodity demanded as trade input
PDS_c	Supply price for commodity produced and sold domestically	QVA_a	Quantity of (aggregate) value-added
PE_c	Export price (domestic currency)	QX_c	Aggregated quantity of domestic output of commodity
PER_{cr}	Export price by region (domestic currency)	$QXAC_{ac}$	Quantity of output of commodity c from activity a

$PINTA_a$	Aggregate intermediate input price for activity a	RWF_f	Real average factor price
PK_{ft}	Unit price of capital in time period t	$TABS$	Total nominal absorption
PM_c	Import price (domestic currency)	$TINS_i$	Direct tax rate for institution i (i ∈ INSDNG)
PMR_{cr}	Import price by region (domestic currency)	$TRII_{ii'}$	Transfers from institution i' to i (both in the set INSDNG)
PQ_c	Composite commodity price	WF_f	Average price of factor
PVA_a	Value-added price (factor income per unit of activity)	YF_f	Income of factor f
PX_c	Aggregate producer price for commodity	YG	Government revenue
$PXAC_{ac}$	Producer price of commodity c for activity a	YI_i	Income of domestic non-government institution
QA_a	Quantity (level) of activity	YIF_{if}	Income to domestic institution i from factor f
QD_c	Quantity sold domestically of domestic output	ΔK^a_{fat}	Quantity of new capital by activity a for time period t
QE_c	Quantity of exports		

Source: Thurlow (2004)

Table 9 Model equations

Production and price equations	
$QINT_{c\,a} = ica_{c\,a} \cdot QINTA_a$	(1)
$PINTA_a = \sum_{c \in C} PQ_c \cdot ica_{ca}$	(2)
$QVA_a = \alpha_a^{va} \cdot \left(\sum_{f \in F} \delta_{fa}^{va} \cdot \left(\alpha_{fa}^{vaf} \cdot QF_{fa} \right)^{-\rho_a^{va}} \right)^{-\frac{1}{\rho_a^{va}}}$	(3)
$W_f \cdot \overline{WFDIST}_{fa} = PVA_a \cdot (1 - tva_a) \cdot QVA_a \cdot \left(\sum_{f \in F'} \delta_{fa}^{va} \cdot \left(\alpha_{fa}^{vaf} \cdot QF_{fa} \right)^{-\rho_a^{va}} \right)^{-1} \cdot \delta_{fa}^{va} \cdot \left(\alpha_{fa}^{vaf} \cdot QF_{fa} \right)^{-\rho_a^{va}-1}$	(4)
$QVA_a = iva_a \cdot QA_a$	(5)
$QINTA_a = inta_a \cdot QA_a$	(6)
$PA_a \cdot (1 - ta_a) \cdot QA_a = PVA_a \cdot QVA_a + PINTA_a \cdot QINTA_a$	(7)
$QXAC_{a\,c} = \theta_{a\,c} \cdot QA_a$	(8)
$PA_a = \sum_{c \in C} PXAC_{ac} \cdot \theta_{ac}$	(9)
$QX_c = \alpha_c^{ac} \cdot \left(\sum_{a \in A} \delta_{ac}^{ac} \cdot QXAC_{ac}{}^{-\rho_c^{ac}} \right)^{-\frac{1}{\rho_c^{ac}-1}}$	(10)
$PXAC_{ac} = PX_c \cdot QX_c \left(\sum_{a \in A'} \delta_{ac}^{ac} \cdot QXAC_{ac}^{-\rho_c^{ac}} \right)^{-1} \cdot \delta_{ac}^{ac} \cdot QXAC_{ac}^{-\rho_c^{ac}-1}$	(11)
$PER_{cr} = pwer_{cr} \cdot EXR - \sum_{c' \in CT} PQ_c \cdot icer_{c'cr}$	(12)
$QE_c = \alpha_c^e \cdot \left(\sum_{r \in R} \delta_{cr}^e \cdot (QER_{cr})^{-\rho_c^e} \right)^{-\frac{1}{\rho_c^e}}$	(13)
$\frac{PER_{cr}}{PE_c} = QER_{cr} \cdot \left(\sum_{r' \in R} \delta_{cr'}^e \cdot (QER_{cr'}) - \rho_c^e \right)^{-1} \cdot \delta_{cr}^e \cdot (QER_{cr})^{-\rho_c^e-1}$	(14)
$PE_c = pwe_c \cdot EXR - \sum_{c' \in CT} PQ_c \cdot ice_{c'c}$	(15)
$QX_c = \alpha_c^t \cdot \left(\delta_c^t \cdot QE_c^{\rho_c^t} + (1 - \delta_c^t) \cdot QD_c^{\rho_c^t} \right)^{\frac{1}{\rho_c^t}}$	(16)
$\frac{QE_c}{QD_c} = \left(\frac{PE_c}{PDS_c} \cdot \frac{1-\delta_c^t}{\delta_c^t} \right)^{\frac{1}{\rho_c^t-1}}$	(17)
$QX_c = QD_c + QE_c$	(18)
$PX_c \cdot QX_c = PDS_c \cdot QD_c + PE_c \cdot QE_c$	(19)
$PDD_c = PDS_c + \sum_{c' \in CT} PQ_{c'} \cdot icd_{c'c}$	(20)
$PMR_{cr} = pwmr_{cr} \cdot (1 + tmr_{cr}) \cdot EXR - \sum_{c' \in CT} PQ_c \cdot icmr_{c'cr}$	(21)
$QM_c = \alpha_c^m \cdot \left(\sum_{r \in R} \delta_{cr}^m \cdot (QMR_{cr})^{-\rho_c^m} \right)^{-\frac{1}{\rho_c^m}}$	(22)
$\frac{PMR_{cr}}{PM_c} = QMR_{cr} \cdot \left(\sum_{r' \in R'} \delta_{cr'}^m \cdot (QMR_{cr'})^{-\rho_c^m} \right)^{-1} \cdot \delta_{cr}^m \cdot (QMR_{cr})^{-\rho_c^m-1}$	(23)
$PM_c = pwm_c \cdot (1 + tm_c) \cdot EXR + \sum_{c' \in CT} PQ_{c'} \cdot icm_{c'c}$	(24)
$QQ_c = \alpha_c^q \cdot \left(\delta_c^q \cdot QM_c^{-\rho_c^q} + (1 - \delta_c^q) \cdot QD_c^{-\rho_c^q} \right)^{-\frac{1}{\rho_c^q}}$	(25)
$\frac{QM_c}{QD_c} = \left(\frac{PDD_c}{PM_c} \cdot \frac{\delta_c^q}{1-\delta_c^q} \right)^{\frac{1}{1+\rho_c^q}}$	(26)
$QQ_c = QD_c + QM_c$	(27)

(continued)

Table 9 (continued)

Production and price equations	
$PQ_c \cdot (1 - tq_c) \cdot QQ_c = PDD_c \cdot QD_c + PM_c \cdot QM_c$	(28)
$QT_c = \sum_{c' \in C'} (icm_{cc'} \cdot QM_{c'} + icmr_{cc'} \cdot QMR_{c'} + ice_{cc'} \cdot QE_{c'} + icer_{cc'} \cdot QER_{c'} + icd_{cc'} \cdot QD_{c'})$	(29)
$\overline{CPI} = \sum_{c \in C} PQ_c \cdot cwts_c$	(30)
$DPI = \sum_{c \in C} PDS_c \cdot dwts_c$	(31)
Institutional incomes and domestic demand equations	
$YF_f = \sum_{a \in A} WF_f \cdot \overline{WFDIST}_{fa} \cdot QF_{fa}$	(32)
$YIF_{if} = shif_{if} \cdot [YF_f - trnsfr_{row\,f} \cdot EXR]$	(33)
$YI_i = \sum_{f \in F} YIF_{if} + \sum_{i' \in INSDNG'} TRII_{ii'} + trnsfr_{i\,gov} \cdot \overline{CPI} + trnsfr_{i\,row} \cdot EXR$	(34)
$TRII_{ii'} = shii_{ii'} \cdot (1 - MPS_{i'}) \cdot (1 - \overline{tins}_{i'}) \cdot YI_{i'}$	(35)
$EH_h = \left(1 - \sum_{i \in INSDNG} shii_{ih}\right) \cdot (1 - MPS_h) \cdot (1 - \overline{tins}_h) \cdot YI_h$	(36)
$PQ_c \cdot QH_{ch} = PQ_c \cdot \gamma^m_{ch} + \beta^m_{ch} \cdot \left(EH_h - \sum_{c' \in C} PQ_{c'} \cdot \gamma^m_{c'h}\right)$	(37)
$QINV_c = IADJ \cdot \overline{qinv}_c$	(38)
$QG_c = \overline{GADJ} \cdot \overline{qg}_c$	(39)
$EG = \sum_{c \in C} PQ_c \cdot QG_c + \sum_{i \in INSDNG} trnsfr_{i\,gov} \cdot \overline{CPI}$	(40)
$YG = \sum_{i \in INSDNG} \overline{tins}_i \cdot YI_i + \sum_{a \in A} ta_a \cdot PA_a \cdot QA_a + \sum_{c \in CMNR} tm_c \cdot pwm_c \cdot QM_c \cdot EXR + \sum_{r \in R} \sum_{c \in CMR} tmr_{cr} \cdot pwmr_{cr} \cdot QMR_{cr} \cdot EXR + \sum_{c \in C} tq_c \cdot PQ_c \cdot QQ_c + \sum_{f \in F} YF_{gov\,f} + trnsfr_{gov\,row} \cdot EXR$	(41)
System constraints and macroeconomic closures	
$QQ_c = \sum_{a \in A} QINT_{c\,a} + \sum_{h \in H} QH_{ch} + QG_c + QINV_c + qdst_c + QT_c$	(42)
$\sum_{a \in A} QF_{fa} = QFS_f$	(43)
$QFS_f / QFS_f^0 = (RWF_f / RWF_f^0)^{etals_f}$	(44)
$RWF_f = \left(\frac{YF_f}{QFS_f}\right) / \left(\frac{CPI}{CPI^0}\right)$	(45)
$YG = EG + GSAV$	(46)
$\sum_{c \in CMNR} pwm_c \cdot QM_c + \sum_{r \in R} \sum_{c \in CMR} pwmr_{cr} \cdot QMR_{cr} \cdot \sum_{f \in F} trnsfr_{row\,f} = \sum_{c \in CENR} pwe_c \cdot QE_c + \sum_{r \in R} \sum_{c \in CER} pwer_{cr} \cdot QER_{cr} + \sum_{i \in INSD} trnsfr_{i\,row} + FSAV$	(47)
$\sum_{i \in INSDNG} MPS_i \cdot (1 - \overline{tins}_i) \cdot YI_i + GSAV + EXR \cdot FSAV = \sum_{c \in C} PQ_c \cdot QINV_c + \sum_{c \in C} PQ_c \cdot qdst_c$	(48)
$MPS_i = \overline{mps}_i \cdot (1 + MPSADJ)$	(49)
Capital accumulation and allocation equations	
$AWF^a_{f\,t} = \sum_a \left[\left(\frac{QF_{f\,a\,t}}{\sum_{a'} QF_{f\,a'\,t}}\right) \cdot WF_{f\,t} \cdot WFDIST_{f\,a\,t}\right]$	(50)
$\eta^a_{fat} = \left(\frac{QF_{fat}}{\sum_{a'} QF_{fa't}}\right) \cdot \left(\beta^a \cdot \left(\frac{WF_{f,t} \cdot WFDIST_{fat}}{AWF^a_{ft}} - 1\right) + 1\right)$	(51)
$\Delta K^a_{fat} = \eta^a_{f\,at} \cdot \left(\frac{\sum_c PQ_{c\,t} \cdot QINV_{c\,t}}{PK_{f\,t}}\right)$	(52)

(continued)

Table 9 (continued)

Production and price equations	
$PK_{f\,t} = \sum_{c} PQ_{c\,t} \cdot \frac{QINV_{c\,t}}{\sum_{c'} QINV_{c'\,t}}$	(53)
$QF_{f\,a\,t+1} = QF_{f\,a\,t} \cdot \left(1 + \frac{\Delta K^{a}_{f\,a\,t}}{QF_{f\,a\,t}} - \upsilon_f\right)$	(54)
$QFS_{f\,t+1} = QFS_{f\,t} \cdot \left(1 + \frac{\sum_{a} \Delta K_{f\,a\,t}}{QFS_{f\,t}} - \upsilon_f\right)$	(55)

Source: Thurlow (2004)

References

Annabi, N., J. Cockburn, and B. Decaluwé. 2006. *Functional forms and parametrization of CGE models*. PEP MPIA working papers 2006-04. Québec: Poverty and Economic Policy Research Network.

Badiane, O., S. Odjo, and J. Ulimwengu. 2010. *Building capacities for evidence and outcome policy planning and implementation: The example of the Comprehensive Africa Agriculture Development Programme (CAADP)*. IFPRI Discussion Paper 1019. Washington, DC: International Food Policy Research Institute.

Breisinger, C., X. Diao, J. Thurlow, B. Yu, and S. Kalovali. 2008. *Accelerating growth and structural transformation: Ghana's options for reaching middle income country status*. IFPRI Discussion Paper 750. Washington, DC: International Food Policy Research Institute.

Diao, X., M. Nwafor, V. Alpuerto, K. Akramov, and S. Salau. 2010. *Agricultural growth and investment options for poverty reduction in Nigeria*. IFPRI Discussion Paper 954. Washington, DC: International Food Policy Research Institute.

Fan, S., B. Yu, and A. Saurkar. 2008. Public spending in developing countries: Trends, determination, and impact. In *Public expenditures, growth and poverty: Lessons from developing countries*, ed. S. Fan. Washington, DC and Baltimore, MD: International Food Policy Research Institute and Johns Hopkins University Press.

Löfgren, H. 2001. *Less poverty in Egypt? Explorations of alternative pasts with lessons for the future*. IFPRI Discussion Paper 72. Washington, DC: International Food Policy Research Institute.

Löfgren, H., R. Harris, and S. Robinson. 2002. *A standard CGE model in GAMS*. IFPRI Discussion Paper 75. Washington, DC: International Food Policy Research Institute.

Thurlow, J. 2004. *A dynamic Computable General Equilibrium (CGE) model for South Africa: Extending the static IFPRI model*. Working Paper No. 1-2004. Pretoria: Trade and Industrial Policy Strategies.

World Bank. 2008. *World development indicators*. Washington, DC: World Bank. http://data.worldbank.org/sites/default/files/wdi08.pdf. Accessed 25 May 2009.

Ousmane Badiane is the Director for Africa at the International Food Policy Research Institute (IFPRI), based in Washington, DC. He oversees the Institute's regional offices for West and Central Africa, in Dakar, Senegal, and Eastern and Southern Africa, in Addis Ababa, Ethiopia. He received a Master's Degree and PhD in agricultural economics from the University of Kiel in Germany. His awards include being selected as a 2015 Yara Prize Laureate, a Doctoral Degree Honoris Causa from the University of KwaZulu Natal in South Africa and induction as Distinguished Fellow of the African Association of Agricultural Economics.

Sunday P. Odjo is a Research Coordinator in IFPRI's West and Central Africa Office in Dakar, Senegal.

Fleur Wouterse is a Research Fellow in IFPRI's West and Central Africa Office, and is based in Kampala, Uganda. She holds a PhD in Development Economics from Wageningen University, the Netherlands. Her research mainly takes a micro-economic approach and focuses on households in rural West Africa.

3

Oil Revenues in Uganda and their Spending

Manfred Wiebelt, Karl Pauw, John Mary Matovu, Everist Twimukye, and Todd Benson

1 Introduction

With the recent discovery of crude oil reserves along the Albertine Rift, Uganda is set to establish itself as an oil producer in the coming decade. Total oil reserves are believed to be two billion barrels, with recoverable reserves estimated at 0.8–1.2 billion barrels. This is comparable to the level of oil reserves in African countries such as Chad (0.9 billion barrels), Republic of the Congo (1.9 billion barrels), and Equatorial Guinea (1.7 billion barrels) but far short of Angola (13.5 billion) and Nigeria (36.2 billion) (World Bank 2010). Using a conservative reserve scenario of 800 million barrels, peak production, likely to be reached by 2017, is estimated by

---

This contribution heavily draws on IFPRI Discussion Paper 1122. The underlying research was financially supported by the Uganda office of the Department for International Development (DFID) of the Government of the United Kingdom through their support to the International Food Policy Research Institute under the Uganda Agricultural Strategy Support Program (UASSP) project. The authors wish to thank participants of two workshops held in Kampala on November 25, 2010 and in Kiel on July 2–3, 2011 for their valuable comments and suggestions for improvement.

M. Wiebelt (✉)
Kiel Institute for the World Economy, Kiel, Germany
e-mail: Manfred.wiebelt@ifw-kiel.de

K. Pauw
Food and Agriculture Organization, Addis Ababa, Ethiopia

J.M. Matovu
Research for Transformation and Development, Kampala, Uganda

E. Twimukye
Economic Policy Research Centre, Kampala, Uganda

T. Benson
International Food Policy Research Institute, Washington, DC, USA

the World Bank to range from 120,000 to 140,000 barrels per day, with a production period spanning 30 years. A more optimistic scenario in this study is based on 1.2 billion barrels and sets peak production at 210,000 barrels per day (see Wiebelt et al. 2011). Although final stipulations of the revenue sharing agreements with oil producers are not yet known, government revenue from oil will be substantial. One estimate, based on an average oil price of US$75 per barrel, puts revenues at approximately 10–15% of GDP at peak production (World Bank 2010). The discovery of crude oil therefore has the potential to provide significant stimulus to the Ugandan economy and to enable it to better address its development objectives, provided oil revenues are managed in an appropriate manner.

If the experience of other resource-abundant countries is anything to go by, the prospects are alarming. Cross-country evidence suggests that resource-abundant countries lag behind comparable countries in terms of real GDP growth (Sachs and Warner 1995, 2001; Gelb 1988; IMF 2003); that the negative relationship between resource abundance and economic growth is stronger for oil, minerals, and other point-source resources than for agriculture; and that this relationship is remarkably robust (Sala-i-Martin and Subramanian 2003; Stevens 2003). Nonetheless, several countries have managed to avoid this so-called resource curse. Indonesia's economy grew by an average of 4% per year during 1965–1990, while oil and gas exports rose quickly in the 1970s, reaching 50% of exports in the early 1980s (Bevan et al. 1999). Botswana achieved double-digit growth in the 1970s and 1980s despite rapidly growing diamond exports since the 1970s, and this development occurred despite the enclave character of the mineral industry (that is, low backward and forward linkages to other sectors) (Acemoglu et al. 2003). Other resource-rich countries, such as Malaysia, Australia, and Norway, have successfully diversified their production structures, laying the ground for broad-based balanced growth.

The anxiety about the effects of resource booms partly reflects reservations about the absorptive and managerial capacity of public sectors—particularly in developing countries—to manage large-scale investment programs or to rapidly step up service delivery without a loss in quality. In part, it also reflects even deeper reservations about resource dependency and the impact of windfall profits on the domestic political economy (Ross 2001; Leite and Weidmann 1999; Easterly 2001). However, more traditional concerns about the macroeconomics of resource booms also figure large, and these are the focus in this study. Dominating these concerns is the fear that the additional foreign exchange arising from the exploitation and exportation of natural resources may cause an appreciation of the real exchange rate. Although a strong domestic currency is good news for importers, Rodrik (2003) warns of the danger an uncompetitive real exchange rate holds for overall economic growth and development. The subsequent loss of competitiveness in the nonresource tradable goods sectors—or Dutch Disease—may hamper growth in traditional export sectors such as manufacturing or agriculture. These sectors are often major employers in developing countries and serve as the engines of growth. Of course, exportation of natural resources does not inevitably have negative consequences for the economy; for example, if the resource flow emanating from the newly exploited natural resource is small relative to overall trade flows, or there are underemployed factors of production that can be used in the expanding natural resource exploitation sectors with little opportunity cost, or both, an expansion in natural resource exports will not necessarily lead to Dutch Disease (see Hausmann and Rigobon 2002; Sala-i-Martin and Subramanian 2003).

This study considers the impact of crude oil extraction and exportation on the Ugandan economy with a specific focus on how it might affect the agricultural sector. We also consider various options open to the Ugandan government for saving, spending, or investing forecasted oil revenues over the coming three decades. For this analysis we modify a recursive-dynamic computable general equilibrium (CGE) model of Uganda by including crude oil extraction and refining industries. These industries are allowed to grow and shrink over time in line with the forecasted oil production trend, while oil revenues accruing to government are either saved abroad in an oil fund (this sterilizes the exchange rate effect) or spent domestically. Several spending scenarios consider the effects of using the balance of oil funds (that is, after deducting amounts saved) to develop public infrastructure. Here we consider scenarios where infrastructure investments only contribute to long-term growth through raising productive capacity, or where they also have productivity spillover effects in targeted sectors (for example, in agricultural or nonagricultural sectors specifically). Scenarios where oil revenues are distributed to citizens in the form of household welfare transfers or used to subsidize prices (for example, fuel subsidies) are also modeled.

The contribution is structured as follows. We first provide an overview on spending options. Particular attention is given to infrastructural investments and their effects in developing countries. Next, we introduce the CGE model and describes the simulation setup and design, then present and discuss the model results. Last, we draw conclusions.

2 Investing Oil Revenues: Options and Challenges

For the past two decades Uganda has managed its public finances and the macro economy in a prudent manner, yet the prospect of a large influx of oil revenue presents a major challenge to government. Even though Uganda's oil reserves are not massive compared to those of the major oil producers of the world, the expected revenue is still substantial relative to the current size of the economy.

There are at least three dimensions to the oil revenue spending challenge that lies ahead: First, there is the issue of how to manage oil price volatility. Volatile prices imply volatile revenue flows from one year to the next, which makes long-term planning difficult. Second, while increased administrative capacity will be required to manage a much larger infrastructural and social spending budget, the danger exists that government becomes too large and undisciplined in its spending. If service delivery becomes inefficient and administrative expenditures (for example, on salaries) grow too much there will ultimately be less funding available for all-important infrastructural spending. Third, infrastructural spending itself may be inefficient due to a lack of administrative or absorptive capacity within government. While spending will contribute to GDP in the current period, thus creating the perception of growth, it may not translate into increased production capacity and higher levels of productivity in future periods, which ultimately hampers the sustainability of oil revenue spending.

2.1 *Revenue Stabilization Options*

One way to deal with revenue volatility and concerns about spending inefficiency is to transfer oil revenues into a foreign "oil fund" from which a smaller or a more stable revenue flow is extracted. The first option is to set up a budget stabilization fund (SF), which involves allocating a certain share of government oil revenues to a fund that can be tapped when low oil prices cause revenues to drop below projected flows. Examples include the SF of the Russian Federation or the State Oil Fund in Azerbaijan. When using an SF government may still plan to spend all oil revenues during the oil extraction period, in which case the SF is only used to smooth the revenue flow as it deviates from projected revenues. However, such a fund could also be used to extend the spending period beyond the oil extraction period by saving a greater share of annual revenue and continuing to draw on accrued savings that remain at the end of the oil extraction period. A second option is a permanent income fund (PIF) or heritage fund. Here all revenue from oil is transferred to the fund and only the interest earned on accumulated funds is allocated to the government budget. The Norwegian Government Pension Fund and the Kuwaiti Future Generations Fund are good examples of such PIFs. A PIF provides a much smaller flow of revenue compared to the default option of spending all revenues immediately, but the income stream is perpetual, thus having the potential of benefiting future generations. The revenue stream is also likely to be fairly stable or predictable, especially when long-term fixed interest rates are earned on the accumulated funds.

Although the development challenges loom large in Uganda, a prudent spending approach is desirable. This means not succumbing to the temptation of spending too much too soon. Proponents of a spend-all approach may appeal more to the masses, with arguments that the country cannot afford to hoard revenue amidst crumbling infrastructure and developmental backlogs. However, ideally speaking, spending levels should only gradually increase in line with the pace at which government capacity grows. Uganda has taken advice of this nature on board in announcing that an oil fund will indeed be set up and managed by the Central Bank (see Uganda, Ministry of Energy and Mineral Development 2008). The way in which the fund is managed (that is, how funds are deposited or withdrawn over time) should be explicitly governed by the legal and regulatory framework for oil revenue. Such a framework, combined with a gradually enhanced institutional capacity, should cushion the country from pressure from those who would want to see quick but unsustainable gains from oil.

2.2 *Investment Spending Options*

2.2.1 Investment for Economic Growth and Poverty Reduction

The pace at which public infrastructure is developed is an important determinant of the development process. Numerous studies highlight the importance of the stock of public infrastructure as one necessary ingredient for agricultural productivity growth (Binswanger et al. 1993; Ram 1996; Esfahani and Ramirez 2002). Hulten (1996) argues it is not only the level of public investment that matters, but also the spending efficiency and the effectiveness with which existing capital stocks are used by citizens (see also Calderón and Servén 2005, 2008; Reinikka and Svensson 2002). Microeconomic studies tend to focus more on the latter aspect, and show that improved access to public infrastructure positively influences the adoption of productivity-enhancing technologies by farm households or firms (Antle 1984; Ahmed and Hossain 1990; Renkow et al. 2004). Access to and utilization of public infrastructure also has important welfare effects, including the reduction of rural poverty (Fan et al. 2000; Fan and Zhang 2008; Gibson and Rozelle 2003) and rural inequality (Calderón and Servén 2005; Fan et al. 2003). The strength of these welfare effects, however, depends on the institutional setup in countries (Duflo and Pande 2007), while strong complementarities exist between physical and human capital (Canning and Bennathan 1999). The latter suggests that investments in education, training, or rural extension services would enhance the effectiveness of infrastructural investments.

The overwhelming message is that infrastructural investments matter for development, especially when measures are in place to improve access to that infrastructure. However, it is less clear precisely where to invest in order to maximize growth and poverty outcomes. The agricultural sector stands out as a strong candidate. Agriculture is an important sector in many developing countries in terms of its share of national GDP and employment. Agricultural growth is therefore particularly important in determining the pace of poverty reduction (Diao et al. 2010; Valdés and Foster 2010). In Uganda the agricultural sector is relatively small, contributing less than one-third to national GDP. However, it remains a significant employer, with 81% of the population living in households that are directly involved in agricultural activities (see Benin et al. 2008). Farming is by no means exclusively a rural activity in Uganda (27.8% of urban households are engaged in agricultural activities), but it is clear from population statistics that a focus on rural agriculture is warranted: 9 in 10 farm households live in rural areas, and one in three rural inhabitants are poor, compared to 13.8% of urban people. This implies that growth in the agricultural sector has the potential to significantly reduce poverty in Uganda. Weak historical agricultural growth, low agricultural yields, and poor infrastructure in Uganda all point to the great potential for this sector to grow rapidly should significant public investments, particularly in infrastructure, reach this sector.

Using a recursive-dynamic CGE model, Benin et al. (2008) are able to demonstrate how rapid agricultural growth achieved through yield improvements under the Comprehensive Africa Agricultural Development Programme (CAADP) in Uganda contributes to overall growth and poverty reduction. CAADP aims to achieve 6% agricultural growth by committing countries to allocate 10% of their overall budgets to the agricultural sector in the form of infrastructure investments, research and development, and extension services. In Uganda the 6% growth target implies a doubling of the agricultural growth rate, which, historically, has remained at just below 3%. Benin et al. (2008) show that if agricultural growth is maintained at 6% over the period 2005–2015, the national GDP growth rate in Uganda will increase by 1% point (that is, from 5.1 to 6.1%). Agricultural growth also has spillover effects into the rest of the economy, with agroprocessing or food-processing and trade and transport sectors benefiting from more rapid growth. More importantly, however, are the poverty-reducing effects of rapid agricultural growth. Benin et al. (2008) show that under an accelerated agricultural growth path the poverty rate in 2015 will be 7.6% points lower than the forecasted level under the *business as usual* growth path. This is equivalent to an additional 2.9 million people being lifted out of poverty by 2015.

Benin et al. (2008) extend their analysis to focus on specific agricultural subsectors' effectiveness at reducing poverty and generating growth through size and economic linkage effects. In this regard they find that horticultural crops, root crops, livestock, and cereals have the greatest poverty-reducing potential in Uganda. This is due both to the crop choices of resource-poor farmers and to the preferences of poor consumers (increased productivity lowers farmers' unit production costs and benefits consumers via price reductions). Given their initial size, growth potential, and economic linkages, growth in subsectors such as roots, *matooke* (cooking banana), pulses and oilseeds, and export crops contribute most to overall growth.

Using a similar methodology, Dorosh and Thurlow (2009) focus more closely on the relative impacts of rural versus urban public investments in Uganda. In general, they find that improving agricultural productivity generates more broad-based welfare improvements in both rural and urban areas than investing in the capital city, Kampala. Although investing in Kampala accelerates economic growth, it has little effect on other regions' welfare because of the city's weak regional growth linkages and small migration effects. In a study in Peru, Thurlow et al. (2008) find that by investing in the leading (more urbanized) region, that country may be undermining the economy in the lagging (mostly rural) region by increasing import competition and internal migration. The authors also show that the divergence between the leading and lagging regions can only be bridged by investing in the lagging region's productivity through providing extension services and improved rural roads.

This brief overview suggests that public investments in rural areas and agriculture should be a critical part of the development strategy in Uganda if the country is to achieve its goals of reducing (rural) poverty and narrowing the welfare gap between urban and rural areas. Studies cited show that investments in cities or major urban centers such as Kampala, although good for growth there, may in fact be harmful or at best neutral for growth or welfare in rural areas. Either way, such investments will lead to rising rural–urban inequality, which is an undesirable socioeconomic outcome. The challenge is to be strategic about how and where to invest so that productivity gains in priority sectors or subsectors are maximized. Certain types of investments have obvious impacts; for example, investments in rural roads, irrigation infrastructure, or water storage will benefit agriculture, and depending on the exact location (or agronomic zone) of those investments, specific subsectors within agriculture. For other types of investments, such as telecommunications, it is likely that urban-based manufacturing sectors would benefit more, but there may still be intended or unintended productivity spillovers into other sectors. It is also important to realize that there may be a lag from the time the investment in agriculture is made until productivity spillovers materialize and rural poverty declines. The immediate beneficiaries of increased agricultural investment spending are more likely to be those nonpoor workers supplying investment services or producing investment goods rather than poor farming households themselves.

2.2.2 Transferring Rents to Citizens

The massive infrastructural spending backlogs in Uganda mean much of the policy discussion around spending of oil revenue has and will continue to focus on public investments. However, infrastructural spending is not the only option open to government. Some argue that oil revenues should be spent on the provisioning of social protection: Since citizens in effect own the oil resource, the most appropriate approach is to transfer revenues back to them. Social protection can be broadly defined. Benefits transferred to citizens can be in the form of tax breaks (for example, income or consumption tax cuts); subsidies (for example, direct price subsidies, employment subsidies, or investment subsidies); job creation schemes; or direct transfers (Gelb and Grasmann 2010). Not all these transfer mechanisms necessarily involve a direct transfer from government to households; some work indirectly via employment or consumption.

Gelb and Grasmann (2010, 12–16) briefly review the merits of and justification for each of these benefits while Gelb and Majerowicz (2011) consider the strengths and limitations of cash transfers in Uganda. A lower tax burden, they explain, might reduce the deadweight costs of taxation, provided the quality of tax administration does not decline at the same time. Lower taxes, in general, will encourage economic activity, thus compensating export sectors in particular for the adverse effect of a stronger exchange rate. Domestic price subsidies are popular for obvious reasons. A common type of subsidy in oil-producing economies is one on petroleum products; in fact, in many countries petroleum prices are kept far below market levels at a subsidy cost equivalent to "several percentage points of GDP" (Gelb and Grasmann 2010, 13). An approach that is used "more widely in the Middle East than elsewhere" (Gelb and Grasmann 2010, 14) is public-sector job creation. One estimate suggests that around 80% of jobs in Gulf are in the public sector (for example, in Kuwait, employment for nationals is virtually guaranteed).

Very few countries have considered the use of oil revenues to finance direct welfare transfers. However, there is *increasing interest* in distribution mechanisms such as those pioneered in Alaska "as the shortcomings of other approaches become more apparent" (Gelb and Grasmann 2010, 14). Cash transfers or grants have two primary functions: They reduce short-term poverty and inequality, and they provide safety nets that enable households to manage risk (Pauw and Mncube 2007). There are several design options. First, grants can be targeted or universal. Targeted grants are more costly to administer, but targeting improves efficiency in terms of reductions in poverty and inequality. Under a universal grant scheme all citizens have access to a grant, irrespective of their socioeconomic status. Second, grants can be conditional or unconditional. Conditional grants, as the name suggests, are only accessible by households that comply with certain provisions, such as attending school or visiting health clinics.

The successes of conditional programs such as Bolsa Familia in Brazil and Opportunidades in Mexico have been widely reported (see, for example, Adato and Hoddinott 2010). However, just like targeting, conditionality increases the administrative burden of these programs, both for administrators who need to determine eligibility of prospective participants and for health and education service providers who need to deal with the mandatory increase in demand for these services. For this reason conditionality may not always be a good idea, especially in countries where administrative capacity is low or where social service delivery is weak (Pauw and Mncube 2007). The alternative (that is, a nontargeted unconditional grant scheme) is costly, but the large influx of oil revenues in Uganda puts the country in a position where it can probably afford such a *basic income grant*. Although a uniformly distributed grant will not improve inequality, it will reduce poverty, while at the same time policymakers can avoid sensitivities that may arise when oil revenues—seen by all as a national resource—are unequally distributed.

3 CGE Model Simulation Setup

3.1 The Ugandan Recursive-Dynamic CGE Model

This study applies a single-country recursive-dynamic CGE for Uganda (also used by Benin et al. 2008) to investigate the effects of oil production and to consider alternative options for spending oil revenue. This modeling tool is useful as it captures the important direct and indirect effects associated with oil production and the spending of oil revenues. In a similar study to this one, Breisinger et al. (2009) also use a CGE model to examine the potential trade-offs between spending and saving of oil revenues in Ghana. The CGE model is a member of the class of single country neoclassical CGE models first developed by Dervis et al. (1982) and features endogenous prices, market clearing, and imperfect substitution between domestic and foreign goods. Below we highlight some of the key features of the Ugandan model. A detailed model description and equation listing can be found in Thurlow (2004).

3.1.1 Private Production and Consumption

Producers and consumers in the model are assumed to enjoy no market power in world markets, so the terms of trade are independent of domestic policy choices.

Firms in each of the 52 economic sectors (or activities) are assumed to be perfectly competitive, producing a single good that can be sold to either the domestic or the export market. Production in each sector i is determined by a constant elasticity of substitution (CES) production function of the form.

$$Q_i = A_i \, \Sigma_f \left\{ \delta_{fi} F_{fi}{}^{-\rho i} \right\}^{-1/\rho i}, \tag{1}$$

where f is a set of factors consisting of land, cattle, capital, and different labor categories; Q_i is the sectoral activity level; A_i the sectoral total factor productivity; F_{fi} the quantity of factor f demanded from sector i; and δ_{fi} and ρ_{fi} are the distributional and elasticity parameters of the CES production function, respectively. Only agricultural crop production requires land. Sectoral supply growth of land is fixed. Sector capital endowments are fixed in each period but evolve over time through depreciation and investment. Capital and labor markets are competitive so that these factors are employed in each sector up to the point that they are paid the value of their marginal product. Private-sector output is also determined by the level of infrastructure, which is provided costless by the government. We assume that total sector factor productivity A_i depends on the availability of public infrastructure.

Consumption for each household type is defined by a constant elasticity of substitution linear expenditure system, which allows for the income elasticity of demand for different goods to deviate from unity. The CGE model endogenously estimates the impact of alternative growth paths on the incomes of various household groups. These household groups include farm and nonfarm households and are disaggregated across rural areas, the major city of Kampala, and other smaller urban centers. Each of the households questioned in the 2005/06 Uganda National Household Survey (UNHS5) are linked directly to their corresponding representative household in the CGE model. This is the microsimulation component of the Ugandan model. Changes in representative households' consumption and prices in the CGE model are passed down to the corresponding households in the survey, where standard poverty measures and changes in poverty are calculated.

3.1.2 Macroeconomic Closures and Dynamics

The model has a neoclassical closure in which total private investment is constrained by total savings net of public investment. Household savings propensities are exogenous. This rule implies that any shortfall in government savings relative to the cost of government capital formation, net of exogenous foreign savings, directly crowds out private investment. Likewise, any excess of government savings directly crowds in private investment.

The model has a simple recursive-dynamic structure. Each solution run tracks the economy over 40 periods. Each period may be thought of as a fiscal year (that is, from year 2007 to 2046). Within-year capital stocks are fixed, and the model is solved given the parameters of the experiment (for example, exogenous growth in the oil production or refining sector, or changes in import tariffs on fuels). This solution defines a new vector of prices and quantities for the economy, including the level of public- and private-sector investment, which feed into the equations of motion for sectoral capital stocks. The equation is specified as

$$K_{i,t} = K_{i,t-1}(1 - \mu_i) + \Delta K_{i,t-1}, \tag{2}$$

where $K_{i,t}$ is the capital stock, μ_i denotes the sector-specific rate of depreciation, and $t-1$ measures the gestation lag on investment.

The final element is an externality resulting from public investment in infrastructure. Public investment is assumed to generate an improvement in total factor productivity. Specifically, equation (1) assumes that $A_{i,t} = A_i$ for nonspillover sectors, whereas in the spillover sectors, denoted s, total factor productivities evolve according to

$$A_{s,t} = A_s \cdot \Pi_g \{(I^g{}_t/I^g{}_0)/(Q_{s,t}/Q_{s,0})\}^{\rho}{}_{sg}, \tag{3}$$

where g denotes a set of public investments defined over rural and urban infrastructure, health and education, and so on; I^g and Q_s are real government investment and sectoral output levels; and $I^g{}_0$ and $Q_{s,0}$ are the correspondingly defined public investments and output levels in the base period. The terms ρ_{sg} measure the extent of the spillovers. If $\rho_{sg} = 0$, there is no spillover from public investment in infrastructure or health and education. The higher ρ_{sg}, the higher are spillovers.

The total population, workforce, area of arable land, number of livestock, and income from abroad are examples of other variables that evolve over time according to exogenously defined assumptions. The growing population generates a higher level of consumption demand and therefore raises the supernumerary income level of household consumption within the linear expenditure system (LES) specific to each household and subject to the constraints of available income and the consumer price vector. Labor, land, cattle, and foreign capital supply are updated exogenously.

3.2 *Simulation Setup*

3.2.1 Baseline Scenario

The baseline scenario serves as the counterfactual against which other scenario results are compared. Scenarios are solved over the period 2007–2046, which roughly coincides with the forecasted crude oil extraction period. The baseline (simulation name BASELINE) is a no oil scenario, which assumes a continuation of the *business as usual* growth path for Uganda over the coming decades (that is, without the establishment of crude oil extraction and refining industries). Growth rates for total factor productivity, factor supply, foreign capital inflow, and real government consumption follow recent historical trends or are set at levels such that GDP at factor cost is targeted to grow at an annual average rate of 5.1% until 2046 (see Table 2: Part A). The table further provides a breakdown of this growth into its different components. Absorption, which includes private consumption (5%), investment expenditure (4.4%), and government expenditure (exogenously set to grow at 3%), grows at 4.7% per year. Export growth outpaces import growth, mainly due to domestic factor productivity growth, which makes exporters more competitive in international markets. The result is a declining trade deficit, while the exogenously imposed 3% growth in foreign capital inflows causes the real exchange rate to appreciate on average by 0.9% per year.

The results in *BASELINE* reveal the so-called Balassa-Samuelson effect, where tradable sectors with higher than average productivity increases and lower income elasticities of demand grow less than nontradable sectors, such as services. Thus, as expected under this growth scenario, the economic structure will continue to change in favor of services and industry. Table 2 (Part B) shows that the share of the agricultural sector in total GDP decreases from 22.6% in 2007 to 15.8% in 2046, which is a result of a relative decline in agricultural prices driven primarily by relatively lower domestic demand for agricultural products and domestic terms of trade effects, which cause an appreciation in the real exchange rate. In contrast, the services sector continues to expand, contributing 62.5% of GDP by 2046.

3.2.2 Modeling Oil Production and Refining

Several oil production and refining scenarios are modeled. All involve the same fairly rapid growth path for oil production. Growth is fastest between 2007 and 2017 when peak oil production is reached. Peak production levels are then maintained for about a decade, before production is gradually phased out over the next two decades until recoverable reserves are exhausted by 2046. The expansion is simulated by exogenously raising or lowering the level capital stock available to the crude oil refining sector. The implicit assumption is that capital stock expansion is funded (almost) entirely by foreign direct investment. However, although the decision to invest is made exogenously by foreign investors, the oil sector still has to compete with other sectors for intermediate inputs and, to a much lesser extent, for labor resources. Furthermore, depending on how government spends its oil revenue (for example, government may spend more on public infrastructure or government services), the demand for labor will rise rapidly in those sectors required to satisfy government demand (for example, suppliers of machinery and equipment, construction services, or public service providers). All crude oil is supplied to the refining sector. Supply bottlenecks are avoided by applying a similar capital stock growth rate to the refining sector as the one that determines crude oil production levels.

Profits—or returns to capital stock—generated in the oil production and refining sectors are shared between the foreign owners of capital (their share is repatriated) and the Ugandan government (revenue is transferred via a 74.4% tax on returns to capital). All crude oil is supplied to the oil refineries, and for the sake of simplicity all refined oil is assumed to be exported. Domestic demand for petroleum products is, in turn, met by imports. In reality, some of the refined oil product will be retained for domestic consumption and the country will cease to import petroleum products, but modeling it in this manner is simpler and does not affect results since the balance of payments effect is symmetrical.

3.2.3 Oil Simulation Experiments

In all the oil simulations, oil production and refining capacity is increased and then gradually phased out to replicate the forecasted production path, which assumes peak production of about 210,000 barrels of oil per day between 2017 and 2025. The main objective in this study is not to compare the contributions of alternative oil production and revenue scenarios to the economy, but instead to evaluate economic and socioeconomic outcomes under alternative spending options. All oil simulations therefore assume the same oil production path and government revenue stream, but they differ in terms of how government saves or spends the revenue. A total of six oil scenarios are modeled. We elaborate below, and Table 1 summarizes.

We start off with a set of basic investment scenarios where we assume all oil revenue is invested domestically, or, alternatively, part of oil revenue is invested and the balance is transferred to a foreign oil fund. Also included in this set of scenarios is one where part of the revenue is transferred to households in the form of a welfare grant. The first simulation, named FND00INV, is a typical Dutch Disease scenario. It assumes that all public revenue is immediately used to finance public infrastructure investment spending. This means none of the government oil revenue is saved abroad in a fund. In general, in this scenario, additional foreign exchange revenue from oil production and exportation increases national income, which is used by private and public agents for consumption (this is an endogenous effect) and investment (via increased private savings, or by design via the government closure selected). The latter increases the economy's total capital stock until peak oil production is reached, but the increased public capital does not sustain significantly higher output over the entire simulation period, as the capital stock in the oil sector is subsequently reduced to replicate declining output as oil reserves are gradually depleted. The simulation therefore allows the pure demand-side effects of the price boom to be isolated: Absorptive capacity constraints are binding and the demand effects lead to a real appreciation and the typical restructuring of production observed during an oil boom.

We start off with a set of basic *investment scenarios* where we assume all oil revenue is invested domestically, or, alternatively, part of oil revenue is invested and the balance is transferred to a foreign oil fund. Also included in this set of scenarios is one where part of the revenue is transferred to households in the form of a welfare grant. The first simulation, named *FND00INV*, is a typical Dutch Disease scenario. It assumes that all public revenue is immediately used to finance public infrastructure investment spending. This means none of the government oil revenue is saved abroad in a fund. In general, in this scenario, additional foreign exchange revenue from oil production and exportation increases national income, which is

Table 1 Summary of modeled baseline and oil scenarios

Simulation name	Long name	Share of revenue invested	Productivity spillover effects modeled	Share of revenue saved to oil fund
0. BASELINE	"Business as usual" baseline scenario with no oil production and refining capacity	N/A	N/A	N/A
Public investment scenarios with no productivity spillover				
1. FND00INV	Fund 00 investment scenario	100%	No	0%
2. FND50INV	Fund 50 investment scenario	50%	No	50%
3. FND00I&H	Fund 00 investment and household transfer scenario[a]	50%	No	0%
Public investment scenarios with productivity spillover effects				
4. FND50NTR	Fund 50 investment scenario with neutral productivity spillover	50%	Yes	50%
5. FND50AGR	Fund 50 investment scenario with agricultural productivity spillover	50%	Yes	50%
6. FND50NAG	Fund 50 investment scenario with nonagricultural productivity spillover	50%	Yes	50%

Source: Authors' estimations
Notes: (a) Uniform cash grant; 50% of oil revenue distributed to citizens

used by private and public agents for consumption (this is an endogenous effect) and investment (via increased private savings, or by design via the government closure selected). The latter increases the economy's total capital stock until peak oil production is reached, but the increased public capital does not sustain significantly higher output over the entire simulation period, as the capital stock in the oil sector is subsequently reduced to replicate declining output as oil reserves are gradually depleted. The simulation therefore allows the pure demand-side effects of the price boom to be isolated: Absorptive capacity constraints are binding and the demand effects lead to a real appreciation and the typical restructuring of production observed during an oil boom.

The second simulation, *FND50INV*, examines the case where only half of the oil revenue is invested immediately in public infrastructure while the remainder is deposited in a foreign oil fund. Government may choose this option in an attempt to mitigate or *sterilize* the Dutch Disease effects associated with a spend-all approach. Sterilization will reduce the growth effects relative to the experience of a massive spending boom, but at the same time the real exchange rate appreciation will be less pronounced since not all oil revenue from exports is brought back into the domestic economy. Although this may benefit export sectors in the short run, the net effect in the long run is not certain since investment flows and capital stock formation is lower in this scenario.

A third simulation, *FND00I&H*, investigates the option of using oil revenues to finance an unconditional uniform cash transfer scheme. This simulation assumes no deposit in a foreign oil fund; instead, half of oil revenue is spent on infrastructural investments (as in *FND50INV*) and the remainder is distributed equally among Uganda's citizens. The cash transfer is modeled as a nonuniform income tax cut across all household groups. The extent of the tax break varies across household groups in the model such that each citizen, irrespective of his or her age, receives the same per capita transfer in *absolute* terms (that is, initial average income tax rates and the size of household groups are taken into account in the calculation of the applicable tax cuts). In *relative* terms, therefore, poorer citizens receive a much larger welfare transfer than wealthy citizens. Since average tax rates are low in Uganda, several household groups end up with a negative tax rate, which effectively means their earnings from welfare transfers exceed income tax payments. If such a uniform grant scheme ever became a reality in Uganda it could be justified on the basis that each citizen in Uganda is entitled to an equal share of oil revenue. The design of the transfer mechanism implies that household incomes will rise across the board by the same absolute magnitude, causing poverty rates to decline, but income inequality will remain virtually unchanged. In contrast to the earlier scenarios, this simulation will lead to a significant increase in private disposable income, which is used by households to increase consumption and savings. The latter, in turn, finances private investment formation. Low savings rates, however, suggest that most of the additional income will be spent on household consumption.

Whereas the first set of oil simulations assume zero productivity spillover effects from public investments, the second set of simulations explore the importance of such productivity spillover. The aim here is to demonstrate not only the importance, in general, of ensuring that public investments are indeed *productivity-enhancing*, but also to show how investments that aim to raise productivity in specific sectors in the economy (for example, through direct targeting of agricultural or nonagricultural sectors) may ultimately have important growth and welfare or distributional implications. The scenarios all follow the same basic setup as *FND50INV* (that is, half of revenues are saved abroad and the other half is allocated to public infrastructure investments), but now assume that government infrastructure investment raises productivity relative to the growth already assumed in *BASELINE*. In *FND50NTR* the productivity-enhancing effect is uniform or neutral across sectors, whereas in *FND50AGR* and *FND50NAG* total factor productivity growth is biased in favor of agricultural/food-processing and nonagricultural sectors, respectively.

The extent of the total factor productivity spillover effects in each sector is linked directly to the level of spending on each of several budget items. Equation (3) defines this relationship. Thus, as explained before, any increase (or decrease) in the real government investment index $I^g{}_t/I^g{}_0$ in relation to the sector production index $Q_{s,t}/Q_{s,0}$ raises (or reduces) sectoral total factor productivity $A_{s,t}$, with the extent of the increase (reduction) determined by the spillover parameter ρ_{sg}. In the first set of investment simulations ρ_{sg} was set to zero, whereas in the spillover simulations $\rho_{sg} = 0.1$. Since the structure of government spending is likely to have a bearing on sectoral productivity spillover effects (Fan et al. 2009), *FND50AGR* and *FND50NAG* assume both an increase in total government investment spending (as in *FND50INV*) and also a change in the composition of that spending. Data on the current budget composition are obtained from Sennoga and Matovu (2010) and Twimukye et al. (2010). In *FND50AGR* we increase the allocation to agriculture by 20% (or 0.8% points) from 3.8 to 4.6% of total budgetary resources, while at the same the expenditure share to roads is reduced by 0.8% points. In *FND50NAG* we assume the opposite, that is, the expenditure share on agriculture is reduced by 0.8% and vice versa for roads. Next, growth-expenditure elasticities (from Benin et al. 2008) are applied to calculate the marginal effect of the absolute and compositional shift in public expenditure sectoral productivity. The growth-expenditure elasticity for agricultural spending is 1.4, whereas it is 2.7 for roads. The result is that total factor productivities in agriculture and food-processing sectors increase by about 25% in *FND50AGR*, while they decrease by about 10% in other manufacturing and trade and transport sectors (these changes are relative to the growth rate in *BASELINE*). The effects are the exact opposite in *FND50NAG*. In the neutral spending scenario (*FND50NTR*) there is no compositional shift in spending, hence productivity across all sectors grows by the same margin.

4 Model Results

4.1 Public Investment Scenarios with No Productivity Spillover Effects

4.1.1 Spending All Revenues on Infrastructure (*FND00INV*)

The major effects and transmission channels of the oil boom in Uganda are described with reference to the results of scenario *FND00INV*, which serves as the benchmark for other oil scenarios. Public investment expenditures are linked directly to government oil revenue and will therefore increase until peak oil production is reached in 2017. Thereafter these expenditures gradually decline due to declining government oil revenues (which in turn is linked to the real exchange rate appreciation) and the gradual winding down of oil production activities.

Under *FND00INV* the Ugandan economy grows rapidly at 6.9% per year until 2017, mainly because of the large increase in real public-sector investment (see Table 2: Part A). Overall investment grows at 9.5% per year over this period. Household income also rises in these scenarios, which leads to an increase in private consumption (by 5.1% during 2007–2017) and savings. However, private savings as a share of GDP actually declines (not reported in Table 2), which suggests the oil boom crowds out private-sector investment, at least in relative terms. A further factor is the real exchange rate appreciation. Although in general such an appreciation would mean imported capital goods become less expensive,

Table 2 GDP growth, sectoral composition, welfare, and poverty: *No productivity spillover* scenarios during oil expansion period, 2007–2017, and entire oil extraction period, 2007–2046

	Initial value			No productivity oil scenarios					
		BASELINE		*FND00INV*		*FND50INV*		*FND00I&H*	
	2007	2007–2017	2007–2046	2007–2017	2007–2046	2007–2017	2007–2046	2007–2017	2007–2046
Part A: Annual growth rate of demand[a]									
Absorption	26,584	4.2	4.7	5.8	5.2	5.1	5.0	5.7	4.9
Private consumption	18,743	4.5	5.0	5.1	5.5	4.8	5.3	5.7	5.3
Fixed investment	5014	3.6	4.4	9.5	4.9	7.1	4.7	7.2	4.2
Government consumption	2689	3.0	3.0	3.0	3.0	3.0	3.0	3.0	3.0
Exports	3697	6.9	7.0	12.7	7.8	14.0	7.4	12.7	7.3
Imports	−7260	4.7	5.6	7.2	6.2	6.1	5.9	7.2	5.9
GDP at factor cost	21,318	4.5	5.1	6.9	5.6	6.8	5.3	6.8	5.3
Real exchange rate[b,c]		−0.5 (−5.2)	−0.9 (−30.7)	−1.3 (−12.4)	−1.2 (−37.5)	−0.8 (−7.7)	−1.1 (−34.4)	−1.6 (−15.2)	−1.1 (−34.5)
Consumer price index[c]		0.5 (5.0)	0.9 (40.3)	1.2 (12.9)	1.2 (56.2)	0.7 (7.7)	1.0 (48.7)	1.6 (16.9)	1.0 (49.1)
Part B: Sector share of GDP by 2017 and 2046		(2017)	(2046)	(2017)	(2046)	(2017)	(2046)	(2017)	(2046)
Agriculture	22.6	21.1	13.2	16.8	11.2	16.9	12.1	17.2	12.6
Industry	27.3	24.7	20.7	45.6	21.2	42.7	21.0	43.8	19.7
Mining (including crude oil)	0.4	0.3	0.1	17.6	0.2	17.7	0.2	17.7	0.2
Oil refining	–	–	–	1.3	> 0.1	1.3	0.0	1.3	0.0
Services	50.1	54.2	66.1	37.6	67.6	40.4	66.9	39.0	67.7
	100.0	100.0	100.0	100.0	100.0	100.0	100.0	100.0	100.0
Part C: Equivalent variation[d]		Cumulative growth			Percentage point deviation from BASELINE				
Rural farm	342	56.0	557.8	6.9	109.4	3.1	58.9	24.4	75.4
Rural nonfarm	135	54.9	563.0	9.3	122.9	4.0	65.9	13.6	56.5
Kampala metro	1277	55.4	579.2	9.3	139.8	4.4	74.6	10.0	56.5

Urban farm	1100	50.3	520.9	9.0	126.2	4.6	67.5	17.0	63.5
Urban nonfarm	1249	55.0	575.2	9.6	137.2	4.4	73.3	12.4	59.4
Average	820	54.3	559.2	8.8	127.1	4.1	68.0	15.5	62.2
Part D: Headcount poverty (P_0) (percent)		(2017)	(2046)	(2017)	(2046)	(2017)	(2046)	(2017)	(2046)
National	31.1	22.6	3.5	20.5	1.9	21.7	2.5	16.2	2.4
Rural	34.3	24.8	3.9	22.6	2.2	23.9	2.8	17.7	2.8
Urban	13.8	10.2	1.4	8.5	0.6	9.4	0.9	8.0	0.9

Source: CGE model results

Note:

[a]Initial value in US dollars billions

[b]Trade-weighted real exchange rate

[c]Overall growth rate in parentheses

[d]Initial expenditure per capita in US dollars thousands

capital formation in Uganda is in fact intensive in nontradable goods (for example, nontradable construction goods make up 78% of investments). This means that foreign capital inflows, which are assumed to grow at 3% annually in all scenarios, finance less and less real investment over time. Diminishing oil reserves means the real exchange rate appreciation weakens over time, but this is not sufficient to reverse the trend of declining non-oil exports. In fact, the initial welfare gains associated with the surge in public-sector investment weaken over time as other components of GDP (for example, private investments, consumption, and exports) fail to grow more rapidly when public investments eventually decline.

A comparison of *FND00INV* with *BASELINE* reveals the typical characteristics of Dutch Disease. The consumer price index increases at an average annual rate of 1.2% during 2007–2046, while the (trade-weighted) real exchange rate appreciates by 1.3% between 2007 and 2017 or by 1.2% per year over the entire 2007–2046 period. Relative to *BASELINE*, the spending of windfall revenues leads to a 0.2 and 1.5% point contraction in agriculture and services, respectively, in the medium term. As a result, these two sectors' shares of GDP also decline dramatically by 4.6 and 16.4% points relative to the base (2007–2017; see Table 2: Part B). The services sector regains growth momentum in the long run, but agricultural growth only improves marginally relative to the base. Thus, while real GDP at factor cost increases, the agricultural sector actually suffers a decline in GDP, both absolutely (compared to *BASELINE*) during the oil expansion period and relative to other sectors over the total oil extraction period (Table 2: Part B). The services sector also realizes absolute income losses in the medium term, but a reversal of fortunes sees this sector become the engine of long-term growth.[1]

Table 3 presents more disaggregated sectoral production results (GDP at factor cost), focusing on changes during the oil expansion period (2007–2017). The first column shows the average annual change in *BASELINE*, and the remaining columns show the percentage point changes in production in the various oil scenarios relative to *BASELINE*. The results for *FND00INV* corroborate the picture of Dutch Disease. Crude and refined oil production expand tremendously, while less tradable subsectors in agriculture, industry, and services also expand production. Within agriculture, export-oriented crops and other agriculture (which includes fisheries, a fairly significant exporter) suffer the greatest declines relative to the base, mainly due to the adverse real exchange rate effects on the trade competitiveness of these subsectors. The same is true for sectors such as fish processing and hotels and catering, both of which are highly export-oriented.

Government spending patterns also determine different sectors' relative performance under *FND00INV*. Increased government expenditure on investment goods leads to a sharp increase in demand for construction services (nontraded) and machinery (mostly imported) in particular. This in turn leads to an indirect increase in demand for intermediate input goods typically supplied by manufacturing and

[1]Of course, the observed structural shift is also a feature of the *BASELINE* scenario, and is, to a large extent, a natural outcome for any developing country's growth path.

Table 3 Annual growth rate of sectoral production (GDP at factor cost): all scenarios during the oil expansion period, 2007–2017

		Percentage point deviation from BASELINE					
		No productivity spillovers		With productivity spillovers			
	BASELINE (%)	*FND00INV*	*FND50INV*	*FND00I&H*	*FND50NTR*	*FND50AGR*	*FND50NAG*
GDP	4.50	2.41	2.32	2.30	3.17	3.26	2.98
Agriculture	3.88	−0.18	−0.11	0.02	0.93	1.32	0.44
Cereals	3.56	−0.07	−0.02	−0.06	1.02	1.33	0.59
Root crops	4.16	0.11	0.05	0.22	1.03	1.39	0.56
Matooke	3.75	0.10	0.05	0.20	1.05	1.34	0.66
Pulses	4.54	−0.03	−0.01	0.01	0.96	1.45	0.38
Horticulture	4.10	0.16	0.07	0.30	1.05	1.35	0.64
Export agriculture	4.49	−0.49	−0.14	−0.70	0.88	1.60	0.05
Livestock	3.95	−0.07	−0.05	0.00	0.98	1.27	0.57
Other agriculture	3.34	−0.50	−0.38	0.12	0.78	1.12	0.34
Industry	3.72	9.00	8.26	8.33	8.80	8.84	8.68
Mining	2.29	55.60	55.60	55.58	55.61	55.61	55.61
Crude oil	1.04	85.19	85.21	85.18	85.19	85.20	85.19
Manufacturing	3.35	2.58	2.65	2.54	3.61	3.72	3.40
Food processing	4.20	−0.07	−0.05	0.35	1.03	1.25	0.74
Fish processing	0.68	−8.15	−4.56	−7.88	−1.93	−1.14	−2.91
Nonfood manufacturing	2.40	5.13	5.22	4.71	6.10	6.12	5.95
Refined oil	1.04	85.19	85.21	85.18	85.19	85.20	85.19
Other industry	3.89	4.03	2.40	2.62	3.24	3.28	3.05
Construction	3.67	5.06	3.02	3.14	3.80	3.85	3.62
Services	5.17	−1.46	−0.89	−1.08	0.18	0.20	0.05
Hotels and catering	13.37	−16.52	−8.63	−16.36	−6.02	−6.87	−5.45
Public services	3.91	0.16	0.09	0.77	0.66	0.67	0.57

Source: CGE model results

services sectors. Despite increased economic activity in nonagricultural sectors (that is, industry in particular), the knock-on effects for nontradable agricultural subsectors is almost negligible.

The contraction of production under *FNDOOINV* is most pronounced in cotton; tobacco; flowers; coffee; and tea, cocoa, and vanilla, where most or all of total production is exported. These sectors do not benefit from higher prices as a result of increasing domestic demand but are negatively affected by higher factor costs and higher prices for intermediate inputs. The latter also holds true for import-competing cereals (maize, rice, other cereals), pulses (oilseeds and beans), and livestock. Though these sectors are more oriented toward the domestic market and therefore benefit from generally higher domestic income, demand elasticities are fairly low and the demand effect is not strong enough to compensate for the negative supply effect. Moreover, producers of maize, rice, other cereals, and oilseeds face competition from foreign suppliers. Given the high substitution possibilities for agricultural goods in domestic demand, the expansion of domestic demand is insufficient to counter the substitution effect. The assumption of zero productivity spillover effects in this scenario also explains the weak performance of nontradable agricultural subsectors. As later results show, these adverse effects can be offset by using oil revenues to raise agricultural productivity. The contraction of fisheries results from strong forward linkages to fish processing, a highly export-oriented food-processing sector, which suffers from Dutch Disease effects.

Only a select few agricultural subsectors (root crops, *matooke*, and horticultural crops) and forestry realize an increase in production in *FNDOOINV* relative to *BASELINE*. These benefit from increasing domestic private demand as a result of higher private income. In the former three sectors, private demand expansion is sufficiently strong to induce price increases, which overcompensate cost increases. Forestry is also a pure nontradable, and though not directly consumed, benefits from its forward linkages to the furniture industry, which is an investment-goods industry and therefore directly affected by increased public investment demand.

We next turn to welfare and household poverty results. The equivalent variation (EV) measures welfare improvements after controlling for price changes (see Table 2: Part C). Under *BASELINE* there is a marked improvement in the EV measure, with all household groups experiencing an increase in EV of between 4.8 and 5% on average per year over the 2007–2046 period (or 520–575% on aggregate). Gains are also fairly equally distributed, with rural farm households gaining slightly more thanks to a relatively rapid agricultural productivity growth rate assumed in *BASELINE*. Sustained GDP growth of just over 5% per year will virtually eliminate poverty by 2046 (Table 4: Part D); the national poverty headcount (P0) drops to about 3.5% from 31.1% in the base.[2]

The introduction of oil (*FNDOOINV*) sees more rapid improvements in EV for higher income urban and nonfarm households than for rural farming households.

---

[2]Similar rates of decline are observed for the depth of poverty measure but are not reported in Table 2.

Table 4 GDP growth, sectoral composition, welfare, and poverty: productivity spillover scenarios during oil expansion and peak production period, 2007–2026

		No oil (2007–2026)	No productivity spillover (2007–2026)	With productivity spillover (2007–2026)		
	Initial value 2007	*BASELINE*	*FND50INV*	*FND50NTR*	*FND50AGR*	*FND50NAG*
Part A: Annual growth rate of demand[a]						
Absorption	26,584	4.3	4.9	5.4	5.5	5.2
Private consumption	18,743	4.7	5.1	5.6	5.7	5.4
Fixed investment	5014	3.8	5.3	5.9	6.0	5.7
Government consumption	2689	3.0	3.0	3.0	3.0	3.0
Exports	3697	6.9	9.4	9.7	9.7	9.7
Imports	−7260	5.0	5.8	6.1	6.1	6.1
GDP at factor cost	21,318	4.7	5.7	6.2	6.3	6.0
Real exchange rate[b,c]		−0.9 (−12.1)	−0.9 (−15.6)	−0.6 (−11.0)	−0.4 (−7.1)	−0.9 (−15.5)
Consumer price index[c]		0.6 (13.8)	0.8 (18.5)	0.6 (12.4)	0.4 (7.2)	0.9 (18.5)
Part B: Sector share of GDP by 2026						
Agriculture	22.6	19.9	16.6	17.0	18.2	15.9
Industry	27.3	23.8	35.3	35.2	35.0	35.5
Mining (including crude oil)	0.4	0.2	11.2	10.2	10.1	10.6
Oil refining	50.1	56.2	48.1	47.8	46.8	48.6
Services	22.6	19.9	16.6	17.0	18.2	15.9
	100.0	100.0	100.0	100.0	100.0	100.0
Part C: Equivalent variation[d]			Cumulative growth	Percentage point deviation from FND50INV		
Rural farm	342		155.2	26.7	35.2	13.2
Rural nonfarm	135		156.0	22.9	28.6	12.3
Kampala metro	1277		159.9	24.4	29.8	13.8
Urban farm	1100		145.7	21.4	27.2	11.0

(continued)

Table 4 (continued)

		No oil (2007–2026)	No productivity spillover (2007–2026)		With productivity spillover (2007–2026)					
	Initial value 2007	*BASELINE*	*FND50INV*		*FND50NTR*		*FND50AGR*		*FND50NAG*	
Urban nonfarm	1249		158.6		23.3		28.3		13.0	
Average	820		155.1		23.7		29.8		12.7	
Part D: Headcount poverty (*P0*)			(2017)	(2026)	(2017)	(2026)	(2017)	(2026)	(2017)	(2026)
National	31.1		21.7	12.5	17.3	9.7	16.6	8.9	18.4	11.0
	34.3		23.9	13.8	19.0	10.7	18.2	9.9	20.3	12.1
	13.8		9.4	5.6	7.7	4.1	7.7	3.8	8.0	4.9

Source: CGE model results
Note:
[a]Initial value in US dollars billions
[b]Trade-weighted real exchange rate
[c]Overall growth rate in parentheses
[d]Initial expenditure per capita in US dollars thousands

This relates to oil production, construction, and nonfood manufacturing being more capital and skilled-labor intensive, which means increases in factor returns in these sectors tend to benefit higher income and urban households. Self-employed family labor in the agricultural sector is furthermore assumed to remain in the agricultural sector, which means farm households do not benefit much from increasing labor demand and higher wages in nonagricultural sectors, yet they face the same consumer price increases as all other households in the economy. The uneven distributional outcomes under *FND00INV* are also reflected in poverty outcomes. Although the oil boom leads to a larger overall reduction in poverty relative to *BASELINE*, urban poverty declines faster than rural poverty. For example, by 2017 rural poverty is 22.6% in *FND00INV*, an 8.8% drop from the *BASELINE* rate of 24.8%. In contrast, the urban poverty rate is 16.1% lower by in *FND00INV* relative to *BASELINE* by 2017.

Summing up, channeling windfall oil revenue into the Ugandan economy poses a number of challenges. The first one is the likely appreciation of the real exchange rate—the increase in the price of nontradable goods and services, in particular construction—as demand for them increases with windfall revenue in the face of a limited supply response, and its corollary in terms of lost export competitiveness in agriculture and food processing. The second one is the likely drop in overall productivity, as more factors get concentrated in nontradable sectors where potential productivity gains are much scarcer. The third one is the existence of reallocation (investments, migrations) and transition costs (lost markets and know-how), which can make temporary specialization costly overall if the society has to return to its previous specialization patterns. This risk exists with oil in Uganda, given its exhaustible nature, the shape of the likely extraction path, and the possibility that it conducts to an untenable pattern of specialization if government oil revenues are immediately invested and public investments do not confer any spillovers on private-sector productivity.

4.1.2 Transferring Oil Revenues to a Foreign Oil Fund (*FND50INV*)

In the face of severe Dutch Disease effects, Uganda could consider fixing the share of oil revenue to be transferred to the budget and investing the remainder abroad. The impact of such a sterilization strategy is analyzed in scenario *FND50INV*, which assumes that only half of current oil revenue is used to finance public infrastructure investment while the other half is saved in an oil fund abroad. This fund is assumed to be some variant of a permanent income fund (PIF) from which no withdrawals are made during the simulation period. Since none of the invested oil funds make their way back into the economy over the simulation period, we do not explicitly account for interest earned when calculating the cumulative fund value. However, with the nominal exchange rate as numéraire in the model all deposits into the fund are real values; hence, the fund also does not depreciate in value. As a share of GDP the fund reaches more than 50% of GDP by about 2030. After this the fund as a share of GDP declines as no additional oil revenues are deposited into the fund but GDP continues to grow exponentially.

Sterilizing part of the oil revenue and reducing government investment spending leads to less overall investment, less capital accumulation, and lower private consumption and absorption in the medium term (2007–2017). This causes GDP growth to decline marginally in *FND50INV* compared to *FND00INV*, although growth still exceeds that observed in *BASELINE* (Table 2: Part A). Capital outflows (that is, deposits into the oil fund) cause a much smaller real exchange rate appreciation in *FND50INV*, which means the restructuring of supply from trade-oriented sectors with relatively higher total factor productivity growth (for example, agriculture and certain services sectors) toward domestic-market-oriented industrial sectors with lower total factor productivities is less pronounced. This relative productivity gain coupled with the improved export performance almost entirely makes up for the GDP loss associated with the 50% reduction in oil funds invested and the lower level of capital accumulation, at least in the medium term. In the long run, however, total factor productivity effects in *FND50INV* are insufficient to compensate for the lower levels of capital accumulation, with overall GDP growth now deviating more from that in the previous scenario. At the 3% real government consumption growth rate imposed in all these scenarios the adjustment cost falls on private households, with private consumption growing by only 0.2 and 0.3% points more than in *BASELINE* during 2007–2017 and 2007–2046, respectively, compared to 0.5% points in *FND00INV* (both periods).

Tradable and nontradable agricultural subsectors are affected differently by the sterilization of oil revenues. Relative to *FND00INV*, the lower real appreciation improves the competitiveness of export-oriented and import-competing agricultural subsectors. In both types of subsectors, lower costs for nontradable intermediate inputs improve these sectors' domestic terms of trade. In addition, lower price increases on domestic markets, due to less expansion of private domestic consumption, imply that the spread between domestic prices and import and export prices is less pronounced. Thus, on the supply-side, the extent of export reduction is lower in all export-oriented subsectors, whereas on the demand-side, part of the substitution of domestic supply by imports is avoided. Both types of adjustments—export penetration and import substitution—benefit agricultural producers of export crops and agricultural import substitutes. As a result, the contraction of production in these sectors is less pronounced in *FND50INV* compared to *FND00INV* (see Table 3). In contrast, agricultural nontradable goods, such as root crops, *matooke*, and horticulture, are negatively affected by lower private consumer demand, the latter being the result of lower overall income in the Ugandan economy compared to the full spending scenario.

The welfare (EV) results for *FND50INV* in Table 2 (Part C) indicate that, while all households suffer from welfare losses as a result of sterilization, nonfarm households in Kampala and other urban areas will lose out most from the resultant lower levels of public investment. There are two reasons for this result: First, the positive income effect of a higher capital rental rate (for now scarcer capital) is more than offset by lower capital availability; second, wage increases for skilled labor, which is another primary source of income for urban households, are also lower compared to *FND00INV*. The rate of poverty reduction is also lower in all household groups if part of the oil revenue is sterilized (Table 2: Part D). Thus, while sterilization counters Dutch Disease and possibly allows future generations to benefit from increased spending of oil revenues that are saved now, it also means that fewer benefits are transferred to citizens in the medium term.

4.1.3 Transferring Rents to Citizens (*FND00I&H*)

We next consider a scenario where poverty is targeted directly by redistributing part of oil revenues directly to citizens rather than saving funds in an external oil fund. As a variation of *FND00INV*, FND00I&H evaluates the option of investing half of oil revenue in infrastructure while the other half is distributed to citizens as a direct welfare transfer. Each citizen receives the exact same per capita transfer. Households use this windfall to finance additional consumption spending or to save, depending on the average savings propensities specified for different household groups in the CGE model. The grant being uniformly distributed implies that poorer households receive a larger relative transfer. Figure 1 shows the impact of the welfare grant on average per capita income in 2017 when peak production is reached and the transfer value is at a maximum.

The figure shows that prior to receiving the welfare grant, rural farm households have a per capita income of USh900,000 per year in 2017 (approximately $375, or just more than $1 per person per day). The welfare transfer, modeled as a tax rebate, adds a further USh129,000 to their income ($50–60 per person per year); thus, as a share of income the transfer is worth 14.4% to these households. At the other end of the income spectrum are citizens of Kampala with a per capita income of USh5.4 million. To these people the transfer of USh129,000 is worth only 2.4% of their

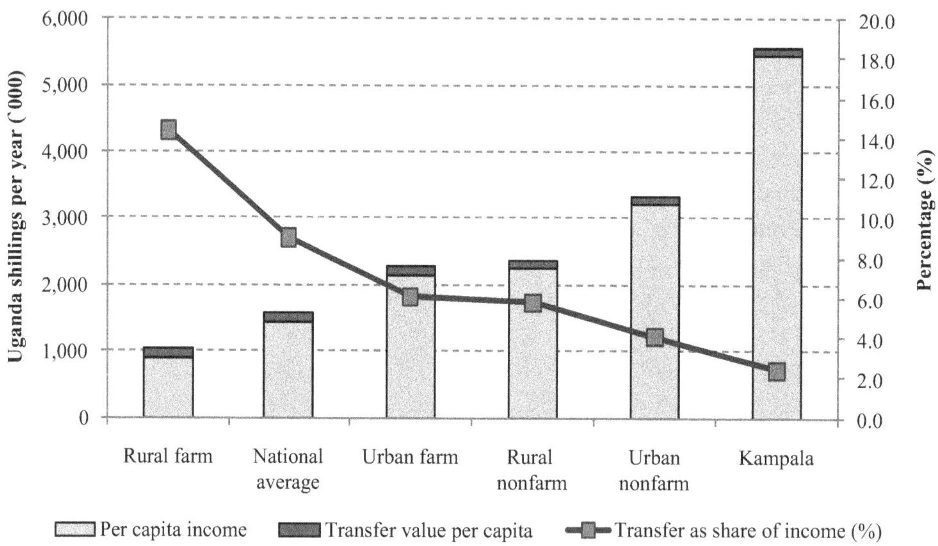

Fig. 1 Average per capita income and per capita transfer values (FND00I&H), 2017. Source: CGE model results

income. About three-quarters of Ugandans live in rural farm households; hence, the national average per capita income is only slightly above that of rural farm households (USh1.4 million), whereas the transfer is worth 9% of income.

Despite price increases, the expansion of private household consumption benefits the agricultural sector as a whole, with overall agricultural GDP growth in *FND00I&H* marginally higher than in *BASELINE* (agricultural growth declined relative to *BASELINE* in both *FND00INV* and *FND50INV*). However, the real exchange rate appreciation accompanying the expansion of private consumption induces structural changes both across and within agricultural subsectors in terms of production for the domestic and world markets. In particular, the expansion of private consumption benefits producers of nontradable agricultural goods such as root crops, *matooke*, horticulture, livestock, and forestry. Export agriculture is now even more negatively affected compared to *FND50INV* due to production cost increases and a stronger real exchange rate. Similarly, import-competing agricultural subsectors, such as cereals and oilseeds, also contract as a result of production cost increases and stronger competition from abroad. In all these subsectors, the demand effect from increased private consumption is not sufficiently strong to compensate for the negative import substitution effect that results from the real exchange rate appreciation. With relatively inelastic demand and strong substitution possibilities between domestic and imported agricultural foodcrops, the substitution effect overcompensates the demand effect.

Compared to the first two experiments, the redistribution of rents creates more employment opportunities in agriculture and leads to significantly higher land rentals and prices for livestock. Thus, a larger share of factor income accrues to rural households, who in turn spend a larger share of their incomes on goods produced domestically and in rural areas. This is corroborated by changes in the EV presented in Table 2 (Part C). These results indicate that welfare improves more rapidly for lower income rural and urban farm households than for higher income nonfarm households. Of course, this result also stems directly from the welfare transfer itself, which in relative terms causes incomes of poorer households to increase more than that of wealthier households (Fig. 1). Moreover, the redistribution of oil rents leads to more consumption by all households, and since production of consumption goods (agricultural and food products in particular) is more land and unskilled-labor intensive, the resulting increases in these factor returns benefit lower income and rural households more.

The uneven distributional impacts are also reflected in poverty outcomes (Table 2: Part D). Between 2007 and 2017 the redistribution of oil rents leads to a significant decline in poverty at the national level, and also relative to *BASELINE* and the first two oil production scenarios. Moreover, rural poverty declines more rapidly than urban poverty. In fact, redistribution is twice as effective at reducing poverty among rural households compared to other rent spending options considered. By 2046, however, poverty outcomes under *FND00INV* are superior to those under *FND00I&H*. This suggests that investments have longer lasting benefits in terms of production capacity and employment in the future. This benefits the poor more in the longer term than welfare handouts in the medium term. Of course, there are several caveats, one of which is the fact that we assume households' expenditure patterns remain unchanged after receiving welfare transfers. In reality, households may choose to invest extra income earned in (say) education, which will raise their productivity and future employability. We also do not consider productivity spillover effects of the investments themselves, which is the focus of the next set of experiments.

4.2 Public Investment Scenarios with Productivity Spillover Effects

In this set of simulations we once again model an increase in public investments, now assuming that these investments have productivity spillover effects in the private sector. All scenarios use *FND50INV* as the basis, with productivity spillover effects determined by both the level of investment spending and its structure. The first simulation, *FND50NTR*, assumes a *neutral* allocation of public investment spending. This assumes increased spending has a uniform productivity-enhancing effect across all sectors of the economy, that is, total factor productivity in all sectors grow by the same margin, in percentage terms, over and above the growth already defined in *BASELINE*. In the second simulation (*FND50AGR*) we model the effect of agricultural-biased public investment spending. This means spending is targeted toward improving agricultural productivity relative to nonagricultural productivity through investing relatively more in (for example) rural and agricultural infrastructure. In this scenario the productivity effects of government infrastructure are restricted to agricultural value-added chains (agricultural sectors and food-processing sectors) and core agricultural inputs, such as communications, banking, and real estate services (this serves to alleviate possible supply constraints in input markets). Finally, *FND50NAG* investigates a restructuring of public investment expenditures toward urban infrastructure at the expense of agriculture-related infrastructure.

In the discussion of results it is important to note that the three scenarios are not necessarily directly comparable as far as overall performance of the economy is concerned. Although a formulaic approach is adopted for determining the productivity shock associated with a certain level and structure of public investment, we do not consider the efficiency of such public spending across different sectors. In reality, cross-sectoral differences in initial productivity rates and productivity growth potential imply that the cost of achieving (say) a 1% increase in productivity may differ from one subsector to the next. What we can (and indeed do) compare are structural differences between the different scenarios. We also compare economic performance in the three productivity spillover scenarios to the no productivity spillover scenario (*FND50INV*).

Table 4 presents the simulation results. Here we only focus on the 2007–2026 period, which includes the run-up to peak oil production as well as the decade during which peak production levels are sustained. All three productivity spillover scenarios assume the same increase in public infrastructural investments as in *FND50INV*. Initially, as public infrastructural investments rise in line with oil revenue increases, the productivity spillover scenarios are exactly the same as *FND50INV*. It is only by 2020 that we assume the productivity spillovers take effect (that is, we allow for a 3-year lag from the time public investments peak in 2017 until a higher level of productivity growth is reached). At this point we observe a fairly substantial additional GDP growth impact in all three scenarios relative to *FND50INV*, such that growth over the 2007–2026 period exceeds growth in *FND50INV* by between 0.3 and 0.6% points across the three productivity spillover scenarios. Even though the same level of oil-funded public investment is assumed in all these scenarios, the increased economic activity means that there is a marked rise in total annual investment as private savings increase.

Real exchange rate and price impacts differ substantially across the three scenarios. Although the real exchange rate appreciates in all these scenarios, it depreciates relative to *BASELINE*, and in *FND50NTR* and *FND50AGR* the real exchange also depreciates relative to *FND50INV*. In contrast, the real exchange rate in *FND50NAG* is virtually unchanged from what was observed in *BASELINE* and *FND50INV*. The combined effect of increased productivity and more favorable terms of trade in at least two of the scenarios mean that export volumes increase in all three productivity spillover scenarios. This is illustrated by the improved performance of sectors such as export-oriented agriculture, livestock, other agriculture, and food processing, all of which grow relative to the decline in GDP observed in *FND50INV* (see Table 3). Other major exporters such as fish processing and hotels and catering show a relative improvement compared to *FND50INV*.

We have previously established that public investment spending in an oil production context and the assumption of no productivity spillovers tends to benefit urban nonfarm households more than rural farm households, since the latter group is largely bypassed as a result of missing backward linkages from rapidly growing industrial and services sectors. The productivity spillover scenarios now suggest a rapid improvement in the outcomes for rural farm households. All households still enjoy increases in welfare (EV) over time if public investment spending does not discriminate between sectors (*FND50NTR*), but, interestingly, the absolute and proportionate gains are now highest for rural farm households (Table 4: Part C). These altered distributional impacts are also reflected in the poverty results (Table 4: Part D), which show that rural poverty declines slightly faster than urban poverty. This relates to the Ugandan economy's ability to produce more tradable and nontradable goods as a result of productivity increases, whereas the reversal of the real exchange rate appreciation shifts the domestic terms of trade in favor of export-oriented and import-competing producers of tradable goods and against producers of nontradable goods. All agricultural sectors now expand their production, whereas export-oriented agricultural sectors increase their export supply. Thus, although many agricultural sectors shrank when public investments were unproductive (for example, in *FND50INV*), the sector is able to expand as a result of productivity spillovers, even when not targeted directly as is the case in *FND50NTR*.

In the case where nonagricultural sectors are targeted (*FND50NAG*), additional public investment spending on urban road infrastructure increases total factor productivity growth in the tradable nonfood-manufacturing sectors (that is, textiles, wood and paper, other manufacturing, machinery, and furniture) and in the trade, hotel and catering, and transport services sectors. At the same time we assume lower levels of spending on rural infrastructure, which reduces total factor productivity growth in all agricultural and food-processing sectors as well as in the less-tradable communications, banking, real estate, and community services sectors. As expected, when productivity growth is lower in sectors that predominantly supply goods for the domestic market (these are also goods that cannot easily be substituted by imports), the spending of oil revenues causes a larger (relative) appreciation of the real exchange rate than in the case of neutral productivity spillovers. Hence, although the manufacturing export performance is slightly stronger in machinery and equipment, hotels and catering, and transport, the agricultural sector is hit relatively hard when productivity gains are biased against it. At 4.1% per year, average agricultural growth in *FND50NAG* is half a percentage point lower than in *FND50NTR*, and the agricultural sector's share in GDP declines by more than a percentage point by 2026 vis-à-vis a neutral allocation of investment spending.

When public investment spending is biased in favor of agriculture and food processing (*FND50AGR*), outcomes are markedly different. Increased supply of agricultural goods and food items is sufficiently strong to more than offset the demand effects of the oil boom, such that the initial real exchange rate appreciation observed in *FND50INV* is reversed within a relatively short time. The effects on exports are a mirror image of those in *FND50NAG*; agriculture exports recover more strongly than in the former experiment, but lower productivity growth in nonfood manufacturing results in a more sluggish recovery in manufacturing exports.

The most striking difference between the two public investment options, though, is the effect on real household disposable incomes, welfare and poverty (Table 4: Parts C and D). Compared to *FND50NTR*, a manufacturing bias (*FND50NAG*) sharply moderates real income and welfare growth in the economy. The total rise in EV relative to *FND50INV* is only 12.7% points in *FND50NAG* compared to 23.7% points in *FND50NTR*. Moreover, the income gain is spread somewhat unevenly across household groups, with rural farm households now faring worse than Kampala households. This contrasts sharply with the outcome under *FND50AGR*, which generates markedly higher aggregate real income gains in the medium term (29.8% points), and one that benefits poorer rural households more. Poverty outcomes for rural and urban households improve in the agricultural-biased scenario relative to the neutral scenario, whereas in the manufacturing-biased scenario poverty rates are higher compared to the neutral growth scenario. In all productivity scenarios, however, poverty rates decline more rapidly than in *FND50INV*.

Given the significant impact on agricultural growth and on the welfare of rural households of the agricultural productivity spillovers from the increased public investments arising from Uganda's oil revenue, it is critical that the Government of

Uganda put in place mechanisms by which these productivity spillovers can be maximized. What is needed, in particular, is a well-coordinated set of interventions aimed at improving competitiveness in the agricultural sector, which would serve as a platform sustainable growth in the economy. However, at 3.8% of the budget, current spending on agriculture in Uganda is well below the 10% target committed to under the Comprehensive African Agricultural Development Program (CAADP). Research by Fan et al. (2009) suggests that agricultural research and development, infrastructure (such as rural roads), and investments in education and skills have the highest payoffs in terms of agricultural productivity gains and increased competitiveness of the sector.

5 Conclusion

Even at conservative prices of $70–80 per barrel, future oil revenue in Uganda will be considerable, potentially doubling government revenue within 6–10 years and constituting an estimated 10–15% of GDP at peak production. The economic impact of oil production on the country's agricultural performance and the livelihood of rural households could be profound, particularly during the first phase of the projected extraction when massive additional inflows of foreign exchange need to be managed by the Ugandan government. The so-called Dutch Disease effects may affect the international competitiveness of export sectors, such as agriculture in particular, and it is likely to make the country's growth strategy—with its emphasis on value-added, export diversification, and manufacturing—harder to achieve. This would threaten to increase, rather than decrease, the urban–rural income gap.

Agriculture and related processing currently contribute about 27% to GDP. Food and agriculture-related processing make up about 50% of household consumption expenditure. Poverty is higher in rural than in urban households and within rural households it is highest among nonfarm households. Even with no oil revenue, agriculture's share of GDP is projected to decrease by 6.8% points from 22.6% in 2007 to 15.8% over the next 40 years, as increasing factor productivities in tradable sectors and increasing per capita income and consumption will be leading toward a restructuring of production in favor of services.

It is important to differentiate between medium- and long-term impacts of oil revenue spending, since structural impacts differ and asymmetric adjustment flexibilities (ratchet effects) in factor markets (investments, migrations) and foreign trade (lost markets and know-how) can make temporary specialization costly if the Ugandan society has to return to its previous specialization patterns because of the exhaustible nature of oil reserves.

The impacts of oil extraction will be felt by Uganda mostly indirectly through higher government expenditures on consumption (largely administration) and investment; direct effects through higher domestic factor income in oil extraction and refining and through backward linkages will be minimal given production technologies and the economic enclave character of the oil industry. Results of this chapter suggest that the extraction and refining of oil will increase overall GDP growth, increase national and rural real household incomes, and benefit the poor in Uganda. In the medium term, that is, from the starting of oil extraction (2011 in this analysis) until reaching peak production (2017), overall average annual GDP growth will be between 2.3 and 3.3% points higher than in a comparable baseline projection without oil. In the long term over the total extraction path of 40 years, the average growth rate will be between 0.2 and 0.5% points higher. The differences depend on how oil revenues are spent, on whether public infrastructure confers any spillovers on private-sector productivity, and in which sectors these spillovers occur.

Several conclusions emerge from the simulations presented in this paper. First, with the projected oil extraction path and recently high oil prices, a real appreciation of the Uganda shilling is almost inevitable. Although policies designed to limit absorption through tight fiscal and monetary policies would reduce the pressure on the exchange rate over the short to medium term, they are unlikely to be sufficient to eliminate it. A rapid buildup of foreign exchange reserves and the accumulation of government oil revenue in some kind of external resource fund could mitigate the pressure but at the expense of domestic investment, the fiscal position, and private household welfare and consumption, as well as poverty reduction. In any case, agriculture and the rural population will be discriminated against by the expected oil boom. As net producers of tradable goods and net consumers of nontradable goods they suffer twice, from increased production costs and higher prices for consumer goods. Only a few select agricultural subsectors that produce exclusively for the domestic market, such as root crops, *matooke*, and horticulture, realize income gains as a result of generally higher income and consumption. Transferring part of the oil rent to citizens—rather than to a foreign oil fund—would directly increase household welfare and accelerate poverty reduction efforts. Moreover, agriculture as a whole would regain growth momentum. However, the real appreciation accompanying the oil-rent-financed expansion of private consumption would induce strong structural changes both across and within agricultural subsectors, which might be difficult to reverse once oil revenues dry out. Thus, there is the real danger of losing long-run competitiveness vis-à-vis foreign suppliers both on world markets for agricultural export commodities as well as on domestic markets for food products.

Second, Uganda's oil discovery comes at an opportune moment as the country battles with the challenges of marked infrastructural backlogs. In this situation of initial scarcity of public infrastructure, oil-funded increases in public infrastructure may lead to potentially large medium-term welfare gains, despite the presence of Dutch Disease effects. This is particularly true when public infrastructure augments the productivity of private factors. Yet, the sectoral and distributional consequences of these investments are highly sensitive to the structure and quality of public investment spending, which has an influence on the location of productivity effects, as well as the characteristics of demand.

Third, a neutral allocation of investment spending, which leads to a balanced sectoral supply response, is broadly beneficial to the Ugandan economy in terms of boosting aggregate growth and investment, welfare, and exports while moderating appreciation of the real exchange rate and reducing poverty on a significant scale, with rural poverty declining even faster than urban poverty. This relates to the Ugandan economy's ability to produce more goods—both tradable and nontradable—as a result of productivity increases, whereas a reversal of the real exchange rate appreciation shifts the domestic terms of trade in favor of export-oriented and import-competing agriculture. Thus, even though many agricultural subsectors would be indirectly discriminated against if there were no productivity-enhancing public infrastructure, these sectors are able to expand as a result of productive public investment, even when not targeted directly. In contrast, agriculture is hit relatively hard when a reallocation of public investment spending leads to a nonagricultural bias in the supply response.

Fourth, outcomes are markedly different when public investment spending is biased in favor of agriculture and food processing. In this case results suggest that (1) the supply response of agriculture would be sufficiently strong to more than offset the demand effects of the oil boom; (2) agriculture exports would recover more strongly than with a neutral or a nonagricultural, industry-biased allocation of investment spending; (3) the supply response would generate higher aggregate real income gains; and (4) poorer rural households will benefit the most, but without sacrificing urban poverty reduction. With respect to the latter, a highly significant outcome is that poverty falls for both rural and urban households under an agriculture-biased public investment spending scenario (relative to a neutral spending strategy), whereas industry-biased spending would lead to comparably higher poverty in both regions.

Although direct comparisons of scenario results should be done with great caution, a simple ranking of public spending options according to growth, real income, and poverty reduction effects suggests an agriculture-biased investment strategy is the preferred option. Such a strategy would not only increase agricultural growth and rural incomes most, but would also have significant and positive spillover effects into the rest of the economy, thereby benefiting all segments of society. The recommendation is less clear in the zero-spillover scenarios. In this case, there is a trade-off between increasing investment (and therefore relatively higher overall growth) and increasing consumption (and therefore relatively higher agricultural growth). The latter (increased consumption), which is achieved by redistributing oil revenues to Uganda's citizens via a welfare transfer scheme, is associated with larger reductions in poverty, at the national level and particularly in poorer rural areas.

These conclusions must, of course, be qualified by a number of caveats. Among these is that absorption capacity and, consequently, the quality and efficiency of public investments for economic growth are critically important. Having oil revenues but then having to incur high economic and social costs in attempting to spend these revenues will lower the net benefits of oil. For balanced growth and poverty reduction to materialize a well-coordinated set of interventions aimed at improving competitiveness in the agricultural sector is needed. These may include investments in agricultural research and development, infrastructure (such as rural roads), and education and skills, with priority afforded to those investment areas that have the highest payoffs in terms of agricultural productivity gains and increased competitiveness of the sector. Any further analysis of the impact of oil in Uganda must pay closer attention to issues of spending efficiency and spending priorities.

References

Acemoglu, D., S. Johnson, and J. Robinson. 2003. Botswana – An African success story. In *In search of prosperity: Analytical narratives on economic growth*, ed. D. Rodrik. Princeton, NJ: Princeton University Press.

Adato, M., and J. Hoddinott. 2010. *Conditional cash transfers in Latin America*. Baltimore: Johns Hopkins University Press.

Ahmed, R., and M. Hossain. 1990. *Developmental impact of rural infrastructure in Bangladesh*. IFPRI Research Report 83. Washington, DC: International Food Policy Research Institute.

Antle, J. 1984. Human capital, infrastructure, and the productivity of Indian rice farmers. *Journal of Development Economics* 14: 163–181.

Benin, S., J. Thurlow, X. Diao, A. Kebba, and N. Ofwono. 2008. *Agricultural growth and investment options for poverty reduction in Uganda*. IFPRI Discussion Paper 790. Washington, DC: International Food Policy Research Institute.

Bevan, D., P. Collier, and J. Gunning. 1999. *The political economy of poverty, equity, and growth: Nigeria and Indonesia, a World Bank comparative study*. New York: Oxford University Press.

Binswanger, H.P., S.R. Khandker, and M.R. Rosenzweig. 1993. How infrastructure and financial institutions affect agricultural output and investment in India. *Journal of Development Economics* 41: 337–366.

Breisinger, C., X. Diao, R. Schweickert, and M. Wiebelt. 2009. *Managing future oil revenues in Ghana. An assessment of alternative allocation options*. IFPRI Discussion Paper 893. Washington, DC: International Food Policy Research Institute.

Calderón, C., and L. Servén. 2005. *The effects of infrastructure development on growth and income distribution*. World Bank Policy Research Working Paper 3643. Washington, DC: World Bank.

———. 2008. *Infrastructure and economic development in sub-Saharan Africa*. World Bank Policy Research Working Paper W4712. Washington, DC: World Bank.

Canning, D., and E. Bennathan. 1999. *The social rate of return on infrastructure investments*. World Bank Policy Research Working Paper W2390. Washington, DC: World Bank.

Dervis, K., J. de Melo, and S. Robinson. 1982. *General equilibrium models for development policy*. Cambridge: Cambridge University Press.

Diao, X., P. Hazell, and J. Thurlow. 2010. The role of agriculture in African development. *World Development* 38 (10): 1375–1383.

Dorosh, P., and J. Thurlow. 2009. *Agglomeration, migration, and regional growth. A CGE analysis for Uganda*. IFPRI Discussion Paper 848. Washington, DC: International Food Policy Research Institute.

Duflo, E., and R. Pande. 2007. Dams. *Quarterly Journal of Economics* 122 (2): 601–646.

Easterly, W. 2001. *The elusive quest for growth. economists' adventures and misadventures in the tropics*. Cambridge, MA: MIT Press.

Esfahani, H., and M.T. Ramirez. 2002. Institutions, infrastructure and economic growth. *Journal of Development Economics* 70: 443–477.

Fan, S., P. Hazell, and S. Thorat. 2000. Government spending, growth, and poverty in rural India. *American Journal of Agricultural Economics* 82 (4): 1038–1051.

Fan, S., T. Mogues, and S. Benin. 2009. *Setting priorities for public spending for agricultural and rural development in Africa*. IFPRI Policy Brief 12. Washington, DC: International Food Policy Research Institute.

Fan, S., and X. Zhang. 2008. Public expenditure, growth, and poverty reduction in rural Uganda. *African Development Review* 20 (3): 466–496.

Fan, S., L. Zhang, and X. Zhang. 2003. *Growth, inequality, and poverty in rural China: The role of public investments*. Research Report No. 125. Washington, DC: International Food Policy Research Institute.

Gelb, A. 1988. *Oil windfalls: Blessing or curse?* New York: Oxford University Press for the World Bank.

Gelb, A., and S. Grasmann. 2010. *How should oil exporters spend their rents?* Working Paper 221. Washington, DC: Center for Global Development.

Gelb, A., and S. Majerowicz. 2011. *Oil for Uganda – Or Ugandans? Can cash transfers prevent the resource curse?* Working Paper 261. Washington, DC: Center for Global Development.

Gibson, J., and S. Rozelle. 2003. Poverty and access to roads in Papua New Guinea. *Economic Development and Cultural Change* 52 (1): 159–185.

Hausmann, R., and R. Rigobon. 2002. *An alternative interpretation of the "resource curse": Theory and policy implications*. NBER Working Paper 9424. Cambridge, MA: National Bureau of Economic Research.

Hulten, C. 1996. *Infrastructure capital and economic growth: How well you use it may be more important than how much you have*. NBER Working Paper 5847. Cambridge, MA: National Bureau of Economic Research.

IMF (International Monetary Fund). 2003, September. *World economic outlook*. Washington, DC: International Monetary Fund.

Leite, C., and J. Weidmann. 1999. *Does mother nature corrupt?* IMF Working Paper 99/85. Washington, DC: International Monetary Fund.

Pauw, K., and L. Mncube. 2007. *Expanding the social security net in South Africa: Opportunities, challenges and constraints*. DPRU Working Paper No. 07/128. Cape Town: University of Cape Town, Development Policy Research Unit.

Ram, R. 1996. Productivity of public and private investment in developing countries: A broad international perspective. *World Development* 24: 1373–1378.

Reinikka, E., and J. Svensson. 2002. Coping with poor public capital. *Journal of Development Economics* 69 (1): 51–69.

Renkow, M., D.G. Hallstroma, and D. Karanjab. 2004. Rural infrastructure, transactions costs and market participation in Kenya. *Journal of Development Economics* 73 (1): 349–367.

Rodrik, D. 2003. What do we learn from country narratives? In *In search of prosperity: Analytical narratives on economic growth*, ed. D. Rodrik. Princeton, NJ: Princeton University Press.

Ross, M.L. 2001. Does oil hinder democracy? *World Politics* 53: 325–361.

Sachs, J. D., and A. M. Warner. 1995. *Natural resource abundance and economic growth*. NBER Working Paper 5398. Cambridge, MA: National Bureau of Economic Research.

Sachs, J.D., and A.M. Warner. 2001. The curse of natural resources. *European Economic Review* 45 (4-6): 827–838.

Sala-i-Martin, X., and A. Subramanian. 2003. *Addressing the natural resource curse: An illustration from Nigeria*. IMF Working Paper 03/139. Washington, DC: International Monetary Fund.

Sennoga, E. B., and J. M. Matovu. 2010. *Public spending composition and public sector efficiency: Implications for growth and poverty reduction in Uganda*. Research Series No. 66. Kampala: Economic Policy Research Centre.

Stevens, P. 2003. Resource impact—Curse or blessing? A literature survey. *Journal of Energy Literature* 9 (1): 1–42.

Thurlow, J. 2004. *A dynamic computable general equilibrium (CGE) model for South Africa: Extending the static IFPRI model.* TIPS Working Paper 1–2004. Pretoria: Trade and Industrial Policy Strategies.

Thurlow, J., S. Morley, and A. N. Pratt. 2008. *Lagging regions and development strategies.* IFPRI Discussion Paper 898. Washington, DC: International Food Policy Research Institute.

Twimukye, E., J. M. Matovu, S. Levine, and P. Birungi. 2010. *Sectoral and welfare effects of the global economic crisis on Uganda: A recursive dynamic CGE analysis.* Research Series No. 73. Kampala: Economic Policy Research Centre.

Uganda, Ministry of Energy and Mineral Development. 2008. *National oil and gas policy for Uganda.* Kampala: Ministry of Energy and Mineral Development.

Valdés, A., and W. Foster. 2010. Reflections on the role of agriculture in pro-poor growth. *World Development* 38 (10): 1362–1374.

Wiebelt, M., K. Pauw, J. M. Matovu, E. Twimukye, and T. Benson. 2011. *Managing future oil revenue for agricultural development and poverty reduction: A CGE analysis of challenges and options.* IFPRI Discussion Paper 1122. Washington, DC: International Food Policy Research Institute.

World Bank. 2010. *Country assistance strategy for the Republic of Uganda for the period FY 2011–2015.* Washington, DC: World Bank.

Manfred Wiebelt is a Senior Research Fellow at the Kiel Institute for the World Economy, an Adjunct Professor of Economics at Kiel University, and Director of the Poverty Reduction, Equity and Growth Network (PEGNet). He holds a PhD in Economics from Heidelberg University. His research focuses on trade and agricultural policies, pro-poor growth, and management of natural resources, primarily based on empirical general equilibrium analysis with a focus on sub-Saharan Africa and the Middle East and North Africa.

Karl Pauw is the Regional Coordinator for the Monitoring and Analyzing Food and Agricultural Policies (MAFAP) program of the United Nations Food and Agriculture Organization (FAO), based in Addis Ababa, Ethiopia. At the time of writing his respective contributions in this book he was a Research Fellow at the International Food Policy Research Institute (IFPRI) and manager of IFPRI's Malawi country program in Lilongwe. He holds a PhD in development economics from the University of Cape Town, South Africa, and his research interests include: development and agricultural policy analysis; microeconomic analyses of labor markets, poverty, welfare outcomes, and nutrition; and policy impact analysis using computable general equilibrium and micro-simulation models.

John Mary Matovu is a Senior Economist at Research for Transformation and Development, based in Uganda. Before he held posts at the International Monetary Fund, Washington, DC and at the Economic Policy Research Centre in Kampala. He obtained his PhD in Economics from Oxford University. His research focuses on the incidence of tax reforms, fiscal response to commodity price shocks, climate-change induced productivity shocks, and domestic resource mobilization in Uganda, primarily using computable general equilibrium models.

Evarist Twimukye at the time of writing this article, Everist Twimukye was a Senior Research Fellow at the Economic Policy Research Centre, based in Kampala, Uganda. He holds a PhD in Applied Economics from Clemson University, USA. His main areas of research and publication include growth and employment, financial economics, fiscal policy, foreign direct investment, food policy analysis, and trade and integration economics.

Todd Benson is a Senior Research Fellow in the Development Strategy and Governance Division at the International Food Policy Research Institute, based in Washington, DC. He obtained his PhD in Geography from the University of Minnesota. His research focuses on policy analysis for poverty reduction, agricultural development, food security, and improved nutrition, primarily using microeconomic and spatial data sets with a focus on sub-Saharan Africa.

4

Agricultural Extension System: A Combined Approach to Study Treatment Effects

Samuel Benin, Ephraim Nkonya, Geresom Okecho, Joseé Randriamamonjy, Edward Kato, Geofrey Lubade, and Miriam Kyotalimye

An important problem in causal inference and estimation of treatment effects is identifying a reliable comparison group (control observations) against which to compare those that have been exposed to the treatment (treated observations). It is common knowledge that the estimate obtained by the difference in the values of the indicator of interest associated with the two groups could be biased due to lack of overlap in the covariate distributions or common support between the treated and control observations (Dehejia and Wahba 2002; Imbens and Wooldridge 2009). This is especially problematic with non-experimental control observations (Dehejia and Wahba 2002) in which case combining propensity score matching and regression methods has been suggested to yield more consistent estimates of the treatment effect than using either method alone (Imbens and Wooldridge 2009). Matching removes

---

This chapter is a re-print of: Benin, S., Nkonya, E., Okecho, G., Randriamamonjy, J. and E. Kato (2012). Impact of the National Agricultural Advisory Services (Naads) program of Uganda: Considering Different Levels of Likely Contamination with the Treatment, American Journal of Agricultural Economics, 94(2), 386–392.

S. Benin (✉) • E. Nkonya • J. Randriamamonjy • E. Kato
International Food Policy Research Institute (IFPRI), Washington, DC, USA
e-mail: s.benin@cigar.org

G. Okecho
National Agricultural Advisory Services, Kampala, Uganda

G. Lubade
National Agricultural Research Organization, Kampala, Uganda

M. Kyotalimye
Association for Strengthening Agricultural Research in Eastern and Central Africa, Kampala, Uganda

self-selection bias due to any correlation between the observable (pre-treatment) covariates and the dependent variable, while regression isolates the effect of change in the covariates on change in the dependent variable over the period of the treatment. Using the combined approach, this paper discusses the effect of using different sets of control groups on estimates of treatment effects of the agricultural extension system in Uganda, the National Agricultural Advisory Services (NAADS) program.

The goal of the NAADS program, which was initiated in 2001, is to increase incomes through increased adoption of profitable agricultural enterprises and improved technologies and practices, agricultural productivity, and marketed output. The program aims at targeting the economically-active poor—those with limited physical and financial assets, skills and knowledge—through farmer groups based on specific enterprises identified by farmers (NAADS 2007). Although the program is a public intervention, farmers have to decide whether to participate in the program or not. When a farmer decides to participate, he or she has to do so through membership of a NAADS-participating farmer group. Then, together with the members of the group, and with members of other NAADS-participating groups, they request for specific technologies and advisory services associated with their preferred enterprises and obtain grants to procure those technologies and related advisory services. The grant is initially used to finance the establishment of a technology development site (TDS) for demonstrations and training, and proceeds (outputs or sale of outputs) from the TDS become a revolving fund for members of the group. The main channel of impact of the program is thus via farmers' access to this grant. Knowledge and skills gained from the activities surrounding the TDS, as well as from select farmers trained to provide follow-up advisory services [community-based facilitators (CBFs)], are also very important.

The program is expected to generate indirect or spillover effects to the extent that the TDSs, NAADS service providers and CBFs are accessible as sources of knowledge and skills to other farmers in the community where the program is implemented. Estimating these indirect effects involves identifying farmers that have benefited from the program in such a manner, which is potentially challenging due to possible misclassification of service providers. For example, the government's regular extension service and NGOs operated in the same areas as the NAADS program. Since some ex-government extension workers and NGOs are occasionally contracted to provide NAADS services, it is possible for them to be wrongly associated with the NAADS program even when they are operating outside the NAADS framework. Spillovers across program boundaries or communities through information flow among farmers and from non-NAADS service providers using the NAADS framework are also possible. We discuss the implications of these from using different controls groups. Next, we present the data and evaluation method, followed by the results, conclusions, and implications.

1 Data and Methods

1.1 Data

The data are from two rounds of household surveys conducted in 2004 and 2007. The 2004 survey served as the baseline on which a stratified sample was based according to the year when the NAADS program was first implemented in the community (sub-county) where the program: began in 2001/02; began in 2002/03; began between 2005 and 2007; or had never been implemented at the time of the 2007 survey. This was done to account for the effect of the rollout of the program that may result in a modified treatment among later entrants to the program due to learning from previous treatments among earlier entrants of the program (supply-side effects of the program), as well as from nonrandom preparedness of later entrants prior to receiving the treatment (demand-side effects). About 400, 300, 100, and 100 households were surveyed from each of the four strata (see Benin et al. 2011 for details). This paper is based on the panel of 719 household observations. The indicator of interest for estimating the treatment effect is agricultural income (INC)—details of this and other variables used are presented later.

1.2 Estimation Approach

What we are interested in is the average treatment effect of the treated (ATT_j):

$$ATT_j = E\left[INC_{1j}|NAADS_j = 1\right] - E\left[INC_{0j}|NAADS_j = 1\right] \quad (1)$$

where INC_{1j} is agricultural income of farm household j due to participation in the program and INC_{0j} is agricultural income of the same farm household j if it did not participate in it. Although, we cannot observe the counterfactual, the underlying estimation problem can be represented as a treatment-effects model of the form:

$$INC_{jt} = \alpha_j + \tau_t + \delta NAADS_j + \boldsymbol{\beta}'\boldsymbol{x}_{jt} + \epsilon_{jt} \quad (2)$$

$$NAADS_j^* = \boldsymbol{\gamma}'w_j + u_j \quad (3)$$

$$NAADS_j = \begin{cases} 1, & \text{if } NAADS_j^* > 0 \\ 0, & \text{otherwise} \end{cases} \quad (4)$$

where: $NAADS_j^*$ is a latent unobserved variable whose counterpart, $NAADS_j$, is observed in dichotomous form; $\boldsymbol{x}_j$ and $\boldsymbol{w}_j$ are vectors of variables determining agricultural income and the decision to participate in the program, respectively; $NAADS_j = 1$ and $NAADS_j = 0$ represent participation (or treatment) and non-participation (or control), respectively; α and τ capture the individual and time specific effect, respectively; β and γ are the vectors of parameters measuring the relationships between the dependent and independent variables; ϵ and u are the random components of the equations with joint normal distribution of means $(\mu, 0)$ and covariance matrix $\begin{bmatrix} \sigma_{\varepsilon}^2 & \sigma_{\epsilon u} \\ \sigma_{\epsilon u} & 1 \end{bmatrix}$.

We apply a two-stage weighted regression (2SWR) method (e.g. Robins and Rotnitzky 1995). In the first stage, we estimate Eq. (3) by probit to obtain propensity scores, which are used in selecting a matched sub-sample of treatment and control observations. In the second stage, the propensity scores are used as weights in a weighted least squares regression of Eq. (2) on the matched sub-sample according to:

$$\Delta INC_j = \hat{\alpha} + \hat{\delta}_B NAADS_j + INC_{jt0} + e_j \tag{5}$$

$$\Delta INC_j = \hat{\alpha} + \hat{\delta}_F NAADS_j + INC_{jt0} + \hat{\boldsymbol{\beta}}'_{2SWRT} \Delta \boldsymbol{x}_j + e_j \tag{6}$$

where: $\Delta INC = INC_{t1} - INC_{t0}$, and INC_{t0} and INC_{t1} are the incomes in the initial (2004) and later (2007) periods, respectively; $\Delta x = x_{t1} - x_{t0}$, and x_{t0} and x_{t1} are the initial and later period values of the covariates, respectively. Equations (5) and (6) represent specifications without and with the covariates, and the impact of the program is measured by $\hat{\delta}_B$ and $\hat{\delta}_F$ for the two model specifications, respectively. In any two-stage estimation procedure, it is important to address the identification of the second-stage regression or endogeneity of the first-stage regression. A common procedure used is excluding some of the explanatory variables used in estimating the first-stage probit from the second-stage regression (i.e. having $\boldsymbol{x} \subset \boldsymbol{w}$ or $\boldsymbol{x} \neq \boldsymbol{w}$ and corr $(w, \varepsilon/x) = 0$). In general, nonlinearity of the first-stage probit model renders exclusion restrictions unnecessary (Wilde 2000). Further, since we apply a fixed-effect or difference estimator in the second-stage regression, the condition is satisfied in the sense that $\Delta \boldsymbol{x} \neq \boldsymbol{w}$.

Participation is measured using the status observed in 2007 to avoid crossover in different years so that a treatment household is always a treatment household and cannot switch status; the same for a control household. Of the 719 observations, 66 are treated and 653 are controls, which we split into three. The first control sub-group is made up of those in the same area where the program is implemented and claimed to have benefited indirectly from the program, labeled $\text{NAADS}_{\text{NON-1}}$. The second sub-group also is made up those in the area where the program is implemented but did not claim any benefits (labeled $\text{NAADS}_{\text{NON-2}}$), while the third sub-group is made up those in areas where the program was never implemented (labeled $\text{NAADS}_{\text{NON-3}}$). These three sub-groups make up 256, 284, and 113 observations, respectively. Because matching with the nearest neighbor only can limit any potential gain from matching participants with more than one non-participant with similar attributes, we consider and report estimated treatment effects based on matching with one, three, and five nearest neighbors.

1.2.1 Variables

Agricultural income (INC) is agricultural income per adult equivalent and measured as the total gross value of households' crop, livestock, beekeeping and aquaculture output (or agricultural gross revenue) divided by the total number of adult equivalents in the household. The choice of covariates was guided by the principles and design of the NAADS program as well as the literature on agricultural household models (e.g. Singh et al. 1986) and adoption of agricultural technologies (e.g. Feder et al. 1985). The variables used include: human capital (gender, age, education and size structure of household); financial capital (livelihood and income strategies); physical capital [land owned and value of agricultural productive assets (e.g. equipment, livestock, etc.)]; social capital (membership in other organizations); access to infrastructure and services (distance to nearest financial services, road, market); location in the four administrative regions of Uganda (Central, Eastern, Northern and Western); and dummy variables representing the year when the NAADS program was introduced in the sub-county. Physical capital may be potentially endogenous and so we estimate the second-stage regression with and without them to analyze the effect of this problem. All monetary values were converted into year 2000 constant prices to help exclude the influence of inflation and other temporal monetary and fiscal trends.

To improve matching, it is common practice to try different variables and transformations of the variables such as logarithms and higher order and interaction terms, because matching is a nonparametric method of preprocessing data to reduce imbalance between treated and control groups (Imbens and Wooldridge 2009). We follow this practice and use: histograms of the propensity scores between the two groups to select the sub-sample with adequate common support; and balancing tests to check the extent to which any differences that existed between the two groups prior to matching have been reduced in the matched sample.

2 Results

2.1 *Determinants of Participation in the Program: Overlap in Covariate Distributions*

Selected results on common support and balancing tests for different combinations and transformations (squared and interaction terms) of the covariates using matching with three nearest neighbors are shown in Fig. 1 and Table 1, respectively. We find that different covariates and transformations yield different outcomes of common support and balance between the two groups after matching. The general pattern is a skewness of the propensity scores toward one for participants and zero for non-participants. The situation is most perverse when no transformations of the variables are included or when the covariates on the length of program presence are included (Fig. 1a–c). Regarding the latter, different propensity scores are generated for different controls who are identical in all aspects except location in a NAADS sub-county and several treated observations have to be dropped to improve common support. The models associated with the probits when we include transformations of the covariates and exclude the covariates on the length of program presence are preferred because their results show that there is greater common

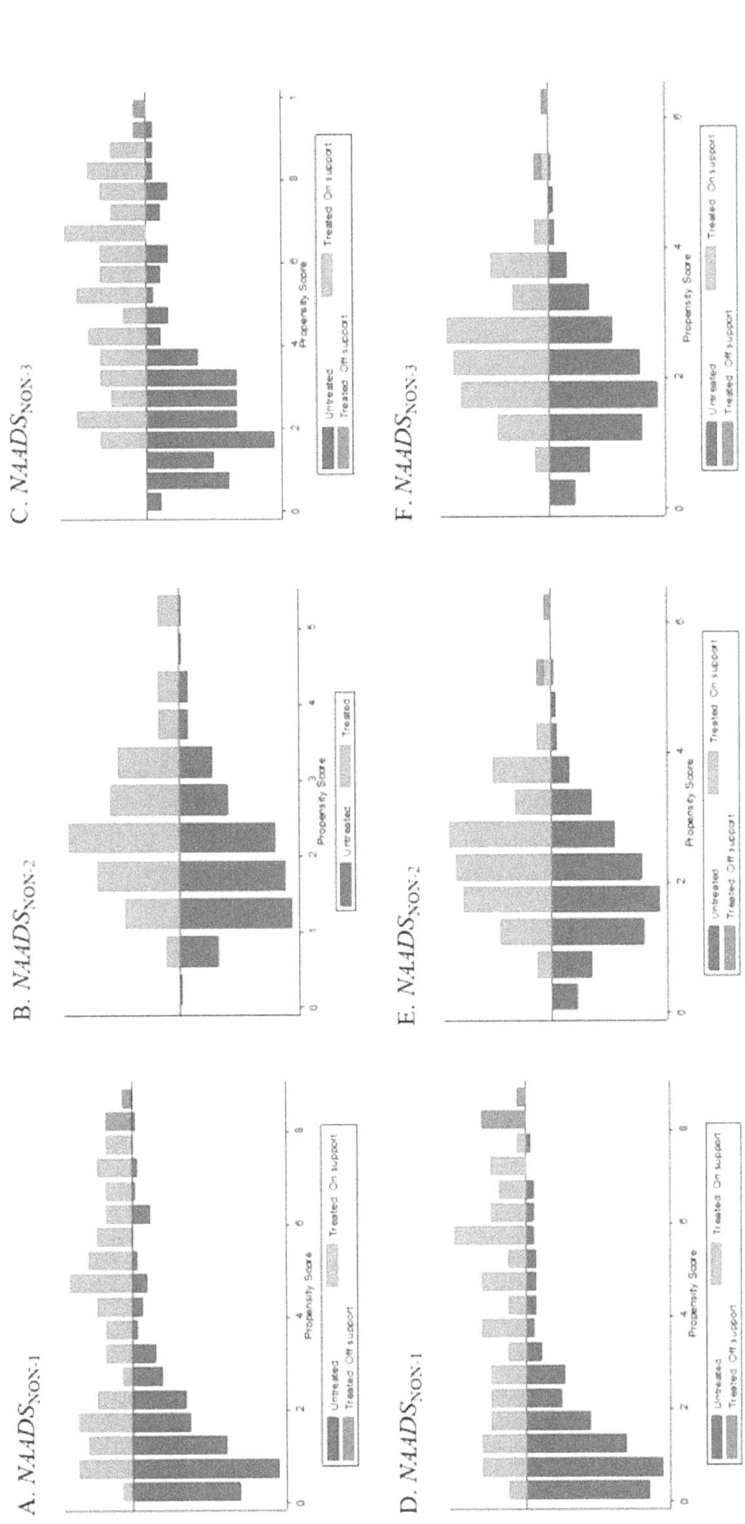

Fig. 1 Histogram of estimated propensity scores between participants and non-participants. Source: Authors' illustration based on probit results. **(a)** to **(c)** excludes squared or interaction terms of the variables in the probits; **(d)** to **(f)** includes them

Table 1 Sample characteristics between NAADS participants (treated observations) and non-participants (control observations)

Variable	Unmatched (mean values)				Matched (% difference in mean values between treated[a] and controls)		
	Treated	$NAADS_{NON-1}$	$NAADS_{NON-2}$	$NAADS_{NON-3}$	$NAADS_{NON-1}$	$NAADS_{NON-2}$	$NAADS_{NON-3}$
Gender of head	0.20	0.13**	0.16	0.24	−3.0	2.7	2.5
Age of head	42.83	45.36**	43.22	42.79	2.3	4.9	−22.8
Primary education	0.64	0.55**	0.66	0.61	−25.0	4.4	5.5
Post-primary education	0.20	0.35***	0.17	0.22	21.3	−10.6	6.4
Household size	4.57	5.41***	4.92*	5.20**	0.7	−0.3	5.5
Membership	0.38	0.83***	0.44	0.44	6.4	3.2	6.4
Income strategy							
Livestock	0.06	0.03*	0.06	0.04	5.2	−4.4	9.3
Other agriculture	0.10	0.17*	0.14	0.16	−6.5	−3.2	4.7
Nonfarm	0.08	0.02***	0.05	0.04*	10.6	−6.4	18.4
Land owned	1.24	3.31	2.61*	1.82	−0.5	−1.5	−4.0
Productive assets	150.00	240.00	290.00	120.00	4.0	2.3	−3.3
Ag revenue per AE	193.14	320.37***	222.86	203.38	11.5	−0.6	8.1
Distance to credit	18.73	19.88	16.78	28.34***	9.6	27.9	7.3
Distance to road	2.61	2.38	2.55	2.75	17.3	9.3	29.2*
Distance to market	6.92	9.35***	7.67	9.24**	−0.3	−3.4	7.8
Eastern region	0.24	0.12***	0.28	0.64***	−8.7	−5.9	−46.4**
Northern region	0.20	0.28*	0.13**	n.a.	−9.1	7.0	n.a.
Western region	0.42	0.42	0.40	0.09***	3.4	4.2	20.8
Number of observations	66.00	256.00	284.00	113.00	93.00	125.00	55.00

Source: Based on probit results including squared and interaction terms of the variables and matching with nearest three neighbors

[a]The numbers of treated observations are 60, 64 and 63 for the sub-samples with $NAADS_{NON-1}$, $NAADS_{NON-2}$ and $NAADS_{NON-3}$, respectively. N.a. means not applicable. *, ** and *** means statistical significance at the 10%, 5% and 1% level, respectively, of the difference in the mean values between treated and control observations

support and only up to six treated observations have to be dropped in any sub-sample (Fig. 1d–f). The sample characteristics in Table 1 also show that any statistically significant differences that existed between the treated and control groups prior to the matching were eliminated or reduced. Together, the results suggest that pooling observations for the different unique control groups as done in Benin et al. (2011) could lead to different policy implications and, as we shall see next, limit any potential gain in knowledge from matching each participant with multiple non-participants that are similar in several attributes but different in others.

2.1.1 Estimated Treatment Effects of the Program on Agricultural Income (INC)

Estimates of the treatment effect are summarized in Table 2 (detailed selected second stage regression results are shown in the annex Table 3). The results show that the NAADS program has had positive impact on agricultural revenue per AE, particularly when participants are compared with those who did not claim any benefits ($NAADS_{NON-2}$) or with those located where the program was never implemented ($NAADS_{NON-3}$). The estimated impacts are statistically weak for the former and insignificant for the latter, however. The positive effect on agricultural revenue per AE is consistent with the estimated effects on other outcomes such as adoption of crop and livestock improved varieties, crop and livestock productivity,

Table 2 Estimated treatment effects (% difference between participants and non-participants in 2004–2007 change in agricultural revenue per adult equivalent)

	Sub-sample of control observations		
	$NAADS_{NON-1}$	$NAADS_{NON-2}$	$NAADS_{NON-3}$
2SWR (without covariates)			
1 nearest neighbor	9.3	59.9*	90.3*
3 nearest neighbors	−5.0	47.5*	64.4
5 nearest neighbors	−19.1	40.6*	50.2
2SWR (with covariates, including change in physical capital)			
1 nearest neighbor	−10.5	56.0*	58.7
3 nearest neighbors	−24.2	45.5*	30.4
5 nearest neighbors	−31.1	36.7	30.4
2SWR (with covariates, excluding change in physical capital)			
1 nearest neighbor	5.8	53.1*	69.7
3 nearest neighbors	−7.3	53.3**	30.5
5 nearest neighbors	−10.4	48.1**	30.5

Source: Based on model results. Number of observations: $NAADS_{NON-1}$ 40, 93 and 119 for matching with nearest one, three and five neighbors, respectively; $NAADS_{NON-2}$ 53, 125 and 164; and $NAADS_{NON-3}$ 32, 55 and 69. *, ** and *** means statistical significance at the 10%, 5% and 1% level, respectively. Detail 2SWR results based on model with covariates, excluding change in physical capital, and matching with nearest three neighbors are presented in the annex, Table 3

Table 3 2SWR results of Δ Ln agricultural revenue per adult equivalent

Variable	$NAADS_{NON\text{-}1}$	$NAADS_{NON\text{-}2}$	$NAADS_{NON\text{-}3}$
Participation in NAADS[a]	−0.08	0.43**	0.27
Δ Gender of head	−0.07	0.46	0.56
Δ Ln Age of head	−0.09	0.26	−0.24
Δ Education (reduction)	−0.50	−0.26	0.37
Δ Education (improvement)	−0.14	−0.31	−0.33
Δ Ln household size	0.12	−0.04	−0.49
Δ Income strategy (to crops)	−0.30	−0.41	−0.89**
Δ Income strategy (to livestock)	0.53	1.25**	1.10**
Δ Income strategy (to other ag)	−0.37	0.16	−1.76**
Δ Income strategy (to non-farm)	−0.12	−0.31	0.39
Δ Ln Distance to credit	0.05	−0.40**	−1.10*
Δ Ln Distance to all-weather road	0.47**	0.81***	−1.12***
Δ Ln Distance to markets	0.23	−0.90*	0.15
Ln Agricultural revenue per AE_2004	−0.68***	−0.83***	−0.90***
Intercept	8.45***	9.92***	10.71***
R-squared	0.34***	0.49***	0.46***

Source: Based on model results using matching with nearest three neighbors. Ln is natural logarithm. Δ is difference in 2004 and 2007 values. *, ** and *** means 10%, 5% and 1% statistical significance, respectively

[a]Percentage change in agricultural revenue per AE associated with participation is calculated by: (exponent (coefficient) − 1) × 100

Table 4 Estimated treatment effects in other selected outcomes

Outcome Variable	$NAADS_{NON\text{-}1}$	$NAADS_{NON\text{-}2}$	$NAADS_{NON\text{-}3}$
Adoption of improved crop varieties[a]	−0.19	0.24	0.31*
Adoption of livestock improved breeds[a]	−0.12	0.18	0.18
Value of crop output per hectare[b]	−44.46**	9.53	140.50*
Value of livestock output per tropical livestock unit[b]	−38.43	33.78	166.45**
Percent of crop output that is sold on the market[b]	−1.11	1.01	5.06
Percent of livestock output that is sold on the market[b]	−0.09	3.61	7.82***

Source: Based on model results of second stage regression with covariates, excluding change in physical capital, and matching with nearest three neighbors

[a]Panel random-effects probit regression results of adoption in 2004 and 2007; estimates are difference between participants and non-participants in probability of adoption in 2004 and 2007

[b]Weighted regression results of change between 2004 and 2007 in logarithm of outcome; estimates are % difference between participants and non-participants in 2004–2007 change in outcome. *, ** and *** means 10%, 5% and 1% statistical significance, respectively

and sale of output; although the statistical significance of the estimates are reversed for $NAADS_{NON\text{-}2}$ and $NAADS_{NON\text{-}3}$ however, which is surprising (see annex Table 4). The estimated effects when direct participants are compared with $NAADS_{NON\text{-}1}$ were consistently negative for the different outcomes analyzed, suggesting that the impacts of the program on direct participants were not as large as the change observed for indirect participants. Because farmers in this group are not very familiar with the NAADS program, they may have confused NAADS service providers with agents of other programs, leading to an overestimation of NAADS program effects for this group, as was likely the results in Benin et al. (2011).

The estimates from the model specification without the covariates are generally larger, suggesting that changes in other factors have been important, particularly changes in sources of income and access to infrastructure and services, particularly roads and markets (see annex Table 3).

The lower estimates associated with the model specification with the covariates including change in physical capital suggest that the impact of the program was also via its effect on these assets. The u-shaped or inverted u-shaped relationship between the estimates and increasing number of nearest neighbor matches is consistent with the literature that greater number of matches generally increases precision, but at the cost of increasing bias (Dehejia and Wahba 2002).

3 Conclusions and Implications

In this paper we used different sets of control groups and different propensity score matching specifications combined with regression to estimate the average treatment effect of the agricultural extension system in Uganda on households' agricultural revenue. By breaking up the control observations into sub-groups reflecting likely differences in potential contamination with the treatment, we show how matching each treatment observation with multiple controls that are similar in several attributes but different in others can yield more insights on estimates of average treatment effects. Unfortunately, the results were mixed and weak, in terms of consistent sign and statistical significance across the different methods, model specifications, and outcomes analyzed, making it difficult to draw definitive conclusions regarding the direct impact of the program and, particularly, its indirect impact. Our underlying assumption was that participation in the NAADS program confers benefits via material inputs that will lead to subsequent outcomes. But this assumption was not consistently validated in the results obtained. While changes in other factors (sources of income and access to road and market) are important in raising agricultural revenue, a major limitation with the study is our inability to capture the separate effect of access to non-NAADS extension services.

References

Benin, S., E. Nkonya, G. Okecho, E. Kato, J. Randriamamonjy, G. Lubade, and M. Kyotalimye. 2011. Returns to spending on agricultural extension: the case of the National Agricultural Advisory Services (NAADS) program of Uganda. *Agricultural Economics* 42: 249–267.

Dehejia, R., and S. Wahba. 2002. Propensity score matching methods for non-experimental causal studies. *Review of Economics and Statistics* 84: 151–161.

Feder, G., R. Just, and D. Zilberman. 1985. Adoption of agricultural innovations in developing countries: a survey. *Economic Development and Cultural Change* 30: 59–76.

Imbens, G.M., and J.M. Wooldridge. 2009. Recent developments in the econometrics of program evaluation. *Journal of Economic Literature* 47: 5–86.

NAADS (National Agricultural Advisory Services). 2007. *Facts and figures.* Kampala: NAADS Secretariat.

Robins, J.M., and A. Rotnitzky. 1995. Semi-parametric efficiency in multivariate regression models with missing data. *Journal of the American Statistical Association* 90: 122–129.

Singh, I., L. Squire, and J. Strauss. 1986. *Agricultural household models: extensions, policy and applications.* Baltimore, MD: John Hopkins University.

Wilde, J. 2000. Identification of multiple equation probit models with endogenous regressors. *Economic Letters* 69: 309–312.

Samuel Benin is a Senior Research Fellow in the Development Strategy and Governance Division at IFPRI, based in Davis, California. He earned an MS from the University of Massachusetts, Amherst and a PhD from the University of California, Davis, with specialty in econometrics, natural resource economics and development economics. His research interests focus on policy, institutional and technology strategies for agricultural and rural development.

Ephraim Nkonya is a Senior Research Fellow in the Environment & Production Technology Division at IFPRI, based in Washington, DC. He earned both an MS in agricultural economics and a PhD in natural resources, econometrics, and statistics from Kansas State University.

Geresom Okecho is a Senior Planning Monitoring and Evaluation Officer at the National Agricultural Advisory Services Secretariat in Uganda.

Joseé Randriamamonjy is a Senior Research Analyst in the Development Strategy and Governance Division of IFPRI, based in Washington, DC. She received her MS in Agricultural Economics from Cornell University and her MA in Economic Policy Management from Auvergne University (CERDI) in France. Her research topics cover the driving forces affecting the global food system, their links to agricultural production, and related policy options to better achieve reducing poverty, food insecurity, and malnutrition.

Edward Kato is a Senior Research Analyst in the Environment & Production Technology Division at IFPRI, based in Washington, DC.

Geofrey Lubade is a Researcher at the National Agricultural Research Organization in Uganda.

Miriam Kyotalimye is a Program Assistant at the Association for Strengthening Agricultural Research in Eastern and Central Africa in Uganda.

5

Agricultural Extension System and its Treatment Effects

Karl Pauw, James Thurlow, and Olivier Ecker

1 Introduction

There is widespread agreement that growth is a necessary condition for poverty reduction, although the extent to which poverty declines depends on the level and the structure of growth, and characteristics of the poor (Dollar and Kraay 2002; Ravallion and Datt 1996; Mellor 1999). Agricultural growth has been shown to be particularly effective at contributing to overall growth and reducing poverty in most developing countries, and hence this sector is often afforded priority as a growth sector in developing countries (Diao et al. 2010; Valdés and Foster 2010). This "agricultural growth hypothesis" largely serves as the justification for the Comprehensive Africa Agriculture Development Programme (CAADP), in terms of which signatories agree to allocate at least ten percent of their government budgets to the agricultural sector (for example, in the form of spending on extension services, rural infrastructure, research and development, and so on) with the aim of achieving a target of six percent annual agricultural growth.

While poverty-reduction is one objective of CAADP—and most of the CAADP country-analyses conducted by the International Food Policy Research Institute

---

This chapter extracts from earlier research on agricultural growth and nutrition linkages undertaken by the respective authors, as cited further below. All the authors were affiliated with the International Food Policy Research Institute (IFPRI) at the time of writing. Financial support for the research was provided by the United States Agency for International Development (USAID). Any opinions stated herein are those of the authors and do not necessarily reflect the policies or opinions of IFPRI or USAID.

K. Pauw (✉)
United Nations Food and Agriculture Organization (FAO), Addis Ababa, Ethiopia
e-mail: k.pauw@live.com

J. Thurlow • O. Ecker
International Food Policy Research Institute, Washington, DC, USA

(IFPRI) in recent years used this as one of the key benchmarks against which the policy was evaluated (see Diao et al. 2012)—improved food and nutrition security is arguably equally important as a development goal.

Because agriculture implies food production and because agricultural growth benefits the poor disproportionately in developing countries, there exists a perception among policymakers that the links between agricultural growth and nutrition are inevitably strong. In fact, growth in general is believed to be good for reducing malnutrition in as far as it raises household incomes, thus allowing households to access better or more nutritious food. However, some countries have seen nutrition deteriorate despite growth.[1] In India, for example, rapid income growth has not translated into nutritional improvements, with stunting and wasting remaining widespread and per capita caloric availability declining (Deaton 2010). This is puzzling and hard to explain, confirming, as Timmer (2000) argued a decade before, that the mechanisms through which growth impacts on nutrition are not yet well understood analytically or quantified empirically.

The obvious conclusion is that improved nutrition is not a necessary consequence of growth-induced increases in incomes or reductions in poverty. This reflects the fact that the concept of "food and nutrition security" has several dimensions: "availability" of sufficient quantities of domestically produced or imported food; "access" to sufficient resources to acquire a nutritious diet; and "utilization" of food through adequate diet, water, sanitation and health care (Heidhues et al. 2004). In order to understand how growth impacts on nutrition it is necessary to consider how growth affects all of its dimensions.

This paper compares and summarizes findings from two recent papers, by Pauw and Thurlow (2011) and Ecker et al. (2012) in which at least two of the dimensions of food and nutrition security were modeled (i.e., availability and access). Both studies used a computable general equilibrium (CGE) model complemented with microsimulation nutrition models, and specifically consider how alternative economic growth paths ultimately impact on nutrition. The paper is structured as follows. It first compares the methods used in the respective studies and next summarizes the key results. The chapter ends by drawing general policy conclusions and outlining the way forward for these types of analyses.

2 Methods

2.1 IFPRI's Standard Recursive-Dynamic CGE Model

Both Pauw and Thurlow (2011) and Ecker et al. (2012) use IFPRI's standard recursive-dynamic computable general equilibrium (CGE) model to capture the impact of alternative sectoral growth paths on different households and regions in

[1]See for example Ecker et al.'s (2012) cross-country analysis.

the respective countries.[2] The economywide impact of growth depends largely on the inter-sectoral linkages and the way in which households are linked to different sectors via employment and consumption demand linkages. The social accounting matrix (SAM) underlying a CGE model captures these linkages.

The Tanzania model identifies 58 sectors, 26 of which are in agriculture and 10 in downstream agro-processing. Agriculture is further disaggregated across 20 sub-national regions, which captures variation in agro-ecological conditions and rural livelihood/cropping patterns. The Malawi model, in turn, includes 36 sectors (17 agriculture, 9 industry, and 10 services), while the agricultural sector is disaggregated across eight agroecological zones, urban areas, and small, medium, and large-scale farmers. In both models producers in each sector and region maximize profits when combining intermediate inputs with land, labor and capital. Production is specified using nested constant elasticity of substitution (CES) functions, which reflect region-specific technologies and allow for imperfect substitution between factors. In the Tanzanian model labor markets are segmented into four education groups (i.e., uneducated, primary, secondary, and tertiary), while the Malawi model includes elementary (farm) workers, unskilled workers, and skilled workers.

Economic outcomes are also affected by trade and movements in market prices. The standard CGE model assumes that producers in each region supply their output to national product markets (using a CES aggregation function), which avoids having to model inter-regional trade flows for which data is often unavailable. However, transaction costs separate regional producer and national consumer prices. International trade is captured by allowing production to shift imperfectly between domestic and foreign markets depending on the relative prices of exports and domestic products (constant elasticity of transformation function). Similarly, consumers choose between imported or domestically supplied goods depending on relative import prices (CES Armington function). Since both Tanzania and Malawi are small economies, world prices are fixed. The current account balance is maintained by a flexible real exchange rate.

Household income and expenditure patterns are important in determining how growth and relative price changes affect household incomes in the model. Both models identify farm and non-farm households in rural and urban areas, with further disaggregation by region, per capita expenditure quintiles (in the case of Tanzania) and the extent of households' land holdings (in the case of Malawi). The Tanzania model is highly detailed with 110 representative household groups, while the Malawian model includes 28 household groups. Factor incomes are distributed among households based on their factor endowments. Households save and pay taxes (at fixed rates), and the balance of income is used for consumption expenditure. The latter is based on a linear expenditure system (LES) of demand, which allows for non-unitary income elasticities and fixed marginal budget shares. Income

[2]For a detailed specification of this class of CGE model, see Dervis et al. (1982) and Löfgren et al. (2002).

elasticities determine the responsiveness of demand for different household consumption items to income changes, and are therefore important for determining the nutrition effects of household income changes, at least in the Tanzania model, as we explain further below.

2.2 Macro-Micro Linkages and Microsimulation Modeling

Household poverty and nutrition are affected through both income and expenditure channels. When agricultural production expands, farm households, who derive income from land ownership and on-farm employment, are more likely to benefit from higher crop revenues, although this may be partially offset by falling producer prices and lower returns to factors. Falling prices, in turn, benefit consumers, particularly nonfarm households, but also net-consuming farm households (i.e., those producing less than they consume). We therefore expect that agricultural growth will lead to a decline in both rural and urban poverty, with the relative magnitudes of the changes depending on consumption patterns and price changes faced by either producers or consumers.

In general, however, the use of aggregate household groups in CGE models prevents a nuanced analysis of the differential poverty effects on households. Both the Tanzanian and Malawian models therefore incorporate a poverty module in which changes in prices and consumption at the representative household group level (i.e., as observed in the CGE model) are linked to corresponding member households in the underlying survey data, where changes in standard income poverty measures are computed.

The two studies, however, adopt different approaches to measuring nutrition changes. The Tanzania nutrition module developed by Pauw and Thurlow (2011) is similar to the poverty module already embedded in the CGE model. Specifically, food consumption changes (rather than changes in overall consumption values as in the poverty module) in the CGE model are linked top-down to the household data where changes in caloric availability at the household level are computed based on the nutritional characteristics of different food types. Caloric availability within each household is then compared against a measure of the daily energy requirement, which depends on a household's size and demographic structure. Households below this requirement are deemed calorie deficient or undernourished. The main "nutrition" result in Pauw and Thurlow's (2011) model is therefore changes in the calorie deficiency rate—the term nutrition is therefore used fairly loosely as it only refers to this one dimension—which is expressed either at the national level or for different household subgroups.[3]

[3]Nutritional characteristics of different food groups are derived from detailed Tanzania-specific data in Lukmanji et al. (2008). Equivalence scales in the nutrition module are from UNU, WHO, and FAO (2004). The Household Budget Survey (HBS) 2001 (NBS 2002) forms the basis of both the poverty and nutrition microsimulation modules.

The UNU, WHO and FAO (2004) recommend that energy needs cannot be considered in isolation of other nutrients as "the lack of one will influence the others." Ecker and Qaim (2011) maintain that micronutrient deficiencies, especially in minerals and vitamins, are often even more widespread in developing countries than calorie deficiencies, which contributes to severe health problems in these countries. Looking beyond caloric availability is therefore critical, particularly when people suffer from multiple nutritional deficiencies as is often the case in developing countries, Malawi included. Hence, in the Malawi microsimulation model, Ecker et al. (2012) focus on a wider range of nutritional indicators.

Rather than using consumption changes observed in the CGE model directly in the nutrition model, Ecker et al. (2012) adopt the two-stage micro-econometric model developed by Ecker and Qaim (2011) to first estimate consumption changes in response to household income changes.[4] In the first stage food demand elasticities are estimated assuming a quadratic almost ideal demand system (QUAIDS). In the second stage the technical coefficients from the first-stage estimation are translated into own-price, cross-price and income elasticities for different nutrients, including calories, protein, iron, zinc, and vitamins A, B3 (riboflavin), B9 (folate), B12, and C. Elasticities are estimated separately for rural and urban households across the different household quintiles. These form the basis of the microsimulation model: CGE results on income changes for different household groups are now fed into the microsimulation model where elasticities are applied to estimate new deficiency levels across the various nutrients.

From the discussion it should be apparent that the main difference between the two model frameworks lies in the specification of the microsimulation components and the way in which results from the "macro" model are linked to the "micro" level. In the Tanzania model caloric availability is calculated directly on the basis of changes in consumption quantities for different consumption items included in the CGE model. As discussed, these consumption changes are determined in an LES demand system, subject to relative price and income changes. In contrast, in the Malawi model, only changes in real household income are passed down to the micro-level. Changes in nutrient availability are calculated on the basis of income elasticities derived from a QUAIDS, a somewhat more flexible and advanced demand system, but one that stands distinct from the CGE model's LES demand system.

---

[4]The Integrated Household Survey (IHS) of 2004/05 (NSO 2005) is used as the basis of the microsimulation model (the poverty module embedded in the CGE model also uses the HIS 2004/05).

3 Country Case Studies

3.1 *Tanzania*[5]

Although Sub-Saharan Africa experienced unprecedented economic growth in recent decades, this did not always translate into less poverty or improved nutrition. The Tanzanian economy is one example of a country that failed to reap the benefits of sustained rapid growth. National gross domestic product (GDP) grew at 6.6% per year during 1998–2007 (MOFEA 2008), while agricultural growth, often regarded as instrumental in lowering poverty rates in agrarian-based developing countries, averaged a respectable 4.4% over the period. Yet, between 2001 and 2007 Tanzania's poverty rate only fell from 35.7 to 33.6%, while the share of the population consuming insufficient calories declined marginally from 25.0 to 23.6% (NBS 2002, 2010).

This outcome raises two questions. First, why did rapid growth not translate into more rapid reductions in poverty and malnutrition? And second, what is the contribution of agricultural growth in reducing poverty and malnutrition in Tanzania? To address these questions, an economywide model of Tanzania is linked with poverty and nutrition modules to (i) show how the current structure of growth resulted in the weak poverty and nutrition outcomes; and (ii) examine how accelerated, broad-based agricultural growth can contribute to higher overall growth and more rapid reductions in income poverty and hunger. Finally, the growth, poverty, and nutrition contributions of agricultural subsectors are examined more closely in order to identify priority sectors.

3.1.1 Notes on the Methodological Framework

The general equilibrium framework used for the Tanzania study incorporates both commodity demand and supply, with the latter made up of domestically produced and imported goods. This means the model is useful for considering the availability and access dimensions of food security. Prices are furthermore treated as endogenous in such models, which is important from a consumption modeling perspective. Consumption behavior is modeled on the basis of income and price elasticities estimated for each household group and commodity type. Both poverty and nutrition are affected by changes in income and relative prices. An analysis of nutrition impacts, however, requires a more in-depth look also at relative food price movements. If, for example, the price of calorie-rich maize increases and that of protein-rich meat declines such that the overall food price index does not change, the calorie

[5]This section was originally published as Chap. 7 of the International Food Policy Research Institute (IFPRI) book *Reshaping Agriculture for Nutrition and Health*, and is included with permission from IFPRI.

Table 1 Calorie contents, calorie prices, and caloric availability in Tanzania, 2001

	Average calories per standard serving[a]	Mean price (TSh) per 100 kcal[b]	Average per capita caloric availability		
			Poor[c]	Non-poor	All
Cereals	294	6.3	1390	1885	1687
Root crops	178	5.5	424	423	423
Pulses and oilseeds	443	10.9	196	411	325
Horticulture	49	19.8	106	240	186
Livestock and processed meat	266	26.0	125	318	241
Sugar and other foods	181	23.5	119	424	302

Source: Pauw and Thurlow (2011), based on Lukmanji et al. (2008)
Notes:
[a]No consumption weights were applied in calculating average calories per food group
[b]Mean price is the total expenditure divided by total calorie content per food item
[c]Poverty line is the 40th percentile of per capita expenditure; *kcal* kilocalories; *TSh* Tanzanian shilling

deficiency rate might decline and the protein deficiency rate might increase, even though the poverty rate remains unchanged. The rich (food) commodity–household specification in the CGE model is useful in this regard, as it captures important differences in consumer spending preferences and responsiveness to income and relative price changes across household types.

To avoid the feeling of hunger poorer consumers often allocate a larger share of their income to food types with high calorie contents and lower costs per calorie. Table 1 compares the calorie content of different foods in Tanzania. It shows how the price per 100 kilocalories (kcal) varies by product, and shows average calories available from different food products for poor and nonpoor households. Livestock products have a higher average calorie content per 100 g serving compared to most other food types, but they also have a higher price that makes them an expensive energy source. Cereals offer a similar amount of calories per serving, but cost considerably less than livestock products.

3.1.2 Tanzania's Recent Growth Performance

An examination of recent production trends suggests that although the agricultural sector as a whole grew rapidly during 1998–2007 (at 4.4% per year), growth has been volatile, while the source of this growth has been concentrated among a few crops. Rice and wheat, for example, dominate cereals production trends, and cotton, tobacco, and sugar production grew almost 10% per year. Larger-scale commercial farmers grow these well-performing crops on farms heavily concentrated in the northern and eastern periphery of the country. In contrast, yield for maize, the dominant staple food crop grown extensively by subsistence farmers, remained low due to primitive farming methods. Despite rice and wheat expansion and generally favorable agroecological conditions, Tanzania remains a net cereals importer because production has failed to keep pace with rising consumer demand.

Roots, such as cassava and potatoes, are also important food sources and account for almost 15% of Tanzania's harvested land. Root crops have performed well recently with more than 4% annual growth. By contrast, higher-value pulses and vegetables have stagnated, with pulses production declining by more than 4% each year. This was partly offset by expanded oilseeds production throughout the country and by fruit production in the northern and eastern regions. Non-cereal food crop production has therefore been characterized by slow growth in widely produced crops, and fast growth in regionally concentrated crops.

Some of the fastest growth rates during 2000–2007 were for export-oriented crops, such as cotton, sugarcane and tobacco. However, these crops are highly concentrated in specific regions. Cotton is mainly produced by smallholders in the western and lake regions (81.5% of national output). Tobacco, another smallholder crop, is produced in the western and highlands regions (82.8%). Sugarcane is mostly produced by larger-scale commercial farmers in the eastern and northern regions (83.8%). Together these three crops generated 17.4% of total merchandise exports in 2007. Coffee and tobacco are also major export crops, but their production has declined in recent years. Growth in export agriculture has therefore been driven by the strong performance of a few regionally concentrated crops. Thus, though the aggregate agricultural sector's substantial expansion in recent years suggests broad-based agricultural growth in Tanzania, a closer examination of agricultural production data suggests the opposite.

3.1.3 Comparing Business-as-Usual Growth to Broad-Based Agricultural Growth

To better understand the poverty and nutritional implications of Tanzania's historical growth path, the CGE model is used to produce a baseline scenario that assumes recent production trends continue over the period 2007–2015. These results are compared to a hypothetical scenario with accelerated agricultural growth ("agriculture scenario") in which agricultural GDP growth averages 5.3%. This scenario assumes a more broad-based agricultural growth path, with yields for crops that have performed well in the past (e.g., rice, wheat, and certain export crops) improving only marginally, while poor-performing crops (e.g., maize, pulses, and vegetables) experience larger yield gains, reflecting their greater growth potential.

The effectiveness of growth achieved under the two scenarios is measured with the aid of two types of elasticity: the poverty–growth elasticity and the calorie–growth elasticity. The poverty-growth elasticity is defined as the percentage decline in poverty caused by a one percent increase in per capita GDP. Similarly, the calorie–growth elasticity is the percentage change in the calorie deficiency rate

Table 2 Modeled poverty– and calorie–growth elasticities for Tanzania, 2007–2015

	Initial deprivation rate (%)	Final deprivation rate (%)	Avg. annual % change in deprivation rate (a)	Annual per capita GDP growth (b)	Deprivation–growth elasticity (a)/(b)
Baseline scenario					
Poverty rate	40.0	29.6	−3.7	3.6	−1.03
Calorie deficiency	23.5	17.6	−3.5	3.6	−0.99
Agriculture scenario					
Poverty rate	40.0	25.7	−5.4	4.1	−1.32
Calorie deficiency	23.5	13.8	−4.8	4.1	−1.57

Source: Results from the Tanzania CGE model and poverty/nutrition modules

divided by the percentage change in per capita GDP. Table 2 reports the deprivation–growth elasticity results from the baseline and agriculture scenarios. Average annual per capita GDP grew by 3.6 and 4.1% under the two scenarios respectively, while poverty declined by 3.7 and 5.4% respectively. This suggests a poverty–growth elasticity of −1.03 in the baseline scenario. In the agriculture scenario the poverty–growth elasticity increases to −1.32. The nutrition module, in turn, shows declines in the malnutrition rate of 3.54 and 4.84% in the two scenarios. This yields a baseline calorie–growth elasticity of −0.99, while in the agriculture scenario the calorie–growth elasticity improves significantly to −1.57.

The results confirm that broad-based agricultural growth greatly strengthens the impact of growth on poverty. The calorie–growth elasticity also rises substantially under the broad-based agricultural growth scenario, which is a reflection of the increased production and consumption of calorie-rich maize, sorghum, millet, and pulses.

3.1.4 Identifying Priority Sectors for Agricultural Growth

While the previous section illustrated the benefits of broad-based agricultural growth, ascertaining whether certain agricultural subsectors are more effective than others in improving the poverty and nutritional outcomes of agricultural growth requires further modeling. Growth within different agricultural subsectors can have different impacts on development outcomes for various reasons. First, poorer households may be more intensively engaged in the production of certain crops or agricultural products. Similarly, some subsectors produce products that poorer households consume more intensively. Growth or price fluctuations in these sectors will therefore have a greater impact on poverty than growth or price fluctuations in other sectors. Second, some subsectors produce products that are particularly important for households' nutritional status, such as those that represent

Table 3 Poverty, nutrition, and growth effects of agricultural subsector growth, 2007–2015

	Poverty-growth elasticity	Calorie-growth elasticity	Size and linkage effects
Maize-led growth	−1.174	−1.477	0.152
Sorghum and millet–led growth	−1.139	−1.348	0.033
Rice and wheat–led growth	−1.106	−1.147	0.106
Root crops–led growth	−1.184	−1.350	0.106
Pulses and oilseeds–led growth	−1.146	−1.161	0.101
Horticulture–led growth	−1.126	−1.092	0.186
Export crops–led growth	−1.097	−1.057	0.098
Livestock-led growth	−1.084	−0.977	0.204

Source: Results from the Tanzania CGE model and poverty/nutrition modules

low-cost sources of calories or are consumed intensively by nutrient-deficient households. While these elasticities are by definition growth neutral, growth itself is crucial for reducing poverty and malnutrition. Thus, a third factor concerns growth itself, and the fact that some sectors, due to their initial size in the economy, downstream production linkages (such as their production multiplier effects), or growth potential (signified by current yield gaps) can have a greater impact on overall growth. These three criteria are taken into account when identifying subsectors most effective at reducing poverty and malnutrition in Tanzania.

Comparative results are presented in Table 3. The simulated growth in each subsector achieves the same target agricultural GDP by 2015 in each simulation, thus ensuring that the poverty– and calorie–growth elasticities are directly comparable across subsectors. The three highest poverty–growth elasticities are for growth led by maize, root crops, and pulses and oilseeds. These crops are important expenditure items for households just below the poverty line and are grown more intensively by poorer farm households. In contrast, the poverty–growth elasticity for rice– and wheat–led growth is lower, mainly because these crops are grown in less poor regions of the country and, in the case of wheat, by larger-scale farmers who are less likely to be poor. The calorie–growth elasticities indicate that maize, sorghum and millet, and root crops raise household caloric availability per unit of growth most effectively. Although pulses and oilseeds have high calorie contents, the poor consume these less intensively since the crops are a fairly expensive source of calories. Livestock products have the lowest elasticity—in spite of the relatively high calorie content of meat products—because they are an expensive source of calories and calorie-deficient households consume them less intensively.

Production multipliers provide a useful indicator of the growth linkages of different subsectors. Multiplying each sector's production multiplier by its initial share in agricultural GDP constructs a simple index of the contribution each unit of additional growth within a sector makes to overall GDP. This index, shown in the last column of Table 2, identifies horticulture, livestock, and maize as sectors with the greatest potential to have a meaningful effect on national GDP in Tanzania within the 8-year timeframe of our simulation analysis.

3.1.5 Policy Recommendations

The analysis here suggests Tanzania's low poverty–growth elasticity results from the current structure of agricultural growth, which favors larger-scale production of rice, wheat, and traditional export crops in specific geographic locations. Accelerating agricultural growth in a wider range of subsectors than those currently leading the growth process can strengthen growth's effectiveness at reducing poverty. Faster agricultural growth would also benefit urban and rural households by increasing caloric availability and the ability to pay for food. Such nutritional improvements are best achieved by improving production of key calorie-laden food crops. The staple maize, already grown extensively by subsistence smallholders in Tanzania, has important size and growth linkages in the economy in addition to having large poverty–growth and calorie–growth elasticities. The analysis therefore identifies this sector as a priority sector for achieving growth, poverty, and nutrition objectives.

The modeling analysis by Pauw and Thurlow (2011) did not explicitly consider how increased agricultural productivity might be achieved or what the cost might be in terms of investments, extension services, or subsidies. However, studies for Tanzania and elsewhere have identified various interventions required to improve smallholders' crop yields, such as investing in rural infrastructure, researching and adopting improved seed varieties, and providing extension services. In recent years the Tanzanian government has allocated a relatively small share of its budget to agriculture. However, current development plans indicate a reprioritization of agriculture as a driver of economic growth and socioeconomic development. Pauw and Thurlow's (2011) results provide some indication of which agricultural sectors should be prioritized within this development plan in order to maximize national growth, poverty, and nutrition outcomes.

3.2 Malawi

While economic growth is generally acknowledged as a necessary precondition for reducing poverty, relatively little is known about how growth and nutrition are related. Therefore, questions persist regarding how to leverage economic policies so that they have a larger impact on nutrition. In recent years the Malawian government allocated a large share of its resources to the Farm Input Subsidy Program (FISP). Subsidized fertilizer and seed mainly for maize production led to rapid GDP growth during 2005–2010. It is obvious that an abundant supply of the calorie-laden staple maize is good for reducing calorie deficiency; however, it is less clear how FISP has affected micronutrient deficiencies, which are high in Malawi. This section explores diverse poverty and nutritional outcomes of recent maize-led growth in Malawi, drawing on the analysis by Ecker et al. (2012). Their study comprises two components: first, a cross-country analysis of the links between growth and nutrition outcomes; and second, a modeling analysis which includes case studies on Yemen and Malawi. We focus on those findings that are relevant to Malawi.

3.2.1 Cross-Country Evidence on the Relationship Between Growth and Nutrition

Ecker et al.'s (2012) cross-country analysis reveals that while some countries have been successful in leveraging growth for improved nutrition outcomes, others have seen nutrition deteriorate despite growth. In general, economic growth positively influences nutrition, but it is often not sufficient. During the early stages of development growth helps reduce calorie deficiency rates in particular, and, in most countries, agricultural growth plays a key role.

Calorie deficiency rates become less responsive to growth as its prevalence declines, and at this stage in the development process economic diversification into manufacturing and services is often necessary to leverage further economic growth, especially as rural-to-urban migration intensifies. Growth is generally insufficient to address all aspects of malnutrition, including child undernutrition and micronutrient deficiencies. Strategic investments and special programs are needed in sectors such as health and education.

3.2.2 Malawi's Farm Input Subsidy Program

The Malawian economy is agriculture-based and features limited economic diversity. Maize and tobacco are dominant subsectors, jointly contributing almost 15% to national GDP, and hence the performance of the agricultural sector and the economy as a whole is highly dependent on these sectors. Growth in the predominantly rainfed agricultural sector is volatile due to frequent droughts and floods. During 1990–2005 Malawi suffered at least three severe droughts and four major floods, with the agriculture sector contracting during 4 of these 15 years. The country has experienced at least two major food deficits since the turn of the millennium, leading to famine in 2002 and a serious food emergency in 2005. Frequent poor harvests combined with poor management of grain stocks contribute to food insecurity in Malawi.

During the 2005–2006 growing season, and in response to particularly severe food supply problems experienced in 2005, the government of Malawi initiated the Farm Input Subsidy Program (FISP), a large scale subsidy scheme that significantly reduces fertilizer and hybrid maize seed costs faced by resource-poor smallholders. The program has been lauded for its success in raising maize yields and contributing to overall economic growth, despite legitimate concerns about its fiscal sustainability (program costs have ranged from 5–16 percent of GDP since inception). Rapid maize output growth improved food security and raised caloric availability.

However, it is less clear how FISP may have impacted on micronutrient deficiencies in iron, zinc, vitamin A, and folate, which historically have been high.

The Malawi case study in Ecker et al. (2012) assesses the ways and extent to which FISP-led growth has contributed to nutrition outcomes in the country, and also considers nutritional outcomes under future growth scenarios. In this analysis, they use an economywide ("macro") model which is linked to household and child nutrition simulation ("micro") models. The combined analytical framework thus permits analyses of the effects of policy shocks on sector-level economic growth and household incomes, and how this in turn affects nutritional status.

3.2.3 Modeled Scenarios and Results

Three scenarios are explored. In the first, the period of rapid maize-led agricultural growth experienced under FISP during 2005–2010 is replicated. Under this scenario national GDP growth averages 6.8%, with growth in cereals driving overall economic growth (Table 4). These estimates are largely consistent with preliminary GDP growth estimates from Malawi national accounts.

Two future scenarios (2010–2020) are also modeled. The first assumes a return to long-term growth of around four percent experienced in the decade prior to FISP. This scenario, which serves as the baseline scenario, assumes the country will be unable to maintain the maize-led growth momentum generated under FISP. A second more optimistic scenario assumes a broad-based agricultural growth path as provided for under Malawi's Agricultural Sector-Wide Approach (ASWAp). This policy document outlines Malawi's vision of transforming the agricultural sector from its current overreliance on maize and tobacco to a more diversified one where a broader range of food and export crops are prioritized, and where rapid growth in downstream industrial and service sectors is encouraged through productivity-enhancing investments.

Table 4 Simulated GDP growth paths for selected sector (2005–2010 and 2010–2020)

		Future scenarios			
	Historical maize-led growth path	Return to long-run growth path		Broad-based agricultural growth	
	2005–2010	2010–2015	2015–2020	2010–2015	2015–2020
National GDP	6.8	4.0	4.1	6.4	6.0
Agriculture	8.5	3.3	3.4	6.5	5.1
Cereals	17.3	3.0	3.0	8.9	4.4
Export crops	4.9	4.1	4.0	5.2	7.7
Industry	5.4	4.6	4.5	6.2	6.8
Services	5.7	4.6	4.6	6.3	6.8

Source: Ecker et al. (2012)

Figure 1 shows changes in poverty and nutrition levels for the historical and future scenarios. Maize is grown extensively by poorer smallholder farmers; hence maize-led growth under FISP contributes to the rapid decline in poverty during 2005–2010. The poverty estimate for 2010 is close to the current official poverty rate of 39% (see NSO 2012). Under the slower growth scenario no further significant reductions in poverty emerge; in contrast, the broad-based growth scenario is associated with significant further reductions in the poverty rate, which drops below 30% by 2020.

The remaining panels in Fig. 1 show changes in calorie and various micronutrient deficiency rates. Historical maize-led growth reduces calorie deficiency from 34.8 to 17.1%. The proportions of people affected by iron, zinc, or folate

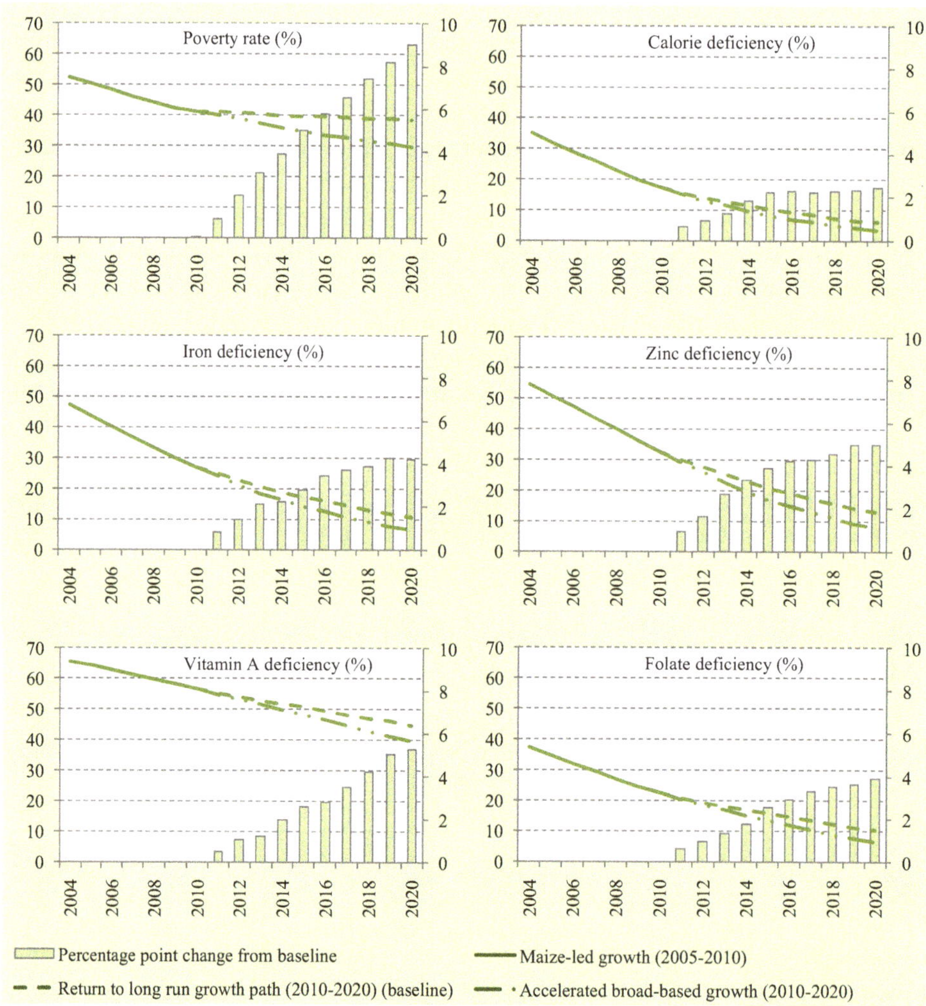

Fig. 1 Poverty and nutritional changes (2005–2020). Source: Based on results in Ecker et al. (2012). Notes: Deficiency rates shown on *left axes*; percentage point difference between slow-growth and accelerated growth paths shown on *right-hand axes*

deficiencies also decline in both absolute and relative terms (i.e., by more than one-third). Vitamin A deficiency, on the other hand, does not decline as rapidly, which reflects limited quantities of meat, fish, vegetable, and fruit in the average diet. In fact, the absolute number of vitamin A deficient people increases by 400,000 over the period. Thus, FISP, coupled with favorable weather conditions, is likely to be successful in reducing calorie and micronutrient deficiencies in relative and absolute terms, with the exception of vitamin A.

The scenarios for 2010–2020 show continued declines in malnutrition rates, albeit generally at a slower pace compared to the historical period. In the baseline scenario the proportion of calorie deficient people drops to under 10% after 2015, while iron, zinc, and folate deficiencies are all estimated to affect less than 15% of the population by 2020. The absolute number of people deficient in calories and most micronutrients also continues to decrease. Vitamin A deficiency, however, remains a concern, with the absolute number of vitamin A deficient people continuing to rise even though their proportion in the total population drops to well below 50% by 2020.

Under the broad-based growth scenario for 2010–2020 nutritional deficiency rates decline considerably faster than in the baseline. Micronutrient deficiencies tend to decline more rapidly than calorie deficiency, at least in percentage point terms. This relates to the high initial incidence of micronutrient deficiencies. From 2015 onwards the rate of decline in calorie deficiency remains stable at around 2% points below the baseline (see bar chart). In contrast, iron, zinc, and vitamin A deficiencies continue to decline at an increasing rate relative to the baseline, such that by 2020 micronutrient deficiency rates will be about 4–5% points below the rates in the baseline. By 2020 the number of people deficient in calories, iron, zinc, and folate is more than one-third lower than in the baseline.

3.2.4 Policy Recommendations

Ecker et al.'s (2012) analysis shows that economic structure and the characteristics of poor or malnourished people determine whether agricultural or nonagricultural growth is more effective at reducing poverty and malnutrition. In countries such as Malawi where agriculture contributes significantly to national income and where the majority of poor people earn a living from farming, agriculture has an important role to play. Nutrition improves not only for those rural households linked to agriculture; urban households also benefit from agricultural productivity growth and the associated reduction in food prices.

However, cross-country evidence shows how the role of growth shifts during the development process. The comparison between the broad-based growth and baseline scenarios for Malawi confirms this and shows how calorie and micronutrient deficiencies become less responsive to growth as prevalence rates decline, at which point economic diversification is needed to leverage further growth and reductions in malnutrition.

Ultimately, however, neither agricultural nor nonagricultural growth is sufficient to eliminate poverty, hunger, or micronutrient malnutrition. For example, in the modeled scenario for Malawi, even after a 15-year period of sustained and rapid agriculture-led economic growth, poverty remains close to 30%. This in part reflects the failure of economic growth to trickle down to all the poor and malnourished households; many individuals simply lack access to jobs or markets and hence fail to benefit from growth. As far as nutrition is concerned, the result also reflects lack of access to information and knowledge about proper nutrition, which diminishes the effect of growth-induced changes in household incomes on nutrition. Individual health status and access to healthcare are equally important for nutrition; if growth is not associated with improvements in health service delivery the nutritional effects of growth will be limited, even if higher incomes mean people can better afford health services. This highlights the need for strategic investments and targeted programs that are complementary to growth policies but explicitly aim to improve health and nutrition outcomes and thus strengthen the growth-nutrition linkages.

4 The Way Forward

The studies by Pauw and Thurlow (2011) and Ecker et al. (2012) are fairly similar in their approach to measuring the links between (agricultural) growth, poverty, and nutrition. The Tanzania analysis explicitly aimed at identifying agricultural subsectors that are most effective at reducing poverty and hunger, while the Malawi study was more focused on how plausible future economic growth paths might affect nutrition across multiple nutrition indicators. Both studies highlight the importance of the structure of growth in determining the pace of poverty reduction and nutritional improvements, with agricultural growth identified as a particularly important sector given its strong ties with rural poor households. Urban households, however, also benefit from increased availability of cheaper food, which is important for countries such as Tanzania where malnutrition levels are higher in urban areas.

Both approaches have strengths and weaknesses. Missing from both is an assessment of how growth affects the "utilization" dimension of food security and nutrition. For example, more rapid growth may be associated with (or the result of) improved infrastructure and better government service delivery in health and education, which either improves nutrition outcomes or raises the responsiveness of nutrition to higher incomes. Such effects are not easily modeled as endogenous outcomes of growth in standard CGE models; moreover, these models typically assume no changes in household consumption behavior over time and hence also not the way in which food is utilized. Analyses that incorporate the utilization dimensions may therefore require a different modeling framework altogether.

A limitation particular to the Malawi study is that it does not consider how consumption responses in the LES (CGE model) compare with those of the QUAIDS (nutrition module); in fact, even the income elasticities are defined and estimated separately. The nutrition module is also not set up to deal with relative price changes (i.e., only real disposable income changes are passed down to the micro-model). Relative prices are therefore implicitly assumed to be unchanged; hence the microsimulation model also disregards changes in the composition of consumption, even if the CGE model's demand system suggests they do change. The model is therefore more suited to analyses of growth-nutrition linkages under a "balanced growth" scenario where relative prices do not fluctuate too much. In essence, therefore, the combined Malawi model framework only considers the demand-side in detail; the supply-side of the nutrition story is reduced to a single measure of income change. In contrast, the Tanzania model explicitly accounts for relative price changes by using the demand system embedded in the CGE model. However, the assumption that all products are gross complements (i.e., cross-price elasticities are negative) is an important limitation of the LES, which means the model is not well suited to analyzing policy shocks leading to large fluctuations in relative prices.

There are, however, some advantages to using a separately-defined demand system for calculating nutrition changes. Whereas demand elasticities in recursive-dynamic CGE models are typically not permitted to change over time, the nutrition demand elasticities in the Malawi microsimulation model are adjusted to account for changes in income levels and the associated behavioral changes (i.e., nutrient demand elasticities are updated to match those of the income cohorts the households move into as their incomes rise). Ecker et al. (2012) are thus able to demonstrate the effect when calorie and micronutrient deficiencies become less responsive to growth as prevalence rates decline over time.

Maize is a widely grown crop in both Tanzania and Malawi, and hence has the potential to significantly contribute to growth and reductions in poverty and calorie deficiency. However, an important question for future research is how a maize-led growth strategy, such as the one followed in recent years in Malawi, might impact on crop diversification and nutrition outcomes across multiple nutrition indicators. The Tanzania study with its narrow focus on calories only cannot answer this question, but neither can the Malawi study, given that the supply of nutrients is not properly accounted for in the microsimulation model (as discussed).

Many of the model limitations can be overcome. Several attempts are underway to introduce a more appropriate demand system into CGE models, specifically one which allows for consumer goods to be treated as genuine substitutes, or a system in which parameters and elasticities can be updated over time to reflect changing consumption behavior (i.e., in recursive-dynamic models). The ultimate aim would be to fully embed a detailed demand system in the CGE model that can be used to evaluate nutrition changes. In the meantime simple model improvements include, in the case of the Malawi model, linking both price and income changes in the CGE model with the microsimulation model, and applying the same set of demand elasticities in both models. The Tanzania model, in turn, can easily be extended to measure changes in the availability of micronutrients as well (data is already available to do so). Ultimately, these studies represent an important step towards better understanding the growth-nutrition linkages.

References

Deaton, A. 2010. Understanding the mechanisms of economic development. *Journal of Economic Perspectives* 24 (3): 3–16.

Dervis, K., J. de Melo, and S. Robinson. 1982. *General equilibrium models for development policy*. New York: Cambridge University Press.

Diao, X., P. Hazell, and J. Thurlow. 2010. The role of agriculture in African development. *World Development* 38 (10): 1375–1383.

Diao, X., J. Thurlow, S. Benin, and S. Fan, eds. 2012. *Strategies and priorities for African agriculture: Economywide perspectives from country studies*. Washington, DC: International Food Policy Research Institute.

Dollar, D., and A. Kraay. 2002. Growth is good for the poor. *Journal of Economic Growth* 7 (3): 195–225.

Ecker, O., C. Breisinger, and K. Pauw. 2012. Chapter 6. In *Reshaping agriculture for nutrition and health*, ed. S. Fan and R. Pandya-Lorch. Washington, DC: International Food Policy Research Institute.

Ecker, O., and M. Qaim. 2011. Analyzing nutritional impacts of policies: An empirical analysis in Malawi. *World Development* 39 (3): 412–428.

Heidhues, F., A. Atsain, N. Hezron, M. Padilla, G. Ghersi, and J. Le Vallée. 2004. *Development strategies and food and nutrition security in Africa. An assessment*. IFPRI 2020 Discussion Paper, 38. Washington, DC: International Food Policy Research Institute.

Löfgren, H., S. Robinson, and R. Harris. 2002. *A standard computable general equilibrium (CGE) model in GAMS*. Washington, DC: International Food Policy Research Institute.

Lukmanji, Z., E. Hertzmark, N. Mlingi, V. Assey, G. Ndossi, and W. Fawzi. 2008. *Tanzania food composition tables*. Dar es Salaam, Tanzania; Boston, MA, Muhimbili University of Health and Allied Sciences (MUHAS); Tanzania Food and Nutrition Centre (TFNC); Harvard School of Public Health (HSPH).

Mellor, J.W. 1999. *Faster, more equitable growth: The relation between growth in agriculture and poverty reduction*. Cambridge, MA: Harvard University Press.

MOFEA (Ministry of Finance and Economic Affairs). 2008. *The economic survey 2007*. Dar es Salaam: Ministry of Finance and Economic Affairs.

NBS (National Bureau of Statistics). 2002. *Tanzania: Household budget survey 2000/01*. Dar es Salaam: National Bureau of Statistics.

———. 2010. *Tanzania: Household budget survey 2007*. Dar es Salaam: National Bureau of Statistics.

NSO (National Statistical Office). 2012. *Integrated household survey 2010/11*. Malawi: National Statistical Office.

Pauw, K., and J. Thurlow. 2011. Agricultural growth, poverty, and nutrition in Tanzania. *Food Policy* 36 (6): 795–804.

———. 2012. The role of agricultural growth in reducing poverty and hunger: The case of Tanzania. In *Reshaping agriculture for nutrition and health*, ed. S. Fan and R. Pandya-Lorch, 55–64. Washington, DC: International Food Policy Research Institute. doi:10.2499/9780896296732.

Ravallion, M., and G. Datt. 1996. How important to India's poor is the sectoral composition of economic growth? *The World Bank Economic Review* 10 (1): 1–26.

Timmer, C.P. 2000. The macro dimensions of food security: Economic growth, equitable distribution, and food price stability. *Food Policy* 25 (3): 283–295.

UNU, WHO, and FAO (United Nations University, World Health Organization, and Food and Agriculture Organization of the United Nations). 2004. *Human energy requirements: Report of a joint FAO/WHO/UNU expert consultation*. Rome, October 17–24, 2001. FAO Food aned Nutrition Technical Report Series 1. Rome: FAO.

Valdés, A., and W. Foster. 2010. Reflections on the role of agriculture in pro-poor growth. *World Development* 38 (10): 1362–1374.

Karl Pauw is the Regional Coordinator for the Monitoring and Analyzing Food and Agricultural Policies (MAFAP) program of the United Nations Food and Agriculture Organization (FAO), based in Addis Ababa, Ethiopia. At the time of writing his respective contributions in this book he was a Research Fellow at the International Food Policy Research Institute (IFPRI) and manager of IFPRI's Malawi country program in Lilongwe. He holds a PhD in development economics from the University of Cape Town, South Africa, and his research interests include: development and agricultural policy analysis; microeconomic analyses of labor markets, poverty, welfare outcomes, and nutrition; and policy impact analysis using computable general equilibrium and micro-simulation models.

James Thurlow is a Senior Research Fellow in the Development Strategies and Governance Division at the International Food Policy Research Institute in Washington DC. James' research focuses on the economy-wide interactions between policies and economic growth, poverty and inequality. James has published more than 80 articles and books that evaluate the contribution of public investments and policies to rural and national development in Africa and Asia.

Olivier Ecker is a Research Fellow in the Development Strategy and Governance Division of the International Food Policy Research Institute (IFPRI), Washington, DC. His research focuses on development policies and programs for poverty reduction and food and nutrition security in Africa and the Middle East.

6

Poverty and Distributional Impact of Macro Events: A Sequential Approach

Jann Lay

1 Introduction

Analyzing the poverty and distributional impact of macro events requires understanding how shocks or policy changes on the macro level affect household income and consumption. It is clear that this poses a formidable task, which of course raises the question of the appropriate methodology to address such questions. This paper presents one possible approach: A sequential methodology that combines a macroeconomic model with a behavioral micro-simulation. We discuss the merits and shortcomings of this approach with a focus on developing country applications with a short to medium run time horizon.[1]

Most analyses of the poverty and distributional impact of macro shocks have turned to Computable General Equilibrium (CGE) models, which typically incorporate different representative household groups with a given within-group income distribution. Yet, recent empirical findings on distributional change indicate that changes within household groups distributions account for an important share of overall distributional change (Bourguignon et al. 2005a, b). At first sight, an obvious solution to this problem seems to increase the number of household groups, or even to incorporate all households from representative household surveys into

This chapter is a re-print of: Lay, J. (2010). Sequential macro-micro modelling with behavioural microsimulations. International Journal of Microsimulation, 3(1), 24–34.

[1]Davies (2009) reviews applications linking macro models to micro-simulation models in developing and transition country contexts. His focus is on the applicability of different types of such models to specific questions and contexts. A more technical survey including applications is provided by Colombo (2010) who concentrates on alternative methods to link macro and micro models.

J. Lay (✉)
GIGA German Institute of Global and Area Studies, Hamburg, Germany
e-mail: jann.lay@giga-hamburg.de

the CGE model. Similarly—yet without providing heterogeneous feedback into the CGE model—micro-accounting techniques on the basis of household survey data that apply changes in factor prices at the individual level using household survey-data could be used to increase household heterogeneity. In an assessment of Russia's accession to the World Trade Organization (WTO), Harrison et al. (2000) however find differences in poverty and distributional outcomes between a model with ten representative household groups and a model with 55,000 households to be negligible.

Such evidence does not imply that household heterogeneity would not matter for a true understanding of the poverty and distributional impacts of macroeconomic shocks. It merely shows that even full heterogeneity of households in terms of factor endowments and consumption patterns does not make a difference in a standard CGE model. Microeconomic evidence on the drivers of changes in income distributions however suggests that applied CGE models (including those combined with household-survey-based micro-accounting models) may fail for a different reason: The importance of individual heterogeneity and decisions taken at the individual level for distributional and poverty outcomes; in other words, the importance of "individual behavior." On the labor market, individual decisions include entry into the labor market, falling into unemployment or switching between sectors or occupations. Of course, CGE models can be extended to include for example unemployment and/or endogenous labor supply. Yet, in order to capture the income distribution implications, decisions would have to be taken by "real" individual household members. This implies to introduce individual "fixed effects" and eventually requires the estimation of structural labor market models (Bourguignon et al. 2005a, b) that would need to be integrated in a general equilibrium framework. The estimation of such structural labor market models is by no means a trivial exercise and embedding them into a general equilibrium framework an additional challenge.[2]

This paper presents a less ambitious and more pragmatic approach. The sequential macro-micro approach that links a macroeconomic model, for example an applied CGE model, to a behavioral micro-simulation model has two distinguishing features. First, it is sequential. A counterfactual scenario is generated in the macro (CGE) model. Then, specific poverty and distribution-relevant link variables, for example wages and employment, are passed to a micro-simulation model. Second, the micro-simulation has behavioral components. For the micro-simulation, individual and household decisions are modeled using microeconometric techniques on household and employment survey data. Through the micro-simulation, the combined model hence incorporates individual "fixed effects" into the analysis.

The paper is structured as follows. We first outline some important characteristics of macro models used as part of a sequential model and present a stylized specification of a labor market that produces the link variables for our illustrative macro-micro model. We then provide a simple representation of household income

[2] See Blundell and MaCurdy (1999) for a survey of structural labor supply models and Creedy and Duncan (2002) for a discussion of their application in micro-simulation models. See Cogneau (2001) and Cogneau and Robilliard (2001) for attempts to integrate such models into general equilibrium models.

generation that forms the core of the of our prototype behavioral micro-simulation. We describe the simulation mechanics of the micro model. The next section presents two applications of this approach before we assess its strengths, weaknesses, and challenges. The final section concludes.

2 A Stylized Macro-Micro Model with a Behavioral Micro-simulation

2.1 The Macro Model and the Link Variables

The sequential approach presented in this paper requires a macro model that produces changes in distribution and poverty-relevant (aggregate) variables that are passed to a micro-simulation model. These variables, which we label "link variables," are prices and quantities on factor and goods markets. Link variables from factor markets include real wages for different types of labor, returns to land and different types of capital. Factor quantities, for example the sectoral composition of labor, may also be passed from a macro model to a micro-simulation. Finally, goods prices and quantities may operate as link variables. The developing country applications presented in this paper use applied trade-focused CGE models.[3] Yet, other types of macro models with very different foci and features, including other forms of general equilibrium models (real business cycle models, and stochastic dynamic general equilibrium models) and macroeconometric models, may be more suitable in different contexts and for different questions. The illustrative framework presented in the following is general enough to allow the reader to imagine the application of a sequential macro-micro approach using very different models both at the macro and micro level, and different link variables.

If a macro model is built as part of a sequential macro-micro model, its labor market specification is the key component and will have to be compatible with the micro-simulation model that we present below. The following representation of a labor market should be thought of as being embedded, for example, in an applied multisectoral CGE model that distinguishes between formal and informal production sectors. The associated labor markets are assumed to exhibit structural imperfections with different clearing mechanisms for these sectors. For the simplicity of exposition, we abstract from other factors of production and assume that the formal and informal sector produce the same good. Let total employment be fixed and assume that factors are fully employed. Hence, total employment will be the sum of formal and informal employment, $L = L^f + L^{if}$. In a simple neoclassical world with full mobility of labor between formal and informal sectors, wages in the formal and informal sectors, which produce with different technologies ($f_f(L^f), f_{if}(L^{if})$), will be the same. Employment in formal and informal sector, respectively, and hence the

[3]See Robinson (1989) for a survey and van der Mensbrugghe (2003) and Lofgren et al. (2002) for standard applied model in the tradition of Dervis et al. (1982).

formal labor share in this economy will be determined by the equation of marginal labor products in formal and informal sectors, as expressed in Eq. (1).

$$\frac{w^f}{p} = \frac{w^{if}}{p} = f'_f\left(L^f\right) = f'_{if}\left(L^{if}\right) \tag{1}$$

Now assume that different wage setting mechanisms exist: In the formal sector, wages are rigid, for example due to the presence of bargaining by trade unions or efficiency wages. This rigidity can be represented by a "wage curve," as in Eq. (2) where the real formal sector wage becomes a function of the ratio of formal to informal employment.

$$\frac{w^f}{p} = g\left(\frac{L^f}{L - L^f}\right) \tag{2}$$

Without unemployment, the informal sector will now absorb the remaining workforce and the informal sector wage will adjust such that labor demand by the informal sector equals "residual" labor supply. This is depicted in Fig. 1 below where Ec illustrates the competitive equilibrium and wc/p0 the corresponding wage. With WC, the wage curve, the equilibrium wage and employment levels are represented by E_0. The formal sector wage w_0^f/p_0 will now be higher than the informal sector wage w_0^{if}/p_0. Accordingly, formal sector employment L_0^f will be lower than in the competitive case L_c^f.

Real wages and employment in formal and informal sector, respectively, constitute the link variables in our illustrative macro-micro model.

$$\frac{w^f}{p}, \frac{w^{if}}{p}, L^f, L^{if}$$

We now consider a policy experiment that shifts formal labor demand and leads to a new equilibrium in E1. The formal sector wage increases to w1f/p1 and formal employment to L_1^f. The informal sector wage will increase as well from w_0^{if}/p_0 to w_1^{if}/p_1. Hence, the counterfactual values for our link variables[4] that will be passed to the micro-simulation will be

$$\frac{w_1^f}{p_1}, \frac{w_1^{if}}{p_1}, L_1^f, L_1^{if}.$$

[4]With real data, the base values for wages and employment levels will typically not be empirically consistent between the macro model, i.e. the SAM, and the micro-simulation model. This inconsistency is "resolved" by passing relative changes from the macro to the micro model. In the simple representation here for example an x percent increase in formal employment and a y(z) percent increase in formal (informal) sector wages.

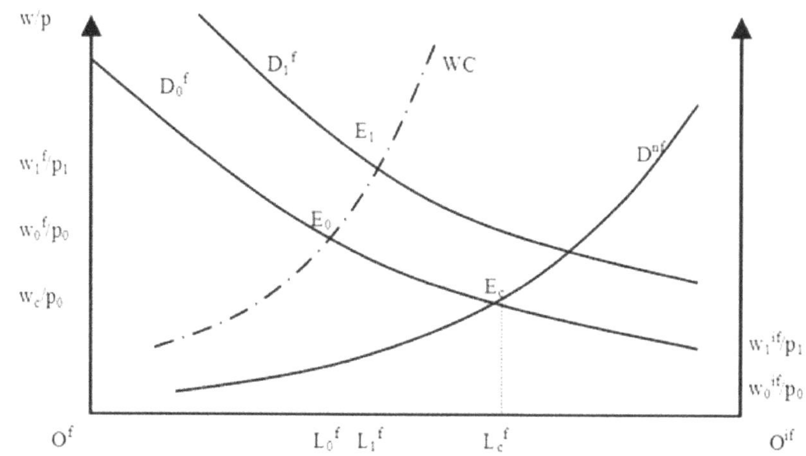

Fig. 1 Formal and informal labor markets. Source: Authors compilation

2.2 *A Prototype Income Generation Model: The Micro-simulation*

This section describes a prototype micro-simulation model that can be used in combination with the above CGE model to simulate the poverty and distributional impacts of shocks. The basis of the micro-simulation is a household income generation model that needs to be compatible with the above CGE model. For good reasons, we avoid the term consistency here and refer to compatibility instead, as the macro and micro models will not be strictly consistent, neither theoretically nor empirically. We will return to this very important issue in more detail later. The household income generation model is estimated from household survey data with individual-level employment information.

In the micro-simulation, we hence model the household income generation process.[5] This implies that individuals make occupational choices and earn wages or profits accordingly. These labor market incomes plus exogenous other incomes, such as transfers and imputed housing rents, comprise household income. The components of the income generation model are thus an occupational choice and an earnings model. In the choice model, individual agents can choose between wage-employment and self-employment.[6] We thus ignore labor market

[5]The following section borrows from Robilliard et al. (2002). A more detailed discussion of a similar labor market specification can be found in Alatas and Bourguignon (2005).

[6]We will use self-employment and informal sector employment interchangeably.

participation choice in this illustrative model. The occupational choice model is assumed to be slightly different for household heads other household members. Once occupational choices are made, earnings are generated accordingly either in the form of wages or as profits for the self-employed. Being self-employed means being part of what might be called a "household-enterprise," in which all self-employed members of a household pool their incomes. The wage-employment market is segmented: the wage setting mechanisms are assumed to differ for skilled and unskilled labor as well as for females and males, which implies that there are four wage labor market segments.

The following set of equations describes the household income generation model. Household income Y_{hh} is earned by k_{hh} members, who are (and remain) active on the labor market [Eq. (3) below]. They are active either in the formal (with $DF_i = 1$, a dummy variable for formal sector employment) or informal sector ($(DF_i - 1)(-1) = 1$ if $DF_i = 0$) and earn the corresponding wages w_i^f, w_i^{if}. In addition, the household receives an exogenous nominal income $\bar{y}_{hh}$, for example transfers or remittances. All these components are real values, i.e. deflated with prices p. In practice, p will be assumed to be one in the initial situation. Per capital income y_{hh} is obtained by dividing household income by household size $Y_{hh}/hsize$ so that $(y_1, y_2, \ldots, y_n)$ denotes the distribution of income when each observation is weighted with household size.

$$Y_{hh} = \frac{1}{p} \sum_{i=1}^{k_{hh}} \left(w_i^f DF_i + w_i^{if} (DF_i - 1)(-1) + \bar{y}_{hh} \right) \tag{3}$$

Individual occupational choices—between informal and formal activities—can be described by the following functions, which are assumed to be different for household heads (h) and other household members (o). We suppress the individual index here. Equation (4) shows that the household head's probability of being employed in the formal sector is a function of a linear expression with a constant term c^h and personal and household characteristics X^h, which can include for example education, age, and households composition variables.

$$P\left(DF^h = 1 | X^h\right) = g^h\left(c^h + X^h \alpha^h\right) \tag{4}$$

The choices of other household members are assumed to depend not only on their own individual characteristics X^o, but also on the household head's occupational choice.

$$P\left(DF^o = 1 | X^o, DF^h\right) = g\left(c^o + X^o \alpha^o + \gamma^o DF^h\right) \tag{5}$$

Equations (6) and (7) express wages w in the formal (f) and informal (if) sectors, respectively, in log-linear form with X, a vector of personal characteristics, and u, a random error.

$$\ln\frac{w^f}{p} = c^f + X\beta^f + u^f \tag{6}$$

$$\ln\frac{w^{if}}{p} = c^{if} + X\beta^{if} + u^{if} \tag{7}$$

The model just described gives the household income as a non-linear function of observed and unobserved individual and household characteristics. This function depends on two sets of parameters, which include the parameters of the wage equations for informal and formal activities and the parameters in the utility associated with different occupational choices for household heads and other family members. The occupational choice equations as well as the corresponding wage equations can be estimated from standard household survey data. Estimating Eqs. (4) and (5) using discrete choice models (with dichotomous choices hence logit or probit models) and (6) and (7) using Ordinary Least Squares (OLS) (or other adequate estimation techniques[7]) yields the following parameter vector:

$$\left(\widehat{c}^h, \widehat{\alpha}^h, \widehat{c}^o, \widehat{\alpha}^o, \gamma^o, \widehat{c}^f, \widehat{\beta}^f, \widehat{c}^{if}, \widehat{\beta}^{if}\right).$$

In addition, we obtain $\widehat{u}^f$ and $\widehat{u}^{if}$ as observed residuals from the wage equations. However, we only observe formal wages for individuals employed in the formal sector. As the micro-simulation will allow individuals to switch between formal and informal activities, we simulate a residual for the non-observed wage, here by a random draw from a normal distribution with the respective (formal or informal) observed variance.[8] We face a similar problem in the latent utility models necessary to estimate Eqs. (4) and (5). In these models, residuals cannot be observed and are hence generated from the distribution underlying the respective model, here either a normal (probit) or logistic (logit) distribution. Residuals have to be drawn consistent with the observed occupational choice, i.e. the utility an observed formal wage earner relates to formal employment has to be higher than the utility associated with informal employment. Statistically, this implies to draw these residuals conditional on the observed choice. These simulated residuals are denoted $u1_i$ and $u0_i$. With

---

[7]Selection bias is a problem in estimating earnings equations in different sectors/occupations (corresponding to different labor market choices) that is difficult to resolve. We return to this point later.

[8]This number does not have to be a random number. It may be reasonable to assume that the observed residual has important informational content with regard to unobserved characteristics, such as ability. A possible alternative to a random draw is then to scale the observed residual in accordance with the observed variances of formal and informal wages, respectively.

ind, an indicator function that assumes a value of 1 (0) if the condition in brackets is (not) fulfilled, we thus have.

$$DF_i^h = ind\left(\widehat{c}^h + X_i^h\widehat{\alpha}^h + u1_i > u0_i\right) \tag{8}$$

$$DF_i^o = ind\left(\widehat{c}^o + X_i^o\widehat{\alpha}^o + \gamma^o DF^h + u1_i > u0_i\right) \tag{9}$$

Here DF_i^h and DF_i^o will hence assume their observed values. This implies that the sum of these two dummies—defined either for household heads or other household members—over all individuals will give the total number formal sector employees L_0^f, consistent with the initial value of this link variable from the macro model. This is illustrated in Eq. (10).

$$L_0^f = \sum_{hh}\sum_{i}^{k_{hh}}\left(DF_i^h \oplus DF_i^o\right) \tag{10}$$

Accordingly, average wages in the formal sector can be expressed as follows.

$$\frac{w_0^f}{p} = \frac{\sum\limits_{hh}\sum\limits_{i}^{k_{hh}}\left[\left(DF_i^h \oplus DF_i^o\right)\cdot \exp\left(\widehat{c}^f + X_i\widehat{\beta}^f + \widehat{u}_i^f\right)\right]}{L_0^f} \tag{11}$$

Similar expressions can be written down for informal sector employment and the corresponding wage, such that we can replicate all link variables in the initial equilibrium $w_0^f, w_0^{if}, L_0^f, L_0^{if}$. Remember that this replication is based on the observed characteristics of the individuals (all X), unobserved and partially simulated characteristics (all u), and the estimated parameters.

Based on this micro replication of the initial situation, we can now micro-simulate the distributional and poverty implications of the changes in the link variables given by the macro model. In the simulation, the link variables $\frac{w_1^f}{p_1}, \frac{w_1^{if}}{p_1}, L_1^f, L_1^{if}$ will hence be used as target values. This implies that individual earnings and occupational choices have to change such that they reproduce these targets on the aggregate level. There are a number of ways how this can be achieved. Obviously, the required individual changes in occupational choices can be obtained by varying the coefficients or the observed or unobserved individual characteristics. A typical choice in applied micro-simulation models is to vary the constant(s). Hence, the chosen parameters are adjusted and occupational choices change accordingly, until the results of the micro-simulation are consistent, at an aggregate level, with the given aggregates. Formally, the following constraint describes the consistency requirement where c_1^h is the constant in the heads' occupational choice equation that is consistent with L_1^f.

$$L_1^f = \sum_{hh} \sum_{i}^{k_{hh}} \left[\left(ind\left(c_1^h + X_i^h \widehat{\alpha}^h + u1_i > u0_i\right)\right) \oplus \left(ind\left(\widehat{c}^o + X_i^o \widehat{\alpha}^o + \gamma^o DF_1^h + u1_i > u0_i\right)\right)\right] \tag{12}$$

Varying only the constant $\widehat{c}^h$ (to c_1^h) implies that we assume that the macro shock only induces household heads to switch occupation. Other household members' occupational choices are only affected through the possible change in the head's occupational choice, i.e. in the case of $DF_1^h \neq DF^h$. As this kind of behavior may not be realistic, we can alternatively assume that the constants of both the heads and other household members vary. However, without an additional restriction, changes in the two constants cannot be uniquely determined. A possible solution is to add a variable Δ to the constant term. In practice—when such equations are solved for real households from a household survey—we will typically be able to find a unique solution for Δ in Eq. (13).

$$L_1^f = \sum_{hh} \sum_{i}^{k_{hh}} \begin{bmatrix} \left(ind\left(\left(\widehat{c}^h + \Delta \right) + X_i^h \widehat{\alpha}^h + u1_i > u0_i \right)\right) \\ \oplus \left(ind\left(\left(\widehat{c}^o + \Delta \right) + X_i^o \widehat{\alpha}^o + \gamma^o DF_1^h + u1_i > u0_i \right)\right) \end{bmatrix} \tag{13}$$

Using either approach to adjust the constant (or both constants) in the occupational choices, will thus enable us to replicate the changes in formal as well as formal employment given by the CGE model. Our very simple income generation model allows us to proceed step-wise. We first solve for changes in occupational choices, and simulate wages in the next step. The reason is that wages do not enter the occupational choices of individuals, as they might in a more complex—or structural—income generation model. However, changes in occupational choices enter the equation for aggregate wages, as the (observed and unobserved) characteristics of the individuals in the respective sectors change. As in the case of occupational choices, we can vary the constants in the respective sectors to equate wages given by the CGE model and those in the micro-simulation.[9] For the formal sector, this requires Eq. (14) to hold with c_1^f, the new formal sector wage equation constant.

$$\frac{w_1^f}{p_1} = \frac{\sum_{hh} \sum_{i}^{k_{hh}} \left[\left(DF_{1\,i}^{\,h} \otimes DF_{1\,i}^{\,o} \right) \cdot \exp\left(c_1^f + X_i \widehat{\beta}^f + \widehat{u}_i^f \right) \right]}{L_1^f} \tag{14}$$

The equation for the average informal sector wage can be derived accordingly. The solutions for the constants in the choice Eq. (13) and the wage Eq. (14) can be obtained using numerical solution algorithms, for example Gauss-Newton techniques. With counterfactual occupational choices and corresponding wages DF_1, w_1,

[9]Alternatively, we may choose to vary the coefficient for education implying that we expect the macro shock to affect wages through its impact on returns to education.

we can now compute the counterfactual household income Y_{1hh}, as illustrated in Eq. (14). We assume that exogenous transfers $\bar{y}_{hh}$ are constant in nominal terms.

$$\begin{aligned} Y_{1hh} &= \frac{1}{p_1} \sum_{i=1}^{k_{hh}} \left(w_{1i}^{f} DF_{1i} + w_{1i}^{if} (DF_{1i} - 1)(-1) + \bar{y}_{hh} \right) \ \ with \ \ DF_1 \\ &= DF_{1_i}^{\ h} \oplus DF_{1_i}^{\ o} \end{aligned} \tag{15}$$

With constant household size these counterfactual household incomes now yield a counterfactual income distribution that can be described by $(y_{11}, y_{12}, \ldots, y_{1n})$.

3 Applications

The above prototype macro-micro model is intended to provide an introduction into the basic mechanics of a macro-micro model with a behavioral micro-simulation. Which macro model to choose and which transmission channels to highlight eventually depends on the research or policy question and the context, in which it is placed. The two applications that we present in the following are based on recursive-dynamic, trade-focused national CGE models.[10] The first application examines the possible poverty impacts of a Doha round scenario of further multilateral trade negotiations for the case of Brazil. The second assesses the poverty and distributional implications of the Bolivian gas shock.

As in the above model and most developing country applications, the focus is on the labor market, as reflected by the link variables that include average wages in different labor market segments, employment levels and the occupational composition of employment. The respective specification of the labor market represents the transmission channels considered to be of particular relevance for the policy and shock under consideration. The Brazilian model focuses on movements between agricultural and non-agricultural sectors, while the Bolivian model concentrates on formal-informal segmentation in the urban labor market. In both applications, the labor market is further segmented along skill levels.

The micro-simulation models used in the subsequent applications share the reduced-form character of the above prototype model. Employment volumes in the respective labor market segments, for example unskilled agricultural employment, and wages are adjusted according to the results from the macro model. These adjustments are not triggered by individual responses to prices, for example relative wages—as they would in a (more) structural labor market model. As above, adjustments are obtained by changing the parameters of the estimated household income generation model.

[10]See van der Mensbrugghe (2003) for a technical description of the basic characteristics of the CGE model used in both applications.

3.1 The Poverty Impacts of Trade Liberalization in Brazil

Using this type of sequential model, Bussolo et al. (2006) ex-ante assess the poverty and distributional impacts of different uni- and multilateral trade liberalization scenarios for Brazil.[11] The labor market specification of the CGE model distinguishes between skilled and unskilled labor. While skilled workers are fully mobile across sectors, the labor market for the unskilled is segmented between agriculture and non-agriculture. This dual labor market for unskilled workers is modeled following a simple Harris-Todaro specification where the decision to migrate is a function of expected income in the non-agricultural sectors relative to the expected income in the agricultural sectors.

The micro model is linked to the macro model through changes in the following set of variables: First, changes in agricultural and non-agricultural labor income of unskilled labor; second, changes in labor income of skilled labor; third, changes in the sectoral (agriculture vs. non-agriculture) composition of the unskilled workforce. In addition, the micro-simulation takes into account that unskilled and skilled labor supplies grow at different rates. These rates—also assumed to be exogenous in the CGE model—are derived from past trends of labor supply growth in the respective categories.

In accordance with the structure of the CGE model, the micro model thus simulates the decision to move from agriculture into non-agricultural sectors (or vice versa) only for unskilled workers. This simulation is based on a sectoral mover-stayer model that is estimated for heads and non-heads separately—as in the above prototype model. For this estimation, Bussolo et al. (2006) make use of a distinguishing feature of the PNAD.[12] In contrast to many other household surveys, the PNAD provides information on employment histories, which allows the authors to identify movers between sectors and their characteristics at the time of moving. These characteristics include the type of land right the movers held or whether they were self-employed before they moved out of agriculture. These characteristics enter as explanatory variables into the mover-stayer model. As in the prototype model, the household income generation model is completed by Mincer-type wage equations for unskilled labor in agriculture and non-agriculture as well as for skilled labor. Individual labor incomes are aggregated as described above.

The mover-stayer model can be used to illustrate the behavioral content of the micro-simulation model. For example, Bussolo et al. (2006) find a strong negative influence of own landholdings on the propensity to move. In contrast, higher educational achievements are making individuals more likely to move into non-agricultural employment. In addition, occupational choices of members of the same household are strongly correlated. In the simulation, individuals with no

---

[11]Changes in global prices and trade flows following multilateral liberalization scenarios are derived from global models. For details see Bussolo et al. (2006).

[12]The Pesquisa Nacional por Amostra de Domicílios (PNAD) is a regularly conducted representative household survey

landholdings, better education and—in case of non-household heads—and moving household heads will hence be the first ones to move from agriculture into non-agricultural employment. Which individuals (landless, but better educated) move first, can make a difference in distributional outcomes. The movers' characteristics will determine the composition of those who remain in agriculture (more with own landholdings, but less educated) as well the earning prospects in the non-agricultural sector (ceteris paribus better with better education).

With these components, the micro-simulation involves two steps: First, unskilled labor moves out of agriculture until the new share of unskilled labor in agriculture given by the CGE is reproduced. Second, wages/profits are adjusted according to the CGE results taking into account the sectoral movements of unskilled labor from agriculture into non-agricultural sectors. Adjustments are achieved through the same procedures as in the above prototype model, i.e. the computation of new constants in the choice and wage equations, respectively, using numerical solution algorithms.

The analysis suggests that the economic effects of multilateral liberalization are rather limited for Brazil. Accordingly, poverty would remain largely unaffected by such reforms. In contrast, a full liberalization scenario implies quite substantial welfare gains that are concentrated among some of the poorest groups of the country, in particular those in agriculture. This scenario is also most interesting from a methodological viewpoint, as it highlights the benefits of a behavioral micro-simulation. Under full liberalization, the rural poor benefit more than proportionately, a result driven—on the macro level—by an export boom in agriculture and agricultural processing industries, growing labor demand and associated higher wages. However, following full liberalization, a larger number of workers remain in agriculture compared to the baseline scenario. Given that moving out of agriculture may substantially improve the income situation of a household, one may expect full liberalization to weaken poverty reduction, an expectation supported by the observation that moving households are on average poorer than those remaining in agriculture (for example because they are landless). However, this is not the case, as the gain in agricultural incomes more than compensates the reduced benefits from lower migration flows (for example because they are better educated than those who stay in agriculture).

3.2 The Poverty Impacts of the Bolivian Gas Boom

Lay et al. (2008) examine the poverty effects of the gas boom Bolivia experienced in the late 1990s and early 2000s. Their analysis attempts to disentangle the effects of the resource-boom/bust from other shocks that the Bolivian economy experienced at the same time. The market for unskilled labor is segmented between rural and urban areas. The two segments are linked through rural-urban migration, modeled as in the Brazilian case as a function of the corresponding wage differential. In contrast, skilled labor is assumed to be fully mobile across all production sectors. Within the urban economy, unskilled workers are mobile between formal and informal sectors, but wage differentials observed in the base period are assumed to persist. These differentials point to systematically lower labor productivity in informal sectors.

Almost as in the prototype model, the macro model is linked to the micro-simulation through the following set of variables: (1) the share of unskilled workers in the formal sector, (2) the share of skilled workers in the formal sector, (3) mean wages for skilled workers, (4) mean wages for unskilled workers, and (5) mean informal profits.[13] Informal profits are understood as mixed income received by self-employed workers. Accordingly, they are calculated as the sum of skilled and unskilled labor income as well as informal capital income.

The two basic components of the income generation model in the Bolivian application are again a model of occupational choices that represents the choice between formal and informal employment as well as earnings functions that correspond to the respective sector of employment. Employment is assumed to be informal if the individual is self-employed/non-remunerated household member and/or works in an enterprise with less than five employees. If individuals happen to be in (or switch to) the formal sector they are assumed to earn a wage, whereas individuals in the informal sector are assumed to be (or become) part of a household enterprise and contribute to the profits earned by this enterprise. The choice between informal and formal activities is modeled separately for household heads, spouses, and other household members. In contrast to the above specifications, the equations of the choice model are interrelated through the head's wage (and choice) that enters the occupational choice model of spouses and other household members. Again, occupational choices are hence assumed to be sequential with the household head deciding first. In line with the CGE model, the micro-simulation distinguishes between unskilled and skilled labor. Separate wage equations for skilled and unskilled labor, respectively, hence describe earnings for individuals employed in the formal sector.[14] The micro-simulation again adjusts the constants to produce counterfactual occupational choices, earnings, and, eventually, household incomes and the corresponding distribution of income.

As in the Brazilian case, the micro-simulation reveals the importance of individual characteristics that determine the sign and the strength of distributional change. Lay et al. (2008) find that—for both unskilled and skilled labor—the very poor are affected most by increasing informality. These results can be rationalized by looking at, first, who moves into informality and, second, the size of the income loss for movers relative to both their initial income and the income losses incurred by other individuals. The size of the income loss depends on individual

[13]The authors note on formal profits (Lay et al. 2008): "Although formal profits account for an important share in value added, they are not passed to the micro-simulation for two reasons. First, most formal profits are retained and invested. Second, capital income is likely to be measured very poorly in household surveys. As formal profits increase considerably during the gas boom, we may systematically ignore an inequality-increasing factor."

[14]Rural incomes are taken into account through a simple micro-accounting exercise.

characteristics (as the returns to these characteristics differ between formal and informal activities) and on whether an individual joins an already existing household enterprise or establishes a new one. The estimation, which underlies the microsimulation, shows that less educated younger (and hence poorer) individuals tend to move into informality first. With regard to the size of the income losses, the estimation results for wages and profit functions indicate that the income loss of moving into informality is higher for more educated individuals, at least in absolute terms, when they move into an existing household enterprise. However, it may also happen that establishing an informal enterprise increases earnings for a skilled individual—conditional of course on other individual characteristics. For an unskilled individual, by contrast, moving into informality will always imply an income loss.

Overall, Lay et al. (2008) find that the gas boom has both unequalising and equalising distributional impacts that tend to offset each other. As net distributional change is limited, growth generated by the boom also reduces poverty and the boom hence does not completely bypass the poorer parts of the Bolivian population. Poverty reduction with little distributional change can be observed despite increasing informality. Additional stylized micro-simulations by Lay et al. (2008) illustrate that lower formal employment can lead to a significant rise in urban poverty and that the very poor are affected most by increasing informality. Yet, considerable overall increases in informal profits compensate this possible negative impact.

3.3 Strengths and Weaknesses

The macro-micro approach presented above and illustrated by the two case studies brings together two strands of literature, macro models, here applied CGE models, on the one hand, and microeconometric poverty and distributional analyses, on the other, which were largely separated from each other. While CGE analyses tend to suffer from being too stylized and not being well informed by micro data, poverty and distributional analyses are often merely descriptive and lack an assessment of the causes of distributional change and the related transmission channels. The sequential approach that combines a CGE model and a behavioral micro-simulation attempts to get the best out of these two "modeling worlds."[15]

A general advantage of a sequential over more complex models is its tractability: While it remains tractable both at the macro and the micro level, it still allows for sufficiently detailed and disaggregated analyses. This is of course more so when the micro model has behavioral components. The case studies above have illustrated the value added of introducing behavior or "individual fixed effects" into the micro-simulation model. In such a micro-simulation, the poverty and distributional impact of policies, as in reality, depend on the characteristics of the households or even individuals.

[15]This section borrows heavily from Lay (2007).

However, getting the best of two fairly different modeling worlds comes at the cost of a lack of both theoretical and empirical consistency. Sequentially combining a macro and micro model typically implies the imposition of a number of ad-hoc assumptions that are not satisfying from a theoretical perspective. While the "degree of consistency" between the macro and the micro model however differs between applications, the combined model will lack the theoretical consistency of a general equilibrium model and it is difficult—if not impossible—to resolve all the data discrepancies between national accounts, on the one hand, and household survey data, on the other. Individual responses from estimated relationships may not be conforming to theoretical expectations and the combined model may have leakages—in contrast to the consistent system of flows of an applied CGE model. Theoretically, changes in the behavior of economic agents are driven by relative price changes, whereas the micro-simulation typically only features a reduced-form representation of labor market behavior where prices do not appear as explanatory variables. Empirically, problems arise from the large differences in national accounts and household data, in particular with regard to labor value added, although some authors, e.g. Robilliard et al. (2002), manipulate survey weights to reach "empirical consistency."

Furthermore, quite a few economists may argue that the combination of an applied CGE model with a micro-simulation based on a reduced-form labor market representation may not be a good idea after all. Both types of models suffer from serious shortcomings and combining the two may compound these problems by adding new problems and distracting the researcher from the shortcomings of the "single" models. This is a critique that should be taken seriously. From our own experience in building sequential models, we have become increasingly aware that the additional problems that arise from combining the models, for example in terms of empirical consistency, leave less time for the scrutiny needed to estimate a household income generation model from household survey data or less time to do the sensitivity analyses so often called for in applied CGE analyses (Harrison et al. 1993). We therefore dedicate the following paragraphs to the weaknesses of the single components of a combined macro-micro model without, however, forgetting about their strengths.

The shortcomings of the income generation models are very specific to the respective application and they are discussed at length elsewhere, for example in Bourguignon et al. (2005b). We just want to highlight two typical problems: Selectivity and parameter validity. Estimating earnings equations that correspond to different sectoral or occupational choices entail selection problems. In the presence of unobserved heterogeneity, for example in terms of entrepreneurial ability, it is fairly likely the same unobserved characteristics that make you choose a specific sector also determine the earnings in the respective sector. This selection on unobservables biases the coefficients of an Ordinary Least Squares estimation of the respective equations and would have to be accounted for. It is not trivial to correct for selectivity bias, although the so-called Heckman correction or one of its variants is very common in applied work. To be empirically valid, however, an instrument is needed that explains the sectoral choice, but not earnings in the respective sectors. Such a variable is typically very difficult to find.

There may also be reasons for challenging the validity of the estimated parameters in the household income generation model. Typically, the behavioral equations, e.g. those governing occupational choices, are estimated from cross-sectional data. It is hence assumed that the observed variation in behavior between individuals is used to simulate behavioral change of (other) individuals in time, for example in the Bolivian case study.[16] The Brazilian model relies on employment histories and therefore avoids this problem, but the type of information used reflects to a certain extent short-term behavior. Even if panel data was available, constant parameters would have to be assumed for the simulation period, which apparently becomes an increasingly problematic assumption the longer time horizon of the analysis.

Despite these problems, micro-simulation models based on household income generation models provide a powerful tool to assess the final distributional impact of changes in "distributional drivers," as they reflect the welfare implications of discrete changes in individual behavior, such as labor market entry or sectoral movements. The impact of individual transitions out of agriculture in the Brazil study demonstrates the possible magnitude of these discrete individual changes on household welfare. Finally, it should be stressed that the household income generation models of the type presented in this paper have been shown to do fairly well in reproducing historical patterns of poverty and distributional change (Lay 2007).

The applications from above both use CGE models to trace the transmission channels and quantify the magnitude of the effects of the respective shock. Although widely applied, these models have been criticized for a number of reasons. Analytically, most CGE models rely on the neoclassical framework, although a number of structural characteristics and rigidities are incorporated in most developing country applications. Whether and how structural characteristics and rigidities are taken into account differs between country applications and the research question at hand, as illustrated by the case studies above. Two areas where applied CGE models do not capture the economic realities very well, are the rural and the urban informal sector. It is well known that neoclassical price setting and supply responses in agriculture, is at best a very rough approximation of the reality in most developing countries. In addition, disaggregated input-output data for agriculture are typically not available and agricultural surveys suffer from a lot of problems related to measurement, seasonality, and temporary shocks. Furthermore, the insights from agricultural household models regarding non-separability of production and consumption in rural households (Singh et al. 1986) have not yet entered standard models.[17] More research effort also needs to be dedicated to modeling the informal urban sector. Its heterogeneity in terms of technology,

[16]Although this assumption seems to be very restrictive, it can be plausibly made e.g. in the context of occupational choices, which are explained mainly by individual educational attainment, age, and household composition variables.

[17]See Lofgren and Robinson (1999), who integrate a rural household model into a standard CGE model, for an exception.

import penetration, export orientation, and linkages to the formal sector are not reflected in applied CGE models.

However, even with all these improvements, eventually the results of a CGE model will be driven by the assumptions made.[18] Econometricians challenge the empirical relevance of applied CGE models on grounds of the calibration technique based on very restricted functional forms, typically (nested) CES functions. McKitrick (1998) shows the choice of the functional form to make a considerable difference in the results. Yet, in the developing country context, data to estimate these functions is typically not available and the calibration approach overcomes these data restrictions. Furthermore, it is well known that model results are very sensitive to the assumed trade and production elasticities. Harrison et al. (1993) therefore suggest to perform systematic sensitivity analyses and to provide confidence intervals for the results. Such sensitivity analyses, however, are not common in applied work.

Finally, an assessment of the validity of CGE model results also depends on the purpose of the model. If the analysis is expected to provide a precise numerical estimate of the effects of a specific policy change, the above criticisms have to be taken very seriously. In contrast, if CGE models are seen as a rather stylized, yet empirically underpinned, analytical tool to better understand the transmission channels of a shock through counterfactual analysis and approximate their relative importance, the critique is less relevant. This is not to say that the numbers resulting from CGE models are without meaning. They should be taken as the results of a model, given a specific set of assumptions.[19]

4 Conclusions

We have presented and discussed a sequential methodology that combines a macroeconomic CGE model with a behavioral micro-simulation. More specifically, we have shown how micro-simulations based on household income generation models allow the researcher to incorporate individual fixed effects into macro-micro analysis. This is achieved by linking aggregate drivers of poverty and distributional change, such as wages and sectoral employment, to a micro-simulation that is being "forced" to reproduce the changes given by the macro

[18]See De Maio et al. (1999) and the reply by Sahn et al. (1999) for an exemplary discussion on specific aspects of CGE models applied to developing countries. These aspects include the macroeconomic and labor market closures as well as the assumption on price setting mechanisms. De Maio et al. (1999) challenge the results of a study by Sahn et al. (1997) on the poverty impacts of structural adjustment in Sub-Saharan Africa as reflecting only the assumptions made in the CGE models, and not reality.

[19]In some CGE applications, including some of those presented in this paper, there is a tendency to treat CGE results as forecasts.

model. We also explain common empirical operationalizations of this link and the micro-simulation procedures commonly used in the literature.

The presented sequential macro-micro approach has been illustrated using two case studies that examine the poverty and distributional impact of macroeconomic shocks, the typical research and policy research to which this kind of model is and should be applied. Examples from these applications have demonstrated the importance of individual heterogeneity in the analysis of these shocks and have underpinned the value added of such methods with behavioral components.

Beyond its ability to capture individual heterogeneity, one of the merits of the approach is its flexibility. However, this flexibility—embodied in a number of fairly ad-hoc assumptions—comes at the cost of theoretical inconsistency. While the macro models rely on consistent theoretical frameworks, the reduced-form models underlying the micro-simulation do not fulfill the requirements, for example in terms of functional forms. Furthermore, empirical inconsistency between national accounts and household survey data that becomes apparent in macro-micro applications is known to be notorious (Round 2003; Robilliard and Robinson 2003).

Finally, we have argued that combining an applied CGE model and a micro-simulation model does not resolve the problems associated to either of those techniques. These problems include a number of typical microeconometric problems that arise from the estimation of income generation models, the basis of the micro-simulation model. Similarly, CGE models suffer from well-known, often-discussed, but less frequently addressed shortcomings. Despite these problems and challenges, the alternative to the proposed models can only be a general equilibrium model that incorporates heterogeneous individuals. As argued in the introduction, researchers are still far from building an applied model based on a micro-based general equilibrium theory. On the route to building such a model, it may be helpful to improve existing macro-micro models through more and better validation exercises. In addition, micro-simulations may also be linked to more different types of general equilibrium models with a more explicit focus on the operation of labor markets.

References

Alatas, V., and F. Bourguignon. 2005. The evolution of income distribution during Indonesia's fast growth, 1980–1996. In *The microeconomics of income distribution dynamics*, ed. F. Bourguignon, F.H.G. Ferreira, and N. Lustig. Washington, DC: The World Bank and Oxford University Press.

Blundell, R., and T. MaCurdy. 1999. Labor supply: A review of alternative approaches. In *Handbook of labor economics*, ed. O. Ashenfelter and D. Card, vol. 3A, 1560–1695. Philadelphia, PA: Elsevier.

Bourguignon, F., A.S. Robilliard, and S. Robinson. 2005a. Representative vs. real households in the macroeconomic modeling of inequality. In *Frontiers in applied general equilibrium modeling*, ed. T.J. Kehoe, T.N. Srinivasan, and J. Whalley. Cambridge: Cambridge University Press.

Bourguignon, F., F.H.G. Ferreira, and N. Lustig. 2005b. A synthesis of the results. In *The microeconomics of income distribution dynamics*, ed. F. Bourguignon, F.H.G. Ferreira, and N. Lustig. Washington, DC: The World Bank and Oxford University Press.

Bussolo, M., J. Lay, and D. van der Mensbrugghe. 2006. *Structural change and poverty reduction in Brazil: The impact of the Doha Round.* World Bank Policy Research Paper 3833. Washington, DC: World Bank.

Cogneau, D. 2001. *Formation du Revenue, Segmentation et Discrimination sur le Marché du Travail d'une Ville en Développement: Antananarivo Fin de Siècle.* DIAL DT/2001/18.

Cogneau, D., and A. S. Robilliard. 2001. Gr*owth, distribution and poverty in Madagascar: Learning from a microsimulation model in a general equilibrium framework.* TMD Discussion Paper 61. Washington, DC: International Food Policy Research Institute.

Colombo, G. 2010. Linking CGE and microsimulation models: A comparison of different approaches. *International Journal of Microsimulation* 3 (1): 72–91.

Creedy, J., and A. Duncan. 2002. Behavioural microsimulation with labour supply responses. *Journal of Economic Surveys* 16 (1): 1–38.

Davies, J.B. 2009. Combining microsimulation with CGE and macro modelling for distributional analysis in developing and transition countries. *International Journal of Microsimulation* 2 (1): 49–65.

De Maio, L., F. Stewart, and R. van der Hoeven. 1999. Computable general equilibrium models, adjustment, and the poor in Africa. *World Development* 27 (3): 453–470.

Dervis, K., J. de Melo, and S. Robinson. 1982. *General equilibrium models for development policy.* Cambridge: Cambridge University Press.

Harrison, G.W., R. Jones, L.J. Kimbell, and R. Wigle. 1993. How robust is applied general equilibrium analysis? *Journal of Policy Modeling* 15 (1): 99–115.

Harrison, G., T. Rutherford, and D. Tarr. 2000. Trade liberalization, poverty and efficient equity. *Journal of Development Economics* 71: 97–128.

Lay, J. 2007. Poverty and distributional impact of economic policies and external shocks. Three case studies from Latin America combining macro and micro approaches. In *Goettingen studies in development economics*, ed. H. Sautter and S. Klasen, vol. 18. Frankfurt: Peter Lang.

Lay, J., R. Thiele, and M. Wiebelt. 2008. Resource booms, inequality, and poverty: The case of gas in Bolivia. *Review of Income and Wealth* 54 (3): 407–437.

Lofgren, H., R. Lee Harris, and S. Robinson. 2002. *A standard computable general equilibrium (CGE) model in GAMS.* Microcomputers in Policy Research No. 5. Washington, DC: International Food Policy Research Institute.

Lofgren, H., and S. Robinson. 1999. *To trade or not to trade: Non-separable farm household models in partial and general equilibrium.* TMD Discussion Paper 37. Washington, DC: International Food Policy Research Institute.

McKitrick, R.R. 1998. The econometric critique of computable general equilibrium modeling: The role of functional forms. *Economic Modelling* 15 (4): 543–573.

Robilliard, A.S., F. Bourguignon, and S. Robinson. 2002. *Crisis and income distribution: A micro-macro model for Indonesia.* Washington, DC: World Bank.

Robilliard, A.S., and S. Robinson. 2003. Reconciling household surveys and national accounts data using a cross-entropy estimation method. *Review of Income and Wealth* 49 (3): 395–406.

Robinson, S. 1989. Multisectoral models. In *Handbook of development economics*, ed. H. Chenery and T.N. Srinivasan, 885–947. Philadelphia, PA: Elsevier.

Round, J.I. 2003. Constructing SAMs for development policy analysis: Lessons learned and challenges ahead. *Economic Systems Research* 15 (2): 161–183.

Sahn, D.E., P. Dorosh, and S.D. Younger. 1997. *Structural adjustment reconsidered: Economic policy and poverty in Africa.* Cambridge: Cambridge University Press.

———. 1999. A reply to De Maio, Stewart, and van der Hoeven. *World Development* 27 (3): 471–475.

Singh, I., L. Squire, and J. Strauss, eds. 1986. *Agricultural household models. Extensions, applications, and policy.* Baltimore: The Johns Hopkins University Press.

Van der Mensbrugghe, D. 2003. *Prototype model for real computable general equilibrium model for the state development planning commission*. PR China: Mimeo.

Jann Lay is an economist and heads the research programme on development and globalization at the GIGA German Institute of Global and Area Studies in Hamburg (Germany). As professor in development studies, he also teaches at the Georg-August-University in Goettingen (Germany). He has published articles in various internationally renowned journals and has worked as consultant for a number of development agencies. His current research interests include informal entrepreneurship in developing countries and the poverty and distributional implications of structural change in developing countries, specifically the impact of large-scale land acquisitions.

Part II
Perspectives on Policy Processes and their Modeling

7

A Quantitative Perspective on Political Processes

Christian Henning and Johannes Hedtrich

1 Introduction

A paradox of low political performance exists in many countries (i.e., suboptimal policies persist despite the existence of specific policy instruments that could generate more desirable outcomes). For example, many developing countries that continue to depend largely on agriculture, particularly countries in Sub-Saharan Africa, underinvest in this sector. Especially in areas of public investment that have high returns in terms of growth and poverty reduction, such as agricultural research and extension, public investments remain below the optimal level (Fan and Rao 2003). Accordingly, in addition to an understanding of socioeconomic responses to new policies, avoiding suboptimal agricultural policy choices requires an understanding of the underlying political processes. An improved understanding of the policy process, including the relevant political institutions and their link with the overall political economy, is essential to determining how the participation of stakeholder groups and the use of credible scientific evidence can be promoted in the design and implementation of efficient, pro-poor agricultural strategies. Filling this gap can help identify practical solutions and tools for reducing political performance gaps and facilitate the implementation of improved policies for reducing poverty and promoting growth.

However, policy processes are complex and dynamic by nature; these processes involve multiple actors (i.e., individuals and organizations) and are defined by national political, social, cultural and institutional realities (e.g., constitutional rules), bureaucratic structures and capacities, and the informal participation of stakeholder organizations. Few studies have explicitly mapped these processes to

C. Henning (✉) • J. Hedtrich
Department of Agricultural Economics, University of Kiel, Kiel, Germany
e-mail: chenning@ae.uni-kiel.de

explain the poor past performance of policy reforms and investment strategies, particularly in the agricultural sector. Most of these studies have offered narratives based on historical accounts, emphasizing the strong role of powerful personalities, vested interests, corruption, and external pressures in influencing policy outcomes (Clay and Schaffer 1984; Juma and Clark 1995; Keeley and Scoones 2003; Young 2005). However, theoretical approaches that analyze determinants of policy processes and their impact on poor political performance also exist. One field of the political economy literature holds that biased incentives are the main source of low political performance. Biased political incentives result from asymmetric lobbying activities (Grossman 1994) or biased voter behavior (Bardhan Mookherjee 2002). Further, Persson and Tabellini (2000) emphasize the role of formal constitutional rules as determinants of politician incentives for choosing inefficient policies.

In addition to biased incentives, the lack of adequate political knowledge has also been considered as an explanation for the poor political performance of countries. For example, Beilhartz and Gersbach (2004), Bischoff and Siemers (2011) and Caplan (2007) emphasize the role of biased voter beliefs about policy impacts as a main determinant of inefficient policy choices. Voter beliefs are defined as agents' simplified mental models to approximate the complex true relation between policy instruments and induced policy outcomes. The work of Caplan is highly recognized in the public choice literature, as he collects an impressive amount of evidence for persistently biased voter beliefs. Based on his empirical findings, Caplan draws the rather pessimistic conclusion that democratic mechanisms of preference aggregation naturally lead to the choice of inefficient policies. However, beyond voters, politicians and lobbyists may also fail to fully understand the complex relation between policy instruments and desired policy outcomes. Hence, the lack of political knowledge (i.e., biased policy beliefs) is another important cause of policy failure.

In response to persisting policy failure in many developing countries, participatory and evidence-based political processes are increasingly promoted as an omnipotent tool/mechanism for guaranteeing unbiased political incentives for political agents and allowing the full use of all available political knowledge at both the academic and practical levels. However, designing such ideal-typical policy processes is challenging in political practice. An applicable model framework must first be developed to not only enable a *political diagnosis* (i.e., the identification of existing incentives and knowledge gaps) but also allow the development of a *political therapy* (i.e., the derivation of adequate strategies for reducing the identified political performance gaps). The latter criterion requires quantitative modeling of political decisionmaking and policy learning processes, including the endogenous formation of legislator's political preferences and policy beliefs. In a dynamic context, explaining the persistence of a lack of political knowledge requires a further explanation of the reasons for which policy learning fails.

In this context, we suggest an evolutionary Computable General Political Economy Equilibrium Model (eCGPE) as a quantitative approach to modeling and evaluating policy processes. This chapter is focused on the derivation of the eCGPE approach, and the chapters that follow use the implementation of the

Comprehensive Africa Agriculture Development Programme (CAADP) reform in Malawi to demonstrate how the eCGPE approach can be applied empirically. This chapter is structured as follows: we describe the main structure of an eCGPE approach, then derive the individual modules of the eCGPE in detail, and conclude by providing an outlook on future research.

2 The Evolutionary Computable General Political Economy Equilibrium Model: An Overview

2.1 General Structure and Characterization of an eCGPE

The eCGPE (Henning and Struve 2008) basically follows the logic of a political economy equilibrium, as proposed by Binswanger and Deininger (1997). This framework makes it possible to examine the economic, political and institutional factors that shape agricultural policy processes. Moreover, the framework allows for the simulation of future policy developments under various economic, political and institutional scenarios.

The CGPE model includes the following modules:

I. A legislative decisionmaking module describing how policy preferences are aggregated to form a final policy choice γ.
II. An economic module describing the transformation of policies γ into outcomes z.
III. An interest mediation module describing the transformation of society's welfare $V(z)$ into political support W(V(z)) via electoral competition and lobbying.
IV. A belief formation module describing how political agents and voters update their political beliefs via communication.

A non-evolutionary (i.e., static) version of a CGPE model is illustrated in Fig. 1. The evolutionary CGPE approach is a recursive dynamic model that combines the static CGPE (i.e., modules I–IV) with a dynamic political belief updating and adaptive policy learning model. Thus, the evolutionary CGPE approach includes a fifth module:

V. A policy learning module describing how political agents and voters update their political beliefs based on observational learning across time periods.

Figure 2 presents the eCGPE model. The derivation of an eCGPE includes five stages: (1) Economic modeling of policy programs, (2) Modeling of voter behavior and lobbying activities and the derivation of political support functions, (3) Derivation of agents' policy preferences based on political beliefs, (4) Modeling of legislative bargaining determined by agents' policy preferences and constitutional rules, (5) Modeling of belief updating based on observed policy outcomes and

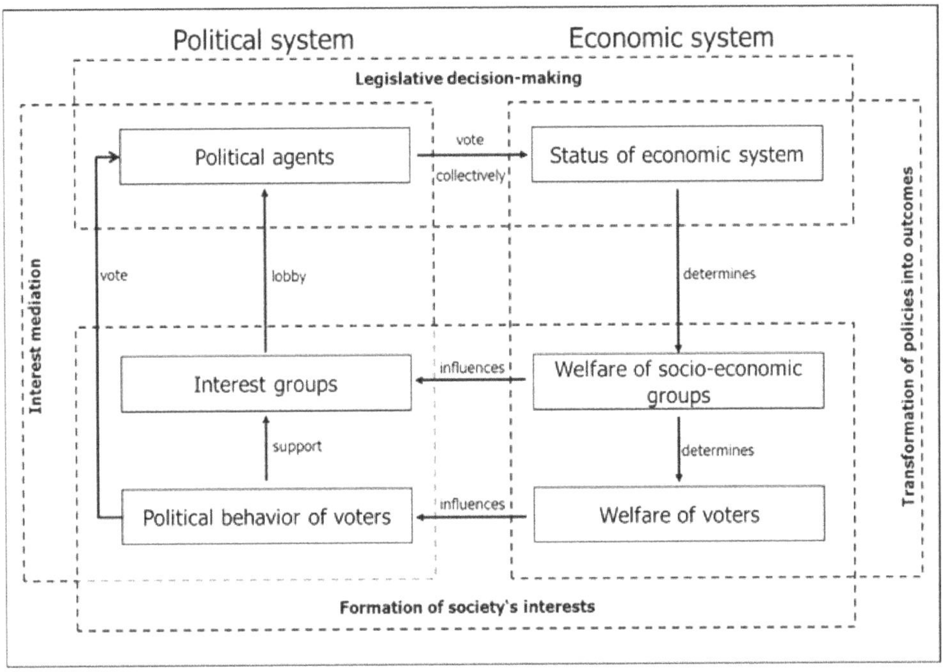

Fig. 1 Computable general political economy equilibrium. Source: Henning (2000)

political communication in networks. The sections that follow will provide the theoretical background required for deriving an eCGPE. However, we will first explain how the tool can be used for policy process evaluation and design.

2.2 *What Is the Purpose and Advantage of a Quantitative Policy Analysis Tool?*

Based on the empirically specified eCGPE model, policy processes can be analyzed, i.e. a political diagnosis identifying political performance gaps can be undertaken. Based on this diagnosis, alternative therapeutic strategies can be simulated.

Specifically, political diagnosis based on a calibrated eCGPE model includes the following steps:

I. Identification of the political performance gap:

- Calculation of the political equilibrium path of sequential eCGPE solutions γ^{**}, where γ^{**} denotes the vector of policy instruments selected over a given simulated time period.
- Calculation of an optimal policy γ^{opt} derived from the maximization of the social welfare function $W(z)$ subject to a "best-estimate" political technology.

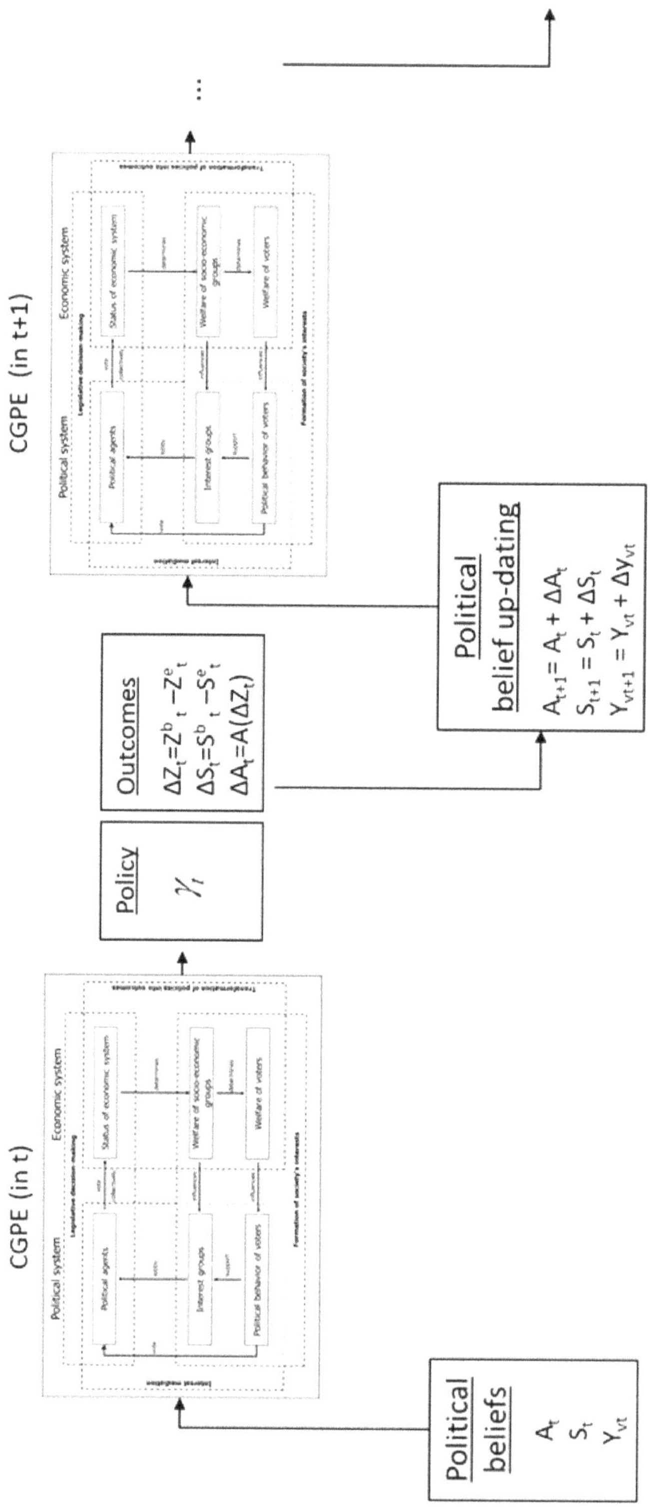

Fig. 2 Evolutionary computable general political economy equilibrium. Source: Author

- Calculation of the total performance gap, which is measured as the difference: W $(\gamma^{opt*}) - W(\gamma^{**})$.

II. Identification of the source of the political performance gap:

- Calculation of the knowledge gap as the difference: $W(\gamma^{opt}) - W(\gamma_1^*)$, where $\gamma_1{}^*$ is the policy outcome resulting from the eCGPE simulation runs, assuming all politicians know the "best-estimate" political technology.
- Calculation of incentive gaps as the difference: $W(\gamma^{opt}) - W(\gamma_2^*)$, where $\gamma_2{}^*$ is the policy outcome resulting from the eCGPE simulation runs, assuming all politicians have unbiased support functions that correspond to the social welfare functions.

III. Identification of the main determinants of performance gaps:

- Impact of formal legislative rules and informal lobbying networks
  - Simulating policy outcomes and the corresponding political performance under various legislative rules.
  - Simulating policy outcomes and the corresponding political performance under various lobbying network structures.
- Impact of policy beliefs of politicians and stakeholders
  - Simulating policy outcomes and the corresponding political performance under various political belief formation mechanisms (i.e., changed political communication networks).
- Impact of policy beliefs of voters
  - Simulating policy outcomes and the corresponding political performance under various mass political belief formation mechanisms (i.e., changing political communication network structures of different voter groups).
- Impact of innovative policy evaluation and monitoring systems
  - Simulating policy learning and implied political performance, assuming the implementation of an effective Monitoring & Evaluation system.

3 Theoretical Background of the eCGPE

3.1 Module I: Legislative Decisionmaking

A policy decision is the result of legislative bargaining among a set of legislators $g \in N^g$ with heterogeneous policy preferences $U^g(\gamma)$.

Technically, the political decisionmaking model corresponds to the mapping of legislators' policy preferences, U^g, and constitutional rules for legislative decisionmaking, φ, into the final policy decision, γ^*:

$$\gamma^* = \Gamma(U^g(\gamma), \varphi), \tag{1}$$

where the properties of the function Γ correspond to a specific political decisionmaking model. A number of different models have been proposed [see for example the literature review of Binswanger and Deininger (1997)]. In particular, two models have become work horse models in political economy: the legislative bargaining model of Baron and Ferejohn (1989) and the interest group model of Grossman (1994). While the latter model has been frequently applied in empirical studies of agricultural protection (Anderson 2010; Rausser et al. 2011), the former model has become a work horse model in theoretical studies of comparative political economy. However, one advantage of the Baron/Ferejohn model (BF model) is that political decisionmaking is explicitly modeled as a collective decision of many legislators, where constitutional legislative decisionmaking rules are explicit determinants of final political decisions. In contrast, the Grossman/ Helpman model (GH model) focuses on the government or a state agency as a common agent controlling policy choices. Accordingly, this model neglects fundamental collective choice problems that are inherent in real political decisionmaking. The advantage of the GH model compared to the BF model is that it can be applied empirically; in contrast, the BF model is a complicated game-theoretical model that cannot be easily applied to real legislative systems.

To combine the advantages of both of these approaches, we suggest a cooperative legislative bargaining model, which can be derived from a modified non-cooperative legislative bargaining model of the Baron-Ferejohn type (Henning 2009). In the following, we briefly describe the main components of the legislative bargaining model; for a more detailed description of the model, we refer the interested reader to our previous work (Henning 2009; Pappi and Henning 1998). Finally, the integration of the GH model into the modified legislative bargaining model is described below in the section that describes Module III.

3.1.1 The Mean Voter Rule

Each agent has spatial preferences, where $\hat{\gamma}_g$ denotes agent g's ideal policy position (i.e., the policy he or she wants to be implemented). However, based on constitutional rules, individual legislators need the support of a winning coalition to make their ideal policy positions the final policy choice. Hence, legislative bargaining corresponds to a competition that involves the formation of winning coalitions among political agents. Following the seminal approach of Baron and Ferejohn (1989), we assume that legislative bargaining is a sequential procedure, as described in Fig. 3.

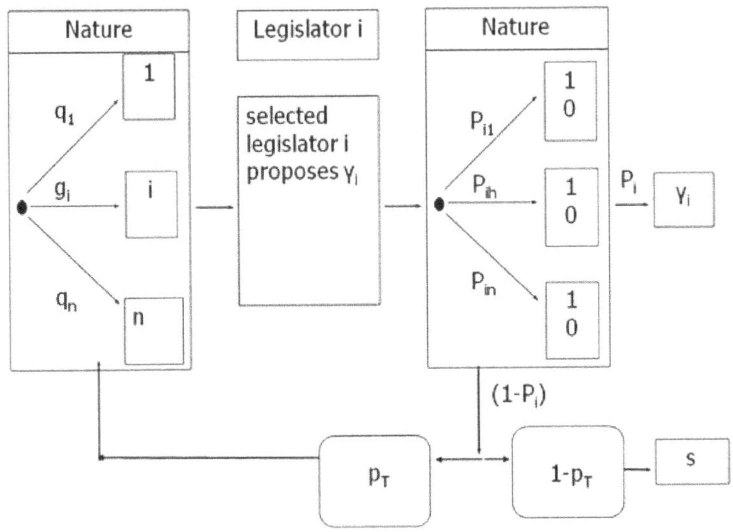

Fig. 3 Game-tree of the modified non-cooperative legislative bargaining game of Baron/Ferejohn. Source: Henning (2000)

Thus, in each bargaining round, a legislator is randomly selected to formulate a policy proposal. This proposal is submitted to the complete legislature for a majority vote. If the proposal wins a majority of votes, it becomes the new policy; if the proposal fails to win a majority of the votes, the legislative bargaining procedure continues (i.e., a new legislator is randomly selected to formulate a proposal, and the process starts over). However, in contrast to the original BF model, we make two different assumptions. First, we assume that voting on a submitted policy proposal is probabilistic and not deterministic, as assumed by Baron and Ferejohn. In the general approach, the voting probabilities of individual legislators for or against a policy proposal are derived from a probabilistic utility function. To demonstrate the main implications of this assumption, we assume for simplicity in this paper that each legislator h votes for any policy proposal γ_g with a fixed probability $P_{gh} = 0.5$. Second, following Henning (2000), we assume that the time to draw a legislative decision is typically limited. This assumption implies that the legislature will not consider proposals regarding a specific decision infinitely. Thus, ex post the number of proposals that have been made is always limited, while the number of proposals that will be considered is ex ante not known by individual legislators. Therefore, it is assumed that after each round, there exists a fixed probability p_T that legislative bargaining continues (i.e., another round will occur). Thus, after each round, the legislative decision procedure stops with a probability $(1 - p_T)$ and the status quo policy sustains.

As we previously described in more detail (Henning 2000), the outcome of the modified BF model corresponds to a lottery of the ideal points of individual legislators and the status quo, where the ex ante probability that the ideal point of an individual legislator g will be the outcome of the non-cooperative bargaining is determined by the constitutional rules, and the probability that the legislative bargaining procedure continues, p_T. Let Q_g denote the ex ante probability that agent g succeeds in forming a winning coalition for her policy proposal, while Q_s denotes the probability that the outcome of the legislative bargaining is the status quo "s". Under these specific assumptions, the outcome of non-cooperative legislative bargaining corresponds to a lottery over agents' ideal positions and the status quo, where Q_g and Q_s equal the probability that agent g's ideal policy and the status quo s are selected as the final policy choice, respectively. Assuming that politicians are risk-averse, non-cooperative legislative bargaining is rather inefficient. Hence, agents have an incentive to agree ex ante on cooperative policy formulation mechanisms that guarantee each political agent a higher pay-off.

In particular, it is straightforward to demonstrate that assuming risk-averse legislators, the following mean voter decision rule is a cooperative decisionmaking procedure that ex ante guarantees each individual legislator a higher expected utility than the expected utility derived from the lottery outcome of the non-cooperative legislative bargaining game (see Henning 2000):

$$\begin{aligned} EU_g &= \sum_h Q_h U_g(\gamma_h) + Q_s U_g(s) \;\leq\; U_g(\gamma^M) \quad \text{with :} \quad \gamma^M \\ &= \sum_h Q_h \gamma_h + Q_s s. \end{aligned} \tag{2}$$

Although the mean voter decision rule is ex ante Pareto-dominant compared to non-cooperative legislative bargaining, the mean voter decisionmaking rule does not generally lead to a Pareto-optimal outcome. In particular, from the viewpoint of a legislative majority, the mean voter decision might still be improved. As can be seen from our simple example below, this assertion follows from two facts. First, even if it is assumed that the legislature continues bargaining with a high probability (i.e., pT is significantly larger than 0.5), the ex ante probability that the outcome of legislative bargaining will be the status quo is still not negligible. Thus, the mean voter position implies that the new policy is still relatively close to the status quo, where the status quo bias does not necessarily correspond to legislatures preferences but results from the fact that the legislature is busy and has only limited time for bargaining on a specific decision. Second, even if the probability Q_s is very low, the mean voter might still be rather inefficient due to the fact that the relative preference intensities for different policy dimensions of different legislators have not been sufficiently taken into account. This scenario is illustrated in Fig. 4, where the mean voter position remains quite distant from the Pareto frontier. Accordingly, Henning (2000) discussed two alternative mechanisms by which legislators can improve the mean voter outcome. As demonstrated in Fig. 4, changing the status quo policy can be considered a two-step procedure, where legislators agree on the direction in which the status quo policy will be shifted in the first step and agree on the distance the status quo policy is shifted towards the agreed direction in the second step. In this context, we suggest the following cooperative policy formulation mechanisms. In a first step, legislators

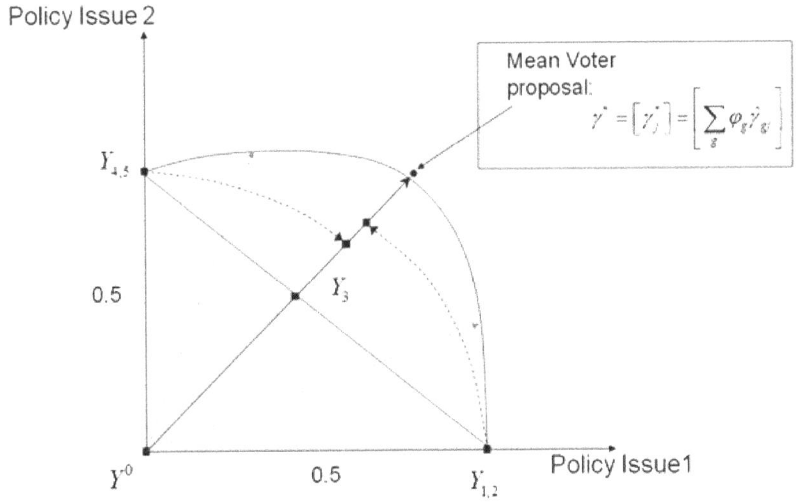

Fig. 4 Utility frontier of a modified non-cooperative legislative bargaining game of the Baron/Ferejohn type. Source: Author

agree on the direction in which the status quo policy will be shifted. In particular, at the first stage, legislative bargaining results in the following mean voter decision rule:

$$\Delta\gamma^* = \sum_g \varphi_g \widehat{\gamma}_g - \gamma_0. \tag{3}$$

$\Delta\gamma^*$ denotes the collectively selected direction, where $\sum_g \varphi_g \widehat{\gamma}_g$ is the mean voter position that corresponds to a compromise of legislators' ideal positions. φ_g corresponds to the relative probability $\frac{Q_g}{\sum_h Q_h}$ that the proposal of a legislator will be the outcome of the non-cooperative legislative bargaining procedure. Hence, φ_g is determined by formal constitutional rules φ and φ_g can be interpreted as the relative political power of a legislator. Technically, under our simplified assumptions, φ_g equals the ratio of the number of winning coalitions in which an agent g is a member and the sum of these numbers for all relevant political agents. Please note that under this assumption, the political power φ_g is quite similar to the classical normalized Coleman-Banzhaf voting power index (Henning et al. 2006). Given the direction $\Delta\gamma^*$, legislators decide on the distance λ_γ at the second stage via voting. As long as legislators' policy preferences, $U^g(\gamma)$, are quasi-concave, it follows that legislators have single-peaked preferences regarding the distance λ_γ. Accordingly, at the second stage, a unique voting equilibrium outcome results.[1]

[1]The proof of single-peakedness is straightforward (Shepsle 1979). Further, please note that even if alternative and more complex voting mechanisms than simple majority voting are assumed, a unique equilibrium outcome results as long as legislators have single-peaked preferences.

3.1.2 How the Mean Voter Rule Works: An Illustrative Example

To demonstrate how this model works, we use a simple example comprised of five legislators g = 1, .., 5. The legislature must make a two dimensional policy choice, where j = 1,2 denote the index of the two policy dimensions (e.g., the policy dimension 1 corresponds to a policy program promoting technical progress in the agricultural sector, while policy dimension 2 corresponds to a policy program promoting technical progress in the non-agricultural sector). Each legislator has a spatial utility function, where $U_g(\gamma) = -\sum_{j=1}^{2} \theta_{gj}\left(\gamma - \widehat{\gamma}_g\right)^2$.

Following the non-cooperative legislative bargaining model of Baron and Ferejohn, legislators are randomly selected, where $q_g = 0.2$ is the probability that a legislator g is selected to formulate a policy proposal. Legislators vote on a suggested policy proposal with a simple majority, where legislators have different voting weights, w_g. Hence, a proposal is accepted if the sum of the voting weights of the legislators voting in favor of the proposal exceeds 0.5. For simplicity, we assume that legislators always vote in favor of their own proposal with probability 1 and that legislators vote with a probability of 0.5 for any other policy proposal[2]. Based on these assumptions, the probability that the proposal suggested by a legislator g will be accepted by a legislative majority depends on the number of winning coalitions of which the proposing legislator is a member. In detail, let wc denote the index of a winning coalition and WC denote the set of all winning coalitions (i.e., all subsets of legislators for which the following holds: $\sum_{g \in wc} w_g > 0.5$). The number of winning coalitions, nc_g, of which a legislator g is a member depends on her voting weight. The voting weights assumed for legislators in our simple example are presented in Table 1. Thus, the number of winning coalitions of which an individual legislator is a member can be calculated as presented in Table 1. Further, given our assumptions, the probability that a specific winning coalition is formed uniquely equals 0.54 for all winning coalitions. Accordingly, the conditional probability that the proposal of a legislator g who was selected to formulate a proposal becomes the final policy outcome can be represented as: $P_g = \sum_{i \in wc} 0.5^4 = nc_g 0.5^4$. Please note that under these specific assumptions, legislators will always propose their ideal policy when selected to formulate a proposal.

Furthermore, given the structure of the modified legislative bargaining game, the ex ante probability Q_s that the status quo will be the policy outcome is (for further details, see Henning 2000):

[2]Please note that in the original approach suggested by Henning (2000), the legislators' probability of voting for or against a proposal are endogenously derived from a probabilistic utility function. To simplify the analysis in this paper, we assume that legislators vote for any proposal with a fixed probability of 0.5.

Table 1 Variables in the simple voting game example

Player	Recognition probability	Probability of voting for proposal	Voting weights	Number of winning coalitions	P_T	P_g	Q_g	Power (φ)
1	0.2	0.5	0.36	12		0.750	0.206	0.245
2	0.2	0.5	0.35	11		0.688	0.189	0.224
3	0.2	0.5	0.15	10		0.625	0.172	0.204
4	0.2	0.5	0.08	8		0.500	0.137	0.163
5	0.2	0.5	0.06	8		0.500	0.137	0.163
Status-quo	0	0	0	0			0.160	0.000
Total	1		1	49	0.70		1.000	1

Source: Author

$$Q_s = \frac{(1 - p_T)\left(1 - \frac{1}{5}\sum_h P_h\right)}{1 - p_T + p_T \frac{1}{5}\sum_h P_h} \tag{4}$$

Moreover, the probability that the ideal point of legislator g will be the final outcome of the legislative bargaining procedure can be calculated as[3]:

$$Q_g = \frac{1}{5} P_g \sum_{t=0}^{\infty} \left(\sum_{h \in N_g} \frac{1}{5}(1 - P_h) P_T \right)^t = \frac{P_g}{\sum_{h \in N_g} P_h}(1 - Q_s) = (1 - Q_s)\frac{nc_g}{\sum_h nc_h} \tag{5}$$

As demonstrated in Table 1, given the assumed voting weights, we can calculate the equilibrium outcome of the modified BF model. Further, we can calculate the mean voter position (i.e., the direction in which the status quo will be shifted). Finally, given the direction $\Delta\gamma^* = (0.127, 0.070)$, we can also calculate the legislators' preferred distance λ_g[4]:

[3]Please note that the following holds: $1 - Q_s = \frac{1/5 \sum_h P_h}{1 - p_T + p_T \frac{1}{5}\sum_h P_h}.$

[4]Please note that Eq. (6) directly follows from the maximization of agent's g spatial policy preferences, assuming each policy proposal must lie on the line connecting the status quo to the mean voter position.

Table 2 Outcomes of the simple voting game example

	Policy position		Policy interest		Direction	Final Outcome	
Player	Issue 1	Issue 2	Issue 1	Issue 2	λ	Issue 1	Issue 2
1	1	0	0.7	0.3	1.678		
2	1	0	0.65	0.35	1.598		
3	0.5	0.5	0.5	0.5	1.166		
4	0	1	0.2	0.8	1.922		
5	0	1	0.3	0.7	1.576		
Status quo	0	0					
Total	0.480	0.360			1.598	0.768	0.576

Source: Author

$$\lambda_g = \frac{\sum_j \theta_{gj}\left(\widehat{\gamma}_{gj} - \gamma_j^0\right)\Delta\gamma_j^*}{\sum_j \theta_{gj}\left[\Delta\gamma_j^*\right]^2}. \tag{6}$$

The voting outcome at the second stage corresponds to the preferred distance of the median legislator, where the median legislator is the legislator for whom it holds that the sum of the voting weights of legislators preferring a lower distance and the sum of the voting weights of legislators preferring a higher distance are both lower than 0.5. In our example, legislator 1 is the median legislator (i.e., the outcome in the second step will be to shift the policy by a distance λ^*= 1.598). Accordingly, the final policy outcome of our bargaining equilibrium will be (see also Table 2 and Fig. 4):

$$\gamma^* = \gamma^0 + \lambda^* \Delta\gamma^* = 0 + 1.598^* \left(0.480, 0.360 = (0.768, 0.567)\right. \tag{7}$$

Please note that our example demonstrates the inefficiency of non-cooperative bargaining (e.g., in Fig. 4, the mean voter position remains rather distant from the Pareto frontier). In general, policy outcomes are stochastic under non-cooperative bargaining (i.e., risk-averse legislators prefer the mean voter rule as a deterministic cooperative decisionmaking procedure). Further, legislators are less able to coordinate their actions under the one-step mean voter rule than under the two-step procedure (e.g., legislators collectively prefer a shift of the status quo beyond the mean voter position (i.e., λ_g is larger than 1 for all legislators) (see Table 2).

3.1.3 Endogenous Derivation of Legislators' Policy Preferences

To calculate legislative bargaining outcomes, the policy preferences of legislators must be known. Legislators' spatial policy preferences $U^g(\gamma)$ are derived from political support maximization:

$$U^g(\gamma) = \text{Max}\{W^g(z)|T(z,\gamma) \equiv 0\}, \tag{8}$$

where $W^g(z)$ denotes the political support function and $T(z,\gamma)$ denotes the political technology transforming policy γ into political outcomes z. $\widehat{\gamma}_g$ denotes legislator g's ideal point [i.e., the policy that maximizes Eq. (8)]. The political technology T is determined by the economic system and is modeled in Module II, while the political support function W is determined by voter behavior and lobbying activities, as described below in the section that describes Module III.

In most existing legislative decisionmaking models, legislators' preferences are exogenously given. However, to derive legislators' spatial policy preferences endogenously from the political support maximization in Eq. (8), we apply a second order Taylor approximation developed at the legislator's ideal position:

$$U_g(\gamma) = \sum_j \sum_k \theta_{gjk}\left(\gamma_j - \widehat{\gamma}_{gj}\right)\left(\gamma_k - \widehat{\gamma}_{gk}\right). \tag{9}$$

θ_{gjk} are the weighting factors of the interaction term of the deviation of the policies j and k, which are technically derived from the second order derivations of the maximization problem in Eq. (8). Please note that this approach for deriving endogenous policy preferences follows Henning and Struve (2008) and that similar approaches exist in the literature (de Gorter and Swinnen 1998; Fafchamps et al. 1993). However, the latter approaches fail to derive complete endogenous policy preferences for individual political agents and integrate them directly into a legislative decisionmaking model.

A simple approach for deriving endogenous policy preferences results from a linear approximation of the political technology:

$$T(z,\gamma) : z = z^0(1 + w_z) \qquad \Leftrightarrow \qquad w_z = A\Delta\gamma + a_0 \tag{10}$$

a_0 denotes the vector of the growth rates of policy concerns z, which are realized assuming the status quo policy sustains, while $A\Delta\gamma = A(\gamma - \gamma_0)$ denotes the vector of growth rates of policy concerns z, which are induced by a change from the status quo policy γ_0 to the policy γ.

Please note that the linear approximation of the political technology (i.e., the matrix A) changes with changing economic framework conditions. Hence, the impact of different economic framework conditions (e.g., changed world market prices) on endogenous policy preferences can be analyzed within this approach (Henning and Struve 2008).

Overall, legislators' policy preferences depend not only on political technology but also on the properties of the political support function (i.e., voter behavior and lobbying activities), which we will discuss in further detail in Module III below. Finally, as we will discuss in more detail in Module IV below, we assume that legislators have very limited knowledge regarding the true political technology.

Accordingly, legislators form political beliefs to approximate the unknown political technology.

3.2 Module II: Transformation of Policy Choices into Policy Outcomes

3.2.1 Computable General Equilibrium Model (CGE)

The economic module corresponds to any economic model that characterizes the general structure and economic responses of the national economy that is under consideration to policy changes. By default, we use the standard recursive dynamic CGE model suggested by International Food Policy Research Institute (IFPRI) (Löfgren 2001). As the model is fully described elsewhere, we will not provide a detailed description of the model here. Interested readers are recommended to read the relevant literature (Löfgren 2001).

3.2.2 Policy Impact Function

The core of a standard CGE application corresponds to the simulation of shocks, where shocks are defined as exogenous shifts in policies or economic framework conditions. To simulate policies within a CGE approach, the policies must be implemented into the CGE model. Some policies (e.g., direct and indirect taxes or tariffs) are already directly implemented in the standard CGE model. However, other policies, (e.g., structural adjustment policies, policy programs aiming to increase technical progress in economic sectors or policies aiming to improve market access for enterprises [i.e., reducing transaction costs]), must be translated into CGE parameters. Dynamic CGE models explicitly incorporate parameters representing sector-specific technical progress, as well as sector-specific transaction costs, subsidy payments and tariffs (see Löfgren 2001). While modeling the impact of technical progress in different economic sectors on the growth of the average per-capita income, on income distribution and on poverty is straightforward, the translation of different policy instruments into sector-specific technical progress or transaction costs is by no means straightforward within a CGE approach.

In this context, we suggest the implementation of a policy impact function. This function is defined as a transformation of policy instruments into relevant CGE parameters that correspond to sector-specific technical progress or transaction costs. Specifically, let β denote the vector of relevant CGE-parameters corresponding to sector-specific technical progress or transaction costs, while γ denotes the vector of relevant policy instruments. We then define a policy impact function as the mapping of policy instruments into relevant CGE parameters: $\beta = PIF(\gamma)$.

To demonstrate how policy impact functions can be applied within the framework of our CGPE approach, we focus below on technical progress, which is a major determinant of future poverty reduction and economic growth (Diao et al. 2007; Fan and Rosegrant 2008). Fan and Rosegrant (2008) emphasize that many African countries spend far too little on the promotion of technical progress in the agricultural sector compared to the non-agricultural sector. The overall effectiveness of total spending depends on the allocation of funds across different policy programs. For example, within the Comprehensive Agricultural Development Plan, four different pillars are specified, including a wide range of policy programs (for details, see Chapter "The Formation of Elite Communication Networks in Malawi: A Bayesian Econometric Approach" below). Moreover, total welfare is also determined by the provision of public goods, such as health, education and other social services. Therefore, at the country level, the overall budget allocation must include the distribution of total financial resources to policy programs promoting economic growth in the agricultural and non-agricultural sectors, as well as the allocation of financial resources for the provision of public goods. For example, Badiane et al. (2011) clearly demonstrate that budget allocation among policies promoting future economic growth and the provision of public goods has a significant impact on present and future welfare developments.

Thus, to identify optimal government budget allocations that promote maximal economic growth within our CGPE framework, we suggest the following two-stage policy impact function approach. Total government expenditure B_{gov} results as the sum of total spending across policy programs:

$$B_{tot} = \sum_{p \in Pol} \gamma_p \tag{11}$$

The effective impact of total government spending on the technical progress tp_s that is realized in a specific economic sector s depends on the allocation of spending across policy programs. All other things being equal, technical progress in the agricultural sector is higher with higher spending on agricultural policy programs. However, total agricultural spending is subdivided across different agricultural policy programs. For example, within CAADP, four key focus areas for agricultural improvement and investment are formulated: (1) Sustainable Land and Water Management, (2) Market Access, (3) Food Supply and Hunger, and (4) Agricultural Research. To account for the effects of different policy programs $p \in P$ on the technological progress realized in a specific sector s, the following two-stage policy impact functions $PIF^s(\gamma)$ are defined for each sector s:

$$PIF^s(\gamma) = \bar{tp}_s \frac{\exp(a_s B_s^{eff} - b_s)}{1 + \exp(a_s B_s^{eff} - b_s)}, \tag{12}$$

$$B_s^{eff} = \omega_s \left[\sum_p \mu_{sp} (\gamma_p)^{-\rho^{IF}} \right]^{-1/\rho^{IF}}. \tag{13}$$

According to the assumed two-stage function, it follows that for each sector, an optimal budget allocation sh_{sp} can be defined by:

$$\frac{sh_{sp}}{sh_{sq}} = \left(\frac{\mu_{sp}}{\mu_{sq}} \right)^{1/(1+\rho)}, \sum_p sh_{sp} = 1. \tag{14}$$

Assuming that ω_s is accordingly normalized implies that for an optimal budget allocation, the effective budget equals total budget $B_s^{eff}(\gamma) = B_{tot}(\gamma) = \sum_p \gamma_p$. In contrast, for any nonoptimal budget allocation, the effective budget is lower than the total budget. At the lower stage, budget allocation is transformed into effective budget allocation following a CES-function specification. At the upper stage, an effective budget is translated into technical progress according to a logistic function (i.e., the maximal technical progress that can be achieved via governmental policy is determined by $\overline{tp}_s$, where the marginal impact of additional effective budget spending is diminishing and approximates zero for a sufficiently large effective budget). Please note that optimal budget allocation across the total set of policy programs varies across different sectors. This scenario implies that the same budget allocation across policy programs in different sectors translates into different effective budgets that induce different rates of technical progress tp.

The suggested policy impact function basically follows the work of Fan and Zhang (2004). However, in contrast to that original approach, our two-stage approach is more general and implies a nonlinear relationship between governmental spending and induced sectoral growth. Moreover, this approach explicitly considers the composition of budget spending for different policy programs. Further, a similar approach was also suggested by Bourguignon et al. (2008a, b) in their MAM model (Maquette for MDG Simulations), which models the impact of different policy instruments on Millennium Development Goals (MDGs).

3.3 *Module III: Interest Mediation Module*

Module III captures the two main channels for the mediation of society's interests in a democracy: electoral competition and lobbying. We apply a modified Baron-Grossman Helpman model to simultaneously capture both voter behavior and lobbying activities.

3.3.1 Modeling Voter Behavior

Voter behavior corresponds to voters' electoral response to governmental policies. According to the probabilistic voter theory, electoral competition implies that legislator g's political support functions, $W^g(z)$, correspond to the weighted social welfare functions of the voter groups represented in his constituency (Persson and Tabellini 2000):

$$W^g(z) = \sum_v w_{gv} V^v(z). \tag{15}$$

In Eq. (15), v denotes the index of voter groups and w_{gv} dentoes the political weight of an individual voter v for the political agent g. In general, the probability that a voter of group v votes for a candidate or party in an election depends on the expected utility $V_v(z)$ that the voter perceives assuming the candidate will be elected.

In a perfect political world, electoral competition would be based on the policy platforms, γ_A and γ_B, suggested by candidates A and B, respectively. Voters would evaluate candidates based on their policy platform (i.e., voters transform policy platforms into their individual welfare according to the political technology, $T(Z, \gamma)$, and vote for the candidate whose policy platform implies the highest utility).

However, because in the real world, the transformation of policies into welfare is rather complex, the calculation of expected utility is also rather complex from the viewpoint of individual voters. Hence, voters apply simple heuristics to estimate their expected utility.

In general, voters apply different types of policy and non-policy indicators to estimate the expected future utility, assuming a candidate is elected. Non-policy-oriented indicators correspond to the concept of valence (Groseclose 2001; Schofield 2004; Stokes 1963), which is based on specific characteristics z_I, such as appearance, charisma, occupation or ethnicity. Based on these characteristics, voters perceive a specific competence or popularity of candidates and parties. Moreover, following Grossman and Helpman (1996), we also assume that voters are at least partially swayed by the relative campaign spending of different parties. These effects may reflect the influence of election advertisements or other efforts made to mobilize support (e.g., election rallies, door-to-door visits by campaign workers, etc.). Assuming, for simplicity, a two-party (i.e., two-candidate) setup below implies that voters perceived the following utility based on non-policy indicators and the relative campaign spending of the candidates:

$$V_I^v(z_I, C^g) = V_0^v(z_I) + \chi\left(C^g - C^{g'}\right). \tag{16}$$

$V_I^v(z_I, C^g\ )$ is the ideological component of voters' perceived utility, where C^g denotes the campaign spending of party g and $C^{g'}$ denotes the campaign spending of party g'.

In addition to non-policy indicators, voters also base their votes on policy indicators. A set of policy indicators corresponds to the concept of retrospective voting (Paldam and Nannestad 2000) (i.e., voters use observable welfare indicators (e.g., income growth or other well-being indicators) that were realized in the past period when an incumbent was in office to update their evaluation of the competence/popularity of the incumbent). Please note that retrospective voting can be interpreted as reinforcement learning. Let $V_R^v(z_r)$ denote the retrospective component of voters' perceived utility.

To the extent that valence indicators and campaign spending are not correlated with political competence, non-policy voting implies a bias. Moreover, non-policy voting implies no incentives for legislators to prefer efficient policies. In contrast, retrospective voting implies such incentives (i.e., based on retrospective voting, support-maximizing legislators prefer policies that lead to a maximal observable social welfare). However, retrospective voting becomes problematic when technological relations between policies and social welfare become more complex (e.g., if time lags occur between the adoption of a policy and its impact on measurable welfare indicators). Public investment in education is a good example, as these investments will increase long-term welfare growth, but positive welfare impacts will not be realized for a decade or more. In the short run, these investments might even reduce welfare. Thus, assuming long-term welfare growth with short-term costs, retrospective voting undermines the incentives for support-seeking legislators to implement long-term growth policy strategies. Analogously, the implementation of environmental policies that promote sustainable welfare growth in the long run might be undermined by retrospective voting.

Therefore, a third component that determines voter choices corresponds to voters' perceived utility that is derived directly from the observed policy platforms of candidates. However, voters have very limited knowledge regarding the true political technology. Accordingly, voters form beliefs (i.e., they apply simple mental models that approximate the true political technology).

In particular, we assume that voters reduce the multi-dimensional policy space γ to a lower dimensional macro-policy space z_p. For example, pro-poor growth policy or agricultural-driven growth can be interpreted as macro-policy strategies. Specific policies γ (e.g., agricultural sector polices, as defined within CAADP) can be mapped into these strategies. At a second stage, voters transform macro-policies into utility, again applying simple linear mapping as a mental model. Under these assumptions, the policy-oriented component of voters' utility can be represented by a spatial utility function $V_p^v(z_p)$, which is defined in the macro-policy space.

Overall, voter behavior is determined by the importance of the non-policy, retrospective and policy-oriented components of voters' perceptions of their utility, which are derived from the election of different candidates or parties. In general, it is possible to estimate the importance of the different utility components by econometrically applying a probabilistic voter approach (for example, see Schofield 2007) Based on the empirically specified probabilistic voter model, we derive the political support function of political agents as follows:

$$
\begin{aligned}
W_g(z, C) &= V_g(z) + \chi\left(C^g - C^{g'}\right) \\
&= \sum_v \alpha_{gv}\left(V_0^v(z_I) + V_R^v(z_R) + V_P^v(z_P)\right) + \chi\left(C^g - C^{g'}\right).
\end{aligned} \tag{17}
$$

3.3.2 Lobbying Activities

Following the Grossman-Helpman model (1996), lobbying groups J = 1,..,n$_J$ contribute to the campaign finances of the relevant parties; these contributions are conditioned on party platforms $C_J^g(\gamma^g)$. The lobbying game has two stages. In the first stage, the lobby offers nonnegative conditional contributions $C_J^g(\gamma^g)$. In a second stage, each party selects a policy to maximize its vote share. In this stage, a party g selects a policy γ^g to maximize:

$$
W^g(z) = V^g(z) + \sum_J \chi_J^g C_J^g(\gamma)\ s.t. T(z, \gamma) = 0. \tag{18}
$$

Further, it can be demonstrated that when the lobbying game is in equilibrium, each lobby group will select a support schedule for each party that induces a policy choice to maximize the net expected utility of a contributing member. Because the legislative bargaining among legislators is a lottery of legislators' ideal points, the net expected utility of changing party g's platform can be expressed as: $\varphi_g V_J(\gamma^g) - \frac{1}{n_J} C_J^g(\gamma^g)$, where n$_J$ denotes the number of members of interest group J. Therefore, in this case, the policy choice $\widehat{\gamma}$ of a legislator g is selected to maximize:

$$
V^g(z) + \varphi_g \sum_J \chi_J^g \frac{n_J}{n} V_J(\gamma^g)\ s.t. T(z, \gamma) = 0. \tag{19}
$$

Furthermore, in a one-shot game, as originally assumed by Grossman and Helpman, interest groups have an incentive to renege on their contribution offers once legislators have announced their platforms. Similarly, legislators have no incentives to pursue their announced positions once the campaign contributions have been paid. Hence, Grossman and Helpman motivate the keeping of premises in a repeated game, where agents would be punished for failure to fulfill their promises. However, even in a repeated game, the potential of agents to commit to their premises is limited and the commitment power depends on the frequency of interaction and the possibility of exchanging information with other agents regarding the opportunistic behavior of an individual agent (Dixit 2003). Accordingly, as long as both participation in the lobby game and reliable information relations with other agents differ across lobby groups and legislators, it follows that not every lobby group can engage in a lobby game with every legislator. Empirically, the access structures among lobbying groups and legislators can be measured via corresponding political network data (Pappi and Henning 1998, 1999; Henning 2009). Formally different access structures are reflected in the relative weights, χ_j^g.

3.4 Module IV: Belief Formation Module

To cope with complexity, laymen, politicians and representatives of interest groups apply naive mental models to understand how policies translate into policy outcomes (i.e., agents form political beliefs). Some scholars (Blendon et al. 1997; Caplan 2002; Rhoads 1985; Walstad 1996) compared the policy beliefs of laymen to the corresponding expert beliefs of trained economists. Based on comprehensive statistical analyses, Caplan concluded that laymen beliefs systematically differ from experts beliefs. In particular, Caplan concluded that these differences result from judgmental anomalies of the general public. In contrast, on average, economic experts hold unbiased and true beliefs. Interestingly, Caplan and other scholars (Akerlof 1989; Caplan 2001; Sachs and Williamson 1994) further concluded that political failure is more likely to be a byproduct of the electorate's systematically biased beliefs about economics than a product of special interest politics.

The mechanism by which actors form their beliefs is of interest. The modeling of belief formation and belief updating has recently become an increasingly acknowledged field of research in economics and social science (see Acemoglu and Ozdaglar 2010; Golub and Jackson 2009; Jackson 2008). Following the relevant literature, we distinguish two types of belief formation: observational and communication learning. Dynamic policy learning corresponds to observational learning, where, as will be shown in detail below, from the viewpoint of an individual actor, it often makes sense to combine observational learning and communication learning. As will be shown in more detail in the following subsections, in our theory, a central determinant of policy learning corresponds to communication structures among agents, which are encapsulated in communication networks. The question of which specific network structure implies effective policy learning and thereby guarantees more efficient policy decisions is central to our theory. In this paper, we focus our analysis on the belief updating of governmental and nongovernmental organizations, leaving the analysis of voter belief formation and updating for future work.[5]

[5]The main reason for not explicitly taking voter beliefs into account at this point follows from the difficulty of collecting reliable data concerning voter communication networks and voter behavior that allow for the estimation of the underlying voter beliefs and the process of voters' belief formation. However, the analysis of political elite networks is a well-established field in the empirical policy network literature (Knoke et al. 1996; Henning 2009; Henning and Krampe 2011; Pappi and Henning 1998; Pappi and Henning 1999).

3.4.1 Communication Learning

Collective belief formation via communication learning corresponds to the mapping of agents' initial individual beliefs $\tilde{A}^0$ into final beliefs, as follows: $\tilde{A} = \Upsilon(\tilde{A}^0)$, where Υ corresponds to a specific communication mechanism. Following recent studies (Acemoglu and Ozdaglar 2010; Golub and Jackson 2009), we assume that agents form their beliefs via communication in local networks. To consider communication structures, we define a binary network M^1 over a set of agents N, where $M^1_{ij} = 1$ indicates that agent i and agent j have an established communication tie. Accordingly, we define the subset $M_i = \left\{j \in N, M^1_{ij} = 1\right\}$ as the neighborhood of agent i and $M = [m_{ij}]$ as a communication network, where $m_{ij} > 0$ indicates that actor i pays attention to actor j. M is a stochastic matrix; for each actor, the sum of the total weights equals 1:

$$\sum_{j \in M_i} m_{ij} = 1 \qquad m_{ij} = \frac{M^1_{ij}}{\sum\limits_{j' \in M_i} M^1_{ij'}}. \tag{20}$$

Within one period, a political communication process occurs, where agents repeatedly update their political beliefs by taking weighted averages of their neighbors' beliefs, with m_{ij} being the weight or trust that actor i places on the current belief of agent j when forming his or her belief for the next period (see also Golub and Jackson 2009). If we let $r = 1, \ldots, R$ denote the communication round, then it follows that:

$$\tilde{A}_i^{r+1} = m_{ii}\tilde{A}_i^0 + \sum_{j \neq i} m_{ij}\tilde{A}_j^r. \tag{21}$$

Rewriting Eq. (21) results in the following:

$$\begin{aligned} \tilde{A}_i^{r+1} &= m_{ii}\tilde{A}_i^0 + (1 - m_{ii}) \cdot \textstyle\sum_j \bar{m}_{ij}\tilde{A}_j^r \\ with: \bar{m}_{ij} &= \frac{m_{ij}}{(1 - m_{ii})}, \end{aligned} \tag{22}$$

where $\tilde{A}_i^r$ is the political belief of agent i that results after r communication rounds, and A_i^0 denotes agent i's initial beliefs prior to communication. The parameter m_{ii} represents the weight actor i puts on her own initial belief. As M is row normalized to one, $(1 - m_{ii})$ is the aggregated weight for all neighbors (i.e., the influence or communication field of other agents). Writing Eq. (22) in matrix notation results in the following, after further rearrangements:

$$\tilde{A} = \left[I - \left(1 - m_{diag}\right)\bar{M}\right]^{-1} \cdot m_{diag} \cdot \tilde{A}^0, \tag{23}$$

with $\widehat{M} = \left[I - \left(1 - m_{diag}\right)\bar{M}\right]^{-1} m_{diag}$ being the network multiplier, which is similar to the Hubbell index (Hubbell 1965). Please note that the belief updating in Eq. (23) corresponds to the Friedkin model (Friedkin and Johnsen 1990) and includes the DeGroot model analyzed by Jackson 2008 as a special case. In particular, for any row stochastic matrix $\widehat{M}$, belief formation converges to a well-defined limit $\tilde{A}$. Accordingly, the limit beliefs of each agent that are reached via communication correspond to the weighted average of the initial beliefs of all agents prior to communication $\tilde{A}^0$, where the weight of agent j's initial opinion $\tilde{A}_j^0$ determining agent i's belief after communication $\tilde{A}_i$ equals the element $\widehat{m}_{ij}$ of the multiplier matrix $\widehat{M}$. The multiplier $\widehat{m}_{ij}$ defines the field strength of agent j's initial belief operating on agent i's final belief.

Note that the multiplier includes all communication loops among actors (i.e., all direct and all indirect effects of j's initial belief on the belief of agent i that result from communication). Overall, the efficiency of communication learning is determined by the extent that communication network structures imply that the relative weights of agents' initial opinions correspond with the agents' relative political knowledge. For the deGroot model, this issue has been analyzed by Golub and Jackson (2009) (see also Jackson 2008). Golub and Jackson (2009) demonstrated that c.p, a random communication process (i.e., agents update their beliefs randomly based on the communicated beliefs of all other actors) implies unbiased beliefs, assuming the number of agents approximates infinity. In contrast, assuming communication is structured in such a way that the weight of an individual agent will not approximate zero when the number of agents approximates infinity implies biased beliefs. However, Golub and Jackson failed to analyze the impact of communication network structures on communication learning in finite societies. Thus, in the following section, we will analyze this interesting relation by applying a simple example.

4 Communication Networks and Policy Learning: A Simple Example

To demonstrate how communication network structures impact the efficiency of policy learning, consider the following simple example of a political elite system comprised of the simple legislative system introduced above and five stakeholder groups. The legislators are labeled L1 to L5, and the stakeholder groups are labeled IG1 to IG5.

For simplicity, we assume that legislators must decide on the expenditure for a specific policy program X. Let X correspond to financing for agricultural extension services. The legislators and stakeholders are concerned about the impact of the policy program X on a political objective Z. Let Z be the reduction of poverty. Assume that a simple linear technical relation describes the impact of budget allocation to agricultural extension services X on poverty reduction Z: $Z = aX$.

Further, assuming quasi-linear preferences V(Z,B):

$$V(Z,B) = \{ Z^{\eta} + \theta(B - X)\}, \tag{24}$$

where B denotes the state budget and θ is a parameter determining the marginal utility of budget expenditures. The optimal expenditure that results from the maximization of V(Z,B) can be expressed as:

$$\widehat{X} = \theta^{\frac{1}{\eta-1}} \eta^{\frac{1}{1-\eta}} a^{\frac{\eta}{1-\eta}}. \tag{25}$$

All other things being equal, the more efficiently the program X impacts poverty reduction (i.e., the larger a becomes), the larger is the amount of financial resources that legislators want to invest into this program. For simplicity, we assume specific parameter constellations ($\eta = 0.5$ *and* $\theta = 0.0625$), such that it follows that: $\widehat{X} = a$.

As described above, the fundamental uncertainty of the technological impact of policy programs on policy targets is a major problem in political decisionmaking. Thus, agents must form beliefs. In particular, we assume that agents observe a signal from which they derive their initial beliefs. The signals are independently but not necessarily identically distributed. As a result, it holds that:

$$a_i = a + \varepsilon_i. \tag{26}$$

ε_i is the bias, which is symmetrically distributed with a mean of zero and a variance σ_i^2. Accordingly, the initial belief is a random variable $\widehat{a}_i$ that is distributed with mean a and a finite variance σ_i^2. Thus, the expected error an agent makes when deriving her policy position form her initial beliefs equals $E(\varepsilon_i{}^2) = \sigma_i^2$.

Next, we analyze the manner in which belief updating via political communication, as described above, impacts the bias of legislators' beliefs and the subsequent error that results for the preferred policy position, $\widehat{X}$. As described above, following our model of communication learning, the final belief of an individual agent corresponds to a weighted mean of legislators' initial beliefs, where the weight of the position of an agent j for the final belief of agent i equals the network multiplier $\widehat{m}_{ij}$. Thus, it holds:

$$\widehat{a}_i^1 = \sum_j \widehat{m}_{ij} \widehat{a}_j^0 = \sum_j \widehat{m}_{ij}(a + \varepsilon_j) = a + \sum_j \widehat{m}_{ij}\varepsilon_j. \tag{27}$$

Define $\mathrm{E}_i = \sum_j \widehat{m}_{ij}\varepsilon_j$ as the bias of agent i's belief after communicational learning. Then, the error an agent i makes when deriving his policy position from his final beliefs corresponds to the weighted sum of the individual errors of all agents:

$$E(\mathrm{E}_i)^2 = \sum_j \widehat{m}_{ij}^{\,2}\ \sigma_j^2. \tag{28}$$

Hence, optimal weights (m_{ij}^{opt}) can be defined by minimizing the error after communication learning:

$$\frac{m_{ij}^{opt}}{m_{ik}^{opt}} = \frac{\sigma_k^2}{\sigma_j^2};\quad m_{ik}^{opt} = \frac{\frac{1}{\sigma_k^2}}{\sum_j \frac{1}{\sigma_j^2}}. \tag{29}$$

Please also note that if individual biases, ε_i, are drawn from an identical distribution with variance σ^2, it directly follows that the optimal weights equal $^1/_n$, where "n" is the number of political agents. Accordingly, communication learning reduces the policy bias by an order of n when compared to an individual updating. Specifically, it holds: $E(\mathrm{E}_i)^2 = \frac{1}{n}\ \sigma^2$. This process basically corresponds to the wisdom of the crowd effect, which was initially identified by Francis Galton (1907).

More generally, we can conclude from our analyses above that an essential precondition for efficient communication learning in networks is that actors' communication structures guarantee that the relative political knowledge of agents is reflected in their relative network multipliers. As can be seen from eq. (29) the relative political knowledge of actors is measured by the ratio of their corresponding error variances. Hence, it is important to identify a strategy for designing policy network structures that imply efficient policy learning. In particular, we must determine under which conditions a stronger participation of stakeholder organizations in the political communication process implies more efficient learning. To this end, we apply our network model to simulate policy learning under different conditions of political knowledge distribution among legislators and stakeholder groups and under different communication network structures. In detail, we simulated three ideal-typical policy network structures corresponding to (1) top-down communication (i.e., stakeholders update based on the communicated beliefs of politicians, not vice-versa); (2) bottom-up communication (i.e., politicians update based on the communicated beliefs of stakeholders, not vice-versa and (3) equal participation of stakeholders (i.e., politicians update based on the beliefs of stakeholders, and stakeholders update based on the beliefs of politicians). The blocked network structure of the three scenarios is presented in Table 3.

The assumption that politicians put a lower weight on their own beliefs (i.e., politicians are generally more open to influence from other actors compared to interest groups) implies the average network multipliers for the three network constellations that are presented in Table 4.

Finally, we assume that the individual bias is the same for all political actors in the scenario "equal-know" and that the relation of the variance of the individual error terms is 4 times higher for the politician than for the stakeholder organizations

Table 3 Ideal-typical political communication structures

	Scenarios					
	Top-down		Equal		Bottom-up	
	L	*IG*	*L*	*IG*	*L*	*IG*
L	1	0	1	1	0	1
IG	1	0	1	1	0	1

Source: Author

Table 4 Network multiplier derived for ideal-typical political communication structures

	Scenarios					
	Top-down		Equal		Bottom-up	
	L	*IG*	*L*	*IG*	*L*	*IG*
L	1	0	0.51	0.49	0.3	0.7
IG	0.4	0.6	0.11	0.89	0	1

Source: Author

in the scenario "IG-expert". We also assume that the average variance across all political actors remains constant. In contrast, we assume in the scenario "pol-expert" that the politicians exhibit a fourfold lower error term variance than the stakeholder organizations. We again assume that the average variance across all agents remains constant.

Following our exposition above, we calculated the average expected belief bias of the legislators for all 9 network and knowledge constellations. Further, we calculated the optimal weighting of agents' initial individual beliefs for all knowledge scenarios. Based on these calculations, we computed the average additional bias that will be realized for a given policy network constellation and a specific knowledge scenario compared to the corresponding optimal communication structure. We expressed this additional bias as the percentage of the bias that is realized under conditions of optimal belief updating. Analogously, we calculated the relative efficiency gain obtained via communicational learning for all three network structures in comparison to individual belief formation. In particular, we compared the average error that results from communication learning to the average error that results assuming individual belief formation among politicians.

Figure 5 clearly demonstrates that the efficiency of policy learning depends on the combination of a specific knowledge distribution and communication structure, where a mismatch between these two components implies extreme losses of efficiency. Assuming that interest groups have more political knowledge than politicians, a top-down communication structure implies an average error due to biased beliefs that is 400% higher than the error that results from an optimal communication structure. However, the corresponding efficiency loss amounts to only 62% when assuming a balanced communication structure. In contrast, assuming politicians have significantly higher knowledge implies an increase in the policy error of 150% for a bottom-up communication structure and 51% for a balanced communication structure (see Fig. 5).

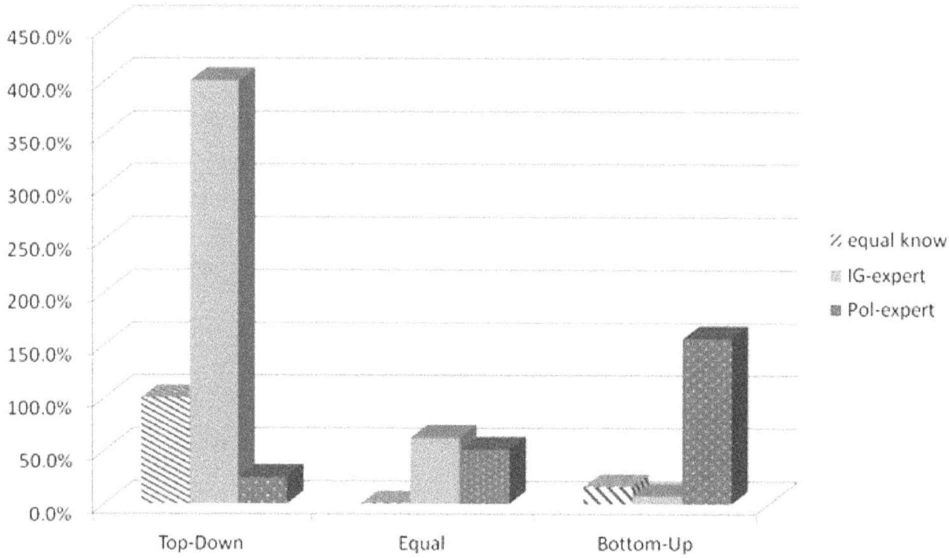

Fig. 5 Efficiency loss resulting from communication policy learning in different knowledge and policy network scenarios. Source: own calculation

Further, a comparison of the policy errors that result from communication learning to the corresponding errors that are implied by individual belief formation emphasizes the efficiency of communication learning. Specifically, communication learning reduces the policy error by over 90% compared to individual learning for all scenarios.

Overall, this simple simulation study implies that stakeholder participation significantly increases the efficiency of communication learning. The ignorance of stakeholder organizations, as assumed for the top-down scenario, only increases the efficiency of policy learning when the relative political knowledge of stakeholder organizations is much lower than that of politicians.

In contrast, focusing policy learning solely on stakeholder organizations, as implied by the bottom-up communication structure, would only be justified if stakeholders have significantly higher knowledge than politicians.

Finally, it is also interesting to identify the conditions under which evidence-based political processes that focus policy learning on a small subset of political experts (e.g., research institutions) increase the efficiency of policies. To this end, we calculated the optimal relative weight of one policy expert, assuming that this expert's relative political knowledge compared to the average agents in the network increases from 1 (i.e., equal knowledge) to 100 (i.e., the error variance of the average agent is 100 times higher than error variance of the expert). Moreover, we calculated the efficiency gain as a percentage comparing the relative error that results under an optimal communication structure to that of a balanced communication structure. The simulation results are presented in Fig. 6. Figure 6 demonstrates that the efficiency gain that results from a focus on political experts increases in a concave manner with the relative expertise of the expert and is dependent on the

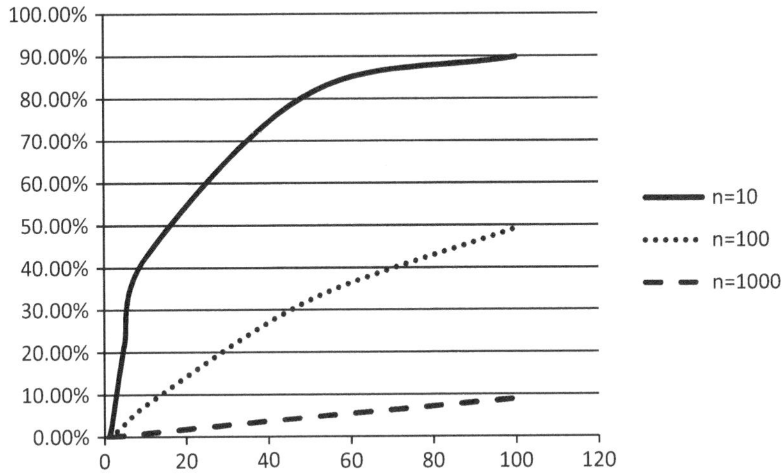

Fig. 6 Efficiency gain resulting from optimal centralization of communication on political experts according to the size of the elite network. Source: Author

size of the total policy elite network. For a small network that includes only ten governmental and nongovernmental organizations, the relative gain amounts to only 10%, assuming that the expert's knowledge is threefold higher. In contrast, the relative gain amounts to nearly 90%, assuming that the expert's knowledge is 100-fold higher.

These gains are significantly lower for larger networks (e.g., for an elite network with 100 organizations, a maximal efficiency gain of 50% is realized, but for an elite network comprised of 1000 organizations, the maximal efficiency gain is reduced to only 9%).

Accordingly, the optimal centralization of political communication on experts decreases significantly with the size of the elite network. Assuming a network size of 10 implies that the optimal communication structures correspond to a significant centralization of the political communication on political experts, with a Herfindahl index ranging from 0.1 for equal knowledge to 0.89 assuming political knowledge is 100 times higher for the expert. In contrast, the corresponding Herfindahl indices range from 0.01 to 0.25 for a network size of 100 and from 0.001 to only 0.009 for an elite network size of 1000 (see Fig. 7).

4.1 *Observational Policy Learning*

While communication learning is possible within a static CGPE approach, belief updating might also occur dynamically (e.g., across time periods). Dynamic policy learning corresponds to a belief updating process that is based on observed policy outcomes. These outcomes can be realizations of political targets (e.g., in our simple example above, agents observe the development of poverty in their

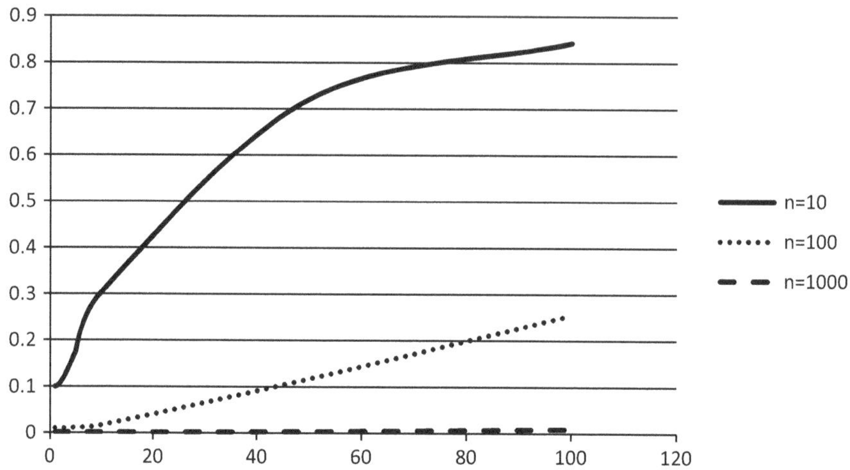

Fig. 7 Optimal centralization of communication on political experts according to the size of the elite network, as measured using the Herfindahl index. Source: Author

constituency after a specific policy X has been implemented). Agents compare the observed policy outcome with the policy outcomes they expected based on their original policy beliefs. Hence, if the observed outcomes differ from the expected outcomes, the agents have an incentive to adapt their beliefs to ensure that expected outcomes match observed outcomes:

$$Z_{it}^{E} = \widehat{a}_{it-1}X_{t-1}, \tag{30}$$

$$\Delta\widehat{a}_{it} = \phi\Delta Z_t = \phi\left(Z_{it}^{O} - Z_{it}^{E}\right), \tag{31}$$

$$\widehat{a}_{it} = \widehat{a}_{it-1} + \Delta\widehat{a}_{it}. \tag{32}$$

Thus, agents update their political beliefs proportional to the relative difference between observed Z^O and expected Z^E policy outcomes, where ϕ denotes the speed of adjustment parameter. Hence, we assume a Nerlovian belief updating process. Nerlovian policy learning that is based on individual observation of policy outcomes becomes complex when more than one policy program impacts policy outcomes. In this case, politicians might update based on available scientific policy evaluation studies (e.g., impact evaluation studies for specific policy programs). These studies deliver direct estimates of specific technical parameters, a.

4.2 *Reinforcement Learning*

While observational policy learning based on observed policy outcomes z implies that political agents actually apply a mental model, which may be simple, to estimate how policies translate into outcomes, reinforcement learning does not require a mental model.

Reinforcement learning implies that agents choose their future behavior based on the perceived gratification received from past behavior (i.e., if this gratification is positive, agents repeat or intensify their past behavior, but agents stop or reduce their past behavior if the perceived gratification is negative). Retrospective voting is a prominent example of reinforcement political learning. In this scenario, a voter's probability of reelecting the government depends on the voter's perceived welfare that was realized while the government was in power. However, in contrast to voters, politicians are interested in reelection. Hence, their observed political support triggers reinforcement learning.

To explain how reinforcement learning works in a policy choice setting, please note that according to the two-stage legislative bargaining procedure described above, politicians perceive multidimensional policy choices in a one-dimensional macro-policy space. The macro-policy space corresponds to the direction in the multidimensional policy space in which agents agree to shift the status quo policy. Given the direction $\Delta\gamma^*$, agents decide on the distance λ_γ, where legislators have single-peaked preferences for this distance, with $\widehat{\lambda}_g$ denoting an agent's ideal distance. Let λ_t^* denote the final policy choice in period t that results from majority voting at the second stage of legislative bargaining. Then, legislators observe the political support feedback that results from the implementation of the policy $\gamma_t^* = \gamma^0 + \lambda_t^* \Delta\gamma^*$. If the feedback is positive, politicians have an incentive to shift the status quo even further in the same direction $\Delta\gamma^*$, but if the support feedback is negative, legislators have an incentive to move the policy back towards the direction of the status quo. Formally, we assume the following reinforcement learning mechanism:

$$\gamma_t = \gamma^0 + \lambda_t^* * (\Delta\gamma^*). \tag{33}$$

Updated policy choices are based on observed changes in political support:

$$\lambda_0 = 0; \qquad 0 < \lambda_1 << 1, \tag{34}$$

$$d\lambda_t^* = \lambda_t^* - \lambda_{t-1}^*, d\widehat{\lambda}_t^g = \widehat{\lambda}_{t-1}^g - \lambda_{t-1}^*, \tag{35}$$

$$dW_t = W_t(\gamma_t) - W_{t-1}(\gamma_{t-1}), \tag{36}$$

$$\Delta\lambda_t = \operatorname{sgn}(dW_t * d\lambda_t), \tag{37}$$

$$\lambda_{t+1}^g = \begin{matrix} \lambda_t^g + \phi\Delta\lambda_t\lambda_1, & if \quad d\lambda_t^* d\widehat{\lambda}_t^g < 0 \\ \lambda_t^g, & otherwise \end{matrix} \quad . \tag{38}$$

where ϕ is again a parameter determining the speed of adjustment. Because political support is a single-peaked function of λ, reinforcement learning will gradually identify the optimal policy strategy. In more specific terms, without an adequate stop strategy, reinforcement learning will lead to an oscillating process in which policy decisions oscillate between $(\lambda^* - \phi\lambda_1, \lambda^* + \phi\lambda_1)$, where λ^* is the support-maximizing policy decision. Thus, the finer the adjustment (i.e., the lower the step length $\phi\lambda_1$) the closer reinforcement learning mechanisms mimic optimal policy choices.

4.3 Combination of Observational and Communication Learning

Analogously, observations of policy outcomes z_t by individual agents are noisy. Thus, if we again assume idiosyncratic measurement errors, which are independent draws from a distribution with a zero mean, the aggregated measurement of policy outcomes is almost correct, but individual measures might be highly biased. Therefore, agents might be willing to combine their individual observational learning with communication learning. To describe the combined learning process, let $\Delta\tilde{a}^0_{it}$ denote the individual parameter update that results from the observational learning of an agent i in period t. Then, combined observational and communication learning implies that the final parameter updates correspond to:

$$\Delta\tilde{a}^1_{it} = M\Delta\tilde{a}^0_{it}. \tag{39}$$

Based on the updated beliefs, a new political decision results from legislative bargaining in period t + 1.

5 Summary and Conclusion

This chapter develops the eCGPE as a theoretical framework and an empirically applicable tool for defining, evaluating and designing efficient participatory and evidence-based policy processes. The eCGPE is a sequential dynamic political economy equilibrium model that incorporates five modules that model legislative decisionmaking, the transformation of policies into socioeconomic outcomes, interest mediation via voting and lobbying, political belief formation and policy learning. In contrast to existing political economy models, which highlight the biased incentives of politicians as a main cause of persisting inefficient policies, the CGPE approach explicitly incorporates the lack of adequate political knowledge as another important source of inefficient policy choices. In particular, the CGPE approach incorporates a model of political belief formation and updating to explain how political agents use a combination of observational and communication learning processes to improve their political knowledge. According to our model, the main determinants of the speed of knowledge are the structures of policy networks that reflect communication patterns between governmental and nongovernmental organizations. Based on empirical policy network data, relevant communication structures can be identified. Combining the identified network structures with the relative political knowledge of the involved governmental and nongovernmental organizations allows for an assessment of the impact of stakeholder participation on the efficiency of policy learning. The knowledge of the involved organizations is derived from the specified economic model, specifically from the political impact function. Moreover, within an extended Grossman-Helpman approach, the impact of lobbying activities and voting behavior on politician incentives is modeled. In this model, the asymmetric lobbying activities of vested interest groups are determined by limited access to powerful politicians. The latter can be empirically identified by applying social network analysis. Furthermore, we demonstrate that based on the eCGPE approach, a political diagnosis can be made (i.e., existing incentives and knowledge gaps can be identified). Furthermore, a political therapy (i.e., adequate strategies for reducing existing political performance gaps) can be derived via simulation analyses based on the eCGPE. To empirically apply a CGPE approach, all five modules must be specified, the model parameters must be empirically estimated and the specified modules must be implemented using an adequate programming framework. In the four sections that follow, we will describe how the CGPE approach can be empirically applied using the policy network study on the CAADP reforms in Malawi as an example. In Chapter "A Network Based Approach to Evaluate Participatory Policy Processes: An Application to CAADP in Malawi", the empirical application of the political belief updating module and the legislative decision-making module is described, while Chapter "The Formation of Elite Communication Networks in Malawi: A Bayesian Econometric Approach", describes the econometric estimation of the network data-generating process of relevant policy networks in Malawi. In Chapter " Voter Behavior and Government Performance in Malawi: An Application of a Probabilistic Voting Model", a probabilistic voter model is estimated using Afrobarometer data from Malawi. Finally, in Chapter "Whither participation? Evaluating participatory policy processes with the CGPE approach: The case of CAADP in Malawi", the complete eCGPE approach is applied to the recent CAADP reform in Malawi to demonstrate how this approach can be applied as a practical tool for analyzing policy processes empirically.

References

Acemoglu, D., and A.E. Ozdaglar. 2010. *Opinion Dynamics and Learning in Social Networks*. MIT Department of Economics Working Paper 10–15. Cambridge: Massachusetts Institute of Technology.

Akerlof, G.A. 1989. The Economics of Illusion. *Economics and Politics* 1: 1–15.

Anderson, K. 2010. *The Political Economy of Agricultural Price Distortions*. Cambridge: Cambridge University Press.

Badiane, O., S.P. Odjo, and F. Wouterse. 2011. *Comparative Analysis of Strategies and Long Term Outlook for Growth and Poverty Reduction among ECOWAS Member Countries*. Discussion paper. West and Central Africa Office.

Bardhan, P., and D. Mookherjee. 2002. *Relative Capture of Local and Central Governments: An Essay in the Political Economy of Decentralization*. Working Paper C99-109. Berkeley: Center of International and Development Economics Research.

Baron, D., and J. Ferejohn. 1989. Bargaining in Legislatures. *American Political Science Review* 83: 1181–1206.

Beilhartz, H.-J., and H. Gersbach. 2004. *General Equilibrium Effects and Voting Into a Crisis.* CEPR Discussion Paper 4454. London: Centre for Economic Policy Research.

Binswanger, H.P., and K.W. Deininger. 1997. Explaining Agricultural and Agrarian Policies in Developing Countries. *Journal of Economic Literature* 35: 1958–2005.

Bischoff, I., and L.-H. Siemers. 2011. Biased Beliefs and Retrospective Voting: Why Democracies Choose Mediocre Policies. *Public Choice* 156: 163–180.

Blendon, R.J., J.M. Benson, M. Brodie, R. Morin, D.E. Altman, D. Gitterman, M. Brossard, and M. James. 1997. Bridging the Gap between the Public's and Economists' Views of the Economy. *Journal of Economic Perspectives* 11: 105–118.

Bourguignon, F., M. Bussolo, and L.A.P. da Silva, eds. 2008a. *The Impact of Macroeconomic Policies on Poverty and Income Distribution.* Washington, DC: World Bank.

Bourguignon, F., C. Diaz-Bonilla, and H. Löfgren. 2008b. *Aid, Service Delivery, and the Millenium Development Goals in an Economy-Wide Framework.* Washington, DC: World Bank.

Caplan, B. 2001. Rational Irrationality and the Microfoundations of Political Failure. *Public Choice* 107: 311–331.

———. 2002. Systematically Biased Beliefs about Economics: Robust Evidence of Judgemental Anomalies from the Survey of Americans and Economists on the Economy. *The Economic Journal* 112: 433–458.

———. 2007. *The Myth of the Rational Voter - Why Democracies Choose Bad Politics.* Princeton, NJ: Princeton University Press.

Clay, E., and B. Schaffer, eds. 1984. *Room for Maneuver: An Exploration of Public Policy in Agriculture and Rural Development.* London: Heinemann.

De Gorter, H., and J.F.M. Swinnen. 1998. The Impact of Economic Development on Public Research and Commodity Policies in Agriculture. *Review of Development Economics* 2: 41–60.

Diao, X., P. Hazel, D. Resnick, and J. Thurlow. 2007. *The Role of Agriculture in Development: Implications for Sub-Saharan Africa.* IFPRI Discussion Paper 153. Washington, DC: International Food Policy Research Institute.

Dixit, A. 2003. Trade Expansion and Contract Enforcement. *Journal of Political Economy* 111: 1293–1317.

Fafchamps, M., E. Sadoulet, and A. de Janvry. 1993. Tariff Seeking in a General Equilibrium Framework. *Journal of International Trade & Economic Development* 2: 167–189.

Fan, S., and N. Rao. 2003. *Public Spending in Developing Countries: Trends, Determination and Impact.* EPTD Discussion Paper 99. Washington, DC: International Food Policy Research Institute.

Fan, S., and X. Zhang. 2004. Investment, Reforms and Poverty in Rural China. *Economic Development and Cultural Change* 52 (2): 395–422.

Fan, S., and M.W. Rosegrant. 2008. *Investing in Agriculture to Overcome the World Food Crisis and Reduce Poverty and Hunger.* IFPRI Policy Briefs 3. Washington, DC: International Food Policy Research Institute.

Friedkin, N.E., and E.C. Johnsen. 1990. Social Influence and Opinions. *Journal of Mathematical Sociology* 15: 193–205.

Galton, F. 1907. Vox Populi. *Nature* 75: 450–451.

Golub, B., and M.O. Jackson. 2009. Naive Learning in Social Networks and the Wisdom of Crowds. *American Economic Journal Microeconomics* 2 (1): 112–149.

Groseclose, T. 2001. A Model of Candidate Location When One Candidate Has a Valence Advantage. *American Journal of Political Science* 45: 862–886.

Grossman, J.B. 1994. Evaluating Social Policies: Principles and U.S. Experience. *The World Bank research observer* 9 (2): 159–180.

Grossman, G.M., and E. Helpman. 1996. Electoral Competition and Special Interest Politics. *Review of Economic Studies* 63: 265–286.

Henning, C.H.C.A. 2000. *Macht und Tausch in der europäischen Agrarpolitik: Eine positive politische Entscheidungstheorie*. Frankfurt/Main: Campus.

———. 2009. Networks of Power in the CAP System of the EU-15 and EU-27. *Journal of Public Policy* 29: 153–177.

Henning, C.H.C.A., and E. Krampe. 2011. *How the European Union Works: Theory and Empirical Evidence from EU Agricultural Policy*. Paper presented at the Political Economy of International Organizations (PEIO), Zurich, Switzerland.

Henning, C.H.C.A., C. Struve, B. Brümmer, and L. Seidel, eds. 2006. Macht und Ideologie in der EU-25: Eine Anwendung eines Generalisierten Banzhaf-Index auf die Europäische Agrarpolitik. In *Schriften der Gesellschaft für Wirtschafts- und Sozialwissenschaften des Landbaues e.V*. Kiel: Agrar- und Ernährungswissenschaftliche Fakultät.

Henning, C.H.C.A., and C. Struve. 2008. The Logic of the European Agricultural Policy: Political Power or Economic Rules? *German Journal of Agriculture Economics* 57: 179–194.

Hubbell, C.H. 1965. An Input-Output Approach to Clique Identification. *Sociometry* 28 (4): 377–399.

Jackson, M.O. 2008. *Social and Economic Networks*. Princeton, NJ: Princeton University Press.

Juma, C., and N. Clark. 1995. Policy Research in Sub-Saharan Africa: An Exploration. *Public Administration and Development* 15: 121–137.

Keeley, J., and I. Scoones. 2003. *Understanding Environmental Policy Processes. In Africa: Cases from Ethiopia, Mali and Zimbabwe*. Earthscan: London.

Knoke, D., F.U. Pappi, J. Broadbent, and Y. Tsujinaka. 1996. *Comparing Policy Networks. Labor Politics in the U.S., Germany, and Japan*. Cambridge: Cambridge University Press.

Löfgren, H. 2001. *Less Poverty in Egypt? Explorations of Alternative Pasts with Lessons for the Future*. Discussion Paper 72. Washington, DC: International Food Policy Research Institute.

Paldam, M., and P. Nannestad. 2000. What do Voters Know about the Economy? A Study of Danish Data 1990-1993. *Electoral Studies* 19: 363–391.

Pappi, F.U., and C.H.C.A. Henning. 1998. Policy Networks: More than a Metaphor? *Journal of Theoretical Politics* 10 (4): 553–575.

———. 1999. The Organization of Influence on EC's Common Agricultural Policy: A Network Approach. *European Journal of Political Research* 36 (2): 257–281.

Persson, T., and G. Tabellini. 2000. *Political Economics—Explaining Economic Policy*. Cambridge: MIT Press.

Rausser, G.C., J. Swinnen, and P. Zusman. 2011. *Political Power and Economic Policy: Theory, Analysis, and Empirical Applications*. Cambridge: Cambridge University Press.

Rhoads, S. 1985. *The Economist's View of the World: Government, Markets, and Public Policy*. Cambridge: Cambridge University Press.

Sachs, J., and J. Williamson, eds. 1994. Life in the Economic Emergency Room. In *The Political Economy of Policy Reforms*, 501–524. Washington, DC: Institute for International Economics.

Schofield, N. 2004. Equilibirium in Spatial Valence Models of Politics. *Journal of Theoretical Politics* 16: 447–481.

Schofield, N.J. 2007. The Mean Voter Theorem: Necessary and Sufficient Conditions for Convergent Equilibrium. *Review of Economic Studies* 74: 965–998.

Shepsle, K.A. 1979. Institutional Arrangements and Equilibrium in Multidimensional Voting Models. *American Journal of Political Science* 23 (1): 27–59.

Stokes, D.E. 1963. Spatial Models of Party Competition. *American Political Science Review* 57: 368–377.

Walstad, W. 1996. Economic Knowledge and the Formation of Economic Beliefs. In *Economic Socialization: The Economic Beliefs and Behaviors of Young People*, ed. P. Lunt and A. Furnham, 162–182. Cheltenham: Edward Elgar.

Young, J. 2005. Research, Policy and Practice: Why Developing Countries Are Different. *Journal of International Development* 17: 727–734.

Christian Henning is professor and chair of agricultural economics, University of Kiel (Germany). He studied economics, agricultural economics, sociology, political science and mathematics. He earned a PhD in economics, in agricultural economics and in political science. His main areas of specialization are applied political economy and applied economic modelling of agricultural policies. To date he has published five books and various articles in refereed journals including PLoS ONE, American Journal of Agricultural Economics, European Review of Agricultural Economics, Journal of Public Policy, Journal of Mathematical Sociology and Journal of Theoretical Politics.

Johannes Hedtrich is a computer scientist and a PhD student in agricultural economics. He studied computer science and agricultural economics at the University of Kiel (Germany). His main areas of specialization are computational economics, Bayesian econometrics and social network analysis.

8

Analyzing Participatory Policy Processes: A Theoretical Framework

Christian Henning and Eva Krampe

1 Introduction

Donor organizations recently engaged in promoting participatory policy processes as a tool for designing efficient policy programs. Participatory policymaking is a process through which stakeholders influence and share control over priority-setting and policymaking (World Bank 2011). The implementation of participatory processes is promoted to increase the efficiency and effectiveness of policy choices, particularly in developing countries. In general, more effective and efficient policy choices are induced via specific mechanisms: 1. Increasing governmental accountability (Keefer and Khemani 2005) (i.e., incentives for governmental agents to serve societal interests and needs). 2. Reducing government capture (Bardhan and Mookherjee 2002) (i.e., government incentives to serve vested interests at the expense of the general public). 3. Increasing evidence-based policy processes (i.e., the degree to which political actors use available political knowledge for making policy choices. Political knowledge is knowledge about the technical relation between policies and induced policy outcomes). 4. Increasing policy ownership (i.e., citizens [civil society] identify with and feel committed to governmental policy); policy ownership implies a higher citizen compliance with the established policy framework and can significantly reduce political implementation costs (Adserà et al. 2003; Jones 2013; Chambote and Shankland 2011).

Any opinions stated herein are those of the authors and do not necessarily reflect the policies or opinions of EIB.

C. Henning
Department of Agricultural Economics, University of Kiel, Kiel, Germany

E. Krampe (✉)
European Investment Bank, Luxembourg, Luxembourg
e-mail:

Accordingly, it is widely accepted that the ownership of policy programs that occurs as a result of participation in policy program formulation leads to more effective implementation and adoption of the policy programs (World Bank 2011).

Understanding the nature of participatory policy processes is not only high on the research agenda at the academic level but also increasingly recognized as a key condition for efficiently providing support for the formulation of effective policy programs in political practice. The Comprehensive Africa Agriculture Development Programme (CAADP), which was initiated by the African Union, is a good example of these new developments. The inclusion of local stakeholder organizations in the planning, formulation and evaluation of sector-specific growth policies is a key principle of the program (NEPAD 2010). However, a CAADP task group focused on the evaluation of non-state actor participation reported that stakeholders had only a limited ability to use the newly created opportunities for participation. Based on information collected via a qualitative stakeholder survey and desk research, the task group emphasized that CAADP has not yet consistently achieved a high quality inclusion of non-state actors at the national, regional or local levels (Randall 2011, p. 2).

Nevertheless, although participatory policy processes are intuitively convincing as a tool for the evaluation of existing policy processes and for the design of more efficient policy processes in the future, the development of a measurement tool that allows for the comprehensive characterization of participation structures inherent to real policy processes that are ongoing in political practice is necessary. Ideally, this measurement tool is grounded in political theory to guarantee that empirically identified participation structures can be consistently related to an intervention logic (i.e., the derivation of a causal link between specific properties of the policy process and desirable policy outcomes). The latter criterion implies that the impact of the identified structures of a policy process on governmental accountability and capture and on the effective use of political knowledge and political ownership can be directly derived.

However, to the best of our knowledge, a comprehensive, micro-political-founded and quantitative evaluation framework for participatory policy processes is not currently available. In this context, the Advocacy Coalition Framework (ACF) proposed by Sabatier and Jenkins-Smith (1993) has attracted attention as an approach for analyzing policy processes, particularly among political scientists at the academic level. More recently, the ACF has been increasingly recognized by development economists (Birner and Resnick 2010). This framework includes a number of interesting aspects (e.g., this framework explicitly identifies beliefs as drivers of coalition formation and final political decisionmaking). Moreover, this framework provides a systematic approach for analyzing stakeholder interactions. However, the ACF is a qualitative approach and provides neither a theoretical model of political decisionmaking nor a theoretical model of belief formation among the actors involved in policymaking. In particular, a quantitative description of real policy processes is a necessary condition for a comprehensive evaluation of the impact of these processes on the effectiveness and efficiency of policy outputs. Hence, the ACF in its present form is not yet an appropriate tool for policy learning (i.e., a tool that is ready to identify causal links between specific patterns of stakeholder interactions and induced governmental performance).

In this context, the aim of this chapter is to initiate the development of a theoretically founded framework for analyzing participatory policy processes that can be applied empirically. In particular, following the literature on policy network analyses (Lauman and Knoke 1987; Pappi et al. 1995; Knoke et al. 1996; Pappi and Henning 1998, 1999; Henning 2000, 2009), we apply social network analysis (SNA) to measure complex interactions among stakeholder and governmental organizations. Moreover, we derive a theoretical framework for the incorporation of policy network theory into political economy models of lobbying and legislative decisionmaking. As we demonstrated in Chapter "Modeling and Evaluation of Political Processes: A New Quantitative Approach", we incorporate a network model of political belief formation into a political bargaining model (see Henning in this volume). The latter model combines a generalized Grossman-Helpman lobbying model and a modified legislative bargaining model of the Baron and Ferejohn type. The central component of such an integrated model corresponds to a generalized mean voter decision rule, where in addition to legislators, interest groups also have political control over policies (Pappi and Henning 1998; Henning 2000, 2009). Political control of nongovernmental organizations results via two different mechanisms: lobbying and communication learning. The first mechanism is determined by the political access structures via which nongovernmental organizations access powerful governmental organizations, and the second mechanism is determined by political communication among organizations. Empirically, the equilibrium outcome of the complete model can be derived from observed political support and communication networks.

Based on our theoretical framework, we undertake a descriptive analysis of the central components that determine policy choices. This analysis includes a network analysis of the underlying communication and access structure, which is encapsulated in the communication network and the political support network. In this regard, social network analyses provide a wide range of local and global network tools and methods for describing the characteristics of an individual network (Wassermann and Faust 1994). Previous political sociology reports demonstrated that network analysis can be used to systematically describe interaction structures among nongovernmental and governmental organizations that are engaged in a specific policy domain (Lauman and Knoke 1987; Knoke et al. 1996; Pappi et al. 1995; Pappi and Henning 1998, 1999; Henning 2000; Henning and Wald 2000). However, with a small number of exceptions (e.g., Pappi and Henning 1998; Henning 2000, 2009), these studies used SNA to describe policy domain network structures without relating the identified structures to political performance. In contrast, our framework offers innovative network tools (i.e., the network multipliers derived in Chapter "Modeling and Evaluation of Political Processes: A New Quantitative Approach") that go beyond a pure descriptive analysis. The framework will allow us to make direct conclusions concerning the impact of the identified network structures on different aspects that determine governmental performance. Specifically, we describe the four previously mentioned aspects of government performance and use our network-based indicators to measure these factors empirically.

The case country selected for the empirical application of our framework is Malawi. Malawi approved a policy reform, the sector investment program Agricultural Sector Wide Approach (ASWAp), based on the principles of CAADP in 2010. Data was collected via a policy network study in 2010.

In the next section, we briefly summarize the theoretical framework for modeling participatory policy processes. We describe in detail the design of the network study, including the collected data and the central network theoretical tools/measures used in our analyses. We then present the principal empirical results, and we conclude by providing an outlook on future research.

2 A Theoretical Framework for Evaluating Policy Processes

In general, we apply the theoretical framework developed in Chapter "Modeling and Evaluation of Political Processes: A New Quantitative Approach". We focus specifically on the combination of a modified legislative bargaining model and the political belief formation model in a policy elite network. This approach considers the political decisionmaking process as an aggregation mechanism of the policy preferences of the involved political actors. In essence, this aggregation mechanism corresponds to a generalized mean voter decision rule:

$$\gamma^* = \sum_j \varphi_j^T \widehat{\gamma}_j^0, \tag{1}$$

where γ^* denotes the final policy decision, φ_j^T denotes the total political power and $\widehat{\gamma}_j^0$ denotes the initial preferred policy position of actor j. The total political power results from political influence on powerful political actors:

$$\varphi_j^T = \sum_i \bar{m}_{ij} \varphi_i^L, \tag{2}$$

where $\bar{m}_{gj}$ denotes the political influence of actor j on agent i. As demonstrated in Chapter "Modeling and Evaluation of Political Processes: A New Quantitative Approach", $\bar{m}_{gj}$ is the network multiplier derived from the communication network among governmental and nongovernmental actors. Accordingly, $\bar{m}_{gg}$ denotes the weight that a legislator g puts on her own initial position, while φ_i^L is the political power of agent i that is derived from the lobbying game, as described in Chapter "Modeling and Evaluation of Political Processes: A New Quantitative Approach". Thus, it holds:

$$\varphi_i^L = \sum_g m_{gi}^S \varphi_g. \tag{3}$$

As described in Chapter "Modeling and Evaluation of Political Processes: A New Quantitative Approach", m_{gi}^{S} is the support network multiplier that corresponds to the outflow of legislative power from legislator g to actor i, resulting in the equilibrium of the lobbying game. Hence, the better access an interest group i has to powerful legislators, the more successful are the lobbying activities of this organization. Further, φ_g denotes the legislative power of legislator g that is derived from the modified legislative bargaining game, as described in Chapter "Modeling and Evaluation of Political Processes: A New Quantitative Approach". Equations (1, 2, and 3) constitute the theoretical backbone of our policy process framework, which we have also illustrated in Fig. 1 below.

As is illustrated in Fig. 1, based on our theory, the policy process corresponds to an aggregation mechanism of the policy positions of the involved governmental and nongovernmental organizations, where the individual weight of an organization is jointly determined by political communication network structures that determine political influence $\bar{m}_{ij}$, informal access structures $\bar{m}_{gi}^{S}$ that determine lobbying power and constitutional rules that determine legislative decisionmaking powerφ_g[1].

Based on our theoretical framework, the underlying communication and access structures, which are encapsulated in the communication network MC and the political support network MS, are central components that determine final policy choices. To describe these networks, we apply social network analysis tools, including methods for identifying overall network structures (e.g., block model analysis) (Wassermann and Faust 1994). However, our framework offers innovative network tools that go beyond a pure descriptive analysis to allow us to draw direct conclusions concerning the impacts of the identified network structures on different aspects that determine governmental performance (i.e., the network multipliers derived in Chapter "Modeling and Evaluation of Political Processes: A New Quantitative Approach". Specifically, we develop the network-based indicators

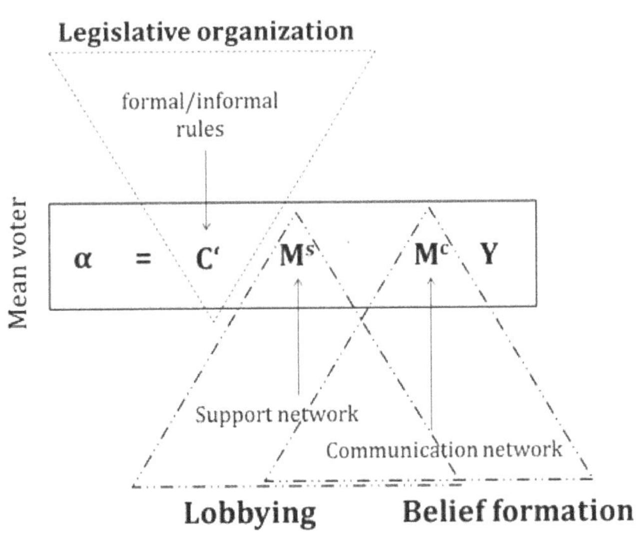

Fig. 1 Overview of the framework. Source: Authors

described below to empirically measure different aspects of governmental performance.

2.1 Government Accountability

The successful functioning of any government depends on the ability of citizens to hold politicians and public administrators accountable for their actions. The existing literature on political accountability describes the machinery of government as a game between a principal (i.e., the public) and an agent (i.e., the politicians or public administrators) in which the former delegates to the latter a given set of instruments to execute certain goals (Adserà et al. 2003). In this game, the principal and the agent may have opposing interests (i.e., even while partially acting based on the interests of their potential electorate, political agents are likely to pursue their own political agenda [e.g., political agents may be interested in enriching themselves while in office or political agents' strategies for enhancing the welfare of the public may differ from the desires of the public]). Hence, with self-interested political agents, the delegation of decisionmaking and policy implementation responsibilities automatically provides the opportunity for significant inefficiencies and corruption among politicians. One could argue that electoral competition induces governmental incentives for acting in line with society's interests; thus, the high concentration of political power in governmental organizations does not contradict political accountability. Though this argument could be true in general, this reasoning is limited because elections fail to guarantee/imply strong governmental accountability. The citizens' (i.e., voters') information concerning governmental policies and their consequences for society's welfare is a factor that impacts the functioning of free and regular democratic elections as an effective mechanism for guaranteeing political accountability. If citizens lack this information, they base their votes on non-policy indicators. As demonstrated in Chapter "Voter Behavior and Government Performance in Malawi: An Application of a Probabilistic Voting Model", this statement is especially true for Malawi, where non-policy voting motives are the principal determinants of vote choices, particularly within the rural population. Thus, voters are swayed by the relative campaign spending of different parties, which reflects the influence of election advertisements more than high governmental performance (i.e., serving voters' true desires and needs). Hence, in addition to elections, the participation of stakeholder organizations in the political process is a second mechanism for holding public officials accountable. The more domestic stakeholder organizations control governmental actions and policy choices via lobbying and political communications, the more these actions and choices correspond to the desires of society.

Therefore, we use the sum of the total political power of national nongovernmental organizations (NGO) as a general indicator of government accountability (GA-total):

$$GA - total = \sum_{j \in NGO} \varphi_j^T \quad (4)$$

Moreover, to understand how policy network structures interact with constitutional rules, we use the power outflows from central political institutions to national NGOs (i.e., from the government, including the president and the ministries, and from the parliamentary parties) as two additional sub-indicators of governmental accountability (i.e., GA-Gov and GA-Par, respectively).

2.2 Government Capture

According to the relevant political economy literature (Bardhan and Mookherjee 2002), governmental capture corresponds to the concept that governmental political actions and policy choices are biased towards the particular interests of organized social groups at the expense of the general public. Thus, even if the government is fully accountable to its electorate, it might respond asymmetrically to the specific interests of particular social groups. In this context, electoral competition induces governmental capture because some social groups are less informed than others (see also Chapter "Voter Behavior and Government Performance in Malawi: An Application of a Probabilistic Voting Model"). However, beyond democratic elections, stakeholder participation is a second channel/mechanism for relaying society's interests to public officials. Hence, the determination of the extent to which this mechanism is biased in favor of the particular interests of vested groups is of interest. Accordingly, we calculate the quadratic distance between the relative total political power of a stakeholder organization and its corresponding share of represented society members in the total population Pop_j and take the square root of the sum of these distances over all relevant stakeholder organizations as an indicator of capture (GC-total):

$$GC - total = \sqrt{\sum_{j \in GNO} \left[\frac{\varphi_j^T}{\sum_{k \in NGO} \varphi_k^T} - Pop_j \right]^2} \quad (5)$$

To guarantee that our capture index GC lies in the [0,1] interval, we normalize GC as follows: $GC^n = \frac{GC}{GC+1}$. Further, we take the square root of the sum of the calculated distances for specific population subgroups that represent specific interests (e.g., small-, medium- and large-scale farmers or urban consumers) as sub-indicators of capture, namely GC-farm and GC-urban.

2.3 Political Knowledge

Understanding the complex relation between policy instruments and induced policy outcomes is difficult; thus, politicians use simple mental models (i.e., political beliefs) to describe the manner in which policies translate into outcomes. Because voters, politicians, and lobby and stakeholder organizations fail to fully understand the complex relation between political instruments and desired policy outcomes, inefficient policy choices are implied. As described in the introductory chapter of this book, an increasing number of publications emphasize the role of biased policy beliefs as a main determinant of inefficient policy choices (Beilhartz and Gersbach 2004; Bischoff and Siemers 2011; Caplan 2007). Hence, beyond biased governmental incentives caused by low accountability or high governmental capture, the lack of political knowledge becomes another important source of policy failure. As described in Chapter "Whither participation? Evaluating participatory policy processes with the CGPE approach: The case of CAADP in Malawi", the individual political knowledge of an actor can be measured by comparing the stated ideal policy positions of an organization with the optimal policy position of an organization. The latter position results from maximizing an organization's support, assuming perfect political knowledge (i.e., CAADP policies translate into policy outcomes based on the specified Computable General Political Economy Equilibirum (CGPE) model, denoting the stated and optimal policy positions by $\widehat{\gamma}_i$ and $\widehat{\gamma}_i^{opt}$ and the Euclidian distance, which is a measure that corresponds to the error variance, as derived in Chapter "Modeling and Evaluation of Political Processes: A New Quantitative Approach", by $\psi_i = \left\| \widehat{\gamma}_y^{opt} - \widehat{\gamma}_i \right\|$). As explained in Chapter "Modeling and Evaluation of Political Processes: A New Quantitative Approach", based on our belief updating model, comparing the total political power distribution to the distribution of political knowledge across organizations allows an assessment of the extent to which the identified participation structures promote or impede evidence-based policy processes. Moreover, we can identify power structures, $\varphi_j^{opt}(\psi)$, that imply an optimal use of political knowledge in the policy network ψ and calculate the loss of efficiency that results under the actual communication structure compared to the optimal communication structure. We take this relative loss as an indicator of the impact of existing policy structures on evidence-based policy (PK-use):

$$PK - use = 1 - \frac{\sigma_\varepsilon^2(\varphi^T)}{\sigma_\varepsilon^2(\varphi^{opt})} = 1 - \frac{\sum_j \left[\varphi_j^T\right]^2 \frac{\psi_j}{\psi_0}}{\sum_j \left[\varphi_j^{opt}\right]^2 \frac{\psi_j}{\psi_0}}, \tag{6}$$

$\sigma_\varepsilon^2(\varphi^T)$ and $\sigma_\varepsilon^2(\varphi^{opt})$ denote the error variance that results from the mean voter decision, assuming the actual and optimal distribution of total political power, respectively. $\frac{\psi_j}{\psi_0}$ is the relative political knowledge of an organization j compared to a reference organization 0. Further, we take the Euclidian Distance between the actual and optimal political power distribution and the sum of the total political power of the domestic research organizations as two additional sub-indicators (i.e., PK-dpow and PK-Res) of the degree of political knowledge use.

2.4 Political Ownership

Political ownership corresponds to the concept that a society identifies with a specific policy and is committed to accomplishing the envisaged policy goals. Hence, a lack of ownership corresponds to an incentive problem on the side of the society. Technically, ownership is related to the involvement of national nongovernmental organizations in political communication. Political ownership increases citizen compliance with policies, decreasing implementation costs and increasing the effectiveness of the implemented policies. In contrast to governmental accountability, the ability of nongovernmental organizations to exert influence on governmental organizations is less important for achieving political ownership. In contrast, even a top-down communication system (i.e., the policy beliefs of civil society are primarily influenced by governmental organizations) implies political ownership because the citizens feel involved in policy formulation. Accordingly, all other things being equal, the higher the level of consensus achieved through stakeholder participation, the higher the political ownership of citizens in the decided policies will be. To measure the political ownership implied by stakeholder participation, we define the following political conflict index from the viewpoint of an organization i (CONi):

$$CON_i(\gamma^*) = \sqrt{\sum_k \theta_{ik}\left(\widehat{\gamma}_{ik} - \gamma_k^*\right)^2}, \tag{7}$$

where θ_{ik} denotes the interest of actor i in the policy dimension k, $\widehat{\gamma}_{ik}$ denotes the ideal position of actor i with respect to dimension k, and γ_k^* is the final policy decision for the dimension k. Accordingly, the average political conflict for all national nongovernmental organizations results as:

$$CON_{NGO}(\gamma^*) = \sum_{j \in NGO} CON_j(\gamma^*). \tag{8}$$

Hence, we can calculate the final policy outcome that would result from legislative bargaining, assuming no lobbying and no belief updating occur. Let $\gamma^{\#}$denote this policy outcome. We can then analogously define the average political conflict $CON_{NGO}(\gamma^{\#})$. The lower the political conflict when including political communication and lobbying in comparison to the political conflict without communication, the higher the involvement of the nongovernmental organizations; thus, we define the following indicator of political ownership (PO-Consens):

$$PO - Consens = 1 - \frac{CON_{NGO}(\gamma^*)}{CON_{NGO}(\gamma^\#)}. \tag{9}$$

Further, because political ownership generally decreases with the dominance of donor organizations in the political process (Chambote and Shankland 2011; Jones 2013), we take the total political power of a donor organization as an additional sub-indicator of ownership (PO-Donor). Moreover, we use the density of the communication network between the national nongovernmental and governmental organizations as a measure of political involvement that corresponds to ownership (PO-involve).[1]

Overall, within our framework, we can first use standard network analysis tools to describe the interaction structures among governmental and nongovernmental organizations that are involved in the political decisionmaking process. Second, we can apply innovative network-based indicators to evaluate the extent to which the identified participation structures impact political performance (i.e., governmental accountability and capture, effective use of political knowledge and political ownership). Please note that trade-offs generally exist among the different aspects of political performance. For example, an increase in the participation of civil society organizations in political communication might increase the governmental accountability and political ownership and simultaneously decrease the effective use of political knowledge. Consistent with this reasoning, Ball (1995) demonstrated that lobbying implies a trade-off between the effective use of political knowledge and government capture. Analogously, an increase of donor involvement in political communication might increase the effective use of political knowledge while reducing political ownership and political accountability.

Finally, we must note that the empirical relevance of this assessment depends on the assumption that our theoretical model accurately describes real political decisionmaking processes. In this regard, we use the empirical prediction power of our theoretical model as a test of the empirical relevance and applicability of our framework.

[1]Please note that the involvement of civil society is also related to accountability. Even if stakeholder organizations monitor governmental actions without controlling these actions, accountability might be increased because stakeholders inform voters. Thus, voter choices are c.p. more informed, strengthening voters' ability to hold the government accountable. Therefore, one could also use the density of political communication between national stakeholder organizations and governmental organizations as a sub-indicator of accountability. However, in this paper, we use this factor as a sub-indicator of political ownership.

3 Analyzing the CAADP Policy Processes in Malawi

3.1 Policy Reform Context

In 2010, the Malawi government approved the sector investment program Agricultural Sector Wide Approach (ASWAp) (The Ministry of Agriculture and Food Security, Republic of Malawi 2010). ASWAp is based on the principles of CAADP. The principal goal of the program is to achieve agricultural growth and poverty reduction using investments in the agricultural sector and reforms of the corresponding institutional framework as the central policy instruments. Moreover, the Government of Malawi follows the comprehensive participatory approach elaborated within CAADP (i.e., the Malawi government attempted to design a CAADP policy process characterized by high involvement of local stakeholder organizations in the design, monitoring and evaluation of all activities and policies decided within ASWAp). Thus, in addition to political actors and donor organizations, the umbrella organizations of the food security civil society organizations and farmer organizations (i.e., CISANET and FUM, respectively) signed the CAADP Compact in April 2010. Despite the potential of CADDP reform processes, the extent to which the real CAADP policy process in Malawi promotes participatory and evidence-based policies remains unclear. We apply our framework to elucidate this issue in the following sections.

3.1.1 Study Design and Data Collection

To collect relevant data, an elite network study was organized. Such a study involves a survey containing questions about networks, policy positions and interests. The survey was completed via personal interviews using carefully constructed survey questionnaires in May 2010. Interviews with representatives of relevant nongovernmental and governmental organizations were conducted in Lilongwe and Blantyre.

The unit of observation in an elite network study is an organization, which is interpreted as a corporative actor (Coleman 1990). The respondents are considered experts of the organizations they represent in the specific policy field. Following an established approach that is used in policy network studies, relevant organizations were identified using a two-step procedure (Laumann and Knoke 1987; Laumann et al. 1989; Pappi et al. 1995; Pappi and Henning 1999). In the first step, a list of potentially relevant organizations was compiled based on desk research and expert interviews.[2] This list included 60 nongovernmental organizations and

[2]In particular, we used available information concerning stakeholder participation in agricultural policy workshops published on the internet. Moreover, we used a list of stakeholder organizations, donors and politicians engaged in the formulation of the Farm Input Subsidy Programme (FISP), which was included in a previous study by IFPRI in 2010 (Aberman et al. 2012).

35 governmental organizations. Based on this list, personal interviews were conducted with representatives of the preselected organizations, beginning with governmental organizations (i.e., Ministry of Agriculture and Food Security (MoAFS) and subordinate agencies) and the most important interest groups (i.e., farm organizations). A reputation question was asked during the interview, and interviewees were instructed to mark all influential organizations on the identified list. Based on the reputation question, new organizations that received more than 3 nominations were interviewed. Overall, we interviewed 17 governmental organizations and 20 nongovernmental organizations.

The elite questionnaires included three parts: (a) policy networks, (b) policy preferences (i.e., information concerning interest and position with respect to relevant ASWAp policy issues, and 9c) organizational characteristics.[3] In the network portion of the questionnaire, we collected data on reputation, expert information, monitoring, social relation and organizational membership networks. To collect reliable networks, we designed our network questions using a format that was extremely helpful in previous network studies (Pappi and Henning 1999; Pappi et al. 1995). Interviewees were asked to check those organizations on the list with which they maintain a specific relation. To facilitate orientation, the list of organizations was organized according to the type of organization or the branch of interest represented by the respective organizations (see Table 5 in the appendix).[4] In the following sections, we describe in more detail the reputation and expert information networks, as these networks are used for the empirical application of the proposed policy framework. Based on our theoretical framework, political support networks are also relevant. However, in the Malawi case study, we did not include political support networks in our policy network survey. Accordingly, we will simulate the support network using collected policy network data.[5] Therefore, we will only briefly describe the simulated political access network structures.

As described above, the reputation network is used to specify the network boundary from the actors' point of view. Respondents were asked to mark organizations on the list that according to their opinion, stand out as especially influential with respect to the agricultural policy process.[6] The expert information network is

[3]Data collection for part (c) is described in detail in Chapter "The Formation of Elite Communication Networks in Malawi: A Bayesian Econometric Approach".

[4]As we did not know in advance whether we identified all relevant organizations, we provided a hybrid type of list. That is, interviewees were presented with a roster of organizations and given the option to add additional organizations that they believed to be important. This approach addresses two problems: under-reporting in a free recall interview and failures in setting the theoretical network boundaries.

[5]Please note that we explicitly collect policy support network data in other empirical applications [e.g., for the European Union (Pappi and Henning 1998, 1999) and within the PEBAP-project for Ghana, Uganda and Senegal (https://pebap.agrarpol.uni-kiel.de/)].

[6]The question was framed in a way that instructed interviewees not to exert great effort on a detailed investigation but to mark those organizations that came to mind instantly. This framing assumes that highly important organizations will come to mind quickly. Further, the interviewees had the option to use blank lines to add missing influential organizations.

the centerpiece of our belief formation model for characterizing the policy process. We consider expert information to be any kind of information about policy impacts that an actor can communicate to another actor (e.g., knowledge about the impact of farm input subsidies on central policy outcomes, such as the welfare of different social groups). To collect data on the information flow in the elite network, the interviewees were asked to check those organizations on the list of organizations with which they share information about the consequences of agricultural policies. Specifically, expert information transfers were collected from a supplier perspective (i.e., an organization delivers information to another organization) and a demander perspective (i.e., an organization receives information from another organization). Therefore, we could construct a confirmed expert knowledge network, which is more reliable from a network theoretic point of view (Pappi et al. 1995). A particular knowledge transfer is considered 'confirmed' if both the supplier and demander of knowledge independently report the transfer.

The weight that an actor places on her own initial belief is another key input in our model. To identify an actor's level of own control, interviewees were asked to ascertain the extent to which they use externally provided expert information as opposed to their own expertise when formulating policy strategies. In detail, the respondents were asked to divide 100 points to indicate the relative importance of external versus internal expert information. Own control is then calculated as the relative importance of own internal expertise.

In part (b), we collected data on the policy preferences of organizations. We asked for the relative interest and the preferred position of an organization with respect to relevant ASWAp policy issues. Specifically, we assumed a nested structure of policy preferences. At the top level, we asked for the relative interest in and preferred position regarding relevant policy concerns z. These policy concerns are relevant policy outcomes determined by ASWAp, including $Z1$ the welfare of small scale-farmers, $Z2$ poverty reduction, $Z3$ state budget expenditures and $Z5$ the welfare of urban consumers (see Chapter "Whither participation? Evaluating participatory policy processes with the CGPE approach: The case of CAADP in Malawi" for a full list of relevant policy concerns). At the second level, we considered interest and positions in specific policy programs formulated in ASWAp. Specifically, ASWAp includes the following four pillars, which are formulated as focus areas in official documents (The Ministry of Agriculture and Food Security, Republic of Malawi 2010): pillar I is "Food security and risk management;" pillar II is "Agri-business and market development;" pillar III is "Sustainable land and water management;" and pillar IV is "Technology generation and dissemination/Institutional strengthening and capacity building." According to the official documents for each pillar, two alternative subprograms are formulated. For example, for pillar I, the first subprogram corresponds to fertilizer subsidy payments for maize; in the alternative subprogram, input subsidies are paid for all crop production to increase the diversification of agricultural production. The subprograms of ASWAps are described in Chapter "Whither participation? Evaluating participatory policy processes with the CGPE approach: The case of CAADP in Malawi". For each pillar and each subprogram, we collected the policy positions preferred by an organization, where a policy position corresponds to the amount of budget expenditures allocated to a specific subprogram or pillar. To obtain a complete picture, we also included budget expenditures allocated to non-agricultural policy programs. Overall, the collected data on policy positions included the allocation of total state budget expenditures to the 8 ASWAp subprograms and to non-agricultural policy programs. Subtracting the sum of the budget expenditures for agricultural and non-agricultural policy programs from the total state budget results in the budget expenditures that are available for the provision of public goods, such as health or other social security services. Within the survey, we collected the interest θ and position $\widehat{\gamma}$ in all nine policy programs. Accordingly, we were able to derive the spatial policy preferences of individual organizations, $U_i(\gamma) = -\sum_{k=1}^{4}\theta_{ik}(\widehat{\gamma}_{ik} - \gamma_k)^2$. To describe the different policy preferences of organizations, we further reduce the nine-dimensional policy space to a two-dimensional policy space by applying a principal component analysis using the collected policy positions as inputs. Based on a factor loading matrix, we interpreted the first principal component as the budget allocation between agricultural and non-agricultural programs, where a high factor score on the first component implies a high budget share for agricultural programs and a negative score implies a high budget share for non-agricultural policy programs. The second component can be interpreted as a budget allocation within ASWAp programs, where a positive factor score corresponds to the reallocation of budget expenditures from pillar I (i.e., input subsidies) and to a lower extent, from pillar III (i.e., water and land policy programs) in favor of pillar II (i.e., programs promoting rural infrastructure) and pillar IV (i.e., extension services and agricultural research). The positions of individual organizations in the two-dimensional macro-policy space are presented in Fig. 9 below.

4 Analyzing the CAADP Policy Process in Malawi: A Network Approach

4.1 Relevant Organizations in the CAADP Policy Domain

Table 5 in the appendix lists the 37 interviewed organizations and their indegree centrality in the reputation network. The indegree centrality summarizes an organization's received nominations, which are standardized by the number of maximal possible nominations (Wassermann and Faust 1994). Overall, our sample represents the top most influential organizations in Malawi, and MoAFS stands out as an especially influential organization, with a maximal indegree centrality of 1.

In Table 5, the stakeholder organizations are further subordinated into different categories according to the social groups they represent. In detail, we consider farmer (farm), agribusiness (AB) and non-agricultural interest group (NA) organizations, as well as research (RES) and civil society organizations.

The latter group includes consumer (con) and church organizations (chur). To facilitate the presentation of the results of our network analyses, we combine the civil society organizations and the NA organizations into one civil society category (CSO) in the following section.

4.2 *Identified Network Structures of Political Participation in Malawi*

4.2.1 Political Communication

Political communication in the CAADP policy domain is comparatively intensive, with a global density of 0.23 for the confirmed expert network. For example, in the policy domain of the European Common Agricultural Policy of the EU-27, the confirmed expert network exhibited a global network density of only 0.11; even for the EU-15, the corresponding density is only 0.14 (Henning 2009).

However, a block model analysis of the political communication network[7] reveals that political communication is clearly structured in Malawi, with a political core (i.e., block 1) that includes central governmental organizations and donor organizations and a political periphery (i.e., block 3) comprised of primarily national civil society organizations (see Fig. 2 and Table 5).

Interestingly, in addition to the leading ministries that determine agricultural policy in Malawi (i.e., MoAFS and Ministry of Finance [MoF]), all seven donor organizations are part of the political core. In contrast, the only national nongovernmental organizations that are part of the political core are the two agribusiness interest groups (i.e., Farmer's world and STAM) and the national peak civil society organization CISANET. The farm interest group FUM in block 4 plays a key role in political communication. This interest group is highly integrated in political communication and functions as a broker between the civil society periphery and the political core. A second broker block (i.e., block 2) that connects civil society with the political core is formed around Bunda College, which is the main research organization involved in the CAADP process. In addition to Bunda College, block 2 also includes the public agency ADD and the ministry of irrigation and water development (MoIWD). Given the specific composition of blocks 2 and 4, block 2 can be interpreted as a technical leader, and FUM functions as the central political link connecting the political core to the civil society periphery. Please note that the periphery is not only weakly connected with the political core, as indicated by a density of only 0.12 between block 1 and

[7]A block model analysis identifies actors in a network that are structurally equivalent (i.e., they have the same pattern of relation to all other actors in the network). Structurally equivalent actors are grouped into the same block, where members have a specific relational pattern to other blocks. Please note that in contrast to a cluster analysis, block members are not necessarily related to each other (Wassermann and Faust 1994).

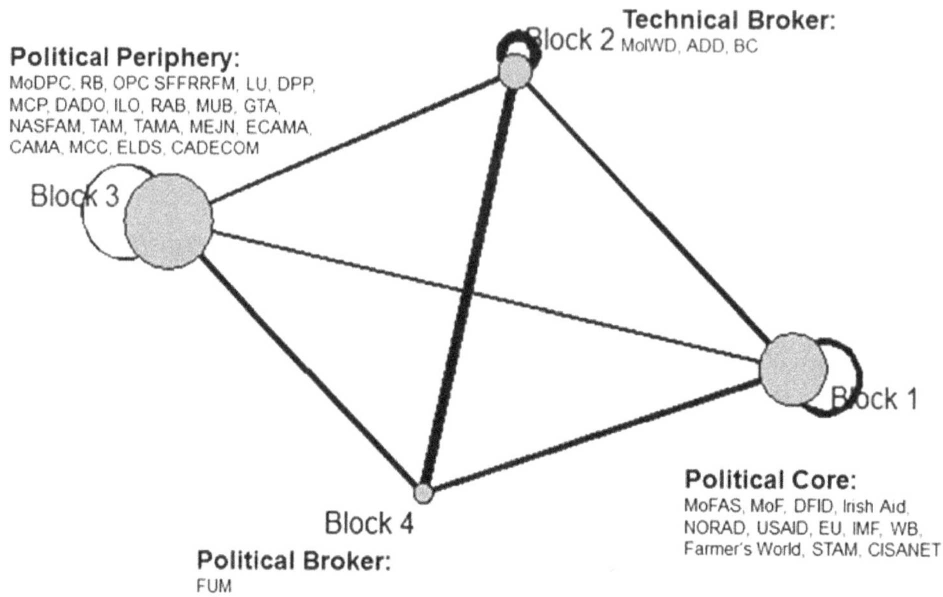

Fig. 2 Block model structure of political communication in Malawi. Source: Authors

3, but even internally peripheral organizations do not communicate with each other very much, as indicated by an internal density of only 0.11 for block 3 (see Table 1). The office of the president (OPC) is a key player within the periphery. The OPC is central within the internal communication of the political periphery, as it is connected to over 30% of the organizations in the periphery. Moreover, the OPC is a strategic link between the periphery and the political core, as it is connected to the political brokers (i.e., blocks 2 and 4) and to MoF in the political core.

4.2.2 Lobbying

According to our modified Grossman-Helpman model, the central determinant of lobbying power is the access of an organization to powerful politicians. Empirically relevant access structures are identified via political support networks. Following Pappi and Henning (1999), we focus on direct access, leaving the analysis of indirect brokerage relations for future work (Henning 2009). The densities of the support network are reported in Table 2. As demonstrated in Table 2, donor organizations have good access to the most powerful governmental organizations, especially MoF and MoAFS, but national stakeholders only have access to MoAFS, MoIWD and the president (i.e., OPC). Interestingly, access to legislative parties is dominated by national stakeholder organizations, primarily CSO, and farm organizations; donors have no access to legislative parties. Moreover, political institutions depend on their mutual political support, and most political institutions exhibit relatively high densities above 0.5 (see Table 2). The mutual dependence of the

Table 1 Block densities of the political communication network in Malawi

	Block 1	Block 2	Block 3	Block 4
Block 1	0.56	0.39	0.12	0.42
Block 2	0.39	1.00	0.37	1.00
Block 3	0.12	0.37	0.11	0.52
Block 4	0.42	1.00	0.52	–

Source: Authors

Table 2 Block densities of the political support network in Malawi

	MoF	MoAFS	MoIWD	MoDPC	OPC	DPP	MCP
Farm	0.000	0.400	0.200	0.000	0.400	0.200	0.000
Donor	0.571	0.429	0.286	0.143	0.286	0.000	0.000
CSO	0.000	0.143	0.571	0.000	0.429	0.000	0.000
Gov	0.500	0.000	0.750	0.500	0.750	0.600	0.200
Leg	0.500	0.000	0.500	0.500	0.500	1.000	1.000
PUB	0.400	0.600	0.400	0.200	0.400	0.200	0.000
AGIND	0.000	0.167	0.333	0.000	0.333	0.167	0.000

Source: Own calculations based on simulated support network data

political support among political institutions is also a common feature in industrialized countries, where in addition to lobbying groups, political parties have a high potential for generating electoral support. The potential of donors to generate political support can be explained by the funds donors provide to national governments, which give the governments leeway to generate electoral benefits.

4.3 Political Influence and Power

According to our network model of political belief updating, communication structures determine political influence among governmental and nongovernmental organizations. Hence, at a descriptive level, an analysis of the ways in which organizations are influenced by each other is of interest. Beyond a descriptive analysis, it is especially interesting to evaluate the impact of political influence structures on different aspects of political performance. For example, evaluating the extent to which the final policy positions of governmental organizations are influenced by the political views of nongovernmental organizations by measuring the effective participation using political power indices. Or, evaluating the extent to which central organizations take political leadership vis-à-vis civil society in a top-down political process using network multipliers. Moreover, a high political influence exerted by donor organizations would characterize a donor-led policy process, which might undermine political ownership if national stakeholder organizations feel ignored. Furthermore, an analysis of the extent to which the identified political influence and power structures reflect the political expertise of the

Table 3 Communication network multipliers

	Gov	Leg	PUB	don	Res	AGIND	farm	CSO	Sum
MoF	0.934	0.009	0.016	0.026	0.002	0.006	0.004	0.003	1.000
MoAFS	0.736	0.002	0.063	0.076	0.012	0.036	0.052	0.025	1.000
oMin	0.832	0.027	0.041	0.032	0.010	0.018	0.013	0.028	1.000
OBC	0.645	0.030	0.051	0.067	0.036	0.030	0.067	0.074	1.000
Leg	0.181	0.733	0.038	0.012	0.006	0.007	0.011	0.012	1.000
PUB	0.108	0.007	0.727	0.059	0.012	0.056	0.019	0.012	1.000
don	0.106	0.002	0.021	0.724	0.034	0.045	0.035	0.034	1.000
Res	0.091	0.003	0.064	0.107	0.530	0.063	0.050	0.091	1.000
AGIND	0.104	0.004	0.068	0.045	0.031	0.701	0.027	0.022	1.000
farm	0.096	0.003	0.055	0.047	0.031	0.034	0.700	0.034	1.000
CSO	0.135	0.004	0.038	0.063	0.086	0.034	0.061	0.579	1.000

Source: Own calculations based on own network survey data

involved governmental and nongovernmental organizations is of interest. To assess these interesting questions, we provide a descriptive analysis of the identified political influence and power structures in the following section, and we evaluate the impact of the identified structures on political performance in the next section.

The network multipliers derived from political communication, as described in Chapter "Modeling and Evaluation of Political Processes: A New Quantitative Approach" above, are the centerpiece of our political influence model. Table 3 presents the communication network multipliers that were calculated for specific categories of governmental and nongovernmental organizations.

The network multipliers presented in Table 3 correspond to the aggregated weight of the policy positions of the row category in determining the final policy position of an average individual organization of the column category. For example, the first column presents the average influence of the row categories on the Ministry of Agriculture (MoAFS). As demonstrated in the first row in Table 3, the final policy position of MoAFS after communication is determined 71% by MoAFS's own initial position; the aggregated weight of the initial position of the donor organizations is 7% compared to only 2.3% for the civil society organizations (CSO). Please note that the relatively high own network multipliers on the diagonal of Table 3 result from the high own control of organizations. Hence, political influence exerted via communication is relatively low in the policy domain of CAADP in Malawi, with own network multipliers ranging from 0.52 for the office of the president (OBC) to 0.91 for the Ministry of Finance (MoF). Interestingly, in Malawi, a particularly high own control was reported by governmental organizations, with own control values above 70% for all organizations expect OBC. Stakeholder organizations are more open to expert information provided by other organizations, with own network multipliers below 65%. Civil society organizations exhibit a relatively low average own control of 56% (CSO in Table 3), while interest groups of the agribusiness and farm sectors exhibit a mid-range average own control of approximately 65%. These structures are partially in contrast to the influence structures in the European Common Agricultural Policy domain (CAP), where elected governmental organizations are particularly open to learning from nongovernmental organizations that represent relevant interests of their electorate (i.e., in the EU, the average reported own control is below 60%). In contrast, interest groups involved in CAP decisionmaking reported a comparatively high average own control of over 70% (Henning 2009); these groups are primarily interested in influencing powerful political actors and less interested in learning about the underlying technological relations. A second interesting feature of the influence structures in Malawi corresponds to the relatively low own control of international donor and national research organizations, with own network multipliers ranging between 66% and 53%, respectively (see Table 3). Like public agencies (Pub-AG), these organizations are supposed to be technological leaders with high political knowledge; hence, these organizations should pay less attention to others' organizational point of view. However, Bunda college (BC) reports a particularly low own control of only 54%. Although public agencies and international donor organizations have significantly higher own control values of 69% and 66%, respectively, these values are relatively low compared to the values reported by the Ministries. This finding indicates that neither research nor public agencies perceive themselves as strong political experts in the field of agricultural policy and development in Malawi.

Beyond own control, the influence profiles of organizations are interesting. Influence profiles identify influential organizations and describe the extent to which other organizations influence the initial policy position of an organization. Formally, influence profiles can be described by the vector of relative network multipliers that operate as an influence field on an organization. Based on our belief formation model, the influence field operating on an actor is determined by her local communication structures. Hence, the more actors are structurally equivalent in the communication network, the more similar c.p. are their influence fields. Accordingly, we conducted a cluster analysis using the influence profiles of the identified organizations. Based on the reported statistical fit values, we preferred a four cluster solution. As expected, cluster membership corresponds nicely to the identified block model structure (see Table 1). Thus, cluster 1 corresponds to the political core (i.e., block 1), while cluster 3 corresponds to the political periphery (i.e., block 3) and the two broker blocks (i.e., blocks 2 and 4) correspond to clusters 2 and 4, respectively. The specific influence profiles of the clusters are described in Figs. 3 and 4.

Figures 3 and 4 demonstrate that on average, governmental organizations exert the highest influence on other organizations, with an average influence share of 39%, followed by donor organizations, with an average influence share of 18%. On average, agribusiness, farm and civil society interest groups exert only moderate influence on other organizations, with shares ranging from 8% (IG-AB) to 12% (IG-farm). A more detailed analysis of the influence of governmental organizations reveals that the main influence on other organizations is exerted by public agencies and other ministries (i.e, MoIWD and MoDPC). In contrast, the central governmental institutions (i.e., MoAFS, MoF and the president) exert little influence on

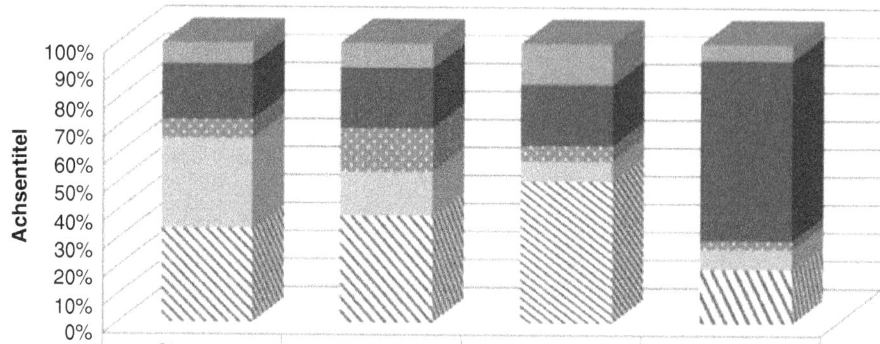

	Cluster1	Cluster2	Cluster3	Cluster4
CSO	8%	9%	15%	6%
IG-AGR	19%	21%	22%	68%
Reseach	7%	15%	6%	3%
Donor	32%	15%	7%	8%
Gov	33%	37%	51%	20%

Fig. 3 Influence profiles in the CAADP policy network in Malawi. Source: Authors

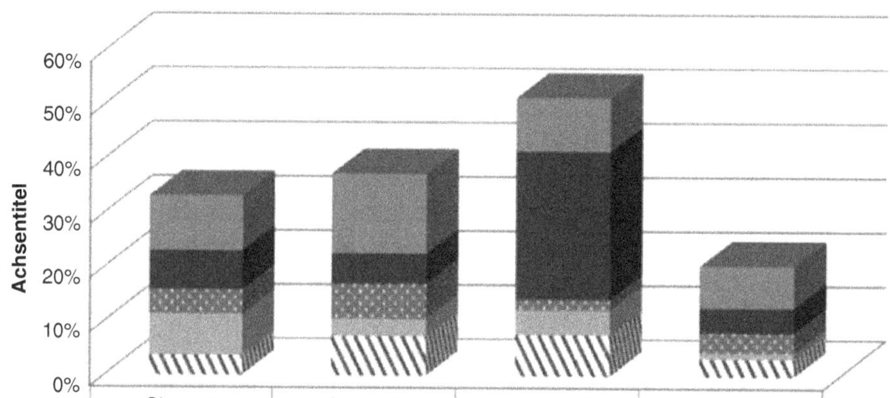

	Cluster1	Cluster2	Cluster3	Cluster4
pub_ag	10%	15%	10%	8%
oMin	7%	6%	27%	5%
MoAFS	4%	6%	2%	4%
MoF	8%	3%	5%	1%
OPC	4%	7%	8%	3%

Fig. 4 Relative influence of governmental organizations in profile clusters. Source: Authors

other organizations (see Fig. 4). A comparison of the average influence across clusters reveals interesting characteristic patterns. Cluster 1, which corresponds to the political core, is strongly influenced by donor organizations, with a share of 32%. Governmental organizations have a particularly low influence compared to the average influence in the network, with a share of only 33% compared to an average of 39% for all organizations.

While it is conceivable that donor organizations that represent the majority in the political core primarily influence each other, please note that the MoF is also highly influenced by donor organizations, which have a share of 30%. Analogously, CISANET and NASFAM, which are both members of cluster 1, are characterized by high influence shares of 31% and 25%, respectively, for donor organizations.

In contrast, cluster 3, which corresponds to the political periphery (i.e., block 3), is extraordinarily influenced by governmental organizations, with a share of 51% compared to an average share of 39% in the entire network. Within governmental organizations, the "other ministries" MoIWD and MoDPC exert a particularly significant influence on the periphery (i.e., cluster 3), with an average share of 27%. Moreover, cluster 3 is the only cluster that is characterized by a significant influence of civil society organizations, with a share of 15% compared to an average of only 10% for all organizations. A significantly different influence profile was observed for the most important national farmer organization (i.e., FUM in cluster 4). Cluster 4 is characterized by a particularly high influence of farm organizations, with an average influence share of 55%. Please note that this share includes only the influence of other organizations. Thus, the farm organizations FUM, TAM and CAMAL in cluster 4 are dominantly influenced by other farm organizations. In contrast, governmental and donor organizations have significantly lower influences of 20% and 8%, respectively, compared to the average influence in the network. Finally, cluster 2 is characterized by an extraordinary influence of national research organizations and a lower influence of public agencies, with an influence share of 15% for both categories. Moreover, agribusiness has a slightly higher influence on cluster 2 compared to the average of all organizations (see Figs. 3 and 4).

Interestingly, although cluster 2 corresponds to the technical block (i.e., block 2) and includes 2 of the 3 members of block 2, some interesting differences can still be observed. In particular, MoAFS is a member of cluster 2. Hence, although MoAFS is an important member of the political core, the influence field operating on MoAFS differs significantly from the influence field operating on the other core members. First, in contrast to MoF, donor organizations exert comparatively less influence on MoAFS. Instead, agribusiness and farmer interest groups exert a significantly higher influence. Second, domestic research organizations exert more influence on MoAFS than MoF.

Overall, the identified influence structures reveal that governmental actors heavily influence other nongovernmental organizations. Interestingly, the main influence is exerted by the ministries MoIWD and MoDPC and organizations in the political periphery, while none of the central governmental institutions (i.e., MoAFS, MoF or the president [OPC]) exert significant influence on other organizations. Moreover, we found clear evidence for a donor-led policy process, where donors exert influence on the lead ministries MoF and MoAFS. Furthermore, public agencies, particularly ADD, take a technical leadership role, exerting relatively high political influence on the political periphery, including OBC, and on the lead ministries (i.e., MoF and MoAFS) in the political core. In comparison to public agencies and donors, the technical leadership of the national research sector (i.e., BC) is less pronounced, with a significant influence on only public agencies and the agribusiness organizations in cluster 2. In contrast, BC's influence on the ministries is rather low. From a society perspective, only agribusiness and farm organizations exert political influence; however, these organizations primarily influence themselves. In contrast, with the exception of MoAFS, governmental organizations are not significantly influenced by agricultural interest organizations. Civil society organizations clearly lag behind other organizations and only exert influence in the political periphery, and the parliamentary parties are completely negligible, with only minor relative influence shares below 3% for nearly all organizations. Thus, in contrast to many parliamentary systems in Western Europe, party leadership of the public political discourse can clearly be denied in Malawi.

It is also important to determine the impact of these specific influence structures on political performance. To answer this question, we must combine the network multiplier with political decisionmaking power to derive the total political power of organizations. As described in Chapter "Whither participation? Evaluating participatory policy processes with the CGPE approach: The case of CAADP in Malawi", we measure political decisionmaking power by applying a composite political bargaining game that includes a modified legislative bargaining game and a modified Grossman and Helpman lobbying game. The solution of the composite game corresponds to a two-step procedure, where we first derive the legislative decisionmaking power of the involved legislators from the modified BF game and subsequently derive the lobbying power of the political agents by applying a generalized political exchange model, as suggested by Pappi and Henning (1998, 1999) and Henning (2009), in a second step. In the modified BF model, legislative power is derived from the set of winning coalitions, where this set is determined by formal constitutional rules and informal legislative norms. By constitution, Malawi is a presidential democracy, where legislative regulations are decided by the parliament under a simple majority rule. By constitution, the president lacks a binding veto power and the government has no binding agenda-setting power vis-à-vis the parliament. Nevertheless, in political practice, the parliament exerts no significant legislative power and is reduced to a pure acclamation machine; the real legislative power rests in the government (Patel and Tostensen 2006). Accordingly, we constructed relevant legislative games, accounting for the dominant role of governmental institutions as legislative norms. However, the literature is ambiguous regarding the specific role of different governmental institutions, namely the power of the involved ministries and the president. Therefore, we constructed different legislative games. In particular, we assumed that agricultural policy in Malawi is decided following the principle of departmental responsibility (PDR) (i.e., MoAFS has agenda-setting power vis-à-vis the cabinet, including the president, and the cabinet decides with a simple majority). Alternatively, in the power scenario PA, we assume that the president functions as a "primus inter pares" in his cabinet (i.e., we assume that the president has agenda-setting power vis-à-vis his cabinet). Furthermore, we assumed that the ministry MoF dominates the political process (i.e., MoF has agenda-setting power vis-à-vis the cabinet [FA]). For all scenarios, we assume that within the cabinet, only the president, MoAFS, MoF and the ministries MoIWD and MoDPC have effective voting power. Please note that

Table 4 Banzhaf power indices

	PDR	PA	FA	PL
President	0.1765	0.2941	0.1765	0
MoAFS	0.2941	0.1765	0.1765	0
MoF	0.1765	0.1765	0.2941	0
MoDPC	0.1765	0.1765	0.1765	0
MoIWD	0.1765	0.1765	0.1765	0
DPP	0	0	0	1
MCP	0	0	0	0
$\sum$	1	1	1	1

Source: Calculated by the authors using IOP 2.0 by Thomas Bräuninger and Thomas König

according to interviewed experts, other ministries that are official members of the cabinet play a minor role in the agricultural process. Therefore, these ministries are excluded from our analysis. Finally, in a contrasting scenario, we assume that legislative decisionmaking in Malawi is characterized by party leadership (PL) (i.e., policies are decided by a majority in the parliament, as foreseen in the constitutions, and the government is not involved). Table 4 summarizes the calculated Banzhaf indices for the different constructed legislative scenarios. This table demonstrates that for the 3 government-led scenarios, legislative decisionmaking power is shifted among MoAFS, MoF and the president. In contrast, assuming party leadership, total legislative power is concentrated on the majority party in the parliament (i.e., DPP).

Following Eq. (3), combining legislative decisionmaking power with the political support network multipliers derived from the political support network generates the political decisionmaking power of an organization. In Fig. 6, we present the simulated support network multipliers assuming different support network structures and varying interest of politicians in political support. In particular, we simulated scenarios in which politicians have no, low and high interest in political support, which are labeled as the autarkic, strong and weak state scenarios, respectively, in Fig. 5. Further, we simulated scenarios in which political access is dominated by donor, farm and CSO organizations, which are labeled as donor, farm and CSO lobbying dominance, respectively, in Fig. 5.[8] Thus, we simulated a total of 4 legislative scenarios for each of the 9 lobbying scenarios. Thus, we simulated a total of 36 political power scenarios, where we used the prediction power of the corresponding political decisionmaking model as a criterion for selecting the empirically relevant model. The best fit to the observed ASWAp decision is achieved by assuming a strong state and donor-dominated lobbying scenario in combination with agenda-setting power for MoAFS (PDR).

[8]Technically, we incorporated the dominance of a specific nongovernmental organization category by multiplying the interest in political support provided by the dominating category by 2 and renormalizing accordingly to derive the corresponding support network multipliers.

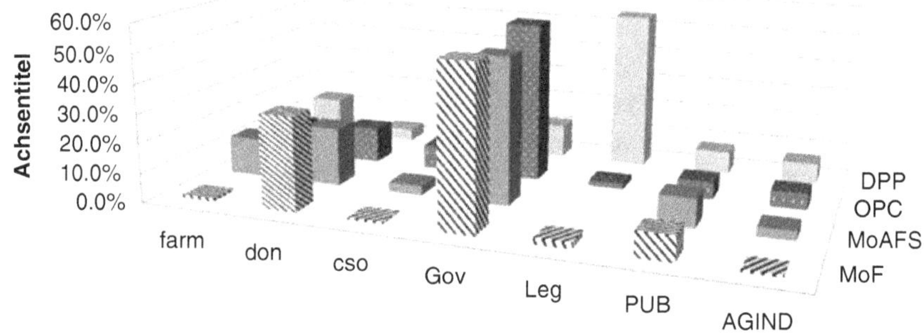

	farm	don	cso	Gov	Leg	PUB	AGIND
MoF	1.2%	31.9%	0.8%	54.7%	2.2%	8.5%	0.7%
MoAFS	13.3%	20.0%	3.3%	50.0%		10.0%	3.3%
OPC	11.0%	12.3%	8.3%	54.9%	1.9%	6.0%	5.6%
DPP	13.5%	4.3%	1.0%	11.7%	54.6%	8.0%	7.0%

Fig. 5 Network multipliers for the political support network of the CAADP process in Malawi. Source: Authors

In Fig. 5, the support network multipliers for different organizational categories are presented for the empirically best-fit scenario (i.e., assuming a strong state with low politician interest in political support and a political support network that is dominated by international donor organizations).[9]

Figure 5 demonstrates that all governmental organizations, especially MoF and MoAFS, strongly depend on the political support provided by international donors. Basically, this pattern reflects the fact that the Malawi government depends on the financial resources provided by donor organizations; in exchange, the government is willing to make political compromises favoring the position of the donors. In contrast to the government, the legislative parties rely less on donor support and more on domestic stakeholder organizations, especially farm interest groups. Overall, the average power outflow from governmental and legislative organizations is approximately 55%, which is moderate compared to other political systems (e.g., for the European Union, an average power outflow of 70% is observed for national members of the agricultural council) (Pappi and Henning 1999).

Following Eqs. (1, 2, and 3), we calculated the total political power by combing the political power derived from the political bargaining game, including lobbying, with the political influence derived from political communication networks. We calculated the total power distribution across organizational categories for the best-fit scenario (i.e., PDR and a donor-dominated lobbying structure) assuming no (i.e., autarkic state), medium (i.e., strong state) and high (i.e., weak state) interest of governmental organizations in political support.

[9]Please note that the average network multipliers calculated for all 9 lobbying scenarios do not significantly differ from the values presented in Fig. 5.

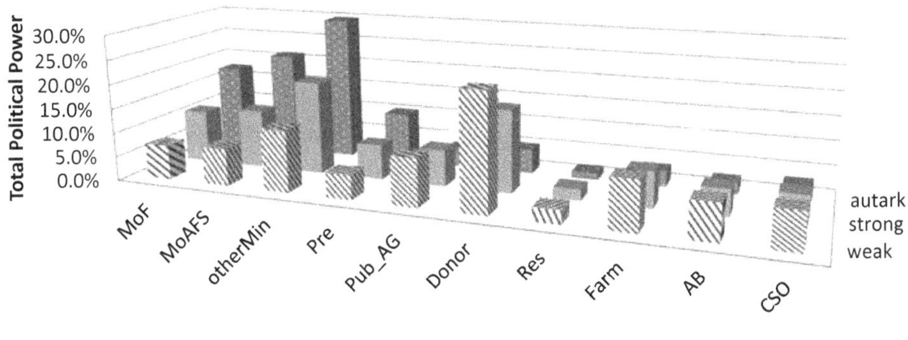

	MoF	MoAFS	otherMin	Pre	Pub_AG	Donor	Res	Farm	AB	CSO
weak	7.1%	7.6%	12.7%	5.1%	9.7%	23.7%	2.9%	10.0%	7.4%	7.6%
strong	10.8%	12.1%	19.1%	7.1%	7.5%	16.8%	2.3%	7.4%	5.4%	5.8%
autark	17.5%	21.2%	29.8%	10.3%	3.7%	5.0%	1.4%	3.2%	2.3%	3.0%

Fig. 6 Total political power distribution in Malawi according to lobbying scenario. Source: Authors

Figure 7 demonstrates that excluding lobbying, the total political power would be highly concentrated on governmental organizations, where MoAFS and MoF are particularly powerful ministries, with individual total powers of 17.5% and 21.2%, respectively. The other two involved ministries (i.e., MoIWD and MoDPC) are comparatively less powerful as individual institutions, with a joint power of 29.8%. In Fig. 6, we interpreted the OBC as the institution representing the president. Following this interpretation, for all lobbying scenarios, the president has a significantly lower total political power than the ministries, ranging from only 5.1% for the weak scenario to 10.3% for the autarkic scenario.[10] Without lobbying, the total legislative power outflow from governmental to nongovernmental organizations is relatively low at approximately 20% (see the autarkic scenario in Fig. 6). Including lobbying power, the outflow increases significantly to 50% assuming a medium interest in political support (i.e., the strong state scenario) and to nearly 70% assuming a high interest (i.e., the weak state scenario). Power outflows directed to national stakeholder organizations are even lower, ranging from only 12% to 34%. International donor organization exhibit nearly the same amount of power outflow as all national stakeholder organizations combined (see Fig. 6). A smaller amount of the total power outflow goes to public agencies that are subordinate to the ministries.

[10]In Malawi, a special case occurred in 2010 in which the President of Malawi and the minister of agriculture were present simultaneously. However, in our analyses, we do not focus on persons but on institutions; therefore, we interpreted MoA and the president as two independent corporate actors. Following this interpretation implies different total political power for the president and the MoA, as reported in Fig. 6.

5 Evaluating Identified Participation Structures

In this section, we discuss how the identified participation structures impact political performance. In particular, we assess governmental performance by applying the derived indicators to measure political accountability, capture, and ownership and effective use of political knowledge. To evaluate different dimensions of political performance, it is important to define adequate benchmark levels. Because by construction, all indicators lie in the [0–1] interval, 1 is a default benchmark value for all indices. However, for some indices, different benchmark values appear to be more appropriate. For example, when measuring accountability by the total political power of national stakeholder organizations (GA-total), it appears unrealistic to assume that perfect accountability corresponds to a situation in which stakeholders control 100% of the total power. Depending on the degree to which democratic elections imply incentives for politicians to represent society's interests, the optimal level of accountability induced through stakeholder participation varies. Given a relatively low level of government accountability induced by elections, as is the case in Malawi (see Chapter "Voter Behavior and Government Performance in Malawi: An Application of a Probabilistic Voting Model"), we assume a benchmark value of 0.5 for all three accountability measures. Analogously, when measuring political knowledge used in the policy process by the power share of national research organizations, it also appears adequate to take a benchmark value below 1. The latter inference results from the fact a benchmark value of 1 implies that the political knowledge of research organizations is infinitely higher than that of other political organizations. Hence, because Bunda College is the only national research organization in Malawi, we took 0.05 as an appropriate benchmark value for our knowledge indicator "PK-research". Finally, when measuring the involvement of national stakeholder organizations in political communication using the network density as an indicator, a benchmark value of 0.5 appears to be more appropriate. Please note that a density of 1 implies that every stakeholder organization communicates with every governmental organization, which would be rather unrealistic and inefficient. This inefficiency results from the fact that brokerage via national peak organizations and subordinated state agencies allows for more efficient communication between government and stakeholder organizations.

Renormalizing the calculated performance indices to the [0–1] interval using appropriate benchmark values, we present the calculated performance indices in an evaluation wheel, as demonstrated in Fig. 7 below. We consider the evaluation wheel a helpful tool for illustrating the impact of the identified participation network structures on the different dimensions of political performance. A closer evaluation of Fig. 7 reveals that overall, the policy process in Malawi implies only a moderate achievement of political performance, where most indicators values reach 50% or less of their benchmark values (see Fig. 7). At first glance, government capture appears to play only a minor rule in the CAADP policy process in Malawi, with a performance level for total capture (GC-total) reaching over 70% of the

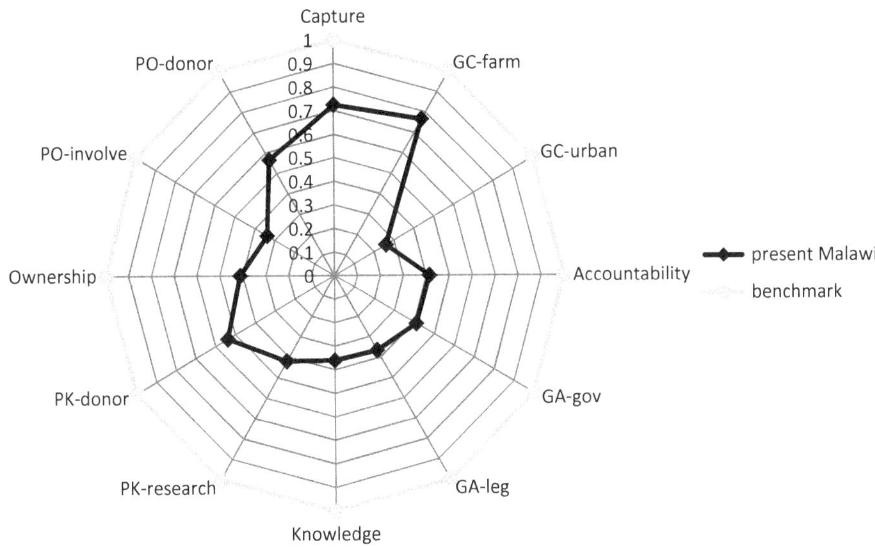

Fig. 7 Participation structures and political performance in the CAADP process of Malawi. Source: Authors

benchmark value, which corresponds to a complete avoidance of capture. However, a close evaluation partially reverses this conclusion. In particular, to construct the capture index, we used the different household types that have been separated in the Malawi CGE (i.e., small-, medium- and large-scale agricultural households and urban consumer households). To calculate the representation of different household types in the political process, we calculated the relative shares of household types in the value-added share of each economic subsector. The higher the value-added share of a subsector that is allocated to a household type, the more the socioeconomic interest groups representing this subsector represent this household type in the political process. Therefore, we matched all agricultural, agribusiness and non-agricultural interest groups in our policy network with economic subsectors. Based on these matches, we could calculate the representation rate of different household types for each organization. Finally, weighting these organizational representation rates by the total power of organizations generates the representation share of a household type in the political process. These shares are compared to the corresponding population shares of household types to derive our capture index. For example, agricultural export crops (i.e., tobacco, coffee and tea) are primarily produced by large-scale farm households (i.e., 30% of the total value-added share of these sectors ends up in the pocket of large-scale farm households, but only 3% of all Malawian households are in this household category). Thus, interest groups like TAM, CAMAL and TAMA that focus on representing these subsectors over-represent large-scale farm households, and general farm organizations, such as FUM, that represent all agricultural subsectors proportionally represent all farm households. A special case corresponds to the National Smallholder Farmers' Association of Malawi (NASFAM), which is focused on representing small- and medium-scale farmers. Therefore, we exogenously assume that NASFAM only represents these two household types. Interestingly, overall, medium farm households (e.g., households that operate farms with a size between 0.75 and 3 hectares of land) are extremely underrepresented, as indicated by a difference of approximately 26 percentage points between the population share and the political representation share for this household type. In contrast, urban households are extremely overrepresented in the political process, with the same difference of approximately 26 percentage points between the representation share of urban households and the urban population share. Thus, political participation is clearly biased against rural households and in favor of urban households. This bias can be observed in the relatively low value of the capture sub-indicator GC-urban. In absolute terms, the share of the total political power that represents the interest of urban households is nearly 3 times higher than the urban population share. However, because urban households comprise only 9% of all Malawian households, the total capture remains low.

Finally, we would like to make one further comment on the interpretation of the impact of the identified participation structures on the achievement of a political consensus. Compared to the benchmark level of 1, the current participation structures imply only a moderate potential for generating a political consensus, as indicated by a level of 41% for the central ownership indicator Ownership. However, as demonstrated in Fig. 8, political communication implies a remarkable reduction of political conflict in the complete network. This reduction is demonstrated in Fig. 8, which compares the range of the convex hull that covers all preferred policy positions before and after communication (see the outer and medium set, respectively, in Fig. 8). Moreover, Fig. 8 demonstrates that the

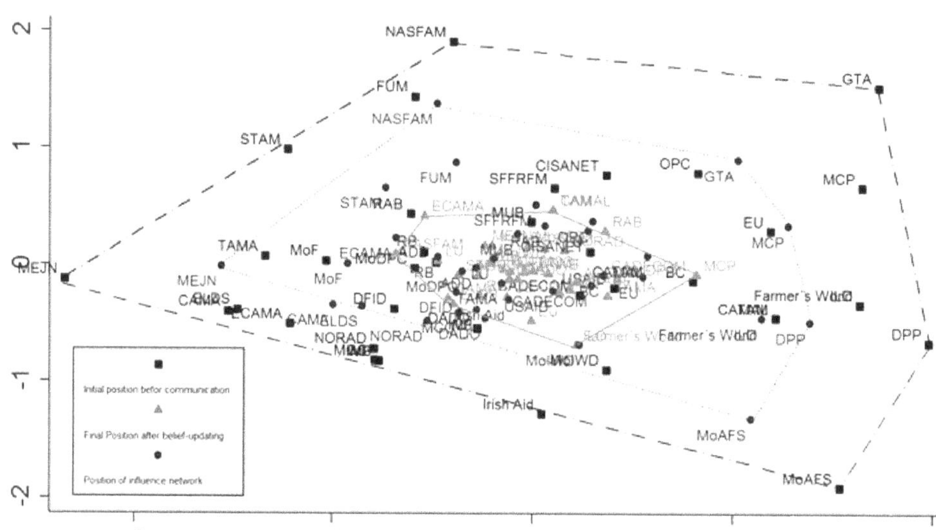

Fig. 8 Participation structures and political consensus in the CAADP process of Malawi. Source: Authors

influence fields that operate on the different organizations imply extremely homogenous policy positions (see the set covering the inner dots in Fig. 8). Thus, if governmental organizations were more open to the opinions and viewpoints that other organizations communicate in the political discourse, the communication network structure in Malawi would imply a political consensus. Therefore, an evaluation of the identified communication structures against a benchmark of 1 might lead to result that is too pessimistic with regard to the potential to achieve political ownership via political consensus.

6 From Diagnosis to Therapy: Lessons Concerning Efficient Design of Participatory Policy Processes

To identify potential strategies for improving participatory and evidence-based policy processes, we simulated the variation of political performance indicators assuming changed formal and informal rules determining participation structures. We simulated political performance for all 45 legislative and lobbying scenarios; however, in the following section, we focus on the most relevant results. First, for both types of participation, we change the level of participation intensity without changing the participation structure. With respect to lobbying, the level of politician interest in political support is changed, keeping both the relative interests of politicians and the access to politicians constant. Accordingly, with respect to political communication, we change the level of own control of politicians, keeping the communication network structure and the relative own control among politicians constant. Second, we change the participation structure (i.e., we shift the participation bias from the identified *donor-dominated* participation structure to a *CSO- and farm-dominated* participation structure. Finally, we simulated how political performance changes assuming a constitutional reform from the present PDR to *party leadership*. We present the results for these four scenarios in Fig. 9. In detail, it is assumed in the "no lobby scenario" that politicians have no interest in political support. In contrast, improved access of national stakeholder organizations is simulated in the "CSO lead" scenario. Technically, the latter scenario is generated by recalculating the support network multipliers under the assumption that the relative interest of politicians in political support provided by national stakeholder organizations[11] is increased. In the "open discourse scenario," we multiplied the own control of politicians by 0.7 and recalculated the communication network multipliers. Finally, in the "party leadership" scenario, we simulated a constitutional reform of the legislative process from the *PDR* to *party leadership* (PL). Please note that with respect to content, such a reform might correspond to a formal constitutional reform from a presidential to a parliamentary system. However, such

[11] Compared to the best-fit scenario, we multiplied the interest in political support of national stakeholders by 2 and divided the interest in support of donor organizations by 2.

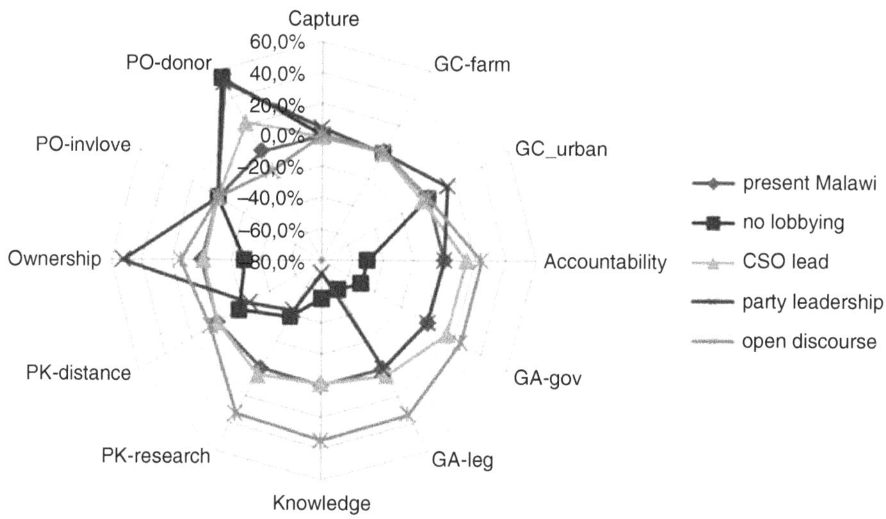

Fig. 9 The impact of changed participation structures on political performance in Malawi, as indicated by percent change in comparison to the base-run scenario. Source: Authors

a reform might also result from changed legislative norms without a formal change of the constitution.[12]

For all simulation scenarios, we take the best-fit scenario (see Fig. 7) as a base-run scenario and present the percent change in political performance indicators in comparison to their corresponding values in the base-run in Fig. 9.

As demonstrated in Fig. 8, lobbying has a significant positive impact on nearly all political performance indicators. Only the dominance of international donor organizations is less pronounced assuming no lobbying occurs (i.e., without lobbying, international stakeholder organizations would not be able to gain much political influence, and Malawi's civil society would take more ownership in CAADP reforms due to a feeling that these reforms are less imposed by the international donor community). However, as demonstrated in Fig. 9, without lobbying, the final political decision regarding CAADP would also be more distant to the desires of Malawi civil society, implying a lower political consensus and less political ownership, as indicated by a decrease of approximately 30% in the indicator Ownership for the "no lobbying scenario" (see Fig. 9). Moreover, increasing the importance of lobbying without changing the relative lobbying power of organizations implies that there will be no impact on capture. Accordingly, for the no lobbying scenario, all capture indices remain unchanged in comparison to their base-run values. The main positive impacts of increased participation via lobbying can be observed for the effective use of political knowledge and for accountability. The use of political

[12]By constitution, even in most presidential systems, the official legislative power resides entirely in the parliament.

knowledge decreased by nearly 60% when comparing the no lobby scenario to the base-run scenario (see Fig. 9).

Analogously, government accountability increases significantly with lobbying, with the accountability level decreasing by approximately 50% for the no lobbying scenario compared to the base-run scenario (see Fig. 9). Interestingly, the positive impact of lobbying does not change significantly if different lobby structures are assumed. Hence, as demonstrated in Fig. 9, for the CSO scenario, the majority of performance indicators remain unchanged (e.g., they lie on the 0% line in Fig. 9). The only exemptions are accountability (GA-total), which improves by 20%, and the dominance of donor organization (PO-donor), which is significantly reduced when changing form donor-dominated to CSO- or farm-dominated lobbying structures.[13]

As described above, the high own control of politicians is a characteristic feature of the CAADP policy process in Malawi, which implies that politicians rely primarily on their own expertise when making policy choices. As demonstrated in Fig. 9, increasing the importance of public discourse for the political belief updating of politicians would imply that wisdom of the crowd effects can be better exploited in Malawi. Thus, in particular, the effective use of political knowledge would increase significantly. Please note that in this context, increasing the physical participation of stakeholders fails to automatically guarantee higher political influence of stakeholders because the political influence of stakeholders only results if politicians in fact update their beliefs based on the political views and opinions communicated by national stakeholders. Thus, as long as stakeholder participation is only formally imposed, as is partially true for the CAADP process in Malawi, the impact on performance is rather limited. A change in the political culture such that politicians increasingly consider the potential political expertise of national stakeholders is needed. However, in this context, a warning also appears necessary. An increase in the effective participation of national stakeholders in political communication only triggers wisdom of the crowd effects and improves political performance if stakeholders have a relatively high political knowledge in comparison to their total political power. Our analysis indicates that this scenario is relevant for Malawi, but this scenario does not necessarily hold true for other countries.

Finally, shifting legislative power from the government to the parliament implies a trade-off between increased political ownership and sharply decreased effective use of political knowledge. In contrast, political incentives (i.e., accountability and capture) are only slightly changed by this power shift (see the party leadership scenario in Fig. 9). Basically, this result follows from the fact that in contrast to governmental organizations, parliamentary parties have significantly less political knowledge (see Fig. 10 in the appendix). Hence, although these parties are generally more open to political opinions communicated by other organizations in the political discourse (i.e., parties have a lower own control), the overall effect of this

[13]Please note, however, that shifting the dominance from donor to farm organizations has a positive impact on government capture, as farmers are better represented.

scenario is negative in Malawi. In contrast, party leadership has a strong positive impact on political ownership. First, deciding budget allocations for CAADP policy programs under a party leadership implies that these allocations would be much closer to the allocations preferred by civil society organizations (i.e., political ownership in CAADP reforms would significantly increase), as indicated by a nearly 60% increase in the indicator Ownership (see Fig. 9). Moreover, the political power exerted by international donor organizations would be significantly lower for the party leadership scenario than for the base-run scenario. Thus, under party leadership, the civil society of Malawi would be less likely to perceive that CAADP reforms are imposed by international donors.

7 Conclusion

Although participatory and evidence-based policy processes are increasingly promoted at the academic level and in political practice, the current understanding of the impact of these processes on political performance is still in its infancy. In this context, this paper proposes a network-based framework for analyzing and evaluating participatory and evidence-based policy processes. Specifically, we consider the following points to be the main contributions of our approach:

1. The approach is theoretically founded. In particular, we derive our theoretical framework by incorporating a network model of political belief formation into a political bargaining model of the Baron-Grossman-Helpman type (BGH). The latter model combines a generalized Grossman-Helpman lobbying model and a modified legislative bargaining model of the Baron and Ferejohn type. The central component of this integrated model corresponds to a generalized mean voter decision-rule, where in addition to legislators, interest groups also have political control over policies (Pappi and Henning 1998; Henning 2000, 2009). Within our approach, the political control of nongovernmental organizations results from two different mechanisms: lobbying and communication learning. The first mechanism is determined by the political access structures by which nongovernmental organizations access powerful governmental organizations, and the second mechanism is determined by political communication among organizations.
2. Our approach is empirically applicable, where the equilibrium outcome of the extended BGH-model can be derived from observed political support and communication networks. Technically, political decisions are determined by three components in equilibrium: constitutional rules and legislative norms captured by legislative decisionmaking power indices, political access structures captured by support network multipliers and political communication structures captured by communication network multipliers. Accordingly, standard social network tools, such as block modeling, can first be applied to describe basic participation structures quantitatively. Second, innovative network-based tools (i.e., network multipliers and total political power) are derived to describe essential participatory structures.

3. Further, based on our model, political performance indicators can be theoretically derived and empirically measured. In particular, based on the empirical application of our approach to the CAADP reform process in Malawi, we can draw the following general conclusions regarding the impact of participation structures on political performance:

   a. Political performance is a multidimensional concept that includes well-established governmental incentive problems (i.e., governmental accountability and capture), as reported in the political economy literature. In addition, the lack of political ownership that corresponds to an incentive problem of the society or to the lack of political knowledge is another important source of policy failure.
   b. We demonstrated that a trade-off typically exists between different aspects of political performance (i.e., a participation structure favoring one specific aspect of political performance simultaneously impedes another). For example, in Malawi, we found a trade-off between political ownership and the use of political knowledge, shifting the legislative power from the government to the legislative parties. Moreover, the high political influence of international donor organizations increases the use of political knowledge but simultaneously decreases political ownership.
   c. The impact of participation structures on political performance depends on specific framework conditions (i.e., the same structure can enhance political performance in one country and impede performance in another). For example, an increase in the political influence of national civil society organizations via lobbying or political communication has a significant positive impact on the effective use of political knowledge in Malawi. However, this positive impact depends on the fact that in Malawi, national stakeholders have relatively high political knowledge in comparison to their actual political influence. Accordingly, no blueprint participation structures are optimal for all countries.

4. Because our approach is theoretically founded, we can perform simulations to identify participation structures that imply higher political performance. However, a concrete strategy for implementing the identified improved participation structures in political practice cannot yet be derived from our approach. With respect to changed policy network structures, such a strategy demands a theory that explains the network-generating process. We address this very interesting topic in Chapter "The Formation of Elite Communication Networks in Malawi: A Bayesian Econometric Approach". However, beyond network structures, participation is also determined by the own control and interest in political support of politicians. Improving our understanding of the determinants of these components is an interesting topic that we leave for future work.
5. Finally, we must admit that the relevance of our assessments to political practice depends on the assumption that our theoretical model correctly describes political decisionmaking in real political systems. In this regard, we use the prediction power of our approach to assess its empirical relevance. With respect to the CAADP reform in Malawi, our best-fit specification nicely predicts the empirically observed budget allocations, with an average prediction error below 20%.

Appendix

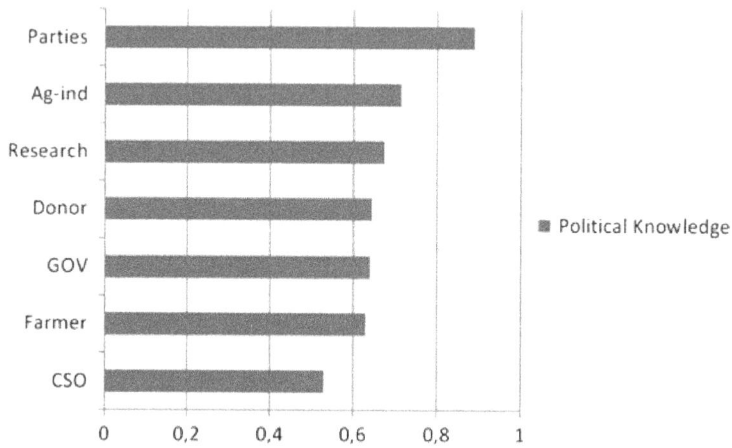

Fig. 10 Average political knowledge in Malawi according to organizational category. Source: Authors

Table 5 Organizations in Malawi: acronym, type and name

Acronym	Type	Name	Reputation	Block	Cluster
MoF	GOV	Ministry of Finance	0.79	1	1
MoAFS	GOV	Ministry of Agriculture and Food Security	1.00	1	2
MoIWD	GOV	Ministry of Irrigation and Water Development	0.67	2	3
MoDPC	GOV	Ministry of Dev. Planning and Cooperation	0.45	3	3
RB	PUB	Reserve Bank	0.27	3	1
OPC	GOV	Office of the President and the Cabinet	0.48	3	3
SFFRFM	PUB	Smallholder Farmers Fertilizer Revolving Fund	0.45	3	3
LU	PUB	Logistics Unit	0.30	3	1
DPP	LEG	Democratic Progressive Party	0.70	3	3
MCP	LEG	Malawi Congress Party	0.33	3	3
ADD	PUB	Agricultural Development Divisions	0.67	2	2
DADO	PUB	District Agricultural Development Offices	0.52	3	3
DFID	DON	Department for International Devel-opment UK	0.82	1	1
Irish Aid	DON	Irish Aid	0.67	1	1
NORAD	DON	Norwegian Agency for Dev. Cooperation	0.58	1	1

(continued)

Table 5 (continued)

Acronym	Type	Name	Reputation	Block	Cluster
USAID	DON	USAID	0.73	1	1
EU	DON	EU	0.85	1	1
IMF	DON	International Monetary Fund	0.55	1	1
WB	DON	World Bank	0.82	1	1
BC	RES	Bunda College	0.82	2	2
FW	IG-AB	Farmer's World	0.55	1	3
ILO	IG-AB	Ilovo Sugar	0.33	3	3
RAB	IG-AB	Rab Processors	0.27	3	2
STAM	IG-AB	Seed Trade Association of Malawi	0.61	1	1
MUB	IG-AB	Mulli Bros.	0.52	3	1
GTA	IG-AB	Grain Trader Association	0.61	3	2
FUM	IG-farm	Farmers Union Malawi	0.79	4	4
NASFAM	IG-farm	National Smallholder Farmers' Ass. of Malawi	0.73	3	1
CISANET	IG-CSO	CISANET	0.58	1	1
TAM	IG-AB	Tea Association of Malawi	0.52	3	4
TAMA	IG-AB	Tobacco Association Malawi	0.52	3	2
MEJN	IG-NAG	Malawi Economic Justice Network	0.55	3	3
ECAMA	IG-NAG	Economics Association of Malawi	0.39	3	3
CAMA	IG-Con	Consumers Association of Malawi	0.52	3	3
MCC	IG-Chur	Malawi Council of Churches	0.39	3	1
ELDS	IG-Chur	Evangelical Lutheran Development	0.36	3	3
CADECOM	IG-Chur	Catholic Development Commission	0.55	3	2

Source: Calculated by authors from own survey data

Notes: GOV: Government, IG- (AB: Agribusiness, farm: Farmers, CSO: Civil society or private sector organization, NAG: Non-Agrar, Con: Consumers Associations, Chur: Churches), PUB: Public sector agency or local government organization, LEG: Political party, DON: Donor organizations, RES: Research organizations

References

Aberman, N.-L., M. Johnson, K. Droppelmann, E. Schiffer, R. Birner, and P. Gaff. 2012. *Mapping the Contemporary Fertilizer Policy Landscape in Malawi*. IFPRI Discussion Paper 01204. Washington, DC: International Food Policy Research Institute.

Adserà, A., C. Boix, and M. Payne. 2003. Are You Being Served? Political Accountability and Quality of Government. *The Journal of Law, Economics and Organization* 19 (2): 445–489.

Ball, R. 1995. Interest Groups, Influence and Welfare. *Economics and Politics* 7 (2): 119–146.

Bardhan, P., and D. Mookherjee. 2002. *Relative Capture of Local and Central Governments: An Essay in the Political Economy of Decentralization*. Working Paper C99-109. Center of International and Development Economics Research (CIDER).

Beilhartz, H.-J., and H. Gersbach. 2004. *General Equilibirium Effects and Voting into a Crisis*. CEPR Discussion Paper 4454. London: Centre for Economic Policy Research.

Birner, R., and D. Resnick. 2010. The Political Economy of Policies for Smallholder Agriculture. *World Development* 38 (10): 1442–1452.

Bischoff, I., and L.-H. Siemers. 2011. Biased Beliefs and Retrospective Voting: Why Democracies Choose Mediocre Policies. *Public Choice* 156: 163–180.

Caplan, B. 2007. *The Myth of the Rational Voter—Why Democracies Choose Bad Politics*. Princeton, NJ: Princeton University Press.

Chambote, R., and A. Shankland. 2011. *Country Ownership, Stakeholder Participation and the Political Economy of Priority-Setting in the Mozambique Pilot Program for Climate Resilience*. Mozambique Case Study Report. Brighton: Institute of Development Studies.

Coleman, J.S. 1990. *Foundation of Social Theory*. Cambridge: Harvard University Press.

Henning, C.H.C.A. 2000. *Macht und Tausch in der europäischen Agrarpolitik: Eine positive politische Entscheidungstheorie*. Campus: Frankfurt/Main.

———. 2009. Networks of Power in the CAP System of the EU-15 and EU-27. *Journal of Public Policy* 29(Special Issue 02):153–177.

Henning, C.H.C.A., and A. Wald. 2000. Zur Theorie der Interessenvermittlung: Ein Netzwerkansatz dargestellt am Beispiel der gemeinsamen Europäischen Agrarpolitik. *Politische Vierteljahreszeitschrift* 41 (4): 647–676.

Jones, H. 2013. *Building Political Ownership and Technical Leadership*. Cambodia: Cambodia Association Centre for Policy Studies.

Keefer, P., and S. Khemani. 2005. Democracy, Public Expenditures, and the Poor: Understanding Political Incentives for Providing Public Services. *The World Bank Research Observer* 20 (1): 1–27.

Knoke, D., F.U. Pappi, J. Broadbent, and Y. Tsujinaka. 1996. *Comparing Policy Networks: Labor Politics in the U.S., Germany, and Japan*. New York: Cambridge University Press.

Laumann, E.O., and D. Knoke. 1987. *The Organizational State*. Madison, WI: University of Wisconsin Press.

Laumann, E.O., P. Marsden, and D. Prensky. 1989. The Boundary Specification Problem in Network Analysis. In *Research Methods in Social Network Analysis*, ed. L.C. Freeman, D.R. White, and A.K. Romney, 61–87. Fairfax, VA: George Mason University Press.

NEPAD. 2010. The Comprehensive Africa Agriculture Development Programme (CAADP). http://www.nepad-caadp.net/about-caadp.php. Accessed 16 Oct 2013.

Pappi, F.U., and C.H.C.A. Henning. 1998. Policy Networks: More than a Metaphor? *Journal of Theoretical Politics* 10 (4): 553–575.

———. 1999. The Organization of Influence on EC's Common Agricultural Policy: A Network Approach. *European Journal of Political Research* 36 (2): 257–281.

Pappi, F.U., T. König, and D. Knoke. 1995. *Entscheidungsprozesse in der Arbeits- und Sozialpolitik*. Frankfurt/Main: Campus.

Patel, N., and A. Tostensen. 2006. *Parliamentary-Executive Relations in Malawi 1994-2004*. Working Paper WP 2006: 10. Norway: Chr. Michelsen Institute.

Randall, I. 2011. *Guidelines for Non State Actor Participation in CAADP Processes*. Midrand: Wasafiri Consulting.

Sabatier, P.A., and H.C. Jenkins-Smith. 1993. *Policy Change and Learning—An Advocacy Coalition Approach*. Boulder, CO: Westview Press.

The Ministry of Agriculture and Food Security, Republic of Malawi. 2010. Agriculture Sector Wide Approach (ASWAp). Malawi's Prioritised and Harmonised Agricultural Development Agenda. http://www.caadp.net/pdf/Investment%20plan%20-%20Malawi.pdf. Accessed 16 Oct 2013.

Wasserman, S., and K. Faust. 1994. *Social Network Analysis: Methods and Applications*. Cambridge, MA: Cambridge University Press.

World Bank. 2011. Participation at Project, Program and Policy Level. http://go.worldbank.org/HKL3IU1T21. Accessed 16 Oct 2013.

Christian Henning is professor and chair of agricultural economics, University of Kiel (Germany). He studied economics, agricultural economics, sociology, political science and mathematics. He earned a PhD in economics, in agricultural economics and in political science. His main areas of specialization are applied political economy and applied economic modelling of agricultural policies. To date he has published five books and various articles in refereed journals including PLoS ONE, American Journal of Agricultural Economics, European Review of Agricultural Economics, Journal of Public Policy, Journal of Mathematical Sociology and Journal of Theoretical Politics.

Eva Krampe is an agricultural sector expert at the European Investment Bank. She studied agricultural economics and earned a PhD in agricultural economics at the University of Kiel (Germany). Her main areas of specialization are Agricultural Policies in the European Union and Sub-Saharan Africa, Applied Political Economy, Agriculture Value Chain Finance, and Economic Analysis of Agricultural Investment Projects.

9

Malawian Elite Communication Networks and their Formation

Christian Aßmann, Eva Krampe, and Christian Henning

1 Introduction

Lobbying is commonly recognized as a public mechanism to induce policy makers to follow the interests of well-organized groups. Therefore, lobbying is criticized for distorting policies in favor of specific interests at the expense of society. Nevertheless, such political influence activities can also be understood as a mechanism by which interest groups signal their policy preferences. That is, lobbying conveys socially valuable information about the consequences of policies from society to political agents. If better-informed political agents now choose policies that increase social welfare, the provision of strategic information through lobbying can outweigh the negative distortionary effects (Ball 1995 and literature cited therein). Such arguments for the informational benefits of lobbying are also in line with the so-called *wisdom of the crowd* hypothesis. The *wisdom of the crowd* hypothesis suggests that a group of relatively uninformed individuals will collectively have much more knowledge than will any single member of the group (Galton 1907). Such a situation would enable political agents to choose better policies if they receive individual information via communication in elite networks.

C. Aßmann (✉)
University of Bamberg, Chair of Statistics and Econometrics, Bamberg, Germany
e-mail: christian.assmann@uni-bamberg.de

E. Krampe
European Investment Bank, Luxembourg City, Luxembourg

C. Henning
Department of Agricultural Economics, Kiel University, Chair of Agricultural Policy, Kiel, Germany

The major factor determining whether the informational benefits in fact outweigh the distortionary costs is the structure of the political elite's communication network. An important issue here is the tradeoff between the efficient policy learning of individual decisionmakers and a potential policy bias in the whole network that induces negative effects on overall economic performance. Political agents learn efficiently about the impacts of policy decisions on the economic system if they choose communication partners similar in political interests to themselves. Festinger (1954) argues that similar others offer relevant information and that similarity in interests is a well-known determinant of, for instance, friendship. In terms of policy learning, having communication ties with organizations that have similar interests to oneself reduces biased information signals and allows for an individually efficient communication process. However, such individually rational information-gathering routines also lead to policy distortions in favor of the group with the same interests as the political decisionmakers.

We suggest an empirical approach allowing for quantitative analysis of the informational value and the distorting nature of real-world knowledge diffusion within a country's political elite.[1] Theoretical and observational studies suggest that political actors choose ties with others in a rational and predictable manner (Carpenter et al. 1998, 2004). In particular, the study tackles the following set of questions in order to provide valuable information for designing evidence-based policy formulation processes. Is the network-generating process individually or globally efficient, i.e., is it not distorted in favor of special interests with regard to policy learning? Do structural factors, similar political views, or the level of an alter's expertise determine the choice of contact? Do individual levels of political expertise lead to higher connectivity with other organizations?

We address these questions based on data collected via a series of face-to-face interviews with Malawi's political elite in 2010. This survey has already been described in detail in Chapter "A Network Based Approach to Evaluate Participatory Policy Processes: An Application to CAADP in Malawi" of this volume. The methodological challenge in assessing determinants of elite communication networks with survey data is dealing soundly with missing data. Despite the highest efforts in fieldwork, survey data is almost inevitably subject to item and unit non-response. Our estimation strategy addresses the mentioned data features by adapting the Bayesian estimation scheme for binary probit models based on the Markov Chain Monte Carlo (MCMC) methodology, namely Gibbs sampling, as suggested by Albert and Chib (1993). Based on a sample from the posterior distribution of the model parameters, obtained via iterative sequential sampling from the full conditional distributions, parameter estimates are given as sample moments. This estimation technique, using the device of data augmentation proposed by Tanner and Wong (1987), is well suited to deal with missing values in

[1]We focus on expert information networks because our main interest lies in understanding information-gathering routines of a country's elite. Studying determinants of political support networks and evaluating the nature of non-informative lobbying is left.

explaining factors and missing values within the dependent network relationship. The vector of model parameters subject to posterior inference is augmented to also include the missing values of explaining variables and missing network relationships, where draws for the missing values within explaining factors are then obtained via sequential regression trees, providing non parametric approximations of the underlying full conditional distributions (Burgette and Reiter 2010). The proposed modeling thereby accounts for the uncertainty within parameter estimation due to missing values, as discussed in Butts (2003). We provide a model fitness criterion that allows for gauging the predictive capability of the suggested empirical framework and comparison of non-nested model specifications.

Empirical results suggest that common meeting opportunities and political influence are important determinants of the probability of observing a tie between a pair of organizations, while knowledge is an important but not leading determinant of communication. There is no evidence that information diffusion is affected by interest bias in Malawi. In terms of designing a political communication process, the results suggest that supporting umbrella organizations should increase information flow in the elite network.

This chapter proceeds as follows. We first describe determinants of political communication and corresponding empirical data. Next, we introduce the estimation strategy and the approach to model comparison. This is followed by study results and conclusions.

2 Determinants of Political Communication Networks

In this section, we first review determinants of elite communication structures as typically discussed in literature on political influence of interest groups and social network formation. Next, we provide a description of the variables used to assess empirically the determinants of communication.

2.1 *Theoretical Considerations*

Models used to describe the evolution of ties within networks commonly fall into two groups: preference-driven models and structure-driven models. To accommodate both approaches, we propose three main categories of determinants of political communication: (i) homophily in political interests, (ii) political knowledge or expertise, and (iii) structural factors (see Fig. 1). The first two categories rely upon the preference-driven approach to explain tie formation, while the third category summarizes the structural constraints organizations face in making contacts.

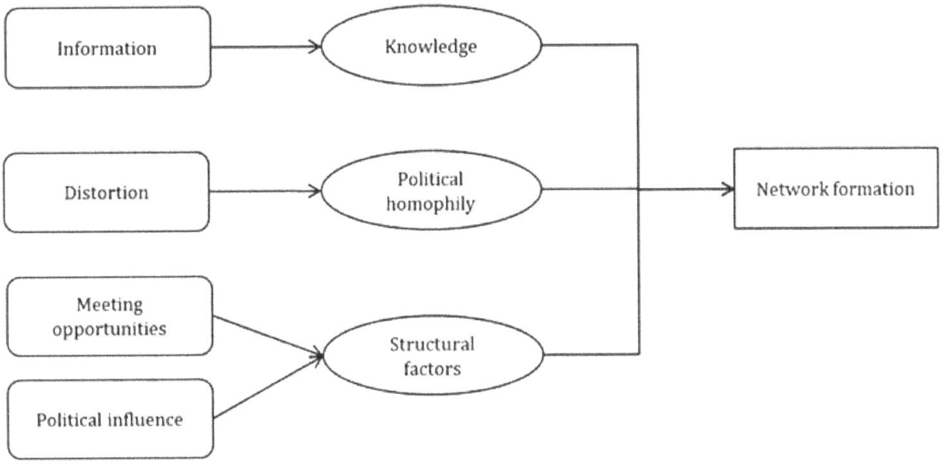

Fig. 1 Determinants of network evolution. Source: Authors

With regard to the first two categories, it is important to consider the two main roles of lobbying, i.e. informing and distorting. Several studies argue for the informational role of lobbying based on theoretical derivations from signaling games (Austen-Smith 1993; Ball 1995; Lohmann 1993). They emphasize that politicians are better able to choose efficient policies if they are being lobbied. Thus, it is rational for political agents to contact nongovernmental organizations with high expertise in a specific policy domain in order to reduce the uncertainty inherent in policy choices. For example, a political goal of agricultural policy is to achieve food security. Based on the dominance of knowledge in tie choice, policymakers should seek advice from organizations with high expert knowledge on, e.g., how a fertilizer subsidy affects food production, household income, and food prices, in order to launch goal-oriented policies.

With regard to expertise as a driver of nongovernmental–nongovernmental relations, consider that expert information is costly and not always publicly available. Nevertheless, an organization's influence on the beliefs of decisionmakers depends primarily on the organization's expertise. Therefore, an organization has the incentive to invest in contact making with experts to reduce uncertainty in their policy beliefs and to increase their reputation as well-informed communication partners.

However, getting informed comes with a price, according to lobbying theories. Information is seldom unbiased and mostly reflects an organization's position, which is biased according to political interests. This bias component leads to policy distortions at the expense of the public interest, if interests are not represented equally. Additionally, it determines a political actor's information-gathering routines. The latter results from the fact that receiving information from sources with similar interests to oneself lowers the likelihood of receiving information that does not match one's own interests in the state of the world (Festinger 1954;

Austen-Smith 1993).[2] Accordingly, communicating with organizations with similar political interests reduces the fiscal, emotional and processing costs of policy learning. It becomes rational for individuals to systematically choose alters that are similar in interests. Therefore, a commonly accepted determinant of tie choice, homophily, can also be applied to understand policy network evolution (for experimental evidence on political homophily as a driver of tie choice, see Knoke (1990), Pappi and Henning (1999), and Moody (2001).[3] In summary, political homophily as a determinant of political communication lowers the likelihood of biased signals for the receiver of information but, assuming an unequal representation of interests and a negative correlation between knowledge and bias, increases the probability of biased, low-value information diffusion in the overall network.

Structural approaches argue that contact opportunities influence an actor's ties. Consider overlapping membership in organizations as well as formal and perceived political influence and human resources as structural determinants of communication choices. Theoretical arguments for overlapping membership in organizations as determinant are twofold. First, we lean on McPherson et al. (2001), who point out that meeting opportunity determines the formation of friendships in school. Transferring this idea to political communication, membership in umbrella organizations or common membership in organizations, as indicators for meeting opportunities, increases the probability that a pair of organizations forms a communication tie. At the same time, a common worldview might determine membership in an (umbrella) organization and thereby increase the trust an organization has in the information of other organizations with the same memberships. That is, an organization will seek information from another organization if a third party links them both (Holland and Leinhardt 1971).[4]

Another important determinant is an organization's power to influence legislation (Huckfeldt and Sprague 1995; Knoke et al. 1996). Given the purpose of lobbying as an interest-mediation mechanism, lobbying organizations contact highly influential actors within the political elite in order to ensure that their members benefit from final policy decisions. We therefore expect that the higher the perceived influence of an actor receiving information is in a specific policy domain, the more likely it is that organizations will contact this actor. We choose perceived influence and not formal political power for two main reasons. First, we argue in line with Shepsle and Weingast (1987) that formal institutional rules cannot explain observed power distributions. With regard to developing countries,

---

[2] Austen-Smith and Wright argue for the contrary effect of preference similarity in tie creation. Interest groups, i.e. organizations try to contact organizations with whom they disagree in order to convince them.

[3] On the concept of homophily in network evolution theories, see Lazer et al. (2008), McPherson et al. (2001) or Huckfeldt and Sprague (1995).

[4] The informational efficiency model contradicts the idea that a common link to a third party increases the likelihood of information exchange between a pair of organizations. On the contrary, this model states that organizations will drop ties to organizations with whom they are linked by a third party due to information redundancies (Carpenter et al. 2004).

consider also the work of Bratton (2007), who argues that the rule of law is often weakly developed even if it is not completely absent in developing countries. Political power tends to be intensely concentrated around the president, and as a result his cabinet becomes more powerful in policymaking (van der Walle 2003). Further, considering only formal political power would dismiss the informal influence of international organizations in developing countries. Second, we argue that using perceived influence instead of formal power will not bias results. Formal political power usually is highly correlated with the perceived influence of actors endowed with formal power. Moreover, employing the concept of perceived influence has the advantage of reflecting both informal and formal political power distributions with one measure.

Finally, consider networking time as a scare resource of an organization, as hiring and paying staff is cost intensive and budgets are usually constrained. Given the time-consuming nature of forming and maintaining relationships, the number of staff, therefore, determines the contact opportunities that exist between a pair of organizations (Carpenter et al. 1998, 2004).

In summary, theoretical considerations offer two insights on the evaluation of participatory policy processes. First, as network formation can be preference-driven, bias in favor of a specific group can occur and resulting policy decisions will be at the expense of the public. Nevertheless, expertise can be a major determinant of tie formation, as all actors seek to reduce uncertainty inherent to policy belief formation. Second, according to structuralist approaches, exogenous actors can influence the network structure by means of increasing meeting opportunities, e.g., joining umbrella organizations and increasing the number of staff.

2.2 Empirical Determinants of Communication

According to our theoretical considerations, our set of empirical variables is differentiated into three classes: (i) variables describing political homophily, (ii) variables indicating individual knowledge, and (iii) variables related to structural factors. For further information on the study that collected data for these variables, see Chapter "A Network Based Approach to Evaluate Participatory Policy Processes: An Application to CAADP in Malawi".

Political Homophily We approximate political homophily by a distance index of political interests (*distance*). Such an index provides dyad-specific information on the probability of observing communication between elite members due to similarity in policy interests. The index summarizes the distances in interest between two actors concerning the preferred dimension of the state of the world. We selected eight dimensions for representing the state of the world that actors address with designing agricultural policy programs (see Table 1). The index is calculated as a Euclidean distance function based on the policy interests of actor i and actor j in dimension $X^{(z)}$ with z=1,..,8:

Table 1 Description of interests: state of the world

Dimension	Common interests	Conflicting positions	Ø interest
Welfare: smallholders	Reduce hunger and malnutrition	Political market interventions	21
Poverty reduction	Poverty reduction	Achievable poverty level (short-term)	18
Welfare: agr. export sector	Foreign currency earnings	Political market intervention	14
Budget	Development of the agricultural sector	Share of agr. budget in total budget	13
Environmental sustainability	Conservation of natural resources	Budget priority of environmental sustainability	12
Gender issues	Lessen the vulnerability of the poor	Gender specific policy programs	10
Welfare: non-agr. industry	Economic growth	Political market intervention	6
Welfare: urban consumers	Food provision to urban population	Level of food prices	5

Source: The Ministry of Agriculture and Food Security, Republic of Malawi (2010), Government of Malawi (2006), own data

$$distance_{ij} = \sum_{z=1}^{8} \left(X_i^{(z)} - X_j^{(z)} \right)^2 \quad (1)$$

Official policy documents provide the basis to extract the dimensions of the state of the world in a respective country. In the case of Malawi, consider the Malawi Growth and Development Strategy (MGDS) and the Agriculture Sector Wide Approach (ASWAp) as important policy programs (Government of Malawi 2006, The Ministry of Agriculture and Food Security, Republic of Malawi 2010). Table 1 describes which policy interests evolve in society that drive political behavior according to these two major policy documents. Interests are listed in descending order of average interest over interviewed organizations. Further, Table 1 lists common interests and conflicting positions that occur within one specific dimension of the state of the world. While common interests will drive political homophily and thereby communication, conflicting positions increase the potential for policy deadlocks but allow also for policy learning. Consider, for example, the welfare of smallholders. Actors might be equally interested in reducing hunger and malnutrition but have different experiences and information about the political strategy to reach their common aim. One actor might favor input subsidies to increase maize yields, the other one might consider budget spending on extension services as a more efficient policy strategy. Information exchange between these two actors can help to choose a strategy that best fits their common interests.

Knowledge Our strategy to identify an organization's level of knowledge is twofold. First, as knowledge is hardly observable, we use the age of the organization (*age*) and the organization's degree of specialization in agriculture (*specialization*) to approximate political knowledge. In our study, *age* equals 2000 minus *year of foundation*, and *specialization* relates to an organization's effort spent on agricultural issues.

Second, we use an alternative indicator that directly measures the technological knowledge of actors regarding the transformation of CAADP policies into policy outcomes based on a computable general equilibrium (CGE) model. In particular, Henning (2012) models the impact of different CAADP policies on the eight relevant policy concerns within an extended CGE approach calibrated for Malawi. As described in detail in Chapter "Whither participation? Evaluating participatory policy processes with the CGPE approach: The case of CAADP in Malawi" of this volume, based on this CGE approach, the optimal CAADP policy positions from the viewpoint of different governmental and nongovernmental organizations can be identified—where optimality involves maximizing the organizations' political support functions—while modeling the technical translation of CAADP policies into policy concerns evolves according to the extended CGE. Comparing the theoretically derived optimal policy positions with the policy positions stated by organizations during our interview implies a measure of an organizations' political knowledge. In particular, Henning (2012) calculates the Euclidean difference between the theoretically implied and empirically stated policy position (see Chapter "A Network Based Approach to Evaluate Participatory Policy Processes: An Application to CAADP in Malawi"). We use this measure as a direct indicator of the political knowledge of an organization (*expertise*) in our econometric analysis. As documented in detail in Chapter "A Network Based Approach to Evaluate Participatory Policy Processes: An Application to CAADP in Malawi", on average, farm and civil society organizations have the highest political knowledge, while politicians and, in particular, political parties have the lowest political knowledge. Donor organizations take a middle ground in political knowledge.

Structural Factors Because the perception of an organization as influential in policymaking will influence its probability of forming ties, we use a reputation network for identifying an organization's political reputation (*reputation*). This variable will further serve as a proxy of an organization's legislative power. Please note that reputation is highly correlated with the lobbying power calculated in Chapter "A Network Based Approach to Evaluate Participatory Policy Processes: An Application to CAADP in Malawi" based on simulated support network data. To account for the meeting opportunities between two organizations, we include the number of staff working on agricultural policy issues (*staff*) in our analysis. Information about organizational membership allows us to calculate a dyad-specific count variable that indicates how often two organizations were members of the same umbrella organization (*same*). Examples of umbrella organizations in Malawi are the Malawi Economic Justice Network (MEJN) and the Civil Society Agriculture Network (CISANET).We include the determinants as dyad-specific characteristics into our econometric model, i.e., sender- and receiver-specific individual variables are transformed into pair-wise distances. In addition, the individual determinants enter the model as sender- and receiver-specific variables.

Since homophily is a key term of interest in this analysis, we calculate Euclidean distance measures between sender- and receiver-specific values of *specialization, age, staff, reputation* and *policy* concerns (*distance*). The larger the values of these distance measures, the more organizations differ in terms of the respective issue. A negative value of the parameter estimate indicates that the probability of forming a tie increases with homophily in the respective dimension. A positive value suggests that heterophily has positive impacts on the probability of communication.

3 Study Design and Econometric Model Framework

3.1 Study Design

Identified relevant governmental and nongovernmental organizations are reported in Table A1 in the appendix. While Chapter "A Network Based Approach to Evaluate Participatory Policy Processes: An Application to CAADP in Malawi" describes the study design in detail and presents the data collected from parts (a), policy network data, and (b), policy preferences of the policy network survey conducted in Malawi, data collected from part (c) of the questionnaire is described below.

First, however, we explain the measurement of political homophily (*distance*) in more detail, as this variable is important within the analysis of network formation. Given our theoretical framework, political homophily relates to an organization's interests in specific policy concerns. Hence, in this study we use the interview data from the questions about interest, $X_i^{(z)}$ in the eight policy concerns, i.e. $z = 1,\ldots,8$. Interests are ascertained by distributing 100 points across the eight dimensions of the state of world (identified in Table 1). For information on the data used to calculate *expertise*, please see Chapters "Modeling and Evaluation of Political Processes: A New Quantitative Approach" and "A Network Based Approach to Evaluate Participatory Policy Processes: An Application to CAADP in Malawi".

Part (c) of the survey asks questions about organizational attributes that inform about an organization's degree of specialization in agriculture (*specialization*), the year of foundation (to calculate *age*), and the number of staff engaged in agricultural issues (*staff*). Further, we asked organizations to name all umbrella organizations of which they are a member. With this information in hand, we calculate the dyad-specific count variable *same*, which informs about overlapping memberships in umbrella organizations between a pair of organizations. The mean of this variable reveals that, on average, two organizations in Malawi are jointly members of 1.3 organizations.

Summary statistics for all exogenous variables under consideration are given in Table 2.

Table 2 Summary statistics

Variable	Mean	SD
Specialization	0.652	0.305
Age	26.027	20.288
Staff	19.625	34.753
Reputation	0.573	0.179
Same	1.267	0.708
Distance	0.314	0.146
Expertise	0.641	0.177

Source: Calculated by authors from own data

3.2 Econometric Model

We design an empirical model capturing key elements of the communication process between local elite members related to individual characteristics influencing the formation probability of a network tie. Individual characteristics are considered as important network determinants in terms of the prevailing homophily of network agents. For analyzing the process which establishes communication ties δ_{ji} or δ_{ij} between local elite members $i=1, \ldots, n$ and $j=1, \ldots, n$ with $i \neq j$ for the considered directed dichotomous network relationships, determinants of communication relationships are assessed within a probit framework, i.e. $\delta_{ij}=1$, if $\delta_{ij}^* > 0$ and $\delta_{ij}=0$ else. Following Hoff and Ward (2004), the latent variable δ_{ij}^* relating determinants of communication with the observed network tie δ_{ij} is thereby parameterized as

$$\delta_{ij}{}^* = W_{ij}\beta + W_i\kappa_s + W_i\kappa_r + h_{ij} + e_{ij} = Q_{ij}\theta + e_{ij}, \tag{2}$$

where W_{ij} is a set of dyad specific variables, W_i denotes a set of sender specific characteristics for individual i, W_j is a set of receiver specific characteristics for individual j. h_{ij} is assumed to capture distance effects and thus homophily and is hence parameterized in such a way to allow the aggregation of individual specific characteristics to the dyadic level, i.e.

$$h_{ij} = \mid W_i - W_j \mid \gamma, \tag{3}$$

and $\theta = \{\beta, \kappa_s, \kappa_r, \gamma\}$ summarizes all model parameters. Using a probit link, which corresponds to the assumption of a standard normal distribution for the latent error, i.e. $e_{ij} \sim N(0, 1)$, allows for establishing a Bayesian estimation routine facilitated by Markov Chain Monte Carlo (MCMC) techniques. Parameter inference within a Bayesian setup is performed based on the posterior distribution defined via

$$p(\theta|data) \propto L(data|\theta)\pi(\theta), \tag{4}$$

where $L(data|\theta)$ denotes the model likelihood and $\pi(\theta)$ the assumed prior distribution of model parameters. Parameter inference is based on moments and quantiles of the posterior distribution. These are obtained on the basis of sample trajectories drawn from the posterior distribution. Sampling of parameters from their joint posterior distribution is achieved via iterative sampling from the full conditional distributions. The model likelihood is then given as

$$L(data|\theta) = \prod_{i \neq j} \Phi\left(\left(2\delta_{ij} - 1\right)\left(Q_{ij}\theta\right)\right), \tag{5}$$

where $\Phi(\cdot)$ denotes the cumulative standard normal distribution function. Given the above model structure, we adapt conjugate priors for all model parameters, i.e. a multivariate normal prior for parameter vector θ with the corresponding mean set to zero and diagonal covariance with variance set to 100 for each element. More details on Bayesian estimation via Gibbs sampling for this kind of models are given in Aßmann and Boysen-Hogrefe (2011). Next to parameter estimates, interpretation of results is provided by calculation of marginal effects, where the corresponding uncertainty is directly accessibly by means of the Gibbs output, see Aßmann and Boysen-Hogrefe (2011) for a more general discussion.

In addition, the use of Bayesian estimation allows for a conceptually straightforward treatment of missing values within both, the observed network relationship and the explaining variables. As empirical network data is most often based on personal interviews and survey data, missing values occur despite tremendous effort in fieldwork and questionnaire design. Missing values are especially troublesome, as a single missing value for a considered explaining characteristic for individual i causes the potential loss of $n - 1$ observed network relationships for assessing the link between the formation probability of a network tie and the considered individual characteristics as determinants thereof. Additionally, the parameter estimates would no longer reflect information on all network constituents. Thus proper estimation routines facilitating the use of variables with single missing observations are needed to perform proper statistical analysis incorporating the uncertainty in parameter estimation stemming from missing values. Dealing with missing values is performed using the MCMC device of data augmentation as suggested by Tanner and Wong (1987). The parameter vector θ is augmented to include the missing values in the explaining factors. Sampling from the full conditional distributions for these missing values is then incorporated within the iterative sampling scheme providing draws from the posteriori distribution $p(\theta|data)$. For the considered probit model allowing for analysis of a directed dependent network relationship, the sampling proceeds by iterating the following basic steps, see Albert and Chib (1993).

1. Sampling of the latent variable δ_{ij}^* from truncated normal distributions with means given by the linear regression setup and variance of one. The truncation at zero from above is $\delta_{ij} = 0$ and from below if $\delta_{ij} = 1$, see Aßmann and Boysen-

Hogrefe (2011) for details on the corresponding moments of this full conditional distribution.

2. Sampling of the parameters $\beta, \kappa_s, \kappa_r$ and γ from full conditional distributions underlying the linear regression setup for latent variable $\delta_{ij}{}^*$, see Aßmann and Boysen-Hogrefe (2011) for details on the corresponding moments of this full conditional distribution.
3. Sampling from the full conditional distributions of missing values.
   a. In case of missing values in one of the explaining variables, these are obtained using non-parametric approximations for the full conditional distributions as suggested by Burgette and Reiter (2010). Note that for this class of empirical network models, where the set of individual characteristics is assumed to explain the formation probability of a network tie, only few observations are at hand to provide a realistic approximation of the full conditional distribution. If the number of observations required by the non-parametric approach of Burgette and Reiter (2010) is not reached, draws for the missing values are obtained from the observed unconditional distribution as the only approximation of the full conditional distribution at hand to obtain draws for this variables.
   b. In case of missing values in the dependent variable, sampling from a binary distribution with success probability $\phi(Q_{ij}\theta)$ yields a draw from the full conditional distribution.

Successive sampling from the outlined full conditional distributions establishes a sample from the posterior distribution facilitating inference with regard to parameters based on the empirical moments. Although parameter estimates allow for direct assessment of the direction in which explaining factors influence the formation probability of a communication tie, marginal effects provide a quantification of the effect of a change in determining factors on the probability of a communication relation. Marginal effects are conceptually given as $\frac{\partial \Pr\left(\delta_{ij}=1\tilde{Q}\right)}{\partial \tilde{Q}}$, where $\tilde{Q}$ denotes a particular state of the considered control variables, e.g., the mode. An estimate of the marginal effects is readily obtained from the output of the Gibbs sampling scheme as

$$\frac{1}{S}\sum_{i=1}^{n}\phi\left(\tilde{Q}\theta^{(s)}\right)\theta^{(s)}, \tag{6}$$

where $\phi(\cdot)$ denotes the standard normal density and $\theta^{(s)}$, $s=1, \ldots, S$, denote the sampled trajectories of all considered model parameters. In general estimates will be based on 10000 draws, i.e., $S=10000$, where discarding the initial 2000 draws have been found sufficient to mitigate the effect of burn-in.

However, whilst the necessity to deal with missing values within the explaining factors is inherent given the considered empirical network model for the surveyed network data, it is nevertheless important to check carefully the adequacy of the considered empirical model. While valid point and interval estimates are readily available for the above suggested approach for dealing with missing values, other standard measures for gauging model fitness, like e.g. $F - tests$, are not readily available. Note that this applies also to alternative approaches allowing for handling of missing data, see Raghunathan et al. (2001). As a natural approach to gauge model fitness is based on the capability of the empirical network model to provide accurate forecasts, the following outlines one possibility to calculate an overall measure of model fitness. The situation of a network observed with missing values poses a methodological challenge, as the benchmark for assessing the prediction accuracy, i.e. the true relationship between network members, remains unobservable. As a formal prediction criteria, we use the area under the curve (AUC) measure derived from the receiver operator characteristics (ROC) curve approach proposed by Egan (1975). In order to function as a valid criterion of model fitness, the AUC measure has to be combined with a pseudo out-of-sample experiment gauging against possible overparameterization, see Aßmann and Boysen-Hogrefe (2011) for a review of this approach in cross validation experiments for binary panel data. One possibility to design the out-of-sample is to split the network constituents into four quarters forming a partition of the set of network constituents, where other splits are also possible. Parameter estimation is based on the network formed by three quarters of the network constituents, where parameter estimates are then used to predict the network formed by the left quarter of network constituents. Adapting a fourfold split yields a total of four possible combinations. Since in our situation the underlying network involves missing data, the predicted network resulting from complete sample estimation serves as a prediction reference. Note that this approach allows for a comparison of even non-nested model specifications.

4 Empirical Results

Estimation results concerning the explanatory factors suggested by theory are provided in Table 3 below. Although parameter estimates show the direction in which explanatory factors influence the probability of tie formation between two organizations, regression coefficients (columns 3 and 4) provide no correct quantitative description of the relationship between the probability of communication ties and changes within the explanatory factors. The relative importance of the different explanatory factors can be gauged based on marginal effects (columns 6 and 7). The in-sample AUC measure reveals that our approach to dealing with missing values and the suggested model specification result in high prediction accuracy of communication ties between organizations. Using the random graph model as an illustrative benchmark (corresponding AUC measure of 0.5), the out-of sample AUC measures point to the significantly increased prediction accuracy due to the considered set of explaining factors.

Table 3 Estimation results (dependent variable is: if A → B, tie = 1; 0 otherwise)

	Parameter estimates				Marginal effects	
	Mean	SD	2.50%	97.50%	Mean	SD
Constant	−1.254	0.468	−2.185	−0.341	–	
Homophily						
Specialization	−0.672	0.201	−1.068	−0.281	−0.223	0.065
Age	0.001	0.004	−0.007	0.009	0.000	0.001
Expertise	0.423	0.372	−0.315	1.147	0.144	0.128
Staff	−0.01	0.003	−0.016	−0.004	−0.003	0.001
Reputation	−0.949	0.346	−1.619	−0.266	−0.316	0.116
Distance	0.41	0.366	−0.295	1.141	0.142	0.129
Structural						
Same	0.814	0.116	0.585	1.043	0.274	0.054
Sender-specific						
Specialization	−0.3	0.246	−0.776	0.189	−0.105	0.087
Age	0.006	0.004	−0.002	0.013	0.002	0.001
Expertise	−1.593	0.392	−2.329	−0.786	−0.53	0.128
Staff	0.02	0.003	0.014	0.026	0.007	0.001
Reputation	0.241	0.336	−0.413	0.896	0.078	0.111
Receiver-specific						
Specialization	0.339	0.17	0.005	0.662	0.111	0.054
Age	−0.007	0.003	−0.014	−0.001	−0.002	0.001
Expertise	0.062	0.293	−0.517	0.642	0.023	0.099
Staff	0.02	0.003	0.014	0.026	0.007	0.001
Reputation	4.591	0.325	3.93	5.23	1.539	0.191
Predicted (rows)/Observed (columns)	0			1		
0	240			43		
1	429			620		
AUC (in-sample/out-of-sample)	0.7262/0.6724					

Source: Calculated by authors from own data

4.1 Homophily in Interests and Other Determinants

In Table 3, estimated parameters and marginal effects show that homophily in an organization's attributes increases the probability that it will interact. All significant variables have a negative sign. If organizations are similar in terms of *specialization*, *staff*, and *reputation*, the probability of forming a tie increases. Inspection of the marginal effects reveals no high quantitative effect of an increase in the difference of *staff* between two organizations on the probability of forming a communication tie, while increasing homophily in *reputation* and *specialization* has a high quantitative impact. These findings point at the need to look not only at parameter estimates but also at marginal effects to assess the quantitative effects correctly. We find no significance for homophily in *age* or *expertise*.

Political homophily (*distance*) is not an important determinant of communication. With regard to the distortionary effects of political homophily, this finding suggests less biased policy decisions. Nevertheless, organizations need to adopt efficient information-processing routines to filter received information in terms of a sender's special-interest bias.

4.2 Knowledge

Next, we take a closer look at knowledge as a determinant of tie formation. We start with the proxy for an organization's level of knowledge: *specialization*. A receiver's probability of gaining information by communication increases with its level of *specialization*. A sender's level of *specialization* is not significantly associated with tie formation. The negative and significant sign of the difference in *specialization* implies that communication partners are likely to be similar in their level of *specialization* and thereby in their level of knowledge. With regard to expertise transmission in the network, this result points at isolated clusters of knowledge that prohibit the spread of knowledge, where receivers are already well informed about policy impacts.

Age as another proxy reveals that the younger an organization, the higher the probability of receiving information from others. If we now put great age on a high level with knowledge, the process enables transmission of knowledge from the long-established, more experienced organizations to the younger and less experienced ones. Please note that similarity in age does not significantly prohibit tie formation.

As these variables are at best proxies for knowledge, we consider a further advanced indicator *expertise*, which is derived from our own survey data and Malawi's CGE. Note that low values of *expertise* indicate a high level of knowledge about impacts of policy decisions on the state of the world. A sender's high value for *expertise* is especially associated with a greater probability of communication. Since homophily in *expertise* has no significant impact on the probability of forming a communication tie, knowledge will not circulate within a cluster of highly informed organizations. Consequently, less-informed organizations are able to receive information from experts ceteris paribus, and well-informed policy decisions are likely to happen.

We summarize for knowledge as a determinant of communication that young organizations receive information from older ones and that knowledge is spread among organizations with divergent levels of knowledge. In fact, the marginal effect of sender-specific *expertise* states that knowledge highly influences the probability of senders to form ties. However, if specialization in agriculture is well correlated with knowledge, homophily in *specialization* would prohibit knowledge transmission. In our case, we observe the contrary. *Specialization* is not highly correlated with *expertise* (correlation equals 0.069). Hence, we suggest discussing the variable *specialization* more generally in terms of an organization's main activity field. That is, organizations with heterogeneous activity fields but high capacity can still be well-informed organizations. Good cases in point are donor organizations. It is well recognized that donors rarely specialize in a sector but handle several problem areas in a developing country. With this example in mind, the negative impact of homophily in *specialization* does not trigger information transmission but simply reveals that organizations with similar activity fields will form ties more often ceteris paribus.

4.3 Structural Factors

Turning now to structural factors as determinants of communication, we observe several significant variables. One factor that determines an organization's probability of participating in elite communication is the number of staff (*staff*). This finding is in line with other studies, see for instance Carpenter et al. (2004). For senders and receivers an increase in the number of staff increases their probability of communicating with others. We again observe homophily among organizations. That is, organizations of about the same size are more likely to communicate with each other. However, inspection of the marginal effects reveals no high quantitative effect of an increase in the number of staff or in the difference of *staff* between a pair of organizations on the probability of communicating.

A receiver's perceived influence (*reputation*) appears to increase the probability that actors will contact highly influential others. Consider here that *reputation* is highly correlated with formal and informal political power. The result is intuitive, since it suggests that senders try to increase the probability that legislation will favor their interests by providing expert information to highly influential organizations. The observed marginal effect of receiver-specific *reputation* reveals a great influence of this determinant on network evolution. The negative sign on the difference in *reputation* suggests that organizations similar in reputation form communication clusters. Consequently, less influential organizations are less likely to form ties to powerful actors.

Another determinant of communication is overlapping membership in umbrella organizations between a pair of organizations (*same*). The more umbrella organizations are connecting A to B, the more likely organization A is to communicate with organization B. Inspection of marginal effects reveals a high quantitative impact of overlapping membership in umbrella organizations on the probability of communicating. This finding is in line with the theoretical considerations. Common membership in umbrella organizations increases the trust between organizations and thereby increases the probability that the two exchange information.

Further, common membership is a proxy for the opportunity structure to meet and communicate.[5]

5 Discussion

Based on the empirical assessment, we conclude that overlapping membership in organizations and political influence are more important determinants of elite communication ties than knowledge in Malawi. We do not infer that knowledge can be neglected as a determinant or that an elite network does not spread information among actors. However, the high marginal effects of *same* and homophily in *reputation* narrow the impact of knowledge on tie formation, even if *expertise* significantly influences the probability of sending information. For illustration, the following calculations are performed to describe how overlapping membership in organizations (*same*) and their level of knowledge (*expertise*) influence the probability of forming a tie for senders. In fact, we calculate the effect of a change in *same* (*expertise*) from the minimum value to the maximal value observed in our sample. Therefore, probabilities to communicate are computed for each of the two determinants at these extreme positions averaging over all other determinants observed within the sample. The minimum of same corresponds to no overlapping organizations, the maximum to four overlapping organizations. The minimum level of knowledge is given by a value of 1.098 for *expertise* in our sample, while a value of 0.445 for *expertise* denotes the highest level of knowledge among the actors.[6] An inspection of effects, see Table 4, reveals that increasing overlapping membership in organizations increases the probability of observing a tie between a pair of organizations by 29%. However, if an uninformed sender gains as much knowledge as the best-informed actor in the sample, the probability of forming ties, with all other determinants fixed at their means except homophily in expertise, increases by 22 percentage points. Hence, joining other organizations would be ceteris paribus a better means than accumulating knowledge to increase the probability of sending information.

In terms of the bias/information tradeoff of participatory policy processes, results show that political homophily is not a significant determinant of communication. Therefore, at least regarding fundamental policy concerns, participatory policy processes allow for unbiased information diffusion in Malawi. However, two qualifications of this result are necessary. First, although political homophily does

[5]Please note that literature suggests that homophily in attributes might affect the opportunity structure to meet (see Lazer et al. 2008). We leave it to future work to disentangle the effect of meeting opportunity and homophily in interests and remind the reader to interpret the results carefully. Nevertheless, we think that our detailed measure of political homophily is neither correlated with overlapping membership in organizations nor affected by the same factors as the latter. Therefore, our estimations are not plagued by endogeneity or multicollinearity.

[6]Please note that we measure political knowledge via the Euclidian distance between stated and optimal policy position of an organization, i.e. the higher the distance the lower the knowledge.

Table 4 Simulation of marginal effects: same and expertise

Same		Expertise	
Min/max	$\Pr(\delta_{ij} = 1)$	Min/max	$\Pr(\delta_{ij} = 1)$
0	0.700	1.098	0.571
4	0.997	0.445	0.790

Source: Calculated by authors

Notes: All other variables, except the distance in expertise for the effect of expertise, are fixed at their means

not play a role, homophily in general is still an important structural determinant of the network-generating process of political communication among Malawi's political elite. In particular, homophily in reputation as well as in specialization clearly discriminates communication between types of organizations. For example, our estimation results imply that, based on reputational homophily, international donor organizations have a significant higher probability of sending information to central ministries, i.e., the Ministry of Finance (MoF) and the Ministry of Agriculture and Food Security (MoAFS), when compared to an average national civil society organization. Second, despite homogeneous interests in fundamental policy concerns, heterogeneity of preferred policy positions among organizations can still result due to biased political beliefs. Hence, to limit policy biases due to wrong beliefs it is important that communication ties are determined by the political knowledge of the sender. Here, the strong marginal effect for sender-specific political knowledge certainly works in favor of unbiased political beliefs, but overall this effect is alleviated by structural factors as well as homophily effects determining the network-generating process. Thus, overall, only suboptimal political communication structures result.

6 Conclusion

This study analyzes the communication patterns among governmental, local stakeholder and international organizations in Malawi. We present an approach that is novel within network estimation as well as within political science. In terms of econometric analysis of surveyed network data, our approach is based on an extended binary regression framework. In fact, the model relies on a Bayesian estimation framework to handle missing data due to survey non-response. For political consultants, the framework enables learning about political communication processes in a country. Findings will enable them to design communication processes that increase the probability of well-informed, unbiased policy choices.

In addition to this, we explicitly analyze the information/distortion potential of participatory policy processes by employing two variables. First, we use an external measure of an actor's knowledge about policy impacts derived from a CGE model and survey data of the actor's policy preferences in order to analyze the impact of the actor's knowledge on its probability of communicating with others. Second, we employ an index of homophily in policy interests between a pair of organizations to describe the distortion potential. Insights about this tradeoff are valuable in order to evaluate the potential of participatory policy processes to increase the likelihood of improving total welfare delivering undistorted policies.

Empirical findings are presented for a case study in Malawi. Data was gathered in face-to-face interviews with local stakeholders, international organizations, and politicians in 2010. We find strong support for explanatory factors suggested by the two strands of literature about determinants of communication—the preference-driven and structure-driven models. Overall, the most influential determinants of communication processes are an actor's reputation, overlapping membership in organizations and knowledge about policy impacts.

In terms of well-informed policy decisions, it is highly appreciated that knowledge about policy impacts increases a sender's probability of forming communication ties. Nevertheless, this positive result for the potential of participatory policy processes to increase well-informed policy choices is narrowed by the high influence of homophily in reputation on the probability of forming ties. Homophily in reputation will disable well-informed but less influential players to convey valuable information into the policy process. Further, joining other organizations increases the probability of communicating with elite members more than accumulating knowledge ceteris paribus. That is, promoting membership in umbrella organizations is a means to increasing information flow between groups. As overlapping membership in organizations relates to sharing common communication platforms, the CAADP approach of creating working groups on priority issues to work on policy proposals for pro-poor growth policy programs is an adequate intervention in the communication process to increase communication opportunities among organizations. However, at time of the interview round, an effective institutional organization of dialogue among stakeholders and between government and stakeholders was still not implemented.

The empirical analysis also shows that the probability of forming ties does not increase with homophily in relative interests in fundamental policy goals, e.g., poverty reduction via economic growth. Hence, although the identified network-generating process clearly discriminates between types of nongovernmental organizations, it still follows that policy decisions will not be fundamentally biased in favor of special interests. Nevertheless, policy bias might result since organizations have different levels of political knowledge, which is not fully reflected in the probability of sending information to powerful politicians. The latter results especially from the fact that, beyond knowledge, structural factors such as meeting opportunities, as well as reputational homophily, determine communication ties among organizations.

Moreover, even communication ties perfectly determined by political knowledge can still result in biased policies if average level of knowledge is rather low, i.e., political beliefs for all organizations are systematically biased. This point will be further elaborated in Chapter "Whither participation? Evaluating participatory policy processes with the CGPE approach: The case of CAADP in Malawi" below.

Finally, the perceived influence of organizations affects tie evolution in the elite network. Organizations are more likely to be contacted if they are highly influential. This finding is intuitive since organizations want to ensure that final policy decisions consider their knowledge about policy impacts, so that their members benefit from implemented policies.

References

Albert, J.A., and S. Chib. 1993. Bayesian Analysis of Binary and Polychotomous Response Data. *Journal of the American Statistical Association* 88 (422): 669–679.

Aßmann, C., and J. Boysen-Hogrefe. 2011. A Bayesian Approach to Model-Based Clustering for Binary Panel Probit Models. *Computational Statistics and Data Analysis* 55: 261–279.

Austen-Smith, D. 1993. Information and Influence: Lobbying for Agendas and Votes. *American Journal of Political Science* 3 (3): 799–833.

Ball, R. 1995. Interest Groups, Influence and Welfare. *Economics and Politics* 7 (2): 119–146.

Bratton, M. 2007. Formal versus Informal Institutions in Africa. *Journal of Democracy* 18: 96–110.

Burgette, L.F., and J.P. Reiter. 2010. Multiple Imputation for Missing Data via Sequential Regression Trees. *American Journal of Epidemiology* 172 (9): 1070–1076.

Butts, C.T. 2003. Network Inference, Error, and Informant (In)accuracy: A Bayesian Approach. *Social Networks* 25 (2): 103–140.

Carpenter, D.P., K.M. Esterling, and D.M.J. Lazer. 1998. The Strength of Weak Ties in Lobbying Networks: Evidence from Health-Care Politics in the United States. *Journal of Theoretical Politics* 10 (4): 417–444.

———. 2004. Friends, Brokers, and Transitivity: Who Informs Whom in Washington Politics? *Journal of Politics* 66: 224–246.

Egan, J. 1975. *Signal Detection Theory and ROC analysis, Series in Cognition and Perception*. New York: Academic Press.

Festinger, L. 1954. A Theory of Social Comparison Processes. *Human Relations* 7 (2): 117–140.

Galton, F. 1907. Vox Populi. *Nature* 75: 450–451.

Government of Malawi. 2006. *Malawi Growth and Development Strategy—From Poverty to Prosperity, Technical Report*. IMF Country Report No. 07/55.

Henning, C.H.C.A. 2012. *An Evolutionary CGPE-Approach to Assess Governmental Performance Gaps: Theory and Empirical Application to Agricultural Policy in Malawi*. Working Paper presented at the Brown-bag Seminar. Washington, DC: IFPRI.

Hoff, P.D., and M.D. Ward. 2004. Modeling Dependencies in International Relations Networks. *Political Analysis* 12 (2): 160–175.

Holland, P.W., and S. Leinhardt. 1971. Transitivity in Structural Models of Small Groups. *Small Group Research* 2 (2): 107–124.

Huckfeldt, R., and J. Sprague. 1995. *Citizens, Politics, and Social Communication*. New York: Cambridge University Press.

Knoke, D. 1990. *Political Networks: The Structural Perspective*. New York: Cambridge University Press.

Knoke, D., F.U. Pappi, J. Broadbent, and Y. Tsujinaka. 1996. *Comparing Policy Networks. Labor Politics in the U.S., Germany, and Japan*. New York: Cambridge University Press.

Lazer, D., B. Rubineau, N. Katz, C. Chetkovich, and M.A. Neblo. 2008. *Networks and Political Attitudes: Structure, Influence, and Co-evolution*. HKS Faculty Research Working Paper Series RWP08-044, September 2008.

Lohmann, S. 1993. A Signaling Model of Informative and Manipulative Political Action. *American Political Science Review* 87 (2): 319–333.

McPherson, M., L. Smith-Lovin, and J.M. Cook. 2001. Birds of a Feather: Homophily in Social Networks. *Annual Review of Sociology* 27: 415–444.

Moody, J. 2001. Race, School Integration, and Friendship Segregation in America. *American Journal of Sociology* 70 (3): 679–716.

Pappi, F.U., and C.H.C.A. Henning. 1999. The Organization of Influence on EC's Common Agricultural Policy: A Network Approach. *European Journal of Political Research* 36 (2): 257–281.

Raghunathan, T.E., J.M. Lepkowski, J. van Hoewyk, and P. Solenberger. 2001. A Multivariate Technique for Multiply Imputing Missing Values Using a Sequence of Regression Models. *Survey Methodology* 27 (2): 85–95.

Shepsle, K.A., and B.R. Weingast. 1987. The Institutional Foundations of Committee Power. *American Political Science Review* 81 (1): 85–104.

Tanner, M., and W. Wong. 1987. The Calculation of Posterior Distributions by Data Augmentation. *Journal of the American Statistical Association* 92 (398): 528–540.

The Ministry of Agriculture and Food Security, Republic of Malawi. 2010. *Agriculture Sector Wide Approach (ASWAp). Malawi's Prioritised and Harmonised Agricultural Development Agenda.* http://www.caadp.net/pdf/Investment%20plan%20-%20Malawi.pdf

Van der Walle, N. 2003. Presidentialism and Clientelism in Africa's Emerging Party Systems. *Journal of Modern African Studies* 41: 297–321.

Christian Aßmann is a lecturer in statistics and econometrics at the University of Bamberg (Germany). Following his study in economics, he earned a PhD in economics at the University of Kiel (Germany). His main areas of specialization are Bayesian estimations and nonlinear panel data models. To date he has published various articles in refereed journals including *Journal of Econometrics, Computational Statistics and Data Analysis, American Journal of Human Biology, Applied Economics, International Journal of Environmental Research and Public Health, Bulletin of Economic Research* and *Pediatric Research.* Currently he is working on a DFG-project "Analysing relations between latent competencies and context information in the National Educational Panel Study" as part of the priority programme "Education as a Lifelong Process".

Eva Krampe is an agricultural sector expert at the European Investment Bank. She studied agricultural economics and earned a PhD in agricultural economics at the University of Kiel. Her main areas of specialization are Africa's Agricultural Policy, Applied Political Economy and Economic Analysis of Agricultural Investment Projects.

Christian Henning is professor and chair of agricultural economics, University of Kiel (Germany). He studied economics, agricultural economics, sociology, political science and mathematics. He earned a PhD in economics, in agricultural economics and in political science. His main areas of specialization are applied political economy and applied economic modelling of agricultural policies. To date he has published 5 books and various articles in refereed journals including PLoS ONE, American Journal of Agricultural Economics, European Review of Agricultural Economics, Journal of Public Policy, Journal of Mathematical Sociology and Journal of Theoretical Politics.

10

Government Performance and the Impact of Voter Behavior

Christian Henning, Laura Seide, and Svetlana Petri

1 Introduction

A review of the burgeoning literature on participatory policy processes reveals that scholars typically focus on the involvement of stakeholder organizations and interest groups as a prerequisite of efficient development policies and ignore the role of voters and elections (World Bank 2011). This situation is at odds with political theory, which interprets electoral competition as a fundamental democratic mechanism for guaranteeing that governmental policies reflect society's interests. A theoretical justification for neglecting electoral competition and the role of the voter can be found in Becker's seminal contribution to political economy theory, which focuses on interest group competition based on the assumption that voters' electoral choices are completely controlled by interest groups e.g., via campaign spending. Another micro-political foundation for the neglect of voters can be derived from socio-structural theories of voting, i.e., following the theory of Lazarsfeld et al. (1968) or Lipset and Rokkan (1967), voters' electoral choices are completely determined by their social classes; hence, electoral competition does not imply any incentives for elected politicians to perform (i.e., to serve the needs and desires of their electorate). For example, following a socio-structural theory of voting, most scholars of African politics agree that ethnic voting dominates vote choice in multiethnic and nascent African democracies (Horowitz 1985; Bratton et al. 2011; Hoffman and Long 2013).

However, interesting work addressing the impact of voter behavior on governmental performance was recently published in political economy theory (e.g., Keefer and Khemani 2005; Bardhan and Mookherjee 2002). According to this

C. Henning (✉) • L. Seide • S. Petri
Department of Agricultural Economics, University of Kiel, Kiel, Germany
e-mail: chenning@ae.uni-kiel.de

theory, electoral competition is often restricted in reality, leading to biased policy outcomes. In general, policy biases result from two major mechanisms: government capture and a lack of government accountability. The latter mechanism corresponds to a lack of sufficient electoral incentives for elected politicians to implement policies that benefit their constituencies; instead, politicians serve their self-interests. The former mechanism corresponds to the bias of electoral competition in favor of special interests. The application of an extended Baron-Grossman and Helpman (1996) model demonstrates that imperfect government performance in terms of government capture results if one assumes that voters apply different mechanisms to choose between political parties or candidates based on their level of information on politics. In particular, while informed voter base their vote choices directly on observed party platforms or on observed policy outcomes, e.g., economic well-being observed under a specific governmental policy, uninformed voters base their vote choices on non-policy factors, e.g., on socioeconomic characteristics like ethnicity, regional origin, or social class or rely on performance evaluation communicated by mass media or other social peer groups. Hence, politicians seeking for reelection have significantly different incentives to serve the interest of their electorate depending on the share of informed and uninformed voters. Thus, to the extent that the share of informed voters varies across social groups, governmental policy is biased in favor of more informed voter groups. However, although existing theoretical work convincingly emphasize the impact of voter behavior on governmental performance, central conclusions rest on the assumption that people apply different mechanisms to evaluate different parties and candidates running for elections, while a comprehensive empirical analyses that explicitly measure voter behavior to test these assumptions have not yet been performed. Hence, Bardhan and Mookherjee accurately conclude that future work is needed to test their assumptions with respect to voter behavior. On the other hand inspired by the Michigan School (Campbell et al. 1960) as well as the Columbia-School (Lazarsfeld et al. 1968) nowadays a large body of empirical voter studies exists that analyzes the relative importance of different voting motives for specific voter groups, e.g. policy-oriented voting (e.g., Downs 1957a, b; Enelow and Hinich 1984), non-policy oriented voting (Miller and Shanks 1996), as well as retrospective voting (Fiorina 1981). However, these empirical voter studies do not yet relate identified difference in voter behavior with induced governmental performance.

This paper integrates existing political economy approaches that explain the impact of voter behavior on government performance and advanced empirical voter studies that focus on voter behavior to derive theoretical hypotheses that will be empirically tested by estimating a probabilistic voter model. In particular, we provide a theory that relates the relative importance of different voting motives for different social voter groups to induced electoral incentives for politicians and subsequently to government performance. Based on our theoretical model, we derive indices of government accountability and capture that are defined in political equilibrium and measure the government's incentives to implement policies that serve pure self-interest or special interests at the expense of the general public.

In the empirical part of the paper, we estimate a probabilistic voting model by applying a mixed conditional logit (MCL) approach using Afrobarometer data for Malawi. Based on the estimated model, we calculate theoretically derived indices of government accountability and capture. Moreover, we derive indices that measure the relative importance of different policy- and non-policy-oriented voting motives for a number of socioeconomic groups. Further, we evaluate the relationship between the relative importance of different voting motives and government performance (i.e., accountability and capture).

2 Related Literature

The role of the voter in African politics has been addressed by two strands of literature: theoretical analyses of the impact of voter behavior on government performance and empirical studies on voter behavior, respectively. Regarding the former strand of theoretical literature Keefer and Khemani (2005) and Bardhan and Mookherjee (2002) focus on the voter's role to explain the redistribution gap from the wealthy to the poor. These authors identify three aspects that support political market imperfections: (a) asymmetric voter information, (b) social polarization and (c) missing accountability of political actors. The basic theory that explains distorted electoral competition by citing imperfectly and asymmetrically informed voters is based on Baron (1994) and Grossman and Helpman (1996). Baron (1994) distinguishes between informed and uninformed voters. Informed voters vote in a policy-oriented manner, and uninformed voters rely heavily on non-policy indicators (e.g., party loyalty, ethnicity or perceived competence) to evaluate parties. Accordingly, the votes of uniformed voters can be influenced by campaign expenditures that are unrelated to political decisions. Particularly in developing countries, people are only coarsely informed about policies. This lack of detailed knowledge occurs due to illiteracy, limited mobility, restricted media access and a number of other factors. Without information, people are unable to adequately assess politicians based on their political performance; instead, they use proxies to assess politicians. These proxies are typically easily observable policies or previously existing party loyalties. Khemani (2004) finds that policy actions that are easily observable increase the closer a country moves to Election Day. The influence of party loyalties is described by Bardhan and Mookherjee (2002), who assume that a higher level of voter loyalty reduces electoral competition, increasing capture and decreasing government accountability. As a consequence, Mani and Mukand (2002) demonstrate that politicians who maximize their political support have strong incentives to focus on targeted and visible policies at the cost of broad social services. First, this situation occurs because only a small number of voters have enough specific and substantial information to evaluate whether policies have actually contributed to better quality services. Second, measurable benefits may not emerge until several years after a policy has been implemented, which increases voters' difficulties in rewarding or punishing politicians within a particular policy cycle. Third, providing service jobs or building roads and buildings can be easily targeted to the politicians' own constituencies; thus, these policies are highly visible for even poorly informed voters. Gazdar (2000), the World Bank (1998, 2001), and Keefer (2002b) provide empirical evidence for this phenomenon. Another line of evidence for the importance of information for voter behavior and induced governmental performance comes from the literature on electoral cycles in fiscal and monetary policies. Cross-country analyses indicate that electoral cycles in monetary and fiscal policies are significantly larger in developing countries (Block 2002; Schuknecht 2000; Shi and Svensson 2000). Schuknecht (2000) and Shi and Svensson (2000) establish a direct link between electoral budget cycles and the limited availability of information to voters, with the latter factor being measured via access to free media. Analogously, Besley and Burgess (2003) demonstrate that state governments in India respond to declines in food production and to crop flood damage by increasing public food distribution and calamity relief spending in locations that have greater newspaper circulation. Thus, external interventions, such as information campaigns by civic society organizations, may be useful in promoting the diffusion of information that is needed for political accountability, particularly in poorer countries. Further, in line with the Columbia-School of voting (Lazarsfeld et al. 1968) Keefer and Khemani highlight social polarization as another mechanism by which voter behavior impacts governmental performance. Interpreting social polarization as expressive or instrumental voting, a dominance of non-policy voting based on ethnicity or social class might also explain why in many developing countries, where the population is divided into heterogeneous groups, suboptimal policies continue to be executed. However, to the best of our knowledge, a comprehensive empirical test of these hypotheses based on voter survey studies is not currently available in the literature. Keefer and Khemani highlighted a third imperfection of political markets that corresponds to the inability of politicians to make credible promises in elections. Persson and Tabellini (2000) demonstrate that when pre-election premises are not credible, elections become less effective as instruments for holding politicians accountable. When retrospective voting is more important (i.e., the more voters base their votes on their own economic welfare that was realized when a party was in government), politicians' incentives c.p. to implement policies that serve the interests of their electorate are higher. Of course, the more elected politicians discount future benefits from being reelected, the lower is the impact of retrospective voting on accountability. In this context, the existence of stable political parties is highlighted as an institutional environment that decreases political discount factors, as stable political parties correspond to an organizational commitment device for honoring future benefits from reelection. Keefer (2002a) demonstrates that in countries where political parties are weak or not established, politicians tend to make credible promises only to voters with whom they have built a personal reputation. Such ties emerge most clearly as the patron-client relationship that is identified with politics in developing countries by a large body of literature. Several studies provided empirical evidence for clientelistic policies (e.g., Glewwe and Jacoby 1994; Sanmartin 2001; Glaeser and Shleifer 2002).

Overall, interesting theoretical work has been published concerning the impact of voter behavior on government performance, where the theoretical hypotheses of Keefer and Khemani and Bardhan and Mookherjee relate directly to empirical hypotheses on voter behavior, In particular, limited information induces voters to rely less on policy indicators (i.e., *policy-oriented voting*) and more on non-policy indicators that are based on ethnic, religious, social or political characteristics (i.e. *party identity*), party competence based on perceived performance (i.e., *approval voting*), or based on observed economic performance (i.e., *retrospective or economic voting*). In particular, an assessment of the relative importance of different voting motives for different social groups and of the corresponding implications for government performance is of interest. However, although some empirical evidence concerning the impact of voter behavior on government performance is available, a comprehensive micro-politically founded empirical confirmation of central theoretical hypotheses has not yet been provided. Hence, Bardhan and Mookherjee (2002, p. 38) accurately say: "We conclude by stressing the need for empirical research. Are local governments more subject to capture? What are the determinants of absolute and relative capture? Are assumptions and implications of our model validated by data? Perceptions of capture by voters may perhaps be elicited from careful design of voter surveys."

As mentioned above, there exists a second strand of literature focusing on empirical studies of voter behavior. Especially, a large body of empirical voter studies analyzed African voters (For example, see the literature overview of Hoffman and Long 2013; Ferree and Horowitz 2010 or Bratton et al. 2011). But these empirical voter studies mainly focus on the relative importance of different non-policy factors, e.g. ethnicity and regional origin, in determining African vote choices, while these studies do not relate different voting motives with induced government performance (Ferree and Horowitz 2010; Bratton et al. 2011; Hoffman and Long 2013). At the methodological level, the majority of the empirical African voter studies apply socio-structural theories (e.g., the theory of Lazarfeld et al. 1968 or Lipset and Rokkan 1967) or social psychological theories of voter behavior (Campbell et al. 1960). Hoffman and Long (2013) published one of the few studies of voter behavior in Africa to mention the importance of policy issues and the spatial theory of voting (Downs 1957a, b as well as Enelow and Hinich 1984). However, although these authors mention the relevance of policy distances as variables of party choices, they fail to include these factors in their empirical model (see Hoffman and Long 2013). The neglect of policy-oriented voting in African election studies is surprising since spatial theory of voting (Enelow and Hinich 1984) has become the workhorse model of election studies in industrialized countries (Adams et al. 2005).

Moreover, the few existing African voter studies that explicitly consider different voter motives (e.g., economic versus ethnic voting or approval voting) only provide a test of statistical significance without providing a measure of the relative importance of different voting motives. One notable exception is the study by Bratton et al. (2011), who computed the marginal effects of different indicators of ethnic and economic voting. In particular, Bratton et al. (2011) provide empirical evidence from a cross-country panel analysis that includes 16 African countries that in addition to ethnic identification, voters' perception of the economic development achieved under the government is a particularly important determinant of voters' electoral choices.

In this context, this paper contributes to the literature by closing existing research gaps, i.e. we combine the theoretical work on voter behavior and government performance with the existing empirical work on voter behavior. In particular, we apply a Baron-Grossman-Helpman model (BGH) as a theoretical framework to derive theoretically founded indices that measure government accountability and capture. At methodological level to combine the original BGH-model with empirical voter studies we need to extend the former via applying the more general Local Nash equilibrium concept to the electoral equilibrium as suggested by Schofield (2007). Further, based on our theoretical framework, we derive indices that measure the relative importance of different policy and non-policy voting motives. Finally, we apply our theory empirically by using data from the Afrobarometer voter survey in Malawi in 2008 to estimate a probabilistic voter model that includes different voter motives.

3 The Model

3.1 The Voters

Following the literature on the theory of voting, we assume that people vote for different parties based on the utility a voter ascribes to the different parties. Let $v \in NV$ denote the index of an individual voter, *NV* denote the set of voters and n is the total number of voters. Further, let *NP* denote the set of political parties that run for election, where $k \in NP$ denotes the index of an individual party and p is the total number of parties. Then each voter can be described by a vector $v_v = \{v_{vk}, \ldots, v_{vp})$, where it holds:

$$v_{vk} = V_{vk} + \varepsilon_{vk} \tag{1}$$

Here, V_{vk} denotes the observable utility that voter v associates with party *k*, and the terms ε_{vk} are the stochastic errors. Following the literature, we assume that each ε_{vk} is drawn from the same probability distribution. The cumulative distribution of the errors is denoted as Ψ. Because of the stochastic assumption, voter behavior is modeled by a probability vector, where the probability that a voter *v* votes for party *k* is:

$$P_{vk} = \Pr[V_{vk} \geq V_{vl}, for\, all\, l \neq k] = F_k^v(v_v) \tag{2}$$

The expected vote share of a party *k* results as:

$$S_k = \frac{1}{n}\sum_v P_{vk} \tag{3}$$

Pr[] stands for the probability operator associated with Ψ; this probability is a function of the vector of observable utilities that voters associate with the different parties. The specific function F depends on the assumed distribution Ψ. In this regard, different distributions are assumed in the literature, implying different voter models. For example, many theoretical studies assume a uniform distribution in a two-party setup, as these assumptions facilitate formal analyses (for example, see Grossman and Helpman 1996; Bardhan and Mookherjee 2006 or Persson and Tabellini 2000). However, the workhorse model that is applied in empirical voter studies corresponds to the logit model, assuming an extreme value distribution for Ψ. In particular, assuming that each ε_{vk} is independent and identically extreme value-distributed allows the derivation of an analytical form for $F_k^v(v_v)$ (McFadden 1974):

$$P_{vk} = F_k^v(v_v) = \frac{e^{V_{vk}}}{\sum_{l \in NP} e^{V_{vl}}} \tag{4}$$

Following the voter theory, the utility that a voter v associates with a party k incorporates different components (i.e., a valence (V^{NP}), a retrospective (V^R), and a policy-oriented (V^P) component):

$$V_{vk} = \beta_v V_{vk}^P + \delta_v V_{vk}^R + \alpha_v V_{vk}^{NP}, \tag{5}$$

where β, δ and α are the relative weights of the different utility components. In a perfect political world, electoral competition would be based on the policy platforms, say γ_A and γ_B, suggested by candidates A and B, respectively. Voters would evaluate candidates based on their policy platform (i.e., voters would transform policy platforms into their individual welfare according to the political technology, $T(Z,\gamma)$,[1] and vote for the candidate whose policy platform implies their highest utility). Hence, in a perfect world, vote choice is only based on the policy-oriented component $V_{vk}^P(\gamma_k)$. The motive of policy-oriented voting goes back to the classic voting theory created by Davis et al. (1970) and Enelow and Hinich (1984). The spatial voting model formulates voter's utility as a loss function of the weighted distance between a voter's own ideal point x_{dv} on a specific policy dimension d and the position taken by a party k, γ_{dk}.

[1]See Chapter "A Network Based Approach to Evaluate Participatory Policy Processes: An Application to CAADP in Malawi" in this book for the definition of the political technology $T(Z,\gamma)$.

$$V_{vk}^{P} = \sum_{d} \beta_d (\gamma_{dk} - x_{dv})^2 \tag{6}$$

However, because in the real world, the transformation of policies into welfare is rather complex, the calculation of expected utility is also rather complex from the viewpoint of individual voters. Hence, voters apply simple heuristics to estimate their expected utility. Basically, voters apply different types of policy and non-policy indicators to estimate the future utility they expect assuming a candidate is elected. Non-policy oriented indicators correspond to the concept of valence (Schofield 2007), which holds that based on specific characteristics z, such as appearance, charisma, occupation and ethnicity, voters perceive a specific competence or popularity of candidates and parties. Moreover, following Grossman and Helpman (1996), we also assume that voters are at least partially swayed by the relative campaign spending of different parties. This effect may reflect the influence of election advertisements or other efforts made to mobilize support (e.g., election rallies, door-to-door visits by campaign workers, etc.):

$$V_{vk}^{NP}(z, c) = \sum_{I} \alpha_{vkI} z_I + \sum_{l} \alpha_{vkl}^{L} C_l, \tag{7}$$

where C_l denotes the campaign spending of party l and c is the vector of campaign spending of all parties. Parties collect campaign funds from different sources. According to Magee et al. (1989) or Grossman and Helpman (1996), organized interest groups have incentives to provide resources to parties for campaign spending. However, Magee et al. (1989) assume that campaign spending by interest groups is mainly governed by electoral motives, while Grossman and Helpman highlight the influence motive of interest groups (i.e., interest groups provide resources to parties expecting that in exchange, parties will adapt their platforms to the ideal points of the interest groups). In addition to campaign spending by special interest groups, especially in developing countries international donor organizations also provide financial resources to politicians (e.g., via development aid). Development aid is often granted conditional on the implementation of specific policies (Dollar and Easterly 1999). Moreover, financial aid gives national politicians some leeway to generate benefits for their electorate. Thus, from the viewpoint of national politicians, development aid is similar to campaign spending. Therefore, we formally include development aid in C_k, although we are aware that campaign spending by national interest groups and development aid are fundamentally different in many other respects.

A third set of indicators corresponds to the concept of retrospective voting (Fiorina 1981; Katz and Katz 2009) (i.e., voters use observable welfare indicators Z_v^r, such as income growth or other well-being indicators realized in the incumbent's last election period, to update their evaluation of the incumbent's competence and popularity). From the viewpoint of the incumbent party, the welfare indicator is determined by implemented policies, $Z_v^r = z_{vr}(\gamma)$. Hence, the retrospective component of voters' perceived utility is also a function of governmental policy, $V^R_{vk}(z_{vr}(\gamma_G))$, where γ_G indicates the governmental policy. Assuming a linear approximation for V^R implies:

$$V^R_{vk}\left(Z^r_v(\gamma_G)\right) = \sum_r \delta_{vkr} Z^r_v(\gamma_G) \tag{8}$$

Please note that following the empirical voting literature, we assume that perceived economic performance has an impact not only on voters' evaluations of governmental parties but also on all other nongovernmental parties.

3.2 *Parties and the Government*

Parties choose their policy platform, γ_k, to maximize their representation in the legislature. Based on this objective, a party chooses its policy platforms to maximize its vote share, S_k. Due to voter behavior, parties choose their policy platforms recognizing that their policy endorsements will affect their popularity among voters in different ways. First, voters evaluate party platforms based on their policy-oriented utility component (i.e., voters compare party positions on different policy dimensions to their own ideal points; the closer a party's platform to a voter's ideal point, the more she adores this party). Second, parties choose their platforms while considering organized interest groups, which vary their support contributions to a party according to the position a party takes. The parties know that any contributions they collect from interest groups can be used to finance campaign activities. Following Grossman and Helpman (1996) and Bardhan and Mookherjee (2006), we assume that in political equilibrium, interest groups donate locally truthful campaign contribution schedules to parties (i.e., the total contributions collected by a party k correspond to a weighted sum of interest group welfare):

$$C_k = \sum_J \rho_{Jk} W_J(\gamma_k) \tag{9}$$

where $W_J(\gamma_k)$ denotes the average per capita welfare of an individual member of the interest group J and ρ_{Jk} denotes the weight of interest group J. Please note that the sum of the interest group weights is generally lower than one (see Grossman and Helpman 1996).[2] Moreover, we formally treat international donor organizations as

[2]Please note that compared to Grossman and Helpman (1996), our set-up is more general (i.e., we allow for more than two parties and allow the assumption of a non-uniform distribution for Ψ). Therefore, the equilibrium results of Grossman and Helpman (GH) do not directly apply to our more general setup. However, at this stage, we do not prove that the essential results of GH also hold for our more general set-up but instead assume this point exogenously. We leave a rigorous proof of this assumption for future work.

interest groups (i.e., the amount of financial aid provided by these organizations corresponds to their intrinsic policy preferences, $W_j(\gamma)$, with j = donor).

After rearrangement the share equation results in:

$$S_k = \frac{1}{n}\sum_v P_{vk} = \frac{1}{n}\sum_v F_k^v(\gamma_k) \tag{10}$$

Finally, parties have also intrinsic policy preferences (i.e., we understand politicians not as pure office-seeking agents who maximize their political support S_k but also as parties with intrinsic policy preferences). Let $u_k(\gamma_k)$ denote the intrinsic policy preferences of party k. Then the total utility of a party results as:

$$U_k = S_k(\gamma_k) + \vartheta_k u_k(\gamma_k) \tag{11}$$

ϑ_k is a party-specific weight that reflects the relative importance of rents received from political office versus the intrinsic utility derived from a policy. Accordingly, the policy platform chosen by a governmental party $k = G$ to maximize its total utility derived from political support and its intrinsic political utility results from the following first-order condition:

$$\begin{aligned}\frac{\partial U_G}{\partial \gamma_G} &= \frac{\partial S_G}{\partial \gamma_G} + \frac{\partial u_G}{\partial \gamma_G}\\ &= \sum_{v \in NV}\sum_k \frac{\partial F_G^v}{\partial V_{vk}}\left(\beta_v \frac{\partial V_{vk}^P}{\partial \gamma_G} + \delta_v \frac{\partial V_{vk}^R}{\partial \gamma_G} + \alpha_v \alpha_{vGk}^L \sum_J \rho_{kJ} \frac{\partial W_J}{\partial \gamma_G}\right)\\ &\quad + \vartheta_k \frac{\partial u_G}{\partial \gamma_G}\\ &= 0\end{aligned} \tag{12}$$

Rearrangement implies:

$$\frac{\partial U_G}{\partial \gamma_G} = \beta_G \frac{\partial V_G^P}{\partial \gamma_G} + \delta_G \frac{\partial Z_G^r}{\partial \gamma_G} + \alpha_G \frac{\partial W_G}{\partial \gamma_G} + \vartheta_G \frac{\partial u_G}{\partial \gamma_G} = 0 \tag{13}$$

where it holds:

$$\begin{aligned}\beta_G &= \sum_{v \in NV} F_{GG}^v \beta_v;\ \delta_G = \sum_{v \in NV} \delta_G \left|\sum_k F_{Gk}^v \delta_{vkr}\right|;\ \alpha_G\\ &= \sum_J \rho_{JG} \sum_{v \in NV} \alpha_v \left|\sum_k F_{Gk}^v \alpha_{vGk}^L\right|\end{aligned} \tag{14}$$

$$\frac{\partial V_G^{PV}}{\partial \gamma_G} = \sum_v \frac{F_{GG}^v \beta_v}{\beta_G} \frac{\partial V_{vG}^{PV}}{\partial \gamma_G}; \frac{\partial Z_G^R}{\partial \gamma_G} = \sum_v \frac{\delta_v \sum_k F_{Gk}^v \delta_{vkr}}{\delta_G} \frac{\partial Z_v^r}{\partial \gamma_G}; \frac{\partial W_G}{\partial \gamma_G} - \sum_J \frac{\rho_{JG}}{\sum_H \rho_{HG}} \frac{\partial W_J}{\partial \gamma_G} \tag{15}$$

$$F_{Gk}^v = \frac{\partial F_G^v}{\partial V_{vk}} \tag{16}$$

It follows from Eq. (13) that the optimal policy platform chosen by a governmental party G, given the platforms of all other parties, satisfies the necessary condition for maximizing a weighted sum of the average welfare of voters, the aggregated welfare of all interest group members and the intrinsic policy preferences of a party.

3.3 *Political Equilibrium*

Following Schofield (2001), we apply the concept of Local Nash Equilibrium (LNE); a strategy vector $\gamma^*=[\gamma^*_1,\ldots,\gamma^*_p] \in \Gamma$ is a local weak (strict) Nash equilibrium of the profile function $S:\Gamma \rightarrow R$ if, for each party k, there exists a neighborhood Γ_k of γ^*_k in Γ such that:

$$S_k(\gamma_k^*, \gamma_{-k}^*) \geq S_k(\gamma_k, \gamma_{-k}^*) \, for \, all \, \gamma_k \in \Gamma_k \tag{17}$$

The LNE is strict (LSNE) if the inequality holds strictly; otherwise, it is a weak LNE. As Schofield demonstrates nicely, assuming an extreme value distribution for Ψ implies that the first-order condition in Eq. (13) is a necessary but not sufficient condition for an LNE. In particular, second-order conditions must be fulfilled to guarantee that a strategy vector γ is an LSNE.

However, in contrast to our approach, Schofield incorporated neither lobbying behavior nor retrospective voting.

3.4 *Voter Behavior and Government Performance*

Before we present our empirical estimations, we derive indices that describe the implications of voter behavior for government performance. As described in the introduction, according to the relevant literature (e.g., Keefer and Khemani 2005 and Bardhan and Mookherjee 2002), less electoral competition implies incentives for the government to implement policies that do not correspond to the needs and desires of the majority of society (i.e., government performance is c.p. lower). Given our derivations above, the more c.p. voters rely on non-policy indicators when evaluating parties, the less a political support-maximizing government considers voters' preferred policy position when it formulates governmental policies. Formally, the larger the α-parameter in relation to the β—and δ -parameters, the more voters base their vote choice on non-policy factors; thus, more electoral competition implies that the government orients its policy towards organized interest groups and ignores voters. Accordingly, we define an index of governmental accountability (GA) vis-a-vis the voter as the following relation:

$$GA_1 = \frac{\beta_G + \delta_G}{\alpha_G + \beta_G + \delta_G} \tag{18}$$

While GA_1 measures the relative accountability of the government vis-a-vis the voter, a low value for GA_1 does not necessarily imply that the government is not accountable to society because a high α-value only implies that the electoral outcome is significantly driven by campaign spending. Thus, as long as campaign funds are generated primarily by national interest groups, elected politicians might still have strong incentives to represent society's interests, as organized interest groups are constituted by members of society. Only if campaign spending is derived primarily from other organizations (e.g., international donors) does a high α-value imply low government accountability. This effect occurs because international donor organizations do not represent society members. In many cases, donor organizations act in the interest of a specific society group, but from a society perspective, donor-driven policies are at best derived from imposed welfare functions.

Further, as demonstrated by Eq. (13), the larger ϑ_G is in relation to the sum $(\alpha_G + \beta_G + \delta_G)$, the larger is c.p. the incentive of the government to pursue its self-interest. Hence, we derive GA_2 as a second index of government accountability:

$$GA_2 = \frac{\vartheta_G}{\alpha_G + \beta_G + \delta_G} \tag{19}$$

A third intuitively conceivable measure of government accountability corresponds to the incentive for the government to diverge from the policy outcome that results from a perfect electoral competition. Following Schofield (2007), we define the electoral center (γ^{**}) as the policy position that maximizes the electoral support of the government, assuming that no lobbying influence occurs and that the government is solely office-seeking (i.e., the government derives no own intrinsic utility from policies) (i.e., $\vartheta_G = 0$). Thus, it holds:

$$\gamma^{**} = \text{argmax} \sum_v w_v V_v^P(\gamma) \tag{20}$$

w_v denotes the political weight of a voter v and is defined below in Eq. (24). Given the definition of the electoral center, a straightforward measure of government accountability corresponds to the change of party platform a government can make in comparison to the electoral center without losing the elections, as follows:

$$\Delta\gamma = \text{argmax}\left[\Delta\gamma^{'}\beta\Delta\gamma\right] \tag{21}$$

s.t.:

$$S(\Delta\gamma + \gamma^{**}) \geq 0.5 \tag{22}$$

β denotes the vector of the normalized weights of the different policy dimensions taken as the average across all voters. Expressing $\Delta\gamma$ as a percentage of γ^{**} indicates the leeway of the government to select a policy that pursues its own interests against society's will without losing the election. Thus, the larger this percentage, the lower is c.p. the government accountability (GA_3):

$$GA_3 = 1 - \frac{\Delta\gamma}{\gamma^{**}} \tag{23}$$

Moreover the relative weight of the policy position of an individual voter determining governmental policy results from Eq. (13) as:

$$w_v = \frac{F_{GG}^{v}\beta_v + \delta_v \sum_k F_{Gk}^{v}\delta_{vkr}}{(\beta_G + \delta_G)} \tag{24}$$

As explained in detail below the relative political weight of individual voters depends on the relative importance of policy and non-policy voting motives. Please note that a perfect democratic vote corresponds to an equal relative weight for all voters (i.e., the weight of each voter equals $\frac{1}{n}$ if n is the total number of voters). If voters differ in the relative importance of voting motives, they also have different voting weights; in particular, the relative importance of the valence component in comparison to the policy-oriented and retrospective voting component determines the relative weights of voters.

Further, we can also derive the relative political weight of social groups. We define social groups as partitions of the total society (e.g., rich versus poor or rural versus urban voters), where T denotes the index of a social group. Thus, it holds:

$$w_T = \sum_{v \in T} w_v \tag{25}$$

Based on the political weights of social groups, we define governmental capture as the average weight of a member of a social group T compared to the average political weight of a member of another social group $T^{'}$:

$$GC = \frac{w_T}{w_{T'}}\frac{n_{T'}}{n_T} \tag{26}$$

The relative weight of an individual voter and hence of a social group is determined by relative voting behavior, i.e., the relative importance of non-policy versus policy voting motives.

Further, government capture results from the lobbying activities of vested interest groups. Particularly when not all society members are equally organized into interest groups (Grossman and Helpman 1996) or when the relative political weight of different interest groups deviates from the corresponding population shares of the society members organized in these interest groups (Bardhan and Mookherjee 2002). Capture that results from the asymmetric political influence of organized interest groups is analyzed in Chapter "A Network Based Approach to Evaluate Participatory Policy Processes: An Application to CAADP in Malawi", and we do not further explore this subject here. However, please note that given our general theoretical framework, it follows that biased electoral competition might compensate for biased incentives of politicians induced by asymmetric lobbying activities and vice-versa. Thus, at least theoretically, although both channels of interest mediation, election and lobbying, are biased still a unbiased policy might result.

To measure the relative importance of different voting motives, we proceed as follows. First, for voting motives based on indicator variables controlled by parties (i.e., policy-oriented voting based on party platforms and retrospective voting based on observed economic development that is indirectly controlled by governmental party choices), we use relative marginal effects of the different indicator variables. In particular, we define the marginal effect of an indicator variable κ, controlled by a governmental party, as follows:

$$ME_{k\kappa} = \frac{\partial S_k}{\partial \kappa} \tag{27}$$

Then we can define the following directional utility differentials:

$$ME^P = \sum_{\kappa=\gamma} |ME_{k\kappa}| \tag{28}$$

$$ME^R = \sum_{\kappa=z^r} |ME_{k\kappa}| \tag{29}$$

Accordingly, the importance of a utility component corresponds to the sum of the absolute marginal effects of the indicator variables that determine this component. If we mean-scale all indicator variables, the sum of the absolute marginal effects corresponds to the change in the reelection probability that is induced by a 100% change of all indicator variables in a direction that increases the reelection of a party k. In contrast to policy-oriented and retrospective voting, non-policy indicator variables that are used by voters to evaluate a candidate's competence, such as appearance, ethnicity, etc., cannot be easily changed by a party in the short- or medium-run. Hence, non-policy indicator variables determine a constant utility that voters assign to parties. To measure the relative importance of the non-policy utility component, we compute the change in the reelection probability of a party that is derived under the assumption that voters would not apply non-policy indicators to evaluate parties. Technically, this change corresponds to the change in the reelection probability of a party assuming α_v equals zero, e.g. $S_k(v_v, a_v) - S_k(v_v, a_v = 0)$. Accordingly, we can approximate this absolute difference in the reelection probability by the following marginal effect. For notational convenience we derive this marginal effect for the governmental party G:

$$ME_{vG}^{NP} = \left|\frac{\partial S_G^v}{\partial \alpha_v}\right| = \left|\sum_k \frac{\partial S_G^v}{\partial V_{vk}^{NP}} V_{vk}^{NP}\right| \tag{30}$$

The relative importance of voting motives results as the relation of the marginal utilities, e.g. the relative importance of the valence vis-à-vis the policy component results as:

$$RRI^{NP} = \frac{ME^{NP}}{ME^P} \tag{31}$$

With respect to content, the index RRI^{NP} indicates the percentage change by which a governmental party would need to adapt its policy platform to compensate for the electoral advantage or disadvantage implied by non-policy voting.

Analogously, we define the relative importance of retrospective voting vis-à-vis the policy component by:

$$RRI^R = \frac{ME^R}{ME^P} \tag{32}$$

RI corresponds to the rate of substitution (i.e., the percentage change in the policy position of the governmental party that is needed to compensate for a 1% change in the economic satisfaction perceived by a voter). Finally, to assess the relative importance of different voting motives empirically, we relate calculated relative marginal effects (*RRI*) to the sum of all marginal effects:

$$RI^{NP} = \frac{|ME^{NP}|}{|ME^{NP}| + |ME^P| + |ME^R|}; RI^P = \frac{|ME^P|}{|ME^{NP}| + |ME^P| + |ME^R|}; RI^R = \frac{|ME^R|}{|ME^{NP}| + |ME^P| + |ME^R|} \tag{33}$$

4 Econometric Models and Estimation Strategy

Following the probabilistic voter model, we assume that the probability (P_{vk}) that a voter v votes for a party k results from a logit function. For example:

$$P_{vk} = \left[\sum_{l} \exp(V_{vl} - V_{vk})\right]^{-1} \tag{34}$$

where V_{vk} denotes the utility that voter v derives from party k. As described above, we assume different policy and non-policy utility components (i.e., a valence V^{NP} component, a retrospective V^{R} component, and a policy-oriented V^{P} component):

$$V_{vk} = \beta_v V_{vk}^{P} + \delta_v V_{vk}^{R} + \alpha_v V_{vk}^{NP} \tag{35}$$

However, because we cannot observe all of the relevant variables that determine a voter's utility empirically, we use different indicator variables to approximate a voter's utility. In particular, we approximate the different utility components using a set of voter- and party-specific indicator variables:

$$V_{vk}^{P} = \sum_{d} \beta_d (\gamma_{dk} - x_{dv})^2; V_{vk}^{NP} = \alpha_k^0 + \sum_{z} \alpha_k^z Z_v; V_{vk}^{R} = \sum_{r} \delta_k^r R_{vr} \tag{36}$$

Technically, we estimate a probabilistic voter model by taking policy distances as party-specific variables and voter characteristics as individual-specific variables. In particular, x_{dv} denotes voter v's ideal point regarding a relevant policy dimension d, while γ_{dk} denotes the party position on the policy dimension d. Further, we approximate a voter's non-policy utility using a party-specific constant,α_k^0, and a set of voter-specific variables, Z_v, for which we estimate a set of party-specific coefficients, α_k^z. z_v is a vector of voter-specific characteristics, including socioeconomic variables (e.g., age, sex and ethnicity). In the context of this specification, we assume that voters have a common belief regarding the competence valence of parties, which is captured in the party-specific constants. However, we further assume that beyond this common belief, specific voter groups might share a common evaluation bias for a party k. Thus, as described above, to capture potential heterogeneity in a voter's perception of party valence competence, we introduce the vector of socio-demographic characteristics, z_v. Moreover, we use a direct measurement of a voter's perception of government performance,[3] i.e. voter's approval of the work of specific governmental bodies, e.g. the president. We consider this

[3]Please note that a more flexible way to control for potential heterogeneity corresponds to the estimation of a latent class model. We also undertook latent class estimation of the corresponding voter model for Malawi, which basically implied the same results. Therefore, to keep the analyses simple, we focus on a standard logit model in this paper.

measure as an indicator for non-policy voting, as the perceived approval of the quality of the work of a governmental body, like the president, is highly dependent on characteristics, which are not related to policy issues. Furthermore, we assume that perceived approval can be strongly influenced by campaign spending and other interest group activities. Finally, we approximate a voter's retrospective voting component using a set of voter-specific indicator variables, R_v, that corresponds to a voter's retrospective perceptions of the economic well-being realized in Malawi.

Equation (34) allows us to calculate probabilities and marginal effects for each individual party. The derived coefficients will be used to calculate the different indices of government performance and the relative importance of different voting motives.

4.1 Data

Before we present our the data used in the estimation, we first briefly describe the party system of Malawi in the next subsection, as an understanding of the historical development of the country and its party system facilitates the interpretation of the estimation results.

4.1.1 The Party System and Elections in Malawi

Malawi is still a young democracy, with its first free multiparty elections held in 1994. Since 1994, four additional elections took place. During the nineteenth century, Malawi was colonized by the British Empire; until 1964, Malawi was part of the British Commonwealth, when it became independent under the leadership of Dr. Hastings Kamuzu Banda. Banda was the first president of Malawi; he ruled the country with the support of his MCP. In the first multi-party elections in 1994, Bakili Muluzi from the UDF won the majority with 47% of the votes and put an end to the regime of Banda after nearly 30 years. Muluzi succeeded again in the second elections, which occurred five years later. Although by constitution, a two-term limit for presidents exists, Muluzi tried to run for presidential elections a third time. He did not succeed, and was instead forced to choose Bingu Wa Mutharika to become his successor. Mutharika likewise proved to be a very successful leader and won the elections in 2004 and the subsequent elections in 2009. However, Mutharika separated from the United Democratic Front (UDF) shortly after his first electoral success and founded his own party: the Democratic Progressive Party (DPP). To date, the DPP remains very successful in Malawi, holding 114 of the total 160 seats in the national assembly. The opposition is once again led by the Malawi Congress Party (MCP), with 26 seats, and the UDF, with 17 seats. All other parties in Malawi are negligible, gaining only a marginal percentage of votes in the last elections.

Given the relatively short democratic experience in Malawi, the political parties in this country are rather weak (e.g., parties are easily formed and dissolved based on the availability and need of powerful political leaders). Mutharika proved to be a prominent example of this behavior. Nevertheless, three parties (i.e., the MCP, the UDF and the DPP) are currently established as political parties in Malawi. Interestingly, although the political parties appear to be weak, the party identity of Malawian voters appears to be high (i.e., two thirds of the Malawian citizens feel affiliated with a political party). However, the principal reason that people are attached to a political party is not the party itself but the party leader. The Afrobarometer survey demonstrated that while only 50% of respondents trust the DPP as a party, 64% trust Mutharika as the president.

4.1.2 Afrobarometer Voter Survey

After analyzing voting behavior theoretically, the following sections will empirically derive voting behavior in Malawi. A major challenge of estimating probabilistic voter models is the availability of adequate data. For case studies in Africa, the Afrobarometer survey offers such data. Afrobarometer is an independent, nonpartisan research project that measures the social, political, and economic atmosphere in Africa. Afrobarometer surveys have been conducted since 1999, when 12 countries were questioned in a first round. To date, five rounds have been completed, with the last round covering 22 Sub-Saharan African countries. Malawi was part of the survey from the beginning. The data set used in this paper is from the fourth round of the survey, which was conducted in 2008 (Afrobarometer 2008). In round four, 1200 Malawians were interviewed. Using random selection methods and sampling with probability proportionate to population size (PPPS), the sample is a representative cross-section of all citizens of voting age in Malawi. Most of the questionnaires were employed in rural areas (85%), and only 15% were employed in urban areas, which corresponds to the real distribution. The respondents included equal numbers of women and men, with a mean age of 35; the oldest respondent was 88 years old, and the youngest respondent was 18 years old. An evaluation of the educational background of the respondents reveals that 18% of the questioned Malawians have no formal schooling. The majority (43%) had some formal schooling, and approximately 38% completed at least primary school. General census data is confirmed by the Afrobarometer survey. Malawi is one of the poorest countries in the world, listed at rank 171 of 187 in the Human Development Index of 2011. The per capita income was 310 U.S. Dollars in 2010, with 50.7% of the population living below the national poverty line (World Bank 2013a, b).

To analyze voting behavior, the most important variable of the dataset is vote choice. Accordingly, respondents were asked to answer the following question: "If a presidential election were held tomorrow, which party's candidate would you vote for?"

Table 1 shows this variable's distribution compared to the results for the three major parties from the elections in 2009. Compared to the Afrobarometer survey,

Table 1 Election results

	DPP	MCP	UDF
Afrobarometer (2008)	77.14	8.32	14.53
Presidential election (2009)	66.17	30.49	

Source: Afrobarometer (2008), African Elections Database (2014)

the Democratic Progressive Party (DPP) gained even more votes and won the presidential elections in 2009 with more than two thirds of the vote, although the Malawi Congress Party (MCP) and the United Democratic Front (UDF) formed an electoral alliance. While vote choice will be the dependent variable, the independent variables can be classified as indicators of policy-oriented, retrospective and non-policy-oriented voting, as explained above. Additionally, to address heterogeneity, we included several socioeconomic variables of voters.

In particular, to capture policy-oriented voting, policy distances between the voter and each party for relevant policy issues are used as indicators. Unfortunately, Afrobarometer did not ask for policy positions on specific policy issues. However, Afrobarometer included a set of policy-related statements and asked individual respondents to indicate their degree of agreement or disagreement with the different statements. The following statements are examples of the policy-related statements used in the Afrobarometer survey:

Statement 1: Government should be able to ban any organization that goes against its policies

Statement 2: We should be able to join any organization, whether or not the government approves of it (Afrobarometer 2008, question Q19)

Overall, we used 12 policy statements (i.e., Q16, Q19, Q20, Q21, Q31, Q32, Q35, Q36, Q37, Q29A–C) and applied a principal component analysis to identify relevant policy issues as underlying factors. Empirically, the conducted factor analysis implied a one factor solution. Based on the factor-loading matrix of different statements, we interpreted high positive factor values as a preference for a strong state (i.e., a more autocratic political leadership of the government); in contrast, low and negative factor values can be interpreted as a preference for a weak state (i.e., a more participatory leadership of the government).[4]

Based on the factor analysis, we calculated individual factor values for each voter, which we interpreted as voters' preferred policy position (x_{dv}). To calculate the corresponding party positions (γ_{vd}), the mean policy position of all voters who voted for a particular party was obtained. This method is known as partisan constituencies and has been used widely by political scientists (e.g., Schofield 2011). Finally, following the classical proximity model of Downs, the distance between the voter's and the party's policy positions were calculated as the quadratic distance between the voter's policy position and the policy position of a given party

[4]Further details on the results of the factor analysis are available from the author on request.

(POL-DIST). We took this distance as our principal indicator of policy-oriented voting.

To measure retrospective voting, we constructed an indicator variable based on the following question from the Afrobarometer questionnaire: "In general, how would you describe: The present economic condition of this country?" Possible answers were: "Very bad," "Fairly bad," "Neither good nor bad," "Fairly good" and "Very good" (Afrobarometer 2008, question Q4A). To construct an indicator of retrospective voting (RETRO), we scaled the answer from 1 = Very bad to 5 = very good. To incorporate non-policy voting into our empirical model, we estimated a party-specific constant (CONST). Moreover, to capture potential heterogeneity in a voter's perception of party competence, we introduced the following socio-demographic characteristics z_v as alternative specific variables. First, we included regional dummy variables (NORTH, CENTRAL) for voters living in the northern or central regions of Malawi, respectively; the southern region is used as the default region. Second, we included ethnicity (YAO, LOMWE, CHEWA), gender (GENDER) and living in a rural or urban area (RURAL) as additional dummy variables in our econometric estimations. In particular, YAO, LOMWE, or CHEWA = 1 implies that a voter belongs to the corresponding ethnic group, while gender = 1 indicates a male respondent and rural = 1 indicates a respondent living in a rural area. EDUCATION is measures on an ordinal scale (1 = no formal education – 9 = University completed), and AGE is measured in years. To measure income, the Afrobarometer survey provides data to apply the LPI index (LPI) (Mattes 2008).

Table 2 presents the descriptive statistics for all variables included in the preferred model. High LPI values correspond to higher poverty levels, while low values indicate lower poverty levels. Please note that we included all socioeconomic variables as alternative specific variables, where we take the incumbent party DPP as reference party. Moreover, we use the Afrobarometer question, "Do you approve or disapprove of the way the following people have performed their jobs over the past twelve months, or haven't you heard enough about them to say: President Bingu wa Mutharika" (Afrobarometer 2008, question Q70A) to obtain a direct measurement of a voter's general perception of government performance (PRES_APPR).

4.2 *Results*

4.2.1 Goodness of Fit and Model Selection

To further analyze voting behavior in Malawi, we estimated a probabilistic voter model using a mixed conditional logit approach. The results are presented in Table 3. We estimated different specifications. In model 1, we began by using only the party-specific constant and policy distance as explanatory variables. In model 2, we include voters' evaluation of the current economic condition of Malawi, corresponding to the retrospective voting motive, and in model 3, we

Table 2 Descriptive statistics

	N	Mean	sd	se	CI-left	CI-right	min	max
POLICY POSITION	805	0.000	0.881	0.031	−0.061	0.061	−1.185	2.676
POL-DIST-DPP	805	0.777	1.018	0.036	0.706	0.847	0	6.959
POL-DIST-MCP	805	0.775	1.052	0.037	0.703	0.848	0	7.157
POL-DIST-UDF	805	0.777	1.092	0.039	0.701	0.852	0	7.373
RETRO	805	2.965	1.253	0.044	2.879	3.052	1	5
PRES_APPR	805	3.429	0.916	0.032	3.365	3.492	1	4
CHEWA	805	0.322	0.467	0.016	0.289	0.354	0	1
YAO	805	0.130	0.337	0.012	0.107	0.154	0	1
CENTRAL	805	0.398	0.490	0.017	0.364	0.431	0	1
NORTH	805	0.145	0.353	0.012	0.121	0.170	0	1
LPI	805	1.318	0.887	0.031	1.257	1.380	0	3.800
GENDER	805	0.471	0.500	0.018	0.436	0.505	0	1
AGE	805	34.584	13.234	0.466	33.670	35.498	18	87
EDUCATION	805	3.612	1.554	0.055	3.505	3.720	1	9

Source: own calculation

included voters' approval of the president as a non-policy voting motive. Finally, in model specifications 4 and 5, we included additional voter characteristics to take potential heterogeneity in voting behavior into account. In particular, in model 4, we include regional dummy variables, as they were a major explanatory factor during past presidential elections. Moreover, in model specification 5, the socio-economic variables ethnicity, gender, education, age, income and rural were included. Please note that we included all of the additional variables that describe specific voter characteristics as alternative specific variables, with the incumbent party DPP as reference party. As demonstrated in Table 3, goodness of fit significantly increases from model 1 to 5, with McFadden R^2 improving from 0.01 in model 1 to nearly 0.3 in model 3. Thus, the party choice of the average Malawian voter is significantly driven by non-policy factors. We interpret the voter-specific constant as party loyalty, which is a more stable perception of party competence. In contrast, the perceived performance of the president is influenced by time-specific shocks, including lobbying activities. Moreover, we identify significant heterogeneity in party loyalty, where party identity is significantly influenced by ethnicity, as well as regional origin and income. In particular, voters from the central region strongly identify with the MCP (see the estimated parameter of 2.422 for MCP-CENTRAL in model 5), while people living in the northern region of Malawi clearly identify with the incumbent party DPP, as indicated by the strongly negative coefficients for both MCP-NORTH and UDF-NORTH. Finally the south represents a stronghold of the UDF, with a high and significant UDF-CONST of 5.657. Furthermore, for the Yao ethnic group, a significant party loyalty for the UDF, which is the former presidential party, can be observed. The MCP is primarily supported by the Chewa tribe, with parameter estimations of 1.404 for UDF-YAO and 0.843 for MCP-CHEWA in model 5 (see Table 3).

Table 3 Model specifications

	Model 1: Down's Model		Model 2: + Retrospective voting		Model 3: + approval of the president		Model 4: + regional voting		Model 5: + NP-variables		Model 6: optimal model	
	coef	P	coef	P	coef	P	coef	P	coef	P	coef	P
MCP:(INTERCEPT)	−2.235***	0.000	−0.816**	0.007	3.810***	0.000	1.381	0.102	2.175	0.079	1.840	0.055
UDF:(INTERCEPT)	−1.711***	0.000	−0.094	0.700	4.981***	0.000	5.286***	0.000	5.657***	0.000	5.541***	0.000
POL-DIST	−2.734***	0.001	−3.177***	0.000	−2.932**	0.005	−2.139 .	0.052	−1.969 .	0.098	−2.272*	0.049
MCP:RETRO			−0.512***	0.000	−0.330**	0.007	−0.301*	0.035	−0.378*	0.018	−0.355*	0.021
UDF:RETRO			−0.598***	0.000	−0.370***	0.001	−0.276*	0.014	−0.408**	0.002	−0.372**	0.003
MCP:PRES_APPR					−1.553***	0.000	−1.497***	0.000	−1.604***	0.000	−1.534***	0.000
UDF:PRES_APPR					−1.784***	0.000	−1.788***	0.000	−1.806***	0.000	−1.786***	0.000
MCP:NORTH							−15.385	0.994	−15.690	0.993	−15.122	0.994
UDF:NORTH							−2.414**	0.001	−2.071**	0.009	−1.735*	0.021
MCP:CENTRAL							2.991***	0.000	2.224***	0.001	2.422***	0.000
UDF:CENTRAL							−0.923**	0.002	−0.854*	0.022	−0.744*	0.041
MCP:YAO									−0.290	0.701	−0.033	0.964
UDF:YAO									1.404**	0.001	1.603***	0.000
MCP:CHEWA									0.843 .	0.067	1.075*	0.011
UDF:CHEWA									−0.034	0.939	0.121	0.768
MCP:LOMWE									−1.373	0.223		
UDF:LOMWE									−0.477	0.303		
MCP:EDUCATION									−0.087	0.435		
UDF:EDUCATION									0.080	0.472		
MCP:RURAL									0.185	0.703		
UDF:RURAL									0.183	0.639		
MCP:GENDER									−0.298	0.370		
UDF:GENDER									−0.192	0.517		
MCP:AGE									0.023 .	0.074		

UDF:AGE									−0.002	0.877		
MCP:LPI									−0.415*	0.041	−0.314	0.106
UDF:LPI									−0.423*	0.024	−0.433*	0.020
Log-Likelihood:	−547.04		−514.73		−389.33		−333.69		−304.28		−309.79	
McFadden R^2	0.01		0.07		0.30		0.40		0.45		0.44	

Source: own estimation

*** $p < 0.001$, **$p < 0.01$, *$p < 0.05$, . $p < 0.1$

The negative coefficients for MCP-LPI and UDF-LPI in model 5 imply that poor people tend to vote for the DPP with a higher probability than rich people. Other socioeconomic variables (i.e., age, gender and rural) have no significant impact on voting behavior. Therefore, we excluded these insignificant variables to improve the efficiency of our estimation. Accordingly, model 6 corresponds to our preferred model specification, which has the highest statistical fit when compared to all other model specifications (see the log-likelihood values presented in Table 3).

4.2.2 Voting Behavior in Malawi

It follows directly from our estimation results that all voting motives are significant determinants of the party choices of Malawian voters. However, the importance of different voting motives varies. To evaluate the absolute importance of non-policy voting, we approximated the marginal effect by setting the weight of the voting motive equal to zero. Neglecting non-policy voting ($\alpha_v = 0$) implies that the vote shares of parties would significantly change. Interestingly, Malawian voters feel strongly affiliated to their governmental party, although the party only exists for 10 years compared to the well established parties UDC and MCP that exist for 22 and 55 years respectively. Accordingly, ignoring non-policy voting implies that the vote shares of the UDF and the MCP increase by 6% and 13%, while the vote share of the governmental party (i.e., DPP) would decrease by 18% points to just 59%. Economic voting (i.e., retrospective voting based on voters' perception of economic development) has only a moderate impact on election outcomes. Assuming that voters' perception of the economic development under the government increases from 'very bad' to 'very good' implies an increase of the vote share of the DPP by 14% points; the corresponding vote shares of the UDF and the MCP decrease by 8% and 6%, respectively. Thus, in contrast to the findings of Bratton et al. (2011), our estimation results for Malawi imply only a moderate, though certainly significant, importance of retrospective economic voting.

In addition to party identity and economic voting, policy-oriented voting is also an important voting motive of the Malawian voter. At a first glance, this finding appears to be a paradox due to the fact that the policy distances have a rather low explanatory power when compared to other non-policy indicator variables (see Table 3). Competing parties tend to adopt the same party platforms; thus, from the viewpoint of the voter, parties hardly differ in their policy-oriented utility component. This observation underlies the relatively low explanatory power of policy-oriented voting. However, the importance of policy voting is nicely demonstrated by Fig. 1. Assuming that the governmental party shifts its present moderate ideological policy position of 0.038 to an extreme position favoring an extremely weak (−3) or strong (+3) state implies that political support for the DPP decreases from 77% to nearly 0% and only 20%, respectively.

Interestingly, an extreme position favoring a strong state would be less harmful for the DPP than an extreme position favoring a weak state (i.e., an extreme participatory policy style). Regardless, these simulation results demonstrate that

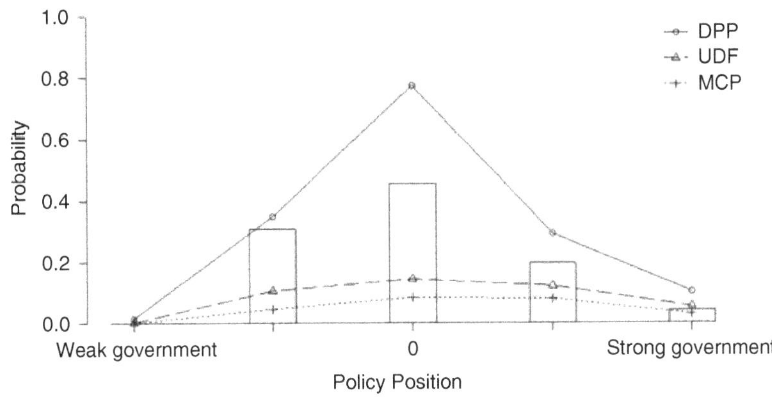

Fig. 1 Importance of policy-oriented voting in the 2008 election in Malawi. Source: Authors

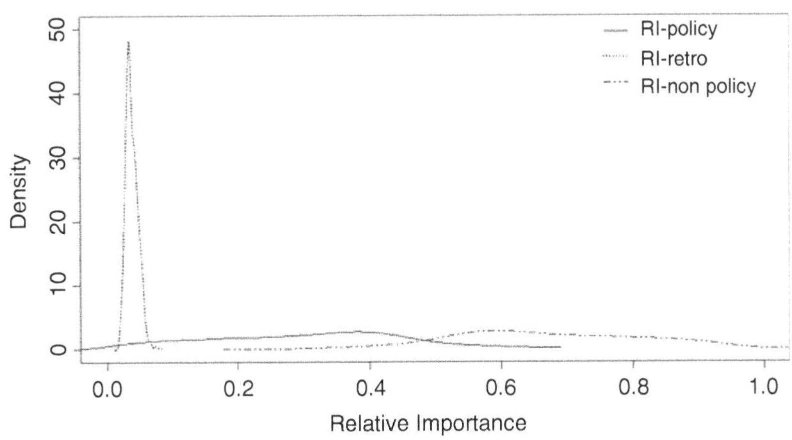

Fig. 2 Relative importance of different voting motives in the 2008 election in Malawi. Source: Authors

Malawian voters discipline support-seeking parties to adopt ideological policy positions that correspond to the preferences of the median voter, as predicted by the Downsian theory of voting.

Furthermore, we calculated the relative marginal effects (RI^P, RI^{NP}, RI^R) based on our preferred model specification (i.e., model 6). In Fig. 2, we present the Kernel distribution of the relative marginal effects of different voting motives. The motives differ strongly in their relative importance. While retrospective voting always has a share lower than 10%, the relative importance of policy and non-policy voting is distributed far more widely, which shows that voting behavior is heterogeneous within a population. Taking the mean relative importance shows that non-policy voting is most important with 66%, followed by policy voting (30%) and retrospective voting with only 4%.

Finally, as described above, the estimation results indicate that significant heterogeneity in voting behavior exists, where in particular, voters' perception of party competence varies significantly with ethnicity, regional origin and income. Moreover, the estimation results imply that the importance of non-policy voting, varies significantly across ethnic groups and regions. As demonstrated in Figs. 3 and 4, non-policy voting is relatively important for the northern region and plays a comparatively minor role for the Yao and Chewa Ethnic Tribes.

However, despite the identified heterogeneity, for most Malawian voters, the second most important voting motive corresponds to policy-oriented voting. This result is remarkable, as most voter studies on African countries that are in the published literature highlight the fact that policies play only a minor role in the party preferences and electoral choices of African voters (Ferree 2004; Hoffman and Long 2013).

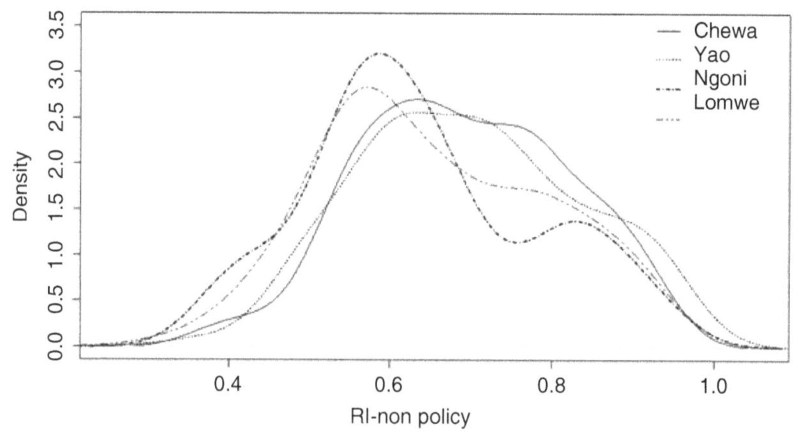

Fig. 3 Relative importance of non-policy voting according to ethnicity. Source: Authors

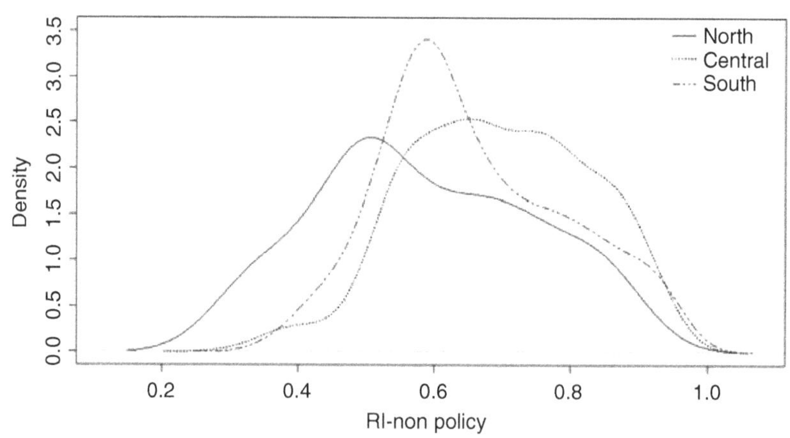

Fig. 4 Relative importance of non-policy voting according to region. Source: Authors

However, at the methodological level, our study differs from existing approaches, as we are estimating a probabilistic voter model by applying a conditional logit specification that takes ideological policy distances between individual voters and parties into account as party-specific attributes. Therefore, future work that empirically tests the extent to which the importance of policy-oriented voting also applies to other African countries or stands as a specific characteristic of the Malawian voter is of interest.

4.2.3 Voter Behavior and Government Performance

We first analyze government capture. Given our expositions above, government capture results from the different average voting weights of different social groups. Individual voting weights are calculated according to Eq. (24):

$$\hat{w}_{vG} = P_{vG}(1 - P_{vG})\left[\beta_v + \delta_{vG} - \sum_{k \neq G} \hat{s}_{vk}\delta_{vk}\right] \tag{37}$$

$$w_{vG} = \frac{\widehat{w}_{vG}}{\sum_v \widehat{w}_{vG}} \approx \frac{P_{vG}(1 - P_{vG})}{\sum_v P_{vG}(1 - P_{vG})} \tag{38}$$

In Eq. (37) s_{vk} denotes the estimated relative vote share of party k. In Fig. 5, we present the relative distribution of the calculated voting weights. As indicated by the Lorenz curve in Fig. 5, the effective voting weights are rather unequally distributed, with a corresponding Gini-coefficient of 0.461.[5]

Given the 805 individual voters in our survey, the average voting weight is 1/805. It follows from the approximation of the individual voting weights in Eq. (38) that swing voters (i.e., voters with a probability to reelect the governmental party that is close to 0.5) have a particularly high voting weight (Fig. 5).

Thus, the higher the share of swing voters in a specific social group, the more government is captured by this social group (i.e., the higher the incentives for a government seeking reelection to deliver policies and policy outcomes that benefit social groups with a high share of swing voters). However, a determination of whether voting weights vary systematically across voter groups is also of interest, e.g., in the literature, it is often assumed that poor people are less represented in the political process than rich people or that rural populations are less represented than urban voters (Keefer and Khemani 2005; Bardhan and Mookherjee 2002). In Fig. 6, we present the calculated capture indices for different social groups. The government of Malawi is significantly captured by the Central region at the expense of the Northern region and the South. Moreover, the Yao and Chewa ethnic tribes are also

[5]The Gini-coefficient measures the relative share of the area between the Lorenz curve and the angle bisecting plane and the total area under the angle bisecting plane. The latter measurement corresponds to a perfect equal distribution. Accordingly, a Gini-coefficient of 1 indicates a maximally unequal distribution, while a Gini coefficient of 0 indicates a perfect equal distribution.

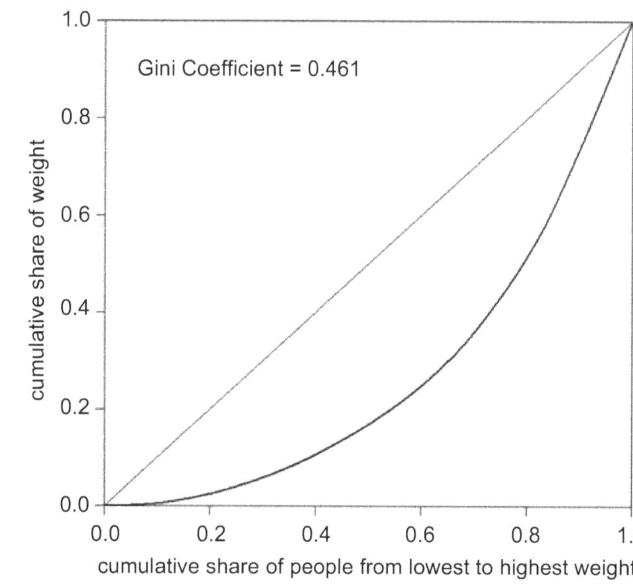

Fig. 5 Distribution of effective voting weights in the 2008 elections in Malawi. Source: Authors

capturing the government significantly. In contrast, there exists only moderate capture of the government by the rich voters compared to the poor, as indicated by a capture index of 1.19, i.e., compared to a rich voter, the average weight of a poor voter is 19% lower. Interestingly, political representation appears not to be biased against neither the rural population nor women. In detail, comparing the political weight of the rural and urban population based on the calculated capture index of 1.09 implies that political representation of a rural voter is only slightly lower when compared to an urban voter. Analogously, comparing the average political weights of men and women a higher weight for women results given a capture index of 0.93. The results are quite surprising as it is usually assumed that in developing countries both women and rural citizen, respectively, are heavily underrepresented in the political process.

Furthermore, as can be seen from Fig. 6 political representation varies significantly across ethnic and regional groups, where the Chewa and Yao tribes as well as the central region seem to be politically overrepresented, while the Northern region of Malawi seems to be politically underrepresented when compared to the average Malawian Voter. Thus, at first glance, our own results appear to confirm the hypothesis that ethno-regional party identity determines the vote choice in multiethnic and nascent African democracies. However, the resulting impact of specific ethno-regional voting patterns on government incentives and on the political representation of social groups is far more complex. For example, in the northern region, voters strongly identify with the governmental party (i.e., DPP), while in the central region, voters significantly identify with the MCP and in the southern region, voters identify with the UDF. But, while party identity with the MCP in the central region is compensated by a strong positive perception of the performance of the president, resulting in a large number of swing voters in the central region, the same positive perception increases voters' commitment in favor of the

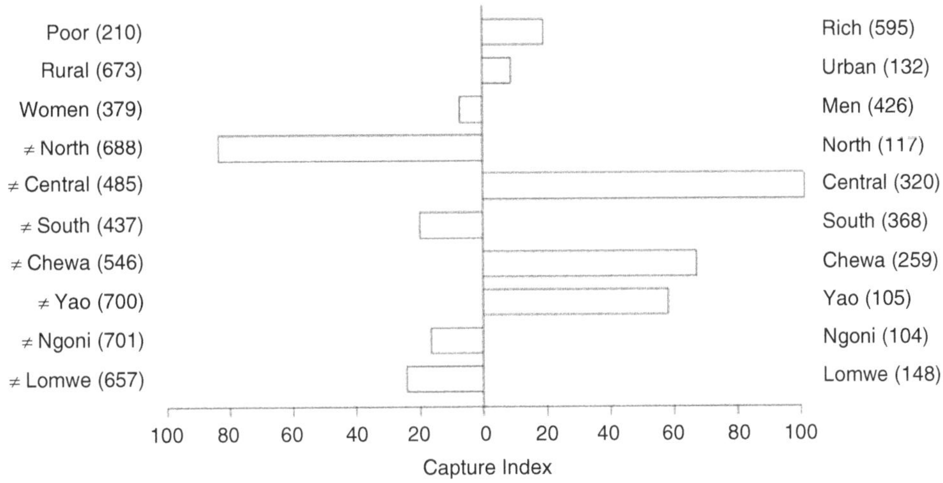

Fig. 6 Government capture by different social groups based on the 2008 elections in Malawi. Source: Authors

DPP and lowers electoral competition and government incentives to deliver policies benefiting Northern voters. Accordingly, the average voter weight is rather low in the northern region and high in the central region. Moreover, please note that a significant variation in voter behavior and in individual voting weights within regions and tribes can still be observed in Figs. 3 and 4 above.

While government capture corresponds to different political weights across social groups, government accountability measures the degree to which electoral competition implies that governmental policies correspond to the needs and desire of voters as a whole or the extent to which these policies are determined by lobbying activities or the intrinsic policy preferences of politicians. Based on our estimation results for our preferred model specification (i.e., model 6), we calculated an accountability index $GA_1 = 0.39$, which indicates that the total political weight of lobbying groups is 61% of the sum of the political weight of all voters and lobbying groups. Hence, in Malawi lobbying plays a major role as a political mechanism for communicating society's interest to politicians. This figure matches with results of the empirical policy network study we conducted in Malawi, where politicians indicate that when formulating their political position, they weight external positions communicated by interest groups between 5 and 90% when compared to their own intrinsic position, with an average weight of the external positions of lobbying groups of approximately 50% (see Chapter "A Network Based Approach to Evaluate Participatory Policy Processes: An Application to CAADP in Malawi"). However, compared to industrialized countries relative importance of lobbying appears to be significantly higher in Malawi, i.e. for EU countries policy network studies of Pappi and Henning reveal an average relative weight of the external positions of lobbying groups of approximately 35% (Pappi et al. 1995; Pappi and Henning 1999; Henning 2009). Thus, the results show that although Malawi has been a democracy for quite some time, the election process is not the most important mechanism in the political process, but interest groups and lobbying activities have the strongest influence. However, to measure the leeway of the government to select policies that do not correspond to the will of the electoral majority, we additionally calculate the accountability index GA_3. The latter is identified as the maximal divergence of the governmental policy position that still guarantees that the government will be reelected (i.e., achieve a vote share higher than 50%). Simulation analyses of the political response function of the governmental party imply that a majority is sustained over the interval $[-1.003, 0.8395]$, where the empirically observed policy position of the DPP is 0.038. Hence, given a maximal policy range of 6, the government can adapt its policy position between approximately -17% and $+13\%$ without losing the electoral majority. Hence, conclusion of a low accountability of the government vis-à-vis its electorate drawn from the calculated GA_1 index seems at least to be moderated based on the index GA_3.

4.2.4 Relating Government Performance and Voting Behavior

While we related governmental performance with voting behavior theoretically in the beginning of the chapter, we did not yet provide quantitative empirical evidence for our theoretical considerations. Therefore, we computed non-parametric regression analyses by regressing the normalized voting weight on the total sub-utility that voters derive from non-policy indicators V^{NP}. The latter factor results as the sum of a voter's party-specific constant and the sub-utility derived from the voter's approval of the government. As demonstrated in Fig. 7, a curve-linear relation exists between non-policy voting and voting weight. In particular, based on Eq. (38), it follows that the voting weight roughly corresponds to the term $P_{vG}(1 - P_{vG})$ (i.e., the more a voter is committed in favor of or against a party at the LNE, the lower is her effective voting weight). Further, as long as the LNE corresponds to a convergent equilibrium in party platforms (i.e., all parties have the

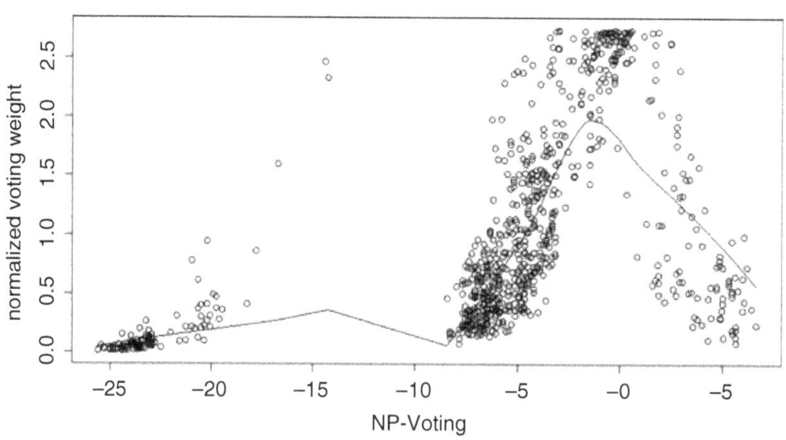

Fig. 7 Non-policy voting and voting weights. Source: Authors

same or very similar policy positions), the effective voting weights are solely determined by non-policy voting. Hence, the larger the differences between the non-policy utility components among parties, the more a voter is committed towards a specific party and the lower is c.p. her voting weight. Please note that the party to which a voter is committed is unimportant (i.e., a large absolute difference in the non-policy utility component among parties implies a high or low probability to vote for the governmental party). Hence, in both cases, a low value for the term $P_{vG}(1 - P_{vG})$ and a low voting weight result. Given the logistic response function, these results make sense, as a voter's local electoral response to political favors is higher when she assesses lower utility differences among political parties.

Beyond lobbying, politicians might also follow their intrinsic policy positions; we capture the relative importance of intrinsic policy preferences using our accountability index GA_2. However, the index GA_2 cannot be calculated based on our empirical estimation because we have no data on politicians' intrinsic policy preferences, parameter ϑ. However, we can estimate the extent to which the relative weight of intrinsic policy preferences would decrease if we assume that voters do not engage in non-policy voting. To this end, we recalculate the parameters $\alpha_G, \beta_G \, and \, \delta_G$, assuming party identity and approval voting is zero for all voters and divide the sum of these recalculated parameters by the sum of the originally estimated parameters. This ratio corresponds to the percentage of accountability that is achieved in comparison to the optimal accountability that would be achieved if all voters based their vote choice on policy indicators and observed economic performance. In the Malawi case, the ratio of actual to optimal accountability is 1.52, indicating that based on actual voting behavior the relative political weight of intrinsic policy preferences of the government is 1.52 times higher when compared to the relative political weight of government's intrinsic preferences induced assuming a perfectly policy-oriented voting behavior. However, without a further cross-country comparison including established democratic systems this accountability measure is hard to interpret. We leave this interesting topic for future research.

5 Conclusion and Outlook for Future Work

This paper integrates theoretical political economy approaches that explain the impact of voter behavior on government performance. We use advanced empirical voter studies to derive and test hypotheses on how the relative importance of different voting motives for different social groups induces electoral incentives for politicians, to serve the needs and desires of their electorate. Based on our theoretical model, we derive different indices of government performance, namely government capture and accountability that measure government incentives in political equilibrium to implement policies that serve special interest or pure self-interest at the expense of the general public.

In the empirical part of this paper, we estimate a probabilistic voting model by applying a mixed conditional logit (MCL) approach using Afrobarometer data for Malawi. Based on the estimated model, we calculate the theoretically derived indices of government accountability and capture. Moreover, we derive indices that measure the relative importance of different policy and non policy oriented voting motives for the electorate as a whole and several socioeconomic groups. Further, we test how the relative importance of different voting motives is related to government performance (i.e., accountability and capture). The principal empirical results are:

1. Beyond party identity Malawian voters apply different policy and non-policy indicators to evaluate parties and candidates, while retrospective voting only plays a minor role.
2. Voter behavior, i.e., the relative importance of non-policy versus policy oriented voting varies significantly across ethnic and regional groups. Accordingly, the estimated voter models imply that government is strongly captured by specific regional and ethnic groups, for which electoral choices are primarily determined by policy-oriented voting and far less by non-policy voting when compared to the average Malawian voter. In particular, the Central region and the Chewa and Yao ethnic groups are able to capture government at the expense of the Northern region and the Ngoni and Lomwe ethnic groups. However, contradicting common assumptions in the literature (Keefer and Khemani 2005; Bardhan and Mookherjee 2002), our estimation results imply that government is not captured by specific socioeconomic groups. Thus, neither the rich nor the urban voters and vice-versa neither the poor nor the rural voters are able to capture government significantly. Interestingly, our estimation results further imply that also Malawian women are not underrepresented in the political process when compared to men.
3. Government accountability vis-a-vis the Malawian voter is strongly limited by lobbying activities. However, this result is moderated by our third accountability index, i.e., assuming constant campaign spending the Malawi government can only shift its current policy by roughly 15% within the feasible policy space without losing its majority.
4. We provide quantitative empirical evidence for our central theoretical hypothesis that government performance is determined by the relative importance of non-policy voting, where applying a non-parametric regression we could perfectly explain observed individual voting weights as a nonlinear function of the sub-utility a voter derives from non-policy indicators.

Finally, the following qualifications of our main conclusion are necessary:

5. Our results clearly imply that the less voters rely on non-policy indicators and the more they base their electoral choices on party policy platforms and evaluate the competence of the government based on observed economic development, the more electoral competition induces incentives for the government to implement policies that correspond to the policy preferences of the majority of the society. However, this definition of government performance in terms of low

governmental capture and high government accountability does not necessarily imply that the government implements the most efficient policies. The latter conclusion results from the fact that voters' policy preferences might be biased. For instance, Beilhartz and Gersbach (2004), Bischoff and Siemers (2011) and Caplan (2007) emphasize the role of biased voter beliefs about policy impacts as a main determinant of inefficient policy choices. Voter beliefs are defined as agents' simplified mental models to approximate the complex true relation between policy instruments and induced policy outcomes. The work of Caplan is highly recognized in the public choice literature, as he collects an impressive amount of evidence for persistently biased voter beliefs. Based on his empirical findings, Caplan draws the rather pessimistic conclusion that democratic mechanisms of preference aggregation naturally lead to the choice of inefficient policies. Interestingly, taking biased voter beliefs into account, a high importance of lobbying in combination with governmental leadership that is driven by its own intrinsic political vision might induce more efficient policy choices while simultaneously decreasing governmental performance, as defined in terms of capture and accountability. Hence, the analysis of voter beliefs is an important topic of our future research.

References

Adams, J., B. Grofman, and S. Merrill. 2005. *A Unified Theory of Party Competition*. Cambridge: Cambridge University Press.

African Elections Database. 2014. *Election Results Malawi Database*. http://africanelections.tripod.com/mw.html. Accessed 8 Jan 2014.

Afrobarometer. 2008. http://afrobarometer.org/. Accessed May 2016.

Bardhan, P., and D. Mookherjee. 2002. *Relative Capture of Local and Central Governments: An Essay in the Political Economy of Decentralization*. Working Paper C99-109. Center of International and Development Economics Research.

———. 2006. Decentralisation and Accountability in Infrastructure Delivery in Developing Countries. *The Economic Journal* 116: 101–127.

Baron, D.P. 1994. Electoral Competition with Informed and Uniformed Voters. *American Political Science Review* 88: 33–47.

Beilhartz, H.-J., and H. Gersbach. 2004. *General Equilibrium Effects and Voting into a Crisis*. CEPR Discussion Paper 4454. London: Centre for Economic Policy Research.

Besley, T., and R. Burgess. 2003. The Political Economy of Government Responsiveness: Theory and Evidence from India. *Quarterly Journal of Economics* 117 (4): 1415–1451.

Bischoff, I., and L.-H.R. Siemers. 2011. Biased Beliefs and Retrospective Voting: Why Democracies Choose Mediocre Policies. *Public Choice* 156: 163–180.

Block, S.A. 2002. Political Business Cycles, Democratization, and Economic Reform: The Case of Africa. *Journal of Development Economics* 67 (1): 205–228.

Bratton, M., R. Bhavnani, and T.-H. Chen. 2011. *Voting Intentions in Africa: Ethnic, Economic or Partisan?* Working Paper No. 127. South Africa: Afrobarometer.

Campbell, A., P.E. Converse, W.E. Miller, and D.E. Stokes. 1960. *The American Voter*. New York: Wiley.

Caplan, B. 2007. *The Myth of the Rational Voter—Why Democracies Choose Bad Politics*. Princeton, NJ: Princeton University Press.

Davis, O., H.J. Melvin, and P.C. Ordeshook. 1970. An Expository Development of a Mathematical Model of the Electoral Process. *American Political Science Review* 64: 426–448.

Dollar, D., and W. Easterly. 1999. The Search for the Key: Aid, Investment and Policies in Africa. *Journal of African Economies* 8 (4): 546–577.

Downs, A. 1957a. *An Economic Theory of Democracy*. New York: Harper and Brothers.

———. 1957b. An Economic Theory of Political Action in a Democracy. *Journal of Political Economy* 65 (2): 135–150.

Enelow, J.M., and M.J. Hinich. 1984. *The Spatial Theory of Voting: An Introduction*. New York: Cambrigde University Press.

Ferree, K. 2004. *The Micro-Foundations of Ethnic Voting: Evidence from South Africa*. Afrobarometer Working Papers 40.

Ferree, K.E., and J. Horowitz. 2010. Ties that Bind? The Rise and Decline of Ethno-Regional Partisanship in Malawi, 1994–2009. *Democratization* 17: 534–563.

Fiorina, M., ed. 1981. *Retrospective Voting in American National Elections*. New Haven: Yale University Press.

Gazdar, H. 2000. *State, Community and Universal Education: A Political Economy of Public Schooling in Rural Pakistan*. London School of Economics: Asia Research Centre.

Glaeser, E. L., and A. Shleifer. 2002. *The Curley Effect*. NBER Working Paper 8942. Cambridge: National Bureau of Economics Research.

Glewwe, P., and H. Jacoby. 1994. Student Achievement and Schooling Choice in Low-income Countries: Evidence from Ghana. *Journal of Human Resources* 29 (3): 843–864.

Grossman, G.M., and E. Helpman. 1996. Electoral Competition and Special Interest Politics. *Review of Economic Studies* 63 (2): 265–286.

Henning, C.H.C.A. 2009. Networks of Power in the CAP System of the EU-15 and EU-27. *Journal of Public Policy* 29: 153–177.

Hoffman, B.D., and J.D. Long. 2013. Parties, Ethnicity, and Voting in African Elections. *Comparative Politics* 45: 127–146.

Horowitz, D. 1985. *Ethnic Groups in Conflict*. Berkeley, CA: University of California Press.

Katz, J.N., and G. Katz. 2009. *Reassessing the Link between Voter Heterogeneity and Political Accountability: A Latent Class Regression Model of Economic Voting*. Paper presented at the Poster Session of the 26th Annual Summer Meeting of the Society for Political Methodology.

Keefer, P. 2002a. Clientelism, Credibility and Democracy. *Journal of Law, Economics and Organization* 24: 371–406.

———. 2002b. *The Political Economy of Public Spending Decisions in the Dominican Republic: Credibility, Clientelism and Political Institutions*. Report prepared for the Public Expenditure and Institutional Review, the Dominican Republic. Washington, DC: World Bank.

Keefer, P., and S. Khemani. 2005. Democracy, Public Expenditures, and the Poor: Understanding Political Incentives for Providing Public Services. *The World Bank Research Observer* 20 (1): 1–27.

Khemani, S. 2004. Political Cycles in a Developing Economy: Effect of Elections in the Indian States. *Journal of Development Economics* 73 (1): 125–154.

Lazarsfeld, P., B. Berelson, and H. Gaudet. 1968. *The People's Choice. How the Voter Makes Up His Mind in a Presidential Campaign*. 3rd ed. New York: Columbia University Press.

Lipset, S.M., and S. Rokkan. 1967. *Party Systems and Voter Alignments: Cross-national Perspectives*. New York: Free Press.

Magee, S.P., W.A. Brock, and L. Young. 1989. *Black Hole Tariffs and Endogenous Policy Theory: Political Economy in General Equilibrium*. New York: Cambridge University Press.

Mani, A., and S. Mukand. 2002. *Democracy, Visibility and Public Good Provision. Mimeo*. Williams College: Williamstown.

Mattes, R. 2008. *The Material and Political Bases of Lived Poverty in Africa: Insights from the Afrobarometer*. CSSR Working Paper No. 216. Centre for Social Science Research, University of Cape Town.

McFadden, D., ed. 1974. The Measurement of Urban Travel Demand. *Journal of Public Economics* 3: 303–328.

Miller, W.E., and J.M. Shanks. 1996. *The New American Voter*. Cambridge, MA: Harvard University Press.

Pappi, F.U., T. König, and D. Knoke. 1995. *Entscheidungsprozesse in der Arbeits- und Sozialpolitik. Frankfurt*. Campus: New York.

Pappi, F.U., and H.C.A. Henning. 1999. The Organization of Influence on EC's Common Agricultural Policy: A Network Approach. *European Journal of Political Research* 36: 257–281.

Persson, T., and G. Tabellini. 2000. *Political Economics—Explaning Economic Policy*. Cambridge: MIT Press.

Sanmartin, M. 2001. Linearity of the Return to Education and Self-Selection. *Applied Economics* 33 (1): 133–142.

Schofield, N. 2001. In *Generic Existence of Political Equilibrium*, ed. M. Lassonde. Heidelberg: Physica.

———. 2007. The Mean Voter Theorem: Necessary and Sufficient Conditions for Convergent Equilibrium. *Review of Economic Studies* 74: 965–980.

———. 2011. Leaders, Voters and Activists in the Elections in Great Britain 2005 and 2010. *Electoral Studies* 30: 484–498.

Schuknecht, L. 2000. Fiscal Policy Cycles and Public Expenditure in Developing Countries. *Public Choice* 102 (1–2): 113–128.

Shi, M., and J. Svensson. 2000. *Political Budget Cycles: Do They Differ between Developed and Developing Countries?* Washington, DC: World Bank, Development Research Group.

World Bank. 1998. *A Framework for Civil Service Reform in Pakistan*. Technical Report, Washington, DC: World Bank, Poverty Reduction and Economic Management, South Asia Region.

———. 2001. *Nepal: Priorities and Strategies for Education Reform*. Technical Report, Washington, DC: World Bank, Human Development Unit, South Asia Region.

———. 2011. *Participation at Project, Program and Policy Level*. Washington, DC: World Bank.

———. 2013a. *Poverty Headcount Ratio at National Poverty Line*. Data retrieved November 15, 2013, from World DataBank: World Development Indicators database.

———. 2013b. *GNI Per Capita, Atlas Method*. Data retrieved November 15, 2013, from World DataBank: World Development Indicators database.

Christian Henning is professor and chair of agricultural economics, University of Kiel (Germany). He studied economics, agricultural economics, sociology, political science and mathematics. He earned a PhD in economics, in agricultural economics and in political science. His main areas of specialization are applied political economy and applied economic modelling of agricultural policies. To date he has published five books and various articles in refereed journals including PLoS ONE, American Journal of Agricultural Economics, European Review of Agricultural Economics, Journal of Public Policy, Journal of Mathematical Sociology and Journal of Theoretical Politics.

Laura Seide works as a commodity trader at Cargill Germany. She studied agricultural economics and earned a PhD in agricultural economics at the University of Kiel (Germany). Her main areas of specialization are Voting Behaviour in Developing Countries, Evaluation of Rural Development Policies and Social Capital and Political Network Analysis.

Svetlana Petri is a senior researcher in agricultural policy department of agricultural economics, University of Kiel (Germany). She studied agricultural economics and mathematics. She earned a PhD in agricultural economics. Her main research interest is probabilistic election models and modelling of capture and accountability of local and central Governments.

11

Evolutionary Computable General Political Economy Equilibrium Model (eCGPE)

Christian Henning, Johannes Hedtrich, Ligane Massamba Sène, and Eva Krampe

1 Introduction

In response to persisting policy failure in many developing countries, participatory and evidence-based political processes are increasingly promoted as an omnipotent mechanism for guaranteeing unbiased and efficient policies. Scholars who advocate participatory policy processes emphasize two points. First, higher stakeholder participation implies that elected politicians have stronger incentives to represent public interests. Second, stakeholder organizations have an improved understanding of the actions required to promote economic growth and improve the welfare of the poor. Alternatively, some scholars highlight the fact that the development of national economies is a complex process and promote evidence-based policy processes because politicians lack the relevant political knowledge and analytical skills to develop an adequate political strategy for promoting economic growth and reducing poverty. Accordingly, scholars who favor evidenced-based policy processes advocate the active participation of national and international research organizations in policy processes and promote the use of economic modelling for providing adequate political knowledge to responsible political agents. Overall, participatory and evidence-based policy processes are designed to induce more efficient policy decisions. However, in political practice, designing effective and efficient participatory and evidence-based policy processes is challenging. On one

C. Henning (✉) • J. Hedtrich
Department of Agricultural Economics, University of Kiel, Kiel, Germany
e-mail: chenning@ae.uni-kiel.de

L.M. Sène
African Union, Addis Ababa, Ethiopia

E. Krampe
European Investment Bank, Luxemborug, Luxembourg

hand, the ability of stakeholder participations to increase the incentives for responsible politicians to implement policies that favor the interest of the general public is questionable. On the other hand, economic modelling is often criticized by political practitioners as a purely academic exercise that fails to provide practical tools for understanding or designing optimal real-life economic processes (Geurts and Joldersma 2001). Accordingly, scholars promote participatory policy analysis that is characterized by an interaction between economic theory and political praxis to combine the 'objective' knowledge derived from economic theories and empirical data with the 'subjective' knowledge of stakeholder organizations as political practitioners (Durning 1993; Joldersma 1997; Geurts and Joldersma 2001). Moreover, inadequate communication between scientific policy analysts and political actors is proposed to be a principal cause of the limited impact of research on policymaking. For example, the 'utilization of knowledge school' emphasizes the fact that policy analysts and policymakers live in two separate communities (Geurts and Joldersma 2001). Hence, to become more efficient, the relationship between scientific experts and policy actors must be redefined. For example, Duke (1974) discusses the role of the interaction between scientific experts and political practitioners within the theoretical perspective of policy learning.

In this context, we suggest the evolutionary Computable General Political Economy Equilibrium Model (eCGPE) as a quantitative approach to modeling and evaluating policy processes. In contrast to standard political economy approaches that focus on political incentive problems and have primarily ignored imperfect political knowledge as a source of inefficient development policies (for example, see Persson and Tabellini 2000), the CGPE approach explicitly allows a quantitative assessment of the impact of both imperfect political incentives and imperfect political knowledge.

While the theoretical CGPE approach has already been introduced in the chapter "Modeling and Evaluation of Political Processes: A New Quantitative Approach" this chapter provides an empirical application of the CGPE approach to the case of the Comprehensive Africa Agriculture Development Program (CAADP) reform in Malawi. CAADP reform in Malawi is a good case in point. First, despite some positive trends, high levels of poverty, poor health, malnutrition and hunger continue to plague Malawi. Second, while it is commonly agreed that these disappointing outcomes are caused in large part by suboptimal public policies, the causes of the continuing failure of the Malawi government to provide optimal public policies remain unknown. Is the Malawi government unwilling to implement the right policies due to biased political incentives or is the government simply unable to implement effective policies due to inadequate political knowledge? For example, by adopting CAADP, the Malawian government, in agreement with the governments of 21 other African countries, committed to a strong role of agriculture in economic development. The pursuit of a 6% annual growth rate in agriculture via the allocation of at least 10% of public resources to the agricultural sector is one of the main principles of CAADP. However, although there is a general agreement among African development specialists that any poverty reduction strategy in Africa must consider rural development and incomes, the role of agriculture in African development is controversial (Brzeska et al. 2012). First, the optimal allocation of public resources to agricultural and non-agricultural policy programs is a complex task, which depends on the specific framework economic conditions of a country and must be supported by adequate evidence-based research. In particular, the extent to which technical progress in agriculture is more effective than progress in non-agriculture in inducing substantial economic growth and poverty reduction remains unclear. Moreover, the optimal allocation of scarce public budget resources among different policy programs that promote technical progress in the agricultural and non-agricultural sectors remains unknown. Finally, beyond the relevant question of which sectors are the most important engines of growth in the Malawi economy (i.e., agriculture versus non-agriculture or within agriculture, food crops versus export crops), another important question relates to the optimal allocation of public resources across different policy programs (e.g., extension services versus fertilizer subsidies) or infrastructure programs to promote maximal technical progress.

Overall, using the CAADP reform in Malawi as a case study, we demonstrate in this paper that the eCGPE is an adequate model framework that not only enables a *political diagnosis* (i.e., the identification of existing incentives and knowledge gaps) but also facilitates the development of a *political therapy* (i.e., the identification of adequate strategies for reducing the identified political performance gaps).

The structure of this chapter is outlined here. In the next section, we explain the manner in which the eCGPE approach is implemented within GAMS and briefly describe how the different eCGPE modules are empirically specified. In particular, we focus on the derivation and empirical estimation of the PIF module and on the econometric estimation of the policy beliefs and political knowledge of different stakeholder organizations. We then describe the principal results of our political diagnosis using the eCGPE model. We also present different simulation analyses that apply the eCGPE to assess different participatory and evidence-based political decisionmaking processes. The chapter concludes by providing an outlook on future work.

2 Technical Implementation and Empirical Specification of the CGPE model

2.1 Technical Implementation in GAMS

The model is implemented in GAMS as a mixed-complementary problem and solved using PATH. The program is a straightforward extension of the existing recursive dynamic CGE of IFPRI type 2 and is structured as described in Fig. 1.

In its current version, the eCGPE includes four modules: a sequentially dynamic CGE model (CGE), the policy impact function module (PIF), the political belief formation module (PBF) and the political decisionmaking module (PDM). The voter module described in Chapter "Voter Behavior and Government Performance in Malawi: An Application of a Probabilistic Voting Model" has not yet been fully implemented. We leave that task for future work. The sequentially dynamic CGE

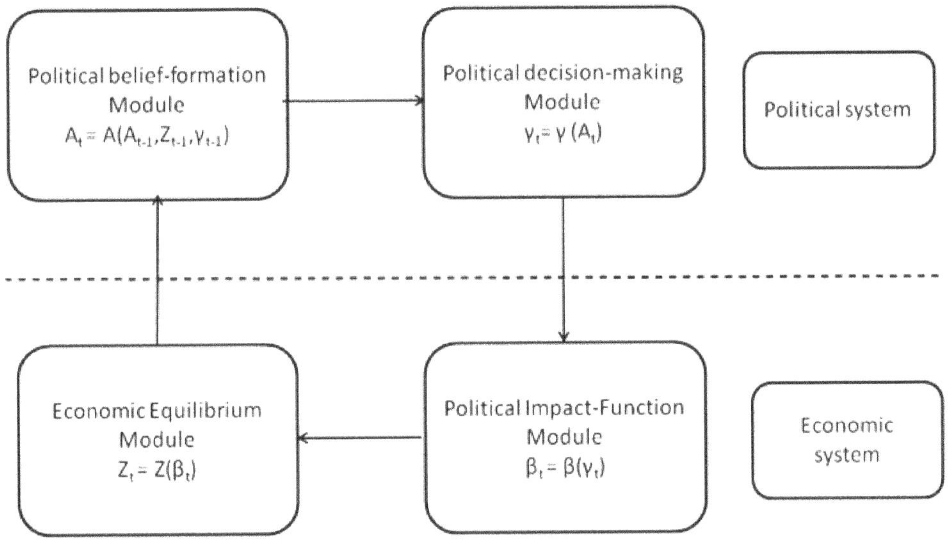

Fig. 1 Model structure of an evolutionary CGPE. Source: Authors

model translates exogenous economic and technological settings into a path of economic outcome variables. For notational convenience, let β denote the economic and technological parameters of the CGE. Relevant outcome variables are denoted by the vector z. Thus, it holds: $z = z(\beta)$. Because we are using a quasi-dynamic CGE, all exogenous and endogenous variables evolve over time, where Z_t and β_t denote the variable values in time period t. Accordingly, we denote by the matrix $Z_T = [z_t]$ the development of the relevant outcome variables, where the vector z_t corresponds to the sequence of values of the outcome variable z over the time periods $t = t_1, \ldots, t_T$. Analogously, the matrix β_T is the matrix of the development of exogenous CGE parameters over the period $t = t_1, \ldots, t_T$. A standard CGE application simulates the impact of exogenous policy shocks on the CGE equilibrium path (i.e., on the development path of Z). In particular, policy parameters (γ) are incorporated into the CGE model. Technically, this incorporation is accomplished via a policy implementation function, which transforms policy parameters into CGE parameters: $\beta = \beta(\gamma)$. Using the PIFs, a sequence of policy shocks (γ_t) is transformed into a sequence of exogenous parameter shocks $\beta_t = PIF(\gamma_t)$, which are translated into a development path of outcome changes dZ_T when solving the sequential CGE. A CGPE model extends the standard CGE model by incorporating a policy-decision module (PDM). The PDM determines endogenously the policy choices γ_t that occur over time. In particular, according to our theoretical CGPE approach the PDM corresponds to a two-stage decision-making model, where at a first stage relevant political actors select a direction, $\Delta\gamma^M$, in which the status-quo policy is shifted and at a second stage political actors vote on a distance (λ) the status quo policy is shifted towards the agreed direction. Let $i=1, \ldots, n_I$ denote the index of relevant political actors including a subset of legislators and a subset of stakeholders, while $g=1, \ldots, n_g$ denotes the index of legislators. Each political agent has spatial policy preferences U(γ). Policy preferences are derived from political support maximization.

According to the mean voter decision rule legislative bargaining implies:

$\Delta\gamma^{M} = \Sigma_{g}\, \varphi_{g}\, Y_{g}$, while the distance results as median, λ^{med} of the individually preferred distances of legislators, λ_{g}.

To include lobbying influence prefered policy positions of legislators result as:

$$Yg = \Sigma_{j}\, M_{gj}\, Y_{j}.$$

Accordingly, lobbying implies an extended mean voter rule:

$$\Delta\gamma^{M} = \Sigma j\; C_{j} Y_{j}, C_{j} = \Sigma_{g}\, \varphi_{g}\, M_{gj}.$$

The final policy choice is gradually implemented for a sufficiently small $d\lambda$:

$$\gamma_{t} = \gamma_{0} + t\, d\lambda\, \Delta\gamma^{M}, \qquad if \;\; \lambda^{med} > (t-1)\, d\lambda + \gamma_{0}$$
$$\gamma_{t} = \gamma_{0} + (t-2)\, d\lambda\;\, \Delta\gamma^{M}, \;\; if \;\; \lambda^{med} < (t-1)\, d\lambda + \gamma_{0}$$

However, we do not assume that politicians have perfect information regarding the political technology (i.e., the transformation of policies into policy impacts); instead, agents are unaware of the true PIF and CGE model.

Hence, we assume that policy choices depend on political beliefs $(\tilde{A}_{t})$. Assuming that beliefs are perfectly exogenous implies that initial beliefs perfectly determine all future policy choices. However, as explained above, politicians engage in policy learning processes, i.e. politicans update their beliefs based on observed policy outcomes and policy beliefs communicated by other actors. Belief-up-dating via communicational and reinforcement learning is modeled in the belief updating module (PBD), which is also incorporated in the eCGPE approach. In particular, communication learning is modeled applying the Friedkin model, while reinforcement learning is applied to the individual preferred distance λ_{i} and is based on agents' political support, $S_{i}(z)$. All CGPE modules are programmed in GAMS and integrated into a sequentially linked eCGPE model, as described in Chapter "Modeling and Evaluation of Political Processes: A New Quantitative Approach" above.

2.2 *Empirical Calibration of the eCGPE and Data*

Empirical calibration of a eCGPE model includes the calibration of all four modules (i.e., the CGE model, the policy impact function [PIF], the belief formation model [PBF] and the political decisionmaking model [PDM]). Because the empirical calibration of the CGE model is a well-known standard procedure, we only describe the empirical calibration of the other three models, including the required empirical data. A detailed description of the empirical estimation procedures for the Malawi case has already been described in Chapters "Modeling and Evaluation of Political Processes: A New Quantitative Approach" and "A Network Based Approach to Evaluate Participatory Policy Processes: An Application to CAADP in Malawi."

As described in detail in Chapter "A Network Based Approach to Evaluate Participatory Policy Processes: An Application to CAADP in Malawi," the main parameters of the PBF and PDM can be specified based on data collected via a policy network survey. This type of survey is a standard approach in political sociology and empirical policy network studies (Henning 2009; Knoke et al. 1996; Pappi and Henning 1999; Pappi et al. 1995). In the first step of the policy network study, the set of relevant governmental and nongovernmental organizations (N), the set of relevant policy concerns (z) and the set of relevant policy instruments (γ), are identified via expert interviews and document analyses.

In the second step of the policy network study, personal interviews will be conducted with all identified relevant organizations. Within the personal interview, policy network relations with other organizations, including political communication, are collected. Based on the stated network relations of all interviewed organizations, the corresponding global networks can be derived directly (Laumann and Knoke 1987; Henning 2009; Knoke et al. 1996; Pappi and Henning 1999; Pappi et al. 1995). Alternatively, an advanced econometric approach can be applied to estimate global network structures based on the stated network relations of the involved agents (Assmann et al. Chapter "The Formation of Elite Communication Networks in Malawi: A Bayesian Econometric by Approach", Snijders 2002). This approach facilitates the identification of the underlying network-generating process and allows an adequate imputation of missing data. Moreover, this approach allows for the identification of determinants of the structure of policy networks and the identification of possible strategies for designing network structures that imply more efficient policy processes. Further, the stated policy preferences of organizations are collected. In the first stage, organizations state their relative interests (X) and their preferred positions $\left(\widehat{Z}\right)$, with respect to identified policy concerns. In the second stage, organizations state their relative interests (Θ^g) and preferred positions with respect to identified policies $(\widehat{\gamma})$.

Based on the stated policy positions of all relevant organizations, the underlying macro policies (γ^P) can be identified as latent variables by conducting a principal component analysis (see below for details). The stated relative interest in policy concerns is used to specify the Cobb–Douglas parameters of the individual support functions ($X^i = [X_{ik}]$).

2.3 Estimation of the Policy Impact Function

The core of a standard CGE application corresponds to a simulation of exogenous shocks. With respect to content, shocks are changes in economic or political framework conditions. Technically, the impact of exogenous shocks is modeled via shifts of exogenous CGE parameters. However, when specific policy shocks are simulated, policies must be incorporated into the CGE model (i.e., shocks must be transformed into changes in CGE parameters). Technically, this transformation is implemented via PIFs. Some policies (e.g., direct and indirect taxes or tariffs) are already directly implemented in the standard CGE model. However, other policies, such as structural adjustment policies, must be translated into CGE parameters. In particular, reducing poverty and promoting overall economic growth is a key factor for achieving the first MDG goal (Diao et al. 2007; Fan and Rosegrant 2008). A range of policy instruments exist that governments can use to promote the required overall economic growth (e.g., technical progress [t.p.] and improving market access by lowering transaction costs). One key factor for sustainable economic growth is t.p. Thus, following Benin et al. (2012), we focus our policy impact analyses on the promotion of t.p. Please note that the PIF approach can be easily extended to include policy impacts on market access and direct transfers to enterprises or households. However, because this chapter aims to demonstrate how a CGPE approach can be applied empirically and to describe the generated results, we restrict the PIF to t.p. When focusing on policy impacts on the promotion of t.p., two questions arise. First, the sectors in which t.p. has the largest impact on the achievement of the envisaged political goals (e.g., poverty reduction or economic growth) remain unknown. Second, the optimal distribution of scarce financial resources across different policy programs for inducing the largest increase in t.p. (e.g., extension services or interest rate subsidies, etc.) must be determined.

With respect to the first question, Fan and Rosegrant (2008) emphasize that many African countries spend too little on promoting agricultural growth compared to non-agricultural growth. Further, with respect to the second question, budget allocations to different agricultural policy programs significantly affect the effectiveness of total budget expenditures. For example, within the Comprehensive Agricultural Development Plan, four different pillars are specified as policy subdomains. Moreover, beyond agricultural growth, overall welfare development is also determined by economic growth in non-agricultural sectors and by the provision of public goods, such as health, education and other social services. Therefore, at the country level, an overall budget allocation must include the allocation of total financial resources for the promotion of economic growth in the agricultural and non-agricultural sectors and the allocation of financial resources for the provision of public goods. For example, Badiane et al. (2011) state that budget allocation to programs that promote future economic growth and the provision of public goods has a significant impact on present and future welfare allocations.

Thus, to identify optimal government budget allocations for promoting economic growth within our CGPE framework, we suggest the following PIF approach. Total government expenditure (B_{tot}) results as the sum of total spending across policy programs: $B_{tot} = \sum_p \gamma_p$. Total government spending determines t.p. realized in the economy, and the effective impact on technical progress (tp_s) that is realized in a specific economic sector s depends on the allocation of governmental spending across policy programs. To capture the importance of different policy programs p to the impact on technological progress that is realized in a specific sector s, the following two-stage policy impact functions ($PIF^s(\gamma)$) are defined for each sector (s):

$$PIF^s(\gamma) = \alpha_s^o E_s \left[B_s^{eff}\right]^{\alpha_s} \tag{1}$$

$$B_s^{eff} = \omega_s \left[\sum_p \mu_{ps} \left[\gamma_p\right]^{-\rho_s}\right]^{-1/\rho_s} \tag{2}$$

$$\frac{sh_{ps}}{sh_{qs}} = \left[\frac{\mu_{ps}}{\mu_{qs}}\right]^{(1+\rho_s)} \tag{3}$$

In the lower stage Eq. (2), budget allocation is transformed into effective budget allocation according to a CES function specification. In the upper stage Eq. (1), an effective budget is translated into t.p. according to a Cobb–Douglas function (i.e., the marginal impact of additional effective budget spending is diminishing and approximates zero for a sufficiently large effective budget). α_s^0 is a normalization parameter that implies that E_s is the maximal rate of t.p. that can be achieved with empirically relevant total budget expenditures for policy programs γ.

The suggested PIF basically follows the work of Fan and Zhang (2004). However, in contrast to the original approach, the PIF approach is more general and implies a nonlinear relationship between governmental spending and induced technical progress in economic sectors. Moreover, this approach explicitly considers the composition of budget spending for different policy programs. Finally, please note that optimal budget allocation to different agricultural and non-agricultural policy programs varies across different economic sectors (i.e., the same budget allocation translates into different effective budgets that induce different t.p. in different sectors).

In general, an empirical estimation of the PIF function demands a large database of budget expenditures for different policy programs and empirical observations of induced technical progress achieved in different economic sectors. Such a large database is not available for most countries. Accordingly, Diao et al. (2012) estimated an aggregated function that relates the total budget expenditures for agricultural and non-agricultural policy programs to the average t.p. realized in the total agricultural sector.

In this context, we suggest a different approach for estimating detailed and sector-specific PIFs. In particular, we apply a Bayesian estimation procedure that uses interview data from political experts to estimate the parameters of the PIFs. According to our theory, governmental and nongovernmental organizations derive their preferred policy positions ($\widehat{\gamma}$) from the maximization of their political support

$S(z)$, where support is generated via policy outcomes z. These outcomes are induced by policy choices, giving the underlying political technology $T(z, \gamma)$. As described above, in the CGPE approach, the political technology corresponds to the CGE model and the PIFs, where the CGE model translates the exogenously given t.p. of different economic sectors into the growth rates of different policy concerns z. Let w_z denote the vector of the annual growth rates of relevant policy concerns that are induced by a vector of technical progress changes (Δtp). Then we can approximate the vector of the annual growth rates of policy concerns implied by exogenously given change in technical progress (Δtp) as follows:

$$w_z = \sum_s \xi_{zs}^{CGE} \Delta tp + w_z^0 + \xi^0 \gamma \tag{4}$$

w_z^0 is the vector of the growth rates that results in the base run, assuming technical progress would not change, while ξ_{zs}^{CGE} denote the CGE elasticities and ξ^0 denotes the vector of direct policy impacts on outcomes. Both ξ_{zs}^{CGE}, ξ^0 and w_z^0 can be derived via CGE simulations.

Given this approximation, the support maximization problem of a political agent i results as:

$$\begin{aligned} &\text{Max} S_i(1 + w_z) \\ &s.t.: \\ &w_z = \sum_s \xi_{zs}^{CGE} (\Delta tp) + w_z^0 + \xi^0 \gamma \\ &tp = PIF(\gamma) \end{aligned} \tag{5}$$

The solution of the maximization problem results in the optimal policy positions $(\widehat{\gamma}_i)$ and the induced preferred policy outcomes (i.e., the growth rates of policy concerns $(\widehat{w}_{zi})$) of a political agent i. Accordingly, based on the observed optimal policy positions and the preferred policy outcomes of a set of political agents, the PIF parameters could be estimated econometrically. However, given the large number of parameters, one would need a large set of relevant political agents. Because the set of relevant political agents is rather small (e.g., 36 governmental and nongovernmental organizations in Malawi) a direct estimation of the PIF parameter is impossible because the econometric model is underdetermined (i.e., the number of parameters is larger than the number of observations). To address the specification of underdetermined models, Golan, Judge and Miller suggested the Generalized Maximum Entropy (GME) and Generalized Cross Entropy (GCE) techniques. In a very interesting paper, Heckelei et al. (2008) discussed an alternative Bayesian estimation approach to the GME and GCE techniques. To understand the Bayesian approach for estimating the parameters of an underdetermined model, let χ denote the vector of the parameters of our PIF functions. Hence, the first order conditions of the political support maximization problem of all relevant political agents correspond to an underdetermined equation system, which we denote $FOC(\chi)$. Further, let $V(\chi)$ denote any prior distribution among the set of PIF parameters χ. Then a solution to the original equation system $FOC(\chi)$ can be obtained from:

$$Max_{\chi}V(\chi)s.t.FOC(\chi) = 0 \tag{6}$$

As long as the prior distribution has a unique maximum within the feasible set of parameters ($FOC(\chi) = 0$), the original parameter estimation problem has a unique solution. Moreover, HMJ demonstrates that the parameter vector χ that maximizes $V(\chi)$ within the subset of feasible parameter solutions is the mode of the posterior distribution and corresponds to the Highest Posterior Density (HPD) estimate of χ (Heckelei et al. 2008). Furthermore, we can also add noise to the first order conditions (i.e., $FOC(\chi) + \varepsilon$, where ε is a vector of error terms). Then assuming that the error terms were independently drawn from N(0,1), the HPD estimator of χ results as:

$$Max_{\chi,\varepsilon}V(\chi)\prod_{i,p} p_e(\varepsilon_{ip})s.t.FOC(\chi) + \varepsilon = 0 \tag{7}$$

where $p_e(.)$ is the standard normal univariate density. Finally, one can also add further restrictions on the parameters χ, which correspond to further prior information regarding the parameters χ. This prior information might correspond to theoretical constraints of the parameters χ or to further empirical information (e.g., expert information regarding minimal or maximal values for specific parameters). Let $RES(\chi) = 0$ denote any further parameter restrictions. Then the HPD estimator of χ is obtained from:

$$\begin{aligned} & Max_{\chi,\varepsilon}V(\chi)\prod_{i,p} p_e(\varepsilon_{ip}) \\ & s.t. \\ & FOC(\chi) + \varepsilon = 0 \\ & RES(\chi) = 0 \end{aligned} \tag{8}$$

Overall, an HPD estimation follows from Eq. (8) using interview data from the policy network survey if a prior probability density function of the model parameters χ, $V(\chi)$, has been specified and if additional relevant parameter restrictions $RES(\chi)$ have been specified.

In particular, we assumed that individual parameters are independently normally distributed [e.g., the corresponding prior density function results as: $vec(\chi) \sim N(\chi^0, \Sigma)$]. We derived the prior means χ^0 based on existing estimations in the literature (Benin et al. 2012), while the covariance matrix was set equal to the diagonal matrix with the elements $[vec(\chi^0)^2]$. The specification of the variance of the prior parameters corresponds to the assumption that the coefficient of variance is 1 for all parameters with a non-zero prior mean. If the prior mean was equal to zero, we set the diagonal element to 0.01.

Given these assumptions regarding the prior density function, the HPD estimator of χ results as:

$$
\begin{aligned}
&Minx[vec(\chi) - vec(\chi^0)]' \sum^{-1} \left[vec(\chi) - vec\left(\chi^0\right)\right] + W_\varepsilon \sum_{i,p} \varepsilon_{ip}{}^2 \\
&s.t. \\
&FOC(\chi) + \varepsilon = 0 \\
&RES(\chi) = 0
\end{aligned}
\tag{9}
$$

W_ε is the relative weight of the interview data in relation to the expert prior information, which we set exogenously. A high relative weight implies that the estimated PIF parameters are more driven by the interview data from the political agents, while a low weight implies that the final parameter estimations are more driven by the prior information obtained from existing studies. The Bayesian estimation procedure was also implemented in GAMS.

2.4 Estimation of Individual Policy Beliefs and Political Knowledge

We understand the policy beliefs of individual political agents as simple mental models for how CAADP policies translate into changes in policy concerns. To capture policy beliefs within the CGPE framework, we estimate for each stakeholder organization the set of PIF parameters and the CGE multiplier that imply that individual political support maximization exactly replicates the policy positions ($\widehat{\gamma}$ and $\widehat{Z}$), that an organization stated in the interview of the policy network survey. Basically, we apply the same Bayesian estimation approach described above using only the data and the first order conditions of the political support maximization of one individual stakeholder. Accordingly, we obtain for each individual political agent an estimation χ_i^* of the parameters χ. Hence, the estimated parameters χ_i^* incorporate the individual policy beliefs of a stakeholder organization. Further, we aggregated estimated individual political technology parameters to common policy beliefs by applying factor and cluster analyses. In particular, we first derived the matrix of first order differentials $A_i = [a_{ij}] = \left[\frac{\partial Z_i}{\partial \gamma_j}\right] = \sum_s \left[\xi_{zs}^{CGE} \ \frac{\partial PIF_s}{\partial \gamma_j}\right]$ as a linear approximation of the estimated individual political technology. Based on the individual matrix elements (a_{ij}), we first conducted a factor analysis. Based on the factor scores derived for individual stakeholder organizations, we conducted a cluster analysis to identify organizations that hold similar policy beliefs.

Beyond policy beliefs, we are interested in the level of political knowledge of relevant stakeholder organizations (i.e., the degree to which stakeholders' policy beliefs correspond to the true political technology). In the CGPE framework, we measure political knowledge as the level of political support an individual organization i realized based on its stated policy position (γ_i) compared to the maximal political support this organization would achieve given the true political technology. If we denote the optimal policy position of an organization as the policy position that maximizes its political support given the true political technology by $\widehat{\gamma}_i^{opt}$, it follows for individual knowledge-gaps:

$$Know - gap_i = 1 - \frac{S_i(\widehat{\gamma}_i)}{S_i(\widehat{\gamma}_i^{opt})} \tag{10}$$

Obviously, individual political knowledge gaps depend on the congruence of stakeholders' policy beliefs and the true political technology. Because it is difficult to identify the true political technology empirically, we will calculate knowledge gaps by simulating different political technologies.

3 Results

3.1 Political Incentives

Empirically, we derive the political incentives of relevant political agents from their relative interest in different policy concerns, which we collected via personal interviews within the policy network survey. As shown in Fig. 2, the main political interest is the welfare of small-scale farmers (Z1), followed by poverty reduction (Z2) and interest in general public services (Z3). In contrast, interest in the welfare of agribusiness (Z4), urban consumer welfare (Z5) and interest in the welfare of agricultural export sectors (Z6) are comparatively low. Interest in environmental

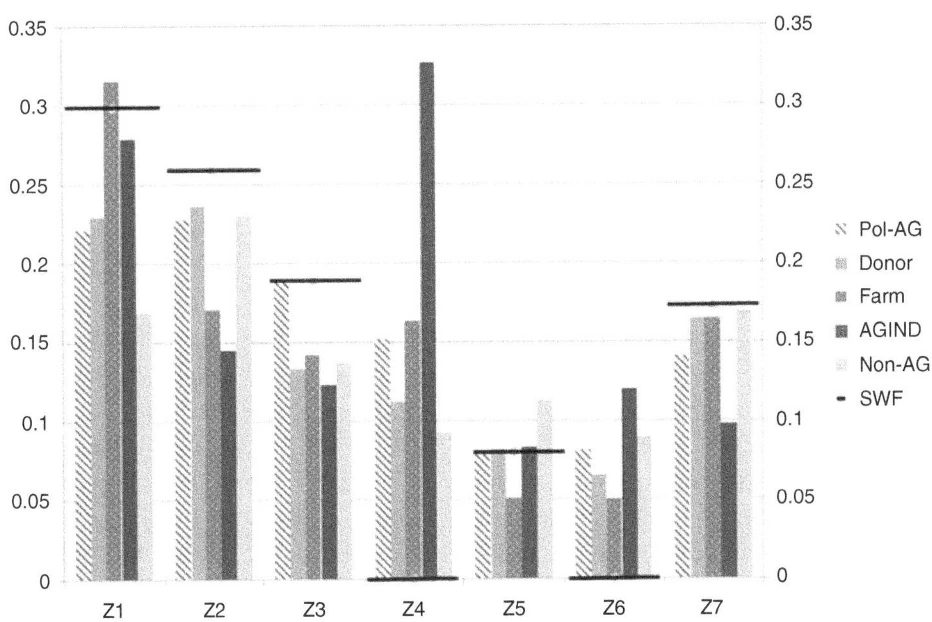

Fig. 2 Interest in policy concerns according to organizational category. Source: Authors

protection (Z7) occupies a middle ground between the high interest concerns Z1–Z3 and the low interest concerns Z4–Z6. Of course, interest group associations that are specialized in the representation of the particular interests of a specific socioeconomic group (e.g., agribusiness and farmer organizations) have extremely high interest in the welfare of their clientele (e.g., farmer associations in Z1 and agribusiness organizations in Z4) (see Fig. 2). In comparison to socioeconomic interest groups, government and international donors and civic society organizations have a relatively higher interest in poverty reduction (Z2) and environmental sustainability (Z7).

Further, we derive a social welfare function based on the collected stakeholder interests. In particular, we set the relative weights of the welfare of particular economic interests (i.e., Z4 and Z6) to zero, while we calculate the relative welfare weights of the remaining policy concerns Z1–Z3, Z5 and Z7 as the average interests of stakeholder organizations. Overall, the following welfare weights result: $Xw_1 = 0.299$, $Xw_2 = 0.259$, $Xw_3 = 0.189$, $Xw_4 = 0$, $Xw_5 = 0.08$, $Xw_6 = 0$, $Xw_7 = 0.173$.

3.2 Policy Beliefs and Political Knowledge

As described above, based on stated policy positions and the achievement of policy goals, we estimated the individual parameters of the PIF and the CGE multipliers that imply that the stated policy positions of relevant governmental and nongovernmental organizations can be replicated from the corresponding political support maximization. Based on the estimated parameters, we calculated the matrix $\left[\frac{dZ}{d\gamma}\right]$ as a linear approximation of the political technology, which we interpret as the policy beliefs of an individual organization. We conducted a factor analysis based on the $7 \times 9 = 63$ matrix entries for the 36 interviewed organizations and derived the factor scores for the organizations. Based on the computed eigenvalues, we preferred a 7-factor solution.

Moreover, we conducted a cluster analyses of the calculated factor scores of all 36 political organizations, where we preferred a 4-cluster solution. The cluster membership of different organizations is presented in Table 5 in the Appendix, where the identified clusters correspond to similar policy beliefs. To illustrate the estimated policy beliefs, we present a two-dimensional policy belief factor space in Fig. 3. Moreover, we also mapped the factor scores calculated for the original prior parameters of the PIF and the CGE multipliers and for the factor scores derived for the empirically identified political technology (labelled new-prior in Fig. 3). As explained above, the latter parameter was estimated based on the stated policy positions and the targeted policy concern achievements of the interviewed political organizations by applying the Bayesian estimation approach described above.

Figure 3 demonstrates that we can identify a governmental belief cluster (cluster1, colored in green) that includes the most powerful political actors: MoFAS,

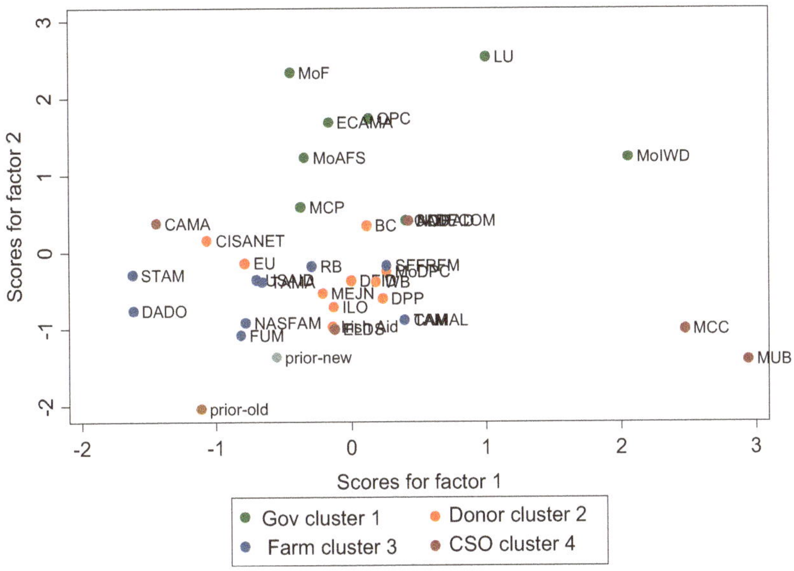

Fig. 3 Factor space of policy beliefs. Source: Authors

MOF and the president, as well as the governmental party MCP, the MOIWD and the governmental agencies LU and ADD (Organization labels are explained in Chapter "A Network Based Approach to Evaluate Participatory Policy Processes: An Application to CAADP in Malawi"). In addition to the governmental belief cluster, we identified a specific agricultural belief cluster (cluster 3, colored in dark gray in Fig. 3) and a civil society belief cluster (cluster 4, colored in blue in Fig. 3); most donor organizations and Bunda College (BC), as the principal national research organization, form a separate donor belief cluster (cluster 2, colored in orange in Fig. 3).

However, not all donor organization appear to hold similar policy beliefs (i.e., USAID is grouped into the farm cluster 3, while the Norwegian donor organization NORAD is grouped in the civil society cluster, e.g. cluster 4, colored red in Fig. 3). Moreover, for comparison, we also mapped the factor scores of the original prior parameters (labelled prior-old in Fig. 3) and the estimated parameters using the stated policy positions of all interviewed organizations (labelled prior-new). Because Fig. 3 only presents the factor scores of the first two factors, while the clustering was conducted using all 7 factors, we will describe the differences between the identified policy beliefs clusters and the prior political technology in more detail in the discussion that follows.

Basically, the impact of CAADP polices on policy outcomes can be separated in three different aspects. First, the relative impact of a specific policy program on the induced technical progress in a specific sector is captured by the CES parameters (μ_{sp}). The second aspect corresponds to the efficiency of effective budget expenditure in the generation of t.p. This aspect is captured by the CD parameters $\left(\alpha_1^s\right)$, which represent the budget elasticity in the production of t.p. (i.e., the percent increase in t.p. change that is induced by a 1% increase in effective budget allocated to promote t.p. in a specific sector s). The third aspect corresponds to the impact of increased t.p. in a specific sector on the change in the achievement of different policy goals. This aspect is captured by the CGE elasticities, where the value of ξ_{ZS}^{CGE} denotes the change in the annual growth rate of a policy concern z that is induced by a change in the rate of t.p. in the sector s. Hence, the larger a sector in terms of the employment share or the share in GDP, the larger will be c.p. the effect of the CGE elasticities on income growth or poverty reduction, respectively. However, beyond the size of an economic sector, the corresponding CGE elasticities are also determined by interlinkages with other sectors and households. The average estimated parameters are reported for all four belief clusters in Table 5 in the Appendix. Moreover, we also report the original prior parameters and the parameters estimated using the complete policy position data for all of the interviewed stakeholder organizations (labeled new-prior in Table 5). Comparing the estimated parameters of the policy belief clusters to the original prior parameters, we can draw the following conclusions:

1. The political beliefs of all stakeholder organizations differ systematically from the prior parameters derived from economic modeling.
2. Interestingly, although some differences exist across belief clusters, we find a remarkably homogeneous pattern of divergences from the prior technology across all belief clusters. In particular, compared to the prior technology, the policy beliefs of all stakeholders correspond to a significantly higher efficiency of policy programs in promoting technical progress. Specifically, while the prior values of the budget elasticity equal 0.35 for all sectors, the policy beliefs of stakeholders correspond to significantly higher values that range between 0.36 and 0.7, where stakeholders commonly believe in a high political potential to induce t.p. in the agricultural crop and livestock sectors as well as in the industrial sector. In contrast, for the trading sectors and the public service sector, stakeholder beliefs frequently correspond to slightly lower budget elasticities when compared to the corresponding prior values (see Table 5). Moreover, stakeholders have common beliefs regarding the impact of t.p. that is realized in different sectors on policy concerns. For example, all stakeholder organizations believe that t.p. in both the livestock sector and the public service sector have a significantly higher impact on poverty reduction (Z2), farm incomes (Z1) and the welfare of urban consumers (Z5) when compared to the prior political technology. With respect to the t.p. in the crop, agribusiness and trading sector, stakeholders believe in a comparatively lower impact when compared to the prior technology. For the industry sector, stakeholder beliefs are mixed. For poverty reduction (Z2), a larger impact of t.p. in the industry sector is commonly believed, while for farm income and urban consumer welfare, a comparatively lower impact of the industrial sectors is believed (see Table 5). Finally, with respect to the importance of different policy programs in the generation of t.p. in specific sectors, a remarkably homogenous pattern results for all belief clusters. For example, according to all belief clusters, general fertilizer subsidies (γ_2) and non-agricultural policy programs are considered to be much more effective in

generating t.p. in the agricultural sectors, especially the livestock sector, when compared to the prior technology. Moreover, compared to the prior political technology, investment in general infrastructure (γ_4) is much more effective in generating t.p. in the trading and public service sectors, according to the policy beliefs of all stakeholders. Analogously, for generating t.p. in the industrial sectors, stakeholder beliefs commonly indicate a comparatively high efficiency of pillar IV policies (e.g., the promotion of extension services (γ_7) and R&D activities (γ_8) (see Table 5 in the Appendix).

3. However, some divergences in policy beliefs also exist between different stakeholder organizations. For example, the civil society cluster (4) believes in contrast to all other stakeholder clusters that investment in infrastructure and the promotion of R&D activities are especially effective in generating t.p. in the agribusiness sector (see Table 5 in the Appendix).
4. Overall, based on our analyses, we conclude that two worlds exist: the scientific world of economic modelers that corresponds to the prior political technology and the world of stakeholders operating as practical experts in Malawi, which is encapsulated in the observed common policy beliefs. These two worlds are nicely illustrated in Fig. 4, where we plotted the factor scores of stakeholder organizations derived from a factor analysis of their stated policy positions, first assuming that policy positions are derived from policy beliefs (blue dots on the left) and second assuming that policy positions are derived from political support maximization assuming that stakeholders adopt the prior political technology as the true political technology (red dots on the right). Hence, our analyses imply a cleavage between the world of economic modeling and the world of political practice.

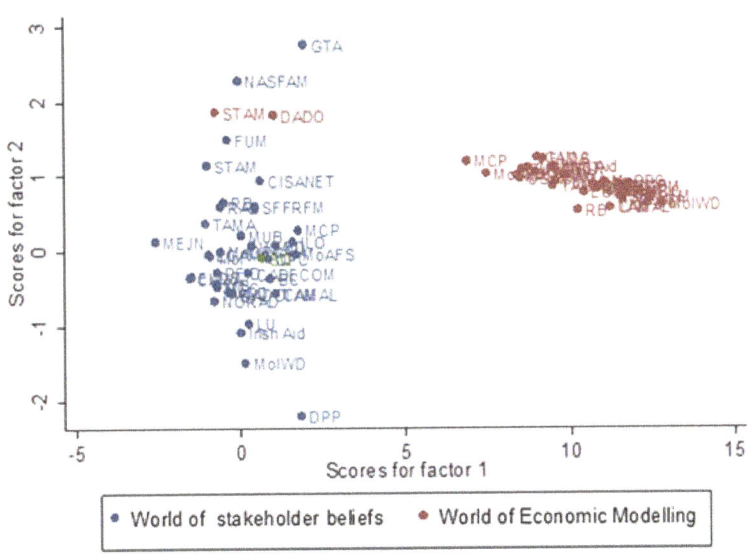

Fig. 4 Preferred CAADP policy positions of Malawi stakeholders in two worlds. Source: Authors

5. The estimated political technology parameters correspond to a compromise between these two worlds, as shown in Fig. 5. Accordingly, assuming this compromise corresponds to the true political technology, the implementation of more research-based policies can hardly be achieved via increased stakeholder participation, because none of the stakeholder organizations hold policy beliefs that correspond with the scientific world of economic modelling. Interestingly, even international donor organizations fail to hold policy beliefs that closely correspond with the wisdom derived from economic modelling. Given the common assumption in the literature on participatory policy analysis (for example, see Greuts and Joldersma 2001, p. 302) that scientific policy analysts and policymakers exist in two separate communities in reality, we consider this finding to be a remarkable result from our analyses that confirms this common assumption.

A determination of which of the three identified worlds best fits reality is of interest (i.e., is the true political technology better represented by the prior parameters derived from scientific models, by the parameters derived from the policy beliefs of stakeholder organizations as political practitioners or by a compromise between these two worlds, as suggested by arguments of the participatory policy analysis?). The latter possibility corresponds to the PIF parameters estimated using the prior parameter distributions and the complete set of stated policy positions of all involved stakeholder organizations. This question is difficult to answer without further empirical data on specific policy strategies and their impact on realized t.p. and implied poverty reduction and income growth. The answer to this question,

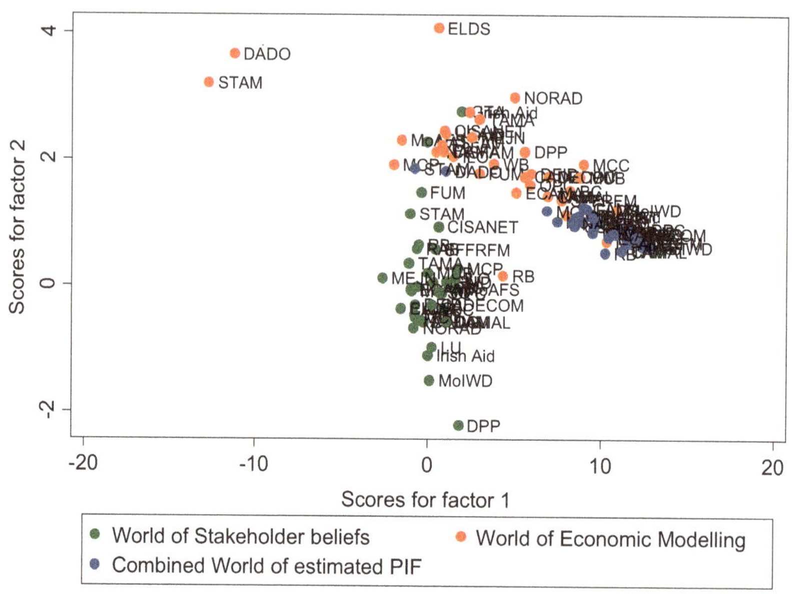

Fig. 5 Preferred CAADP policy positions of Malawi stakeholders in three worlds. Source: Authors

however, is crucial for evaluating policy processes, particularly the impact of stakeholder participation structures on political performance. Therefore, we will assess political knowledge and incentive gaps by assuming different political technologies corresponding to (a) the prior parameters derived from scientific models, (b) the parameters that result from the Bayesian estimation using prior information and expert data from the policy network survey, as well as the political technologies corresponding to the estimated policy beliefs of the four identified stakeholder belief clusters (labelled a–d for belief clusters 1–4 in the text that follows).

3.3 *Assessing Political Knowledge*

In the CGPE framework, we measure political knowledge as the loss of political support that an individual organization i realizes by comparing the political support achieved under its stated policy position (γ_i) to the maximal political support this organization would achieve if it knew the true political technology. Let $\widehat{\gamma}_i^{opt}$ denote the optimal policy position of an organization (i.e., the policy position that maximizes its political support given the true political technology). Then we can calculate the individual political knowledge gaps of each stakeholder organization as defined in Eq. (10) above. In Table 1, we present the average political knowledge gaps calculated for different stakeholder categories for the PIF-Scenarios (a–f) assuming different political technologies. As shown in Table 1, assuming that the true political technology corresponds to the prior-PIF derived from economic modelling, the average political knowledge gaps of stakeholder organizations are high ranging from 30 to 71% with an average gap amounting 60%. However, knowledge gaps are significantly smaller for the PIF-scenarios assuming that stakeholder beliefs match true political technology (scenarios a–d in Table 1).

Table 1 Political knowledge gaps of stakeholder organizations, assuming different political technologies

Assumed PIF—scenario						
Category	(a) Cluster1	(b) Cluster2	(c) Cluster3	(d) Cluster4	(e) Estimated PIF	(F) Prior_PIF
AGIND	18.2	17.4	16.5	16.8	23.1	30.4
Res	9.9	8.3	10.1	6.9	29.8	66.6
Farm	15.5	26.2	9.9	11.3	30.1	57.7
Don	21.3	7.6	15.2	9.7	32.7	56.5
CSO	26.1	18.2	22.1	14	36.3	60.9
Leg	29.2	40.5	29.1	32	38	57.2
PUB	20.2	37.9	17.9	27.4	43.4	61.6
gov	18.8	27.1	23.7	22.2	46.3	70.7
Average	21.8	23.7	19.3	18.1	37.3	60.2

Source: Author's own calculations, based on the CGPE model for Malawi

Accordingly, average political knowledge gaps significantly decrease from 60 to 37% when assuming that the estimated PIF parameter corresponds to the true political knowledge. However, as shown in Table 1, political knowledge gaps vary also significantly across stakeholder categories. On average, the lowest political knowledge gaps are found for national research organizations (Res), followed by national farmer (Farm) and agribusiness organizations (AGIND). Relatively high political knowledge gaps can be found for the central governmental organizations (Gov), particularly MoFAS and MOF, e.g. for the estimated PIF scenario (e) an average knowledge gap of 46.3% results for governmental organizations. Only for the PIF-scenario (a) assuming the true political technology corresponds directly to the policy beliefs of the governmental organizations a relatively low gap of 18.8% is found.

Hence, the political participation of nongovernmental organizations increases the political knowledge used in the political process. In addition, also the political influence of international donor organizations would significantly increase the use of political knowledge. Interestingly, these central results holds true independently of the assumed PIF-scenario with the exception of scenario a.

4 Political Diagnosis

4.1 Assessing Political Performance

The first indicator of the overall political performance of the political system in Malawi corresponds to the difference between the actual budget allocations decided under the CAADP reform in 2010 and the optimal budget allocations derived from social welfare maximization. To this end, we calculated the optimal budget allocations across CAADP programs and non-agricultural policy programs from social welfare maximization assuming different political technologies. Moreover, we calculated the share of budget expenditures for economic policies in total state budget including additionally expenditures for the provision of public good services. As shown in Table 2, observed budget allocations under the status-quo differ significantly from optimal budget allocations derived for all political technology scenarios. In particular, assuming that the prior PIF corresponds to the true political technology implies a rather low efficiency of economic policy programs in generating t.p.. Accordingly, social welfare maximization implies that the state budget is primarily used to provide public services, such as education, health or social security with an optimal budget share of only 2.5% for economic policy programs. Although the optimal budget share of total spending for economic policy programs increases significantly, assuming true political technology corresponds to stakeholder beliefs (scenarios cluster1–4 in Table 2), optimal expenditure shares for economic policy remain low when compared to the status quo. Only following the governmental belief (scenario cluster1) implies a significant higher total state

Table 2 Budget shares under status-quo policy and optimal policy under different political technology scenarios in %

	Pillar I		Pillar II		Pillar III		Pillar IV		Non-agr	Total
Scenario	γ_1	γ_2	γ_3	γ_4	γ_5	γ_6	γ_7	γ_8	γ_9	
SQ	20.7	6.9	2.4	4.0	2.3	3.8	1.5	1.9	56.8	30.0
Cluster1	1.0	3.3	0.3	26.0	1.2	3.1	1.6	28.2	35.3	45.9
Cluster2	1.5	7.4	0.1	36.6	1.9	6.3	1.5	13.1	31.7	17.5
Cluster3	0.6	3.3	0.2	34.6	1.0	2.8	1.1	27.3	29.2	21.2
Cluster4	2.9	7.5	1.5	8.2	2.3	5.2	2.9	1.8	67.5	19.9
Estimated PIF	0.5	1.7	0.0	53.1	0.6	4.7	0.5	8.4	30.4	8.9
Prior_PIF	0.0	0.0	6.7	40.3	0.5	1.7	1.3	24.8	24.8	2.5

Source: Authors

budget share of 45% for economic policy (see Table 2). Interestingly, CAADP budget shares derived for the different PIF-scenarios (cluster1–cluster4) vary also significantly ranging from only 6% under the cluster4 scenario to 30% (64.7% × 0.459) following governmental beliefs (cluster1 in Table 2), while under the status-quo policy Malawi spends 13% of total state budget for CAADP policies (0.432 × 30%, see Table 2). Further, the allocation of budget expenditures across different CAADP pillars differs significantly among political technology scenarios; in particular, spending on subsidy programs under pillar I is drastically reduced under the optimal budget allocation compared to status-quo allocations.

Specifically, under the status-quo policy, a share of over 27% of total expenditures for economic policy programs is allocated to input subsidies under pillar I (γ_1 and γ_2). The corresponding optimal budget shares range from nearly 0% for the Prior-PIF scenario to 10.5% for the PIF-scenario corresponding to the beliefs of the civic society cluster (i.e., cluster 4). Vice versa, budget resources allocated to pillar II, particularly resources allocated to improving the general infrastructure (γ_4), will be much higher according to optimal budget allocations, where the optimal budget shares of pillar II programs range from 10% for the civic society cluster beliefs to over 37% for the donor belief cluster (cluster2). Interestingly, the optimal budget share for pillar II is remarkably higher based on prior and estimated political technology parameters; when compared to the status-quo with a comparatively low budget share of only 6.4%.

To assess the impact of misallocated public budget resources across policy programs, we compare the t.p. induced in different sectors of the Malawi economy under optimal budget allocations to the t.p. induced based on present allocations, as implemented under CAADP by the Malawi government in 2010. In Table 3, the average t.p. rates calculated for different sectors are presented. As demonstrated in Table 3, compared to the status quo scenario, an optimal allocation of public resources across CAADP programs and non-agricultural policy programs implies a significant increase in induced t.p. for most scenarios. Specifically, based on the policy beliefs of stakeholders, the potential t.p. rates that can be maximally induced given optimal budget allocations across policy programs are high for the

Table 3 Simulated technical progress gaps implied by the CAADP reform in Malawi

Scenario	Crop	Livestock	Agri-business	Industry	Trade	Public service
Cluster1	14.9	16.4	7.7	15.8	2.6	3.2
Cluster2	10.8	7.8	3.5	3.9	1.8	2.6
Cluster3	6.4	7.5	4.3	6.6	1.9	3.1
Cluster4	3.6	7.6	3.6	5.3	1.3	2.4
Estimated PIF	2.5	3.1	2.9	2.7	2.7	2.6
Prior PIF	1.3	1.3	1.5	0.9	0.9	0.9
Status-quo	2.0	2.0	2.0	2.0	2.0	2.0

Source: Authors

agricultural and agribusiness sectors, as well as the industry sectors, with t.p. rates ranging between 3.5 and 16.4 (see Table 3). In contrast, following stakeholder beliefs, the potential t.p. rates are comparatively lower for the trading sector and the public service sector, with values ranging between 1.3 and 3.2. In contrast, based on prior PIF-parameters, the optimal t.p. rates are much lower, even lower than under the status quo policy. This follows directly form the fact that for the Prior PIF investments in t.p. are rather inefficient. Accordingly, optimal budget allocations to agricultural and non-agricultural policy programs would be rather low (i.e., only 2.5% of the total state budget), while a major share of the state budget will be more efficiently used to provide public services.

4.1.1 Knowledge or Incentive Gaps?

When using the CGPE framework as a relevant theoretical background, the empirically observed CAADP policies differ from optimal policies (i.e., social welfare-maximizing policies) for two reasons. First, relevant political agents have biased incentives [i.e., S(z) differs from the social welfare function SW(z)]. Second, political agents have biased policy beliefs (i.e., agents' simple mental models approximating the political technology differ from the true political technology). Within the CGPE approach, we can not only estimate the individual policy beliefs and the political incentives of involved stakeholder organizations that determine their stated policy positions, but we can also simulate agents' preferred policy positions derived by assuming different policy beliefs or political incentives. Hence, we can simulate final policy choices by assuming that the policy beliefs of all involved stakeholders correspond perfectly to the true political technology. Comparing the social welfare derived for this scenario to the maximal social welfare derived for optimal policy choices allows us to measure the political incentive gap (i.e., the impact of biased political incentives on political performance). Vice versa, comparing social welfare derived under the assumption that all relevant stakeholder organizations maximize social welfare while maintaining their individual policy beliefs to the corresponding maximal social welfare provides a measure of the knowledge gap (i.e., the political performance gap induced by the lack of political knowledge).

Because we are unaware of the true political technology, we calculated the total political performance gaps and the incentive and knowledge gaps that result for the status-quo policy (i.e., the CAADP reform in 2010 in Malawi) for all six political technology scenarios defined above. Figure 6 presents the calculated performance gaps for different political technology scenarios. As demonstrated in Fig. 6, the political performance of the Malawi governmental system crucially depends on the assumption of the true political technology. In the scientific modeling world, political performance is rated low, with a total political performance gap of 72% (i.e., compared to the optimal budget allocation, the status-quo CAADP policies imply a social welfare that is 72% lower than the maximum achievable social welfare). Moreover, low political performance results from low political knowledge, where the corresponding knowledge gap also amounts to 72%. The social welfare losses induced by biased incentives amount to only 3.7% of the maximum social welfare. In contrast, in the world of stakeholder beliefs, political performance would be significantly higher, with total political performance gaps ranging from 7.5 to 19.4%. Moreover, in contrast to the scientific world of economic modeling, in the world of stakeholders' beliefs, political performance gaps result from both incentive and knowledge gaps.

For example, assuming that governmental policy beliefs (cluster 1) match real economic processes in Malawi implies that political performance primarily results

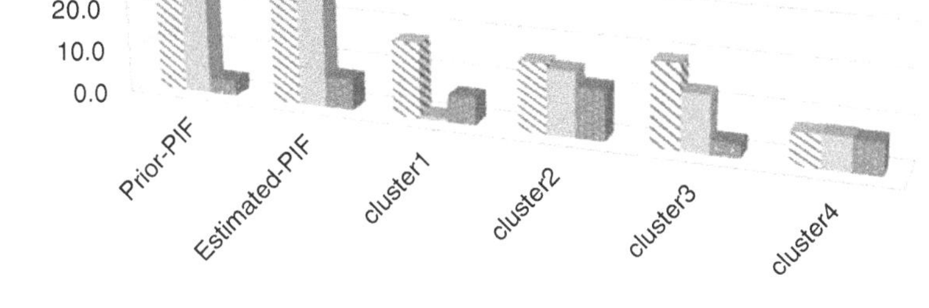

	Prior-PIF	Estimated-PIF	cluster1	cluster2	cluster3	cluster4
Total	72.3	34.7	17.5	16.0	19.4	7.5
Knowledge	72.3	33.8	0.9	15.1	13.2	7.7
Incentives	3.7	7.4	6.5	11.7	3.3	7.4

Fig. 6 Total, knowledge and incentive political performance gaps for different political technology scenarios. Source: Authors

due to biased incentives, while political knowledge gaps are negligible and correspond to only 0.9% of the maximum social welfare (see Fig. 6).

However, we trust that the Bayesian estimation using both prior information from economic modelling and practical expertise from stakeholder organizations best fits the true political technology. Hence, based on the estimated PIF, we identify significant political performance gaps that correspond to social welfare losses of nearly 35% compared to an optimal policy decision. The political knowledge gaps are much more important, with corresponding social welfare losses of nearly 34% in comparison to incentive gaps that correspond to a social welfare loss of only 7.4% (see Fig. 6).

Moreover, an analysis of the differences in realized growth rates with respect to the achievement of different policy concerns that are induced by political performance gaps is of interest. In Fig. 7, the differences between the growth rates of different policy concerns achieved under the optimal policy and the status-quo policy are presented, assuming that the estimated PIF parameters correspond to the true political technology.

As shown in Fig. 7, performance gaps imply significant differences in realized achievement levels for different policy concerns. In particular, Fig. 7 demonstrates that the status-quo policy implies that the achieved growth rates in agribusiness welfare (Z4), reduction in poverty (Z2) and farm income (Z1) are too high when compared to the optimal achievement levels induced by the optimal policy. In contrast, the increase of total budget expenditures (Z3) for public services and the achieved growth rate in urban consumer welfare are too low when compared to the optimal policy. Please note that these CGPE simulations nicely demonstrate the fact

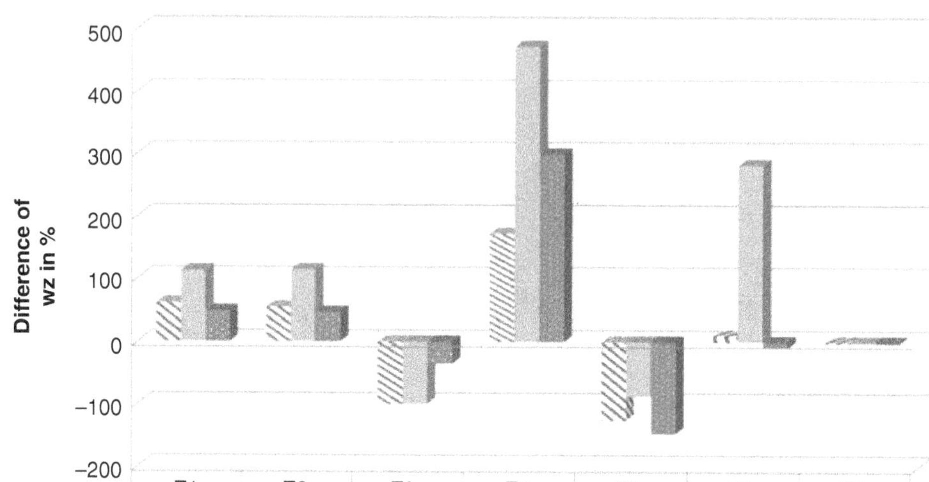

	Z1	Z2	Z3	Z4	Z5	Z6	Z7
Total	61	54	−100	172	−126	10	−2
Knowledge	112	114	−100	472	−87	282	−2
Incentive	48	46	−35	299	−147	−9	−2

Fig. 7 Total, knowledge and incentive gaps in the achievement of policy goals: Differences in the achievement of policy goals as percentages of the optimal policy. Source: Authors

that a rapid reduction of poverty does not necessarily correspond to a maximization of social welfare. This follows intuitively from the fact that a rapid poverty reduction might be realized at the expense of a significantly lower income growth or at the expense of a low growth of the public service sector.

4.2 *From Diagnosis to Political Therapy: Simulating Political Performance Gaps with Increased Stakeholder Participation*

To assess the impact of increased stakeholder participation on political performance, we first analyze the changes in final policy decisions and induced political performance that occur when we exogenously assume that specific stakeholder groups have higher political power. In a second step, we analyze the impact of different formal and informal institutional reforms on the political power of different stakeholder groups. Overall, the first simulation experiment reveals changes in participation structures that could improve political performance and the second simulation identifies potential institutional reform strategies for realizing these changes. At the methodological level, the political decisionmaking module of the CGPE approach integrates a modified legislative bargaining model of a Baron/Ferejohn type with a lobbying model that corresponds to an extended Grossman/Helpman model. Accordingly, as described in detail in Chapter "Modeling and Evaluation of Political Processes: A New Quantitative Approach," we simulate the impact of different constitutional rules via corresponding changes in the legislative decisionmaking power of relevant political agents (i.e., governmental departments and legislative parties in the parliament). We simulate changes in informal lobbying and communication structures via corresponding changes in political network multipliers (for technical details, see Chapter "A Network Based Approach to Evaluate Participatory Policy Processes: An Application to CAADP in Malawi").

4.2.1 Simulation Scenarios

I. To analyze the impact of stakeholder participation on political performance, we run the following simulation scenarios:

   A. Increased political power of international donor organizations (Don).
   B. Increased political power of farmer organizations (Farm).
   C. Increased political power of civic society organizations (Civic).
   D. Increased political power of national research organizations (Res).
   E. Increased political power of agribusiness organizations (Agind).

The political power of stakeholder groups in the base run and in the participation scenarios A–E is reported in Table 4.

Table 4 Simulated political power of stakeholder groups in the CAADP policy domain of Malawi

	Participation scenario					
Group	Base run (%)	A (%)	B (%)	C (%)	D (%)	E (%)
Gov	69.6	43.5	46.4	40.9	51.5	46.4
Leg	2.3	1.5	1.6	1.4	1.7	1.6
PUB	7.7	4.8	5.1	4.5	5.7	5.1
Don	6.1	**41.3**	4.0	3.6	4.5	4.0
Farm	6.1	3.8	**37.4**	3.6	4.5	4.1
CSO	2.6	1.6	1.7	**42.7**	1.9	1.7
Res	1.9	1.2	1.3	1.1	**27.3**	1.3
Agind	3.8	2.4	2.5	2.2	2.8	**35.9**

Source: Authors

To analyze the influence of different formal constitutional rules and informal policy network structures on policy decisions and outcomes, we run the CGPE approach under the scenarios described below.

4.2.2 Benchmark Scenarios

1. **Base run scenario**: The base run scenario corresponds to the institutional set-up that implies the best fit between the CAADP decisions predicted by the CGPE and the observed CAADP allocations in 2010. The best fit results assuming that policy decisions are solely determined by the government (i.e., the parliamentary parties have effectively no legislative decision-making power). Within the government we assume the PF-scenario, i.e., the finance ministry has agenda-setting power vis-a-vis the president, the MoA and all other involved ministries. With respect to the informal influence of nongovernmental organizations, the weak state scenario delivers the best prediction (i.e., political agents are highly interested in the political support of lobbying groups, and average interest in political support is 50%). Moreover, under the weak state scenario, the own control of political agents (i.e., the weight of own political knowledge in comparison to the knowledge of political peer networks) is comparatively low, with an average own control of 50% assumed under the weak state scenario.
2. **Status-quo**: Assuming that CAADP budget allocations correspond to the status-quo allocations for all years from 2010 to 2020.
3. **Optimal**: Assuming that CAADP budget allocations correspond to the budget allocations across CAADP programs that maximize a social Nash welfare function over the true political technology.

4.2.3 Simulating Constitutional Reforms

4. **PF**: For the PF-scenario we assume that the finance ministry has agenda-setting power vis-a-vis the president, the MoA and all other involved ministries.

5. **PDR**: For the principle of departmental responsibility (PDR) scenario, we assume that the legislative organization corresponds to a presidential system, as in the base run scenario, but the government operates under the principle of departmental responsibility, where within the cabinet, the MoA has the total formal legislative decisionmaking power for agricultural policy.
6. **PA**: For the PA scenario, we assume that the president has the total formal decisionmaking power within the government.
7. **Parl**: For the party leadership (Parl) scenario, we assume that the legislative organization corresponds to a parliamentary system, where the parliamentary parties exert total legislative decision-making power.

4.2.4 Simulating the Informal Political Influence of Nongovernmental Organizations

8. ***Autarkic (a):*** Under the autark scenario, we assume that political agents have neither interest in the political support of lobbying groups (i.e., interest in political support is zero) nor interest in the political knowledge of other stakeholders (i.e., own control is one).
9. ***Strong state (s)***: Political agents have 50% lower interest in political support and political knowledge when compared to the base run scenario. Technically, it is assumed that political interest in the political support of lobbying groups is 50% lower, while the own control of political agents is increased by up to 20% for the strong state scenario when compared to the corresponding stated values that were empirically collected in the policy network survey.
10. ***Weak state (w)***: Own control and interest in political support correspond to the stated values of stakeholder organizations, which are comparatively high, with an average interest in political support of 50% for all relevant political agents and an average own control of 70%.

For all scenarios except the status-quo and the optimal benchmark scenarios, we assume that political agents engage in reinforcement and communication learning (i.e., based on marginal political support, stakeholders update their policy beliefs as described in Chapter "Modeling and Evaluation of Political Processes: A New Quantitative Approach"). In particular, as a result of the legislative bargaining process, the direction in which the status quo policy is shifted is determined as the mean voter position, where the constitutional decision-making power, which is measured using the generalized Banzhaf index, corresponds to the weight of individual agents. Before the formal political decision is made, agents engage in communication learning, where agents update their preferred direction according to the communicated positions of other agents with whom they communicate. At the stationary point of political communication, each agent's preferred policy direction results as the weighted average of the agents' initial policy positions, where the weight of agent j's initial position in agent i's final position is determined by the communication network (see the theoretical section above for further details). Accordingly, simulating the impact of formal institutions, we assume different formal decision-making power of governmental organizations according to the calculated Banzhaf indices. To simulate the impact of political influence of nongovernmental organizations, we assume different interest in political support and different own control values for the weak, strong and autarkic state scenarios, as described above.

4.3 Whither Participation?

As demonstrated in Fig. 8 below, it is nearly impossible to identify a vision of participation that could significantly increase political performance. In particular, irrespective of the assumed political technology, neither increased participation of any stakeholder group nor increased participation of international donor organizations implies a significant increase of total political performance when compared to the base run scenario. This result appears surprising at first glance; however, given the fact that the preferred policy positions of stakeholder organizations are primarily determined by policy beliefs, while heterogeneous interests among stakeholders have a comparatively low impact on their preferred policy positions, it follows that any change in participation structures has little impact on policy performance.

The latter conclusion follows directly, because changed participation structures only shift the relative political power of stakeholders and the relative weight of individual stakeholder positions in determining the final policy decision. Thus, because stakeholder positions are empirically similar when compared to the scientific world of economic modelers that is encapsulated in the prior parameters (see Figs. 4 and 5 above), it follows that basically any

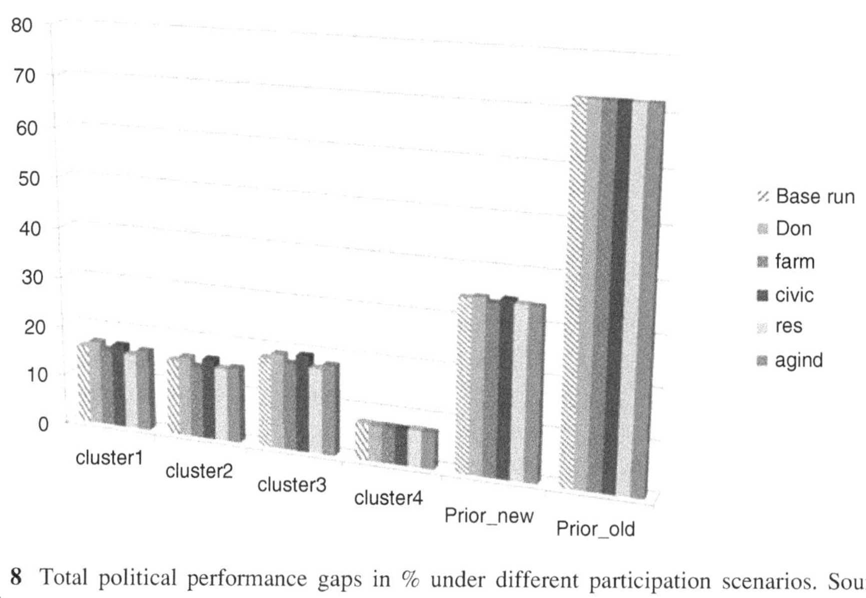

Fig. 8 Total political performance gaps in % under different participation scenarios. Source: Authors

participation structure that corresponds to a linear combination of preferred stakeholder positions merely maps into the world of stakeholder beliefs separated from the scientific world of economic modelers. Hence, assuming that the true political technology corresponds to stakeholder beliefs implies a relatively high political performance for any linear combination of policy positions in the world of stakeholder beliefs. Vice versa, assuming that the true political technology corresponds to the prior parameters derived from economic modeling implies that any linear combinations of policy positions in the subspace of the world stakeholder beliefs is rather distant from the subspace defined by the scientific world of economic modeling.

Hence, political performance is low for the base run, but it can barely be improved by any vision of increased stakeholder participation. Basically, this situation drives the results presented in Fig. 9. Hence, if we assume that the estimated PIF parameters correspond to the best representation of the true political technology, one fundamental implication of our simulation analyses is that the interaction between political practice and theoretical modeling implies a particularly successful strategy for improving political performance in Malawi and likely in many other African countries.

In contrast, increased participation of any stakeholder group, such as national farmer associations, civil society organizations, research institutions or international donor organizations, exerts little if any impact on political performance. Basically, this fundamental conclusion does not change if the political performance gaps of constitutional reforms are analyzed. As shown in Fig. 10, the total political performance changes only slightly when assuming different constitutional reforms.

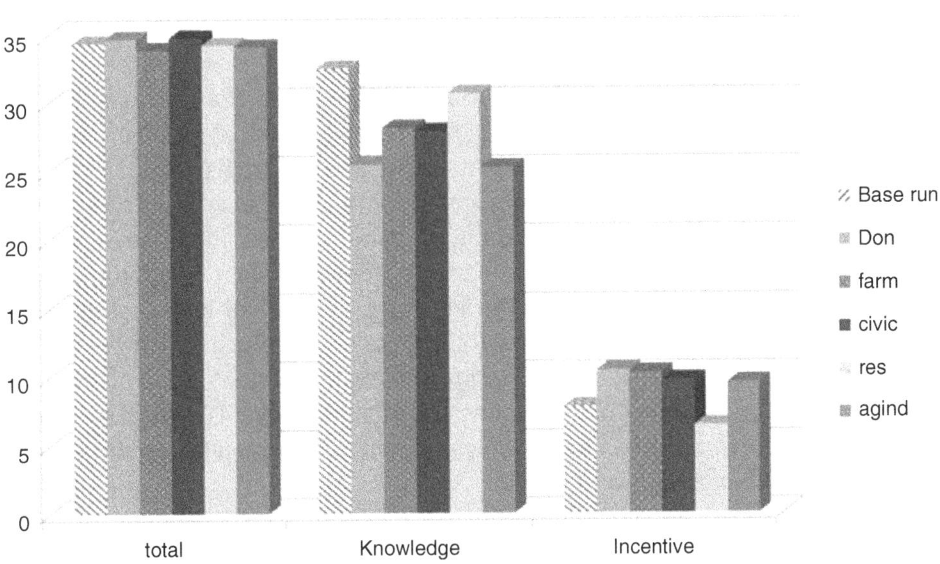

Fig. 9 Total, knowledge and incentive gaps in Malawi (in % of maximum social welfare). Source: Authors

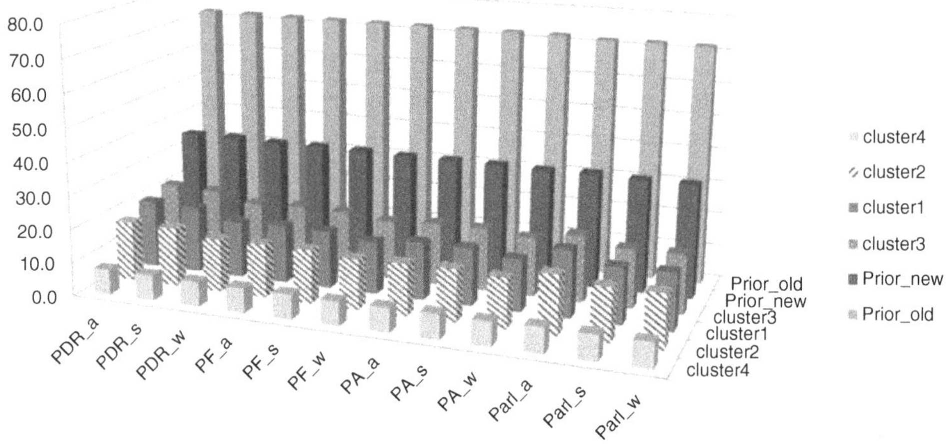

Fig. 10 Total, knowledge and incentive gaps in Malawi (in % of the maximum social welfare). Source: Authors

5 Conclusion and Outlook on Future Research

The common observation that governments persistently fail to implement effective policy and investment strategies that translate into the achievement of development goals in most African countries raises questions about government performance. In particular, low government performance occurs in two forms. First, low government performance occurs as a political incentive gap (i.e., elected politicians lack sufficient incentives to serve public interests and instead serve particular interests or pursue their own interests). Second, low government performance occurs as a political knowledge gap (i.e., the government lacks adequate knowledge and the capacity to identify and implement efficient policies).

In this paper, we develop and apply the CGPE model as a new quantitative approach to analyzing the performance of policy processes with respect to the production of efficient policy choices. In contrast to existing political economy models focusing on biased government incentives the CGPE approach incorporates explicitly the lack of adequate political knowledge as another important source of low government performance. Within the CGPE approach participation of stakeholder organizations is modeled in two ways. First, as classical lobbying influence and second as informational influence within a model of political belief formation. According to our model, the main determinants of the accumulation of political knowledge and the speed of policy learning correspond to policy network structures that reflect the communication and interaction patterns between governmental and nongovernmental organizations.

An empirical application of the CGPE model analyzing the policy processes that underlie the ongoing CAADP reforms in Malawi delivered the following results:

1. In contrast to standard CGE applications, within the CGPE approach the impact of specific policy programs on induced sectoral t.p. is explicitly captured by policy impact functions (PIFs). Empirically, PIFs are specified in a two-step estimation procedure. At a first stage a prior-PIF is specified bases on available statistical data and existing studies in the literature. In a second step a Bayesian estimation procedure is applied to estimate PIF parameters based on expert data collected from relevant governmental and nongovernmental organizations involved in CAADP reform process in Malawi using PIF- parameters estimated at the first stage as priors. Moreover, applying the Bayesian estimation procedure also allows us to identify individual policy beliefs for each stakeholder organizations as the set of PIF parameters that replicates the stated policy positions and desired goal achievements from individual political support maximization.
2. Our estimation results imply that the estimated policy beliefs of stakeholders differ significantly from the corresponding prior parameters. Hence, we conclude that in the context of the CAADP policies in Malawi, practical policymakers and economic policy analysts exist in two separate worlds. In particular, following the prior PIF-parameters, the political technology of Malawi is characterized by a rather low efficiency of policy programs in promoting technical progress. Accordingly, based on the objective knowledge of scientific modeling, the optimal budget spending under CAADP would be rather low, amounting to only 2.5% of the total state budget, compared to an observed agricultural budget share of 30% under the status quo policy in 2010., while the majority of budget resources would be efficiently used for the provision of public services. Moreover, investments in infrastructure and non-agricultural policy programs are most effective in generating t.p. in both the agricultural and non-agricultural sectors. In contrast, based on estimated stakeholder beliefs, CAADP policies are much more effective in promoting t.p., particularly in the agricultural, agribusiness and industrial sectors, ranging between 3.5 and 16.4%. Accordingly, following stakeholder beliefs, total budget spending under CAADP is significantly higher when compared to prior parameters and ranges between 17.5% based on donor beliefs and even 45% based on governmental beliefs. Finally, combing both worlds, i.e. estimated PIF parameters using expert data from stakeholders and scientific knowledge from prior economic studies implies public investments in t.p. that take a middle ground, with an optimal agricultural budget share of nearly 10% and induced t.p. ranging between 2.5 and 3.1%.
3. Moreover, in the scientific world of economic modeling identified political performance gaps are extremely large, i.e. these amount to nearly 73% of the maximally achievable social welfare. In contrast, performance gaps are small based on stakeholder beliefs, ranging between 7.5 and 17.5%. Again, in the third world of estimated PIF parameters that combines the scientific world with the world of stakeholder beliefs, achieved political performance occupies a middle ground, with a total gap of 35%. Interestingly, based on prior and estimated political technology parameters, low political performance results primarily from a lack of political knowledge, while incentive gaps play only a minor role.

4. Interestingly, changing political influence across governmental and nongovernmental organizations has no impact on political performance, regardless of the assumed political technology scenario. Hence, neither assuming an extremely high political influence of national farm or civic society organizations nor assuming an extremely high political influence of national research or international donor organizations would imply a significant change in political performance. This result appears surprising at first glance, especially because the estimated political knowledge of governmental organizations is low when compared to that of nongovernmental organizations. However, the fact that the estimated policy beliefs of policymakers and stakeholders are comparatively homogenous implies that any combination of preferred stakeholder policy positions still maps into the same world of stakeholder beliefs. Therefore, if this world corresponds to the true political technology, political performance is high under the status-quo and remains high for any participation scenario. Vice versa, if the world of stakeholder beliefs does not correspond to the true political technology, any policy position derived from this world does not intersect with the true political technology; thus, political performance remains low for any participation scenario.
5. Therefore, our analyses of the Malawi case establish the following general and fundamental result: if neither the policy beliefs of policymakers nor the prior parameters correspond to the true political technology, adequate political knowledge does not yet exist in the scientific system or in political praxis and must be created in the political process. Therefore, the only effective political therapy corresponds to the application of adequate tools that facilitate interactive communication and policy learning among stakeholders and economic modelers. However, the most effective organization of this interactive communication in political praxis is an interesting question that we leave for future research.

Finally, the following two limitations of our presented CGPE approach must be considered:

First, in its present version, the CGPE does not yet incorporate the voter module (i.e., political support functions are derived exogenously from interview data). Basically, this setup implies that political support is driven by retrospective and non-policy voting only, while policy-oriented voting is neglected. However, as demonstrated in Chapter "Voter Behavior and Government Performance in Malawi: An Application of a Probabilistic Voting Model," policy-oriented voting is an important determinant of voter behavior. Hence, voters' policy beliefs might effectively restrict politicians' policy choices. This aspect is not fully reflected in the presented CGPE analyses. Thus, incorporating the voter module and deriving political support endogenously from estimated voter behavior might imply that observed political performance is actually more restricted by biased political incentives than implied by the presented CGPE analyses.

Second, by construction, we assume that budget spending for a specific policy program (γ_i) is homogenously effective in promoting t.p. in different subsectors. However, in reality, it appears more realistic that even within specific policy programs (e.g., investments in infrastructure), different subprograms can be formulated by focusing on specific subsectors. For example, investing in the infrastructure of specific regions or investing in the railroad system versus the road system might be more or less effective for different subsectors. These differences occur because subsectors might be regionally concentrated or dependent on specific infrastructure systems. Thus, including a third stage in our PIF function that allows for sector-specific subprograms within a specific policy program would imply that preferred policy positions across stakeholder organizations become more heterogeneous; hence, c.p., the induced incentive gaps would also be higher. Again, we leave a more detailed three-stage modeling of PIF functions for future research.

Appendix

Table 5 Overview of CAADP policy programs

		Estimated PIF	Prior PIF	bcluster1	bcluster2	bcluster3	bcluster4
CGE-Elasticities							
ζ_{SZ}^{CGE}	Z1						
	Crop	0.233	0.455	0.256	0.138	0.204	0.248
	Livestock	0.631	0.053	0.878	0.443	0.658	0.904
	Agribusiness	0.216	0.422	0.222	0.212	0.214	0.207
	Industry	0.206	0.270	0.207	0.191	0.187	0.212
	Trade	0.448	0.461	0.465	0.459	0.458	0.451
	Public	0.018	0.001	0.018	0.018	0.018	0.018
	Z2						
	Crop	0.409	0.455	0.543	0.382	0.384	0.405
	Livestock	0.271	0.053	0.344	0.366	0.294	0.240
	Agribusiness	0.216	0.422	0.222	0.228	0.218	0.194
	Industry	0.557	0.270	0.579	0.567	0.560	0.432
	Trade	0.236	0.461	0.241	0.236	0.237	0.240
	Public	0.005	0.001	0.005	0.005	0.005	0.005
	Z4						
	Crop	−2.612	−0.225	−2.339	−4.169	−3.095	−2.548
	Livestock	2.475	−0.050	3.193	3.774	3.747	3.028
	Agribusiness	4.834	4.668	5.291	5.833	5.782	2.675
	Industry	−2.556	−0.113	−3.533	−2.747	−3.398	−2.598
	Trade	−0.400	−0.364	−0.398	−0.399	−0.398	−0.399
	Public	2.569	0.138	2.653	2.541	2.766	2.564
	Z5						
	Crop	0.233	0.455	0.215	0.195	0.220	0.228
	Livestock	1.389	0.053	0.589	0.747	0.867	1.084
	Agribusiness	0.216	0.422	0.212	0.213	0.212	0.200

(continued)

Table 5 (continued)

		Estimated PIF	Prior PIF	bcluster1	bcluster2	bcluster3	bcluster4
	Industry	0.140	0.270	0.134	0.138	0.137	0.137
	Trade	0.236	0.461	0.235	0.236	0.236	0.236
	Public	0.005	0.001	0.005	0.005	0.005	0.005
	Z6						
	Crop	−0.166	−0.159	−0.179	−0.189	−0.185	−0.174
	Livestock	0.612	−0.023	0.287	0.348	0.257	0.381
	Agribusiness	−0.129	−0.149	−0.131	−0.131	−0.133	−0.138
	Industry	0.666	1.006	0.447	0.573	0.440	0.421
	Trade	1.407	2.194	1.397	1.515	1.421	1.602
	Public	0.189	0.367	0.187	0.187	0.182	0.185
	Z7						
	Crop	−0.385	−0.770	−0.342	−0.399	−0.374	−0.366
	Livestock	−0.743	−0.010	−0.531	−0.359	−0.531	−0.418
	Agribusiness	−2.709	−0.418	−2.519	−1.922	−2.127	−3.882
	Industry	2.494	0.029	2.564	2.647	2.441	3.471
	Trade	2.613	0.226	2.622	2.529	2.605	2.576
	Public	−0.024	−0.048	−0.024	−0.024	−0.024	−0.024
α_S^1							
	Crop	0.525	0.350	0.700	0.700	0.591	0.538
	Livestock	0.363	0.350	0.641	0.643	0.585	0.604
	Agribusiness	0.525	0.350	0.542	0.542	0.508	0.675
	Industry	0.469	0.350	0.672	0.447	0.561	0.621
	Trade	0.309	0.350	0.271	0.242	0.251	0.240
	Public	0.312	0.350	0.288	0.283	0.309	0.281
μ_{PS}	Crop						
	γ_1	0.003	0.006	0.003	0.003	0.003	0.003
	γ_2	0.138	0.006	0.123	0.108	0.122	0.136
	γ_3	0.050	0.086	0.049	0.037	0.047	0.047
	γ_4	0.249	0.238	0.246	0.341	0.293	0.261
	γ_5	0.107	0.103	0.097	0.035	0.064	0.090
	γ_6	0.094	0.189	0.104	0.115	0.113	0.099
	γ_7	0.089	0.079	0.077	0.037	0.053	0.082
	γ_8	0.131	0.262	0.148	0.183	0.171	0.134
	γ_9	0.139	0.032	0.152	0.148	0.134	0.148
	Livestock						
	γ_1	0.097	0.037	0.111	0.098	0.080	0.106
	γ_2	0.105	0.031	0.142	0.174	0.149	0.148
	γ_3	0.018	0.036	0.020	0.023	0.020	0.022
	γ_4	0.121	0.241	0.112	0.121	0.131	0.119
	γ_5	0.052	0.104	0.076	0.095	0.085	0.080
	γ_6	0.247	0.174	0.145	0.153	0.139	0.126
	γ_7	0.040	0.080	0.059	0.067	0.057	0.055

(continued)

Table 5 (continued)

	Estimated PIF	Prior PIF	bcluster1	bcluster2	bcluster3	bcluster4
γ_8	0.177	0.265	0.121	0.082	0.120	0.185
γ_9	0.144	0.032	0.214	0.186	0.219	0.160
Agribusiness						
γ_3	0.160	0.183	0.193	0.225	0.209	0.043
γ_4	0.286	0.256	0.292	0.300	0.315	0.346
γ_7	0.068	0.060	0.080	0.086	0.087	0.043
γ_8	0.416	0.403	0.362	0.316	0.311	0.512
γ_9	0.070	0.098	0.072	0.072	0.078	0.066
Industry						
γ_3	0.051	0.103	0.052	0.056	0.049	0.071
γ_4	0.297	0.343	0.261	0.300	0.302	0.244
γ_7	0.049	0.023	0.048	0.054	0.048	0.066
γ_8	0.359	0.075	0.365	0.306	0.369	0.309
γ_9	0.243	0.457	0.274	0.283	0.231	0.310
Trade						
γ_3	0.051	0.103	0.052	0.053	0.052	0.053
γ_4	0.671	0.343	0.668	0.668	0.667	0.668
γ_7	0.011	0.023	0.011	0.011	0.011	0.011
γ_8	0.038	0.075	0.038	0.037	0.038	0.038
γ_9	0.228	0.457	0.231	0.230	0.232	0.230
Public						
γ_3	0.051	0.103	0.052	0.052	0.052	0.052
γ_4	0.488	0.343	0.480	0.484	0.467	0.486
γ_7	0.011	0.023	0.011	0.011	0.011	0.011
γ_8	0.038	0.075	0.038	0.038	0.037	0.038
γ_9	0.411	0.457	0.419	0.415	0.433	0.413

Source: Authors

Table 6 Overview of CAADP policy programs

Pillar I: Agricultural markets
γ_1: Subsidy payment to maize
γ_2: Subsidy payment to all agricultural production
Pillar II: Infrastructure
γ_3: Improvement of infrastructure for agricultural exports
γ_4: General infrastructure improvement
Pillar III: Land and water policy
γ_5: Land policy
γ_6: Water policy
Pillar IV: Supporting institutional environment of the agricultural sector
γ_7: Support of research and development facilities
γ_8: Support of extension services
Other: Non-agricultural policy
γ_9: Non-agricultural policy

Source: Authors

References

Badiane, O., S. P. Odjo, and F. Wouterse. 2011. *Comparative analysis of strategies and long term outlook for growth and poverty reduction among ECOWAS member countries*. Discussion paper. Dakar: West and Central Africa Office.

Benin, S., S. Fan, and M. Johnson. 2012. Estimating public agricultural expenditure requirements. In *Strategies and priorities for African agriculture: Economywide perspective from country studies*, ed. X. Diao, J. Thurlow, S. Benin, and S. Fan. Washington, DC: International Food Policy Research Institute.

Brzeska, J., X. Diao, S. Fan, and J. Thurlow, eds. 2012. African agriculture and development. In *Strategies and priorities for African agriculture: Economywide perspective from country studies*. Washington, DC: International Food Policy Research Institute.

Diao, X., P. Hazel, D. Resnick, and J. Thurlow. 2007. *The role of agriculture in development: Implications for sub-Saharan Africa*. IFPRI Discussion Paper 153. Washington, DC: International Food Policy Research Institute (IFPRI).

Diao, X., J. Thurlow, S. Benin, and S. Fan, eds. 2012. *Strategies and priorities for African agriculture: Economywide perspective from country studies*. Washington, DC: International Food Policy Research Institute.

Duke, R.D. 1974. *Gaming, the future's language*. Beverly Hills, CA: Sage.

Durning, D. 1993. Participatory policy analysis in a social service agency: A case study. *Journal of Policy Analysis and Management* 12 (2): 297.

Fan, S., and M. W. Rosegrant. 2008. *Investing in agriculture to overcome the world food crisis and reduce poverty and hunger*. IFPRI Policy Briefs 3. Washington, DC: International Food Policy Research Institute (IFPRI).

Fan, S., and X. Zhang. 2004. Investment, reforms and poverty in rural China. *Economic Development and Cultural Change* 52 (2): 395–422.

Geurts, J.L.A., and C. Joldersma. 2001. Methodology for participatory policy analysis. *European Journal of Operational Research* 128 (2): 300–310.

Heckelei, T., R. Mittelhammer, and T. Jansson. 2008. *A Bayesian alternative to generalized cross entropy solutions for underdetermined econometric models* (Discussion Paper 2). Bonn: Institute for Food and Resource Economics, University of Bonn.

Henning, C.H.C.A. 2009. Networks of power in the CAP system of the EU-15 and EU-27. *Journal of Public Policy* 29 (02): 153–177.

Joldersma, C. 1997. Participatory policy making: Balancing between divergence and convergence. *European Journal of Work and Organizational Psychology* 6 (2): 207–218.

Knoke, D., F.U. Pappi, J. Broadbent, and Y. Tsujinaka. 1996. *Comparing policy networks. Labor politics in the U.S., Germany, and Japan*. Cambridge: Cambridge University Press.

Laumann, E.O., and D. Knoke. 1987. *The organizational state: Social choice in national policy domains*. Wisconsin: University of Wisconsin Press.

Pappi, F.U., and C.H.C.A. Henning. 1999. The organization of influence on EC's common agricultural policy: A network approach. *European Journal of Political Research* 36 (2): 257–281.

Pappi, F.U., T. König, and D. Knoke. 1995. *Entscheidungsprozesse in der Arbeits- und Sozialpolitik*. Frankfurt: Main.

Persson, T., and G. Tabellini. 2000. *Political economics – Explaning economic policy*. Cambridge: MIT Press.

Snijders, T.A. 2002. Markov chain Monte Carlo estimation of exponential random graph models. *Journal of Social Structure* 3 (2): 1–40.

Christian Henning is professor and chair of agricultural economics, University of Kiel (Germany). He studied economics, agricultural economics, sociology, political science and mathematics. He earned a PhD in economics, in agricultural economics and in political science. His main areas of specialization are applied political economy and applied economic modelling of agricultural policies. To date he has published five books and various articles in refereed journals including PLoS ONE, American Journal of Agricultural Economics, European Review of Agricultural Economics, Journal of Public Policy, Journal of Mathematical Sociology and Journal of Theoretical Politics.

Johannes Hedtrich is a computer scientist and a phd student in agricultural economics.He studied computer science and agricultural economics at the University of Kiel (Germany). His main areas of specialization are computational economics, Bayesian econometrics and social network analysis.

Ligane Massamba Sène is a Research Economist at the African Union. He holds a PhD in Agricultural Economics from the University of Kiel and a MSc Degree—Engineer in Statistics and Economics from ENSAE. He also studied Mathematics, Physics and Computer Science. His research interests include macroeconomic, macrosectoral and economic modeling of development and agricultural policies—Poverty, Inclusive growth and optimizing public expenditures—Taxation, social policies and household welfare—Modeling and Econometrics.

Eva Krampe is an agricultural sector expert at the European Investment Bank. She studied agricultural economics and earned a PhD in agricultural economics at the University of Kiel. Her main areas of specialization are Africa's Agricultural Policy, Applied Political Economy and Economic Analysis of Agricultural Investment Projects.

Part III
Conclusion

12

Conversion of Evidence into Action: Strategic Analysis and Knowledge Support Systems (SAKSS)

Michael E. Johnson

1 Introduction

Many sub-Saharan African countries today have committed to the continent-wide goals of the Comprehensive African Agriculture Development Programme (CAADP) of the Africa Union and New Partnership for Africa's Development (NEPAD). The goals draw attention towards a shared commitment of allocating at least 10% of their national budgets to agriculture in order to achieve a 6% annual sector growth rate and meet the Millennium Development Goal (MDG) of halving poverty by 2015. As a result, policymakers have been called on to allocate more resources and design strategies to accelerate agricultural growth in order to meet these goals. The challenge now is ensuring that selected policies and investment strategies are effective in producing their intended goals of sustaining broad-based growth and poverty reduction.

The desire for more effective policy and investment strategies that translate into the achievement of shared CAADP goals has revived questions about capacities for policy analysis and participatory processes of designing and implementing development strategies in Africa. Many past studies in the region have documented the failure of past central planning or top down approaches of implementation (Brinkerhoff 1996; Crosby 1996; Killick 1976; Montjoy and O'Toole 1979; Wildavsky 1973). Such inadequacies led to calls for more decentralized, evidence-based, and participatory processes, to be complemented by strong monitoring and evaluation (M&E) systems that allow for adaptation to changing conditions over time given the nonlinear and dynamic nature of designing and implementing development strategies.

M.E. Johnson (✉)
CARE USA, Washington, DC, USA
e-mail: mjohnson@care.org

Recognizing the complexities of formulating and implementing effective policies and investment strategies requires a lot of evidence to accurately assess the choices available to a government and the tradeoffs inherent in any choice they make.[1] To supply this evidence, the country must have a solid foundation of analytical capacity throughout its planning agencies and academic institutions. In addition, governments need policymakers who have the motivation and ability to demand and use the information (Omamo 2004). The intersection of these two sides and the knowledge generated describes the state of a national knowledge system, defined here as the existing stock of knowledge and established links between people and organizations on both the supply and demand side in influencing the type of knowledge products generated and utilized in policy dialogue and decisionmaking.

How effective a national knowledge system is in generating and promoting the use of evidence depends on many factors: the perceived credibility and relevance of the evidence generated; the type of relationships and linkages that develop among all individual actors and organizations involved; capacities to comprehend and utilize the evidence, the local policy process and political climate; and local beliefs and norms (Young 2005; Cash et al. 2003). Often, it is the linkage among individuals and organizations that help to bridge the supply and demand for evidence which is especially weak. It requires establishing effective mechanisms by which both sides can be more closely tied as part of ongoing dialogue and decisionmaking processes. These mechanisms effectively link suppliers and users of knowledge through the creation and use of knowledge products.

For many African countries, the state of their national knowledge systems remains very weak and poses a serious challenge for strengthening the effectiveness of future strategy design and implementation efforts. Data collection and analysis continues to suffer from a shortage of attention and resources. Knowledge sharing is often minimal, with planning ministries that operate in isolation and uncoordinated ministries, research institutes, and statistical bureaus. Government agencies, NGOs, and development partners carry out parallel and overlapping processes of information gathering. Often development partners have more input into the strategy process than legislative bodies or the national civil society does. The M&E frameworks of many strategies rarely deal with issues of causality and attribution between investments, policy changes, and outcomes.

The large capacity gaps also exacerbated an inherently weak link between the supply and demand of evidence. For example, local universities rarely undertake research directly relevant to local decisionmaking needs while national institutions and agencies seldom have sufficient capacities and experience to provide relevant information needed to guide strategy formulation and implementation.

[1]By evidence we mean data statistics and analysis of past trends, economic analysis of future policy alternatives, impact assessment of past investments, research findings from a number of disciplines (public policy, socioeconomic and political sciences, and the biophysical sciences), and lessons from practice and experience.

The Strategic Analysis and Knowledge Support System (SAKSS) concept was developed in direct response to these serious capacity gaps in many African countries. Its principle goals are to: (a) bring quality and strategic analysis to bear on identifying key investments, institutional mechanisms, and policy options, as well as the implementation of selected options for agricultural policy and investment strategies (this includes harmonizing and generating standardized information for development planning and M&E, and to be available as global public goods); (b) build and strengthen national and regional capacities for policy analysis, M&E, while helping to bridge the research and policy divide; and, (c) broker the dialogue and links between institutions and individuals who supply and use data and information related to agricultural strategies by establishing network for information exchange and knowledge management.

The SAKSS was developed around two key concepts—'strategic analysis' and 'knowledge support systems' which have since defined its overall purpose and utility for supporting CAADP implementation. The 'strategic analysis' concept describes generating information that is not only scientifically credible but has important relevance to the range of questions and issues being faced by policymakers in formulating and implementing their country's agricultural development strategies. The 'knowledge support system' concept defines a network of individuals and institutions that are linked in ways intended to help bring strategic analysis and research evidence to bear during the design and implementation of the agricultural development strategy. We now review these in more detail.

2 The Strategic Analysis Concept and Approach

Strategic analysis describes a logical series of analyses which help identify policy and investment options for achieving growth and poverty outcomes, beginning with a broader, economywide perspective and ending with a more targeted sector and community level perspective. This type of integrated analysis is intended to guide a credible action plan of development priorities in agriculture which contribute the most to the achievement of desirable targets for growth and poverty reduction. Such prioritization implies finding answers to a range of strategic questions such as: What is the role of agriculture in promoting overall economic growth and poverty reduction in the different stages of development given a country's natural resource endowments? How should public resources be mobilized and allocated among different sectors, sub-sectors, and regions? What have been the lessons and effect of agricultural policies and investments on outcomes and impact? Answers to these questions can help arm policymakers with useful evidence on the kinds of tradeoffs and outcomes associated with their policy and investment choices.

The analysis is considered 'strategic' so long as it contributes to the narrowing down of investment options that will help lead to the achievement of these high-end development targets. It means weighing in the costs and benefits for undertaking one strategy over another. For example, should government focus on promoting a rapid expansion in food staples production? It will definitely benefit consumers, but producers could be devastated if prices drop too fast following a bumper harvest. Or, governments may wish to introduce a policy that is designed to target the poor and yet undercuts private sector participation and long term sustainability, such as in the case of output procurement and the provision of modern inputs.

The sequence and types of analysis are not fixed, however. Different local contexts may require a different set of analyses. Because SAKSS has been primarily developed for African countries with a large agricultural sector, the analysis is focused on identifying options for agriculture as a source of economic growth and poverty reduction. Various economic tools and methodologies exist, but which tools and approaches are used will not only depend on the question being asked but on many other important considerations as well, such as: the availability of data and expertise, time to undertake the analysis, cost, access to analytical tools and economic models, and underlying assumptions and limitations. Johnson and Flaherty (2011) provide a review of some of these tools, as well as a guidance on which tool is most appropriate under what conditions with respect to a range of factors such as data availability, cost, and time to complete the analysis.

To illustrate, we offer a number of very broad but logically sequenced series of 'strategic analysis' type questions to consider when assessing the policy and investment alternatives for achieving goals of agricultural growth and poverty reduction. These include: How can agriculture contribute the most to overall development objectives? How should resources be mobilized and allocated more efficiently? How can individual policies and interventions be better targeted? How can lessons be monitored and evaluated during and after implementation? We review each of these below.

2.1 How Can Agriculture Contribute the Most to Overall Development Objectives?

From the outset, it is useful to first establish the country's current situation and whether its trajectory will lead to the achievement of the CAADP goals. It should do so within the context of the country's overall economy in order to highlight a broad set of strategic options and tradeoffs—e.g. whether simply promoting faster growth is more important than considering poverty and food security, or even environmental degradation. This context is needed because policies at the macro level, such as trade and market liberalization, can have a profound impact on growth, and even more so on agriculture, the rural economy, and poverty (Dorward et al. 2004). At the same time, policies that directly affect rural areas and agriculture can have an impact on the overall economy and in turn have feedback effects on the rural sector. By examining many of these policy options within the context of the broader economy, key relationships and welfare implications can be assessed in ways that lessen any potential adverse impacts on the poor.

The economywide perspective permits other higher-level strategic questions to be posed for shaping an agricultural strategy within the context of overall national development goals, and in so doing, provides the greatest strategic leverage to priority setting (Byerlee 2000). The potential role of agriculture, including individual subsectors in agriculture, can then be explored with respect to how they contribute to economywide growth and national development priorities, such as reducing poverty. Within this normative mode of analysis, questions regarding the long-term distributional consequences of alternative investment and policy choices for meeting these targets can also be explored. Specific to rural sector strategies, sectorwide investment options should be examined more closely, especially with regard to how they affect the incentives for rural agricultural production and commercialization.

Various economic analysis tools can be used. For example, the Computable General Equilibrium (CGE) model is particularly well suited for analyzing a country's progress towards achieving its national development goals through agriculture. CGE models help analyze the effects of policy shifts and alternative sector growth scenarios on overall economic growth and poverty reduction. They have the advantage of capturing both direct and indirect effects of policy changes on poverty and income distribution given a country's overall economic structure. The effects are channeled through changes in employment, wages and relative prices while considering forward and backward linkages in the economy. From this, policymakers can weigh the costs and benefits associated with focusing attention on stimulating growth in different sectors and subsectors.

Existing examples that apply this level of analysis involve the work that has been undertaken by IFPRI researchers in a number of countries in Africa (e.g. Ethiopia, Ghana, Mozambique, Rwanda, Zambia and Malawi). From these studies, for example, it became quickly evident that most countries could not meet the MDG poverty target of halving poverty by 2015, with the exception of Ghana, Mozambique and Uganda. Model results further showed that the additional growth would need to be driven mostly by food staple sectors as these have a larger impact on poverty reduction than similar growth in export-oriented crops (see example for Zambia in Fig. 1). This impact occurs because yield improvements in food crops not only benefit households directly, by increasing incomes from agricultural production, but also by allowing farmers to diversify into higher-value crops. Food crops also typically have stronger growth-linkages to non-agriculture, which stimulates broader economywide growth and poverty reduction.

2.2 *How Should Resources Be Mobilized and Allocated More Efficiently?*

An essential component of a development strategy is its plan for prioritizing investments and mobilizing resources. A strategy grounded in country-specific

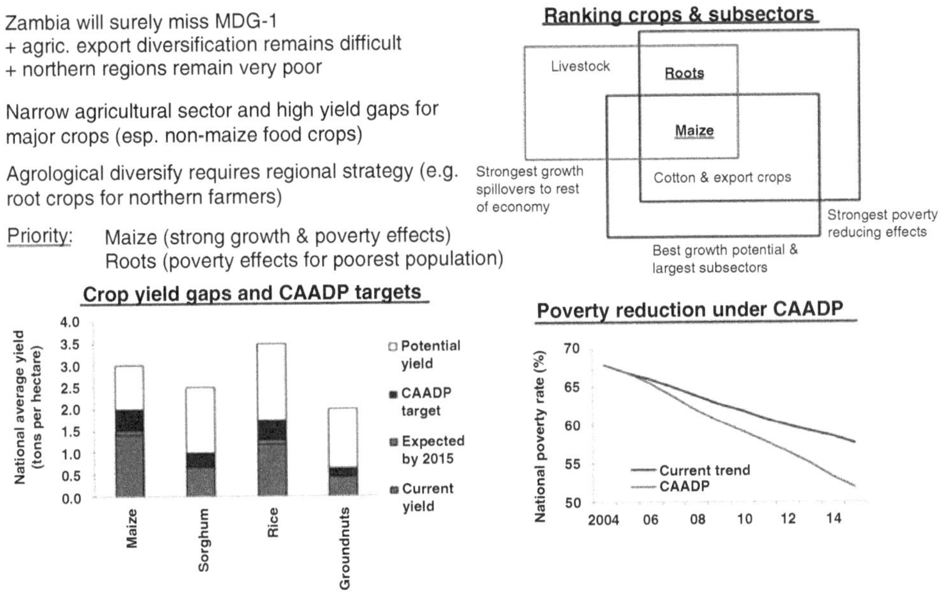

Fig. 1 Example of 'strategic analysis' results of investment options for Zambia. Source: CAADP Modeling results from Thurlow et al. (2008b)

context must be based on a thorough assessment of the public investment situation and potential to contribute to the development goals. Public investments can be thematic (e.g. roads, marketing institutions), sectorwide (e.g. research and extension, irrigation), and subsector specific (e.g. commodity-based research).

All these investments affect rural poverty through many channels. For example, public investment in agricultural research, rural education and health, and infrastructure increases farmers' income directly by increasing agricultural productivity and lowering transaction costs of both inputs and outputs, which in turn reduces rural poverty. Indirect impacts come from higher agricultural wages and improved nonfarm employment opportunities induced by growth in agricultural productivity and increases in market opportunities. Growth in agricultural output from rural investment often yields lower food prices, again helping the poor indirectly because they are often net buyers of food crops. Redistribution of land caused by higher agricultural growth also has important impacts on rural poverty. In addition to their productivity impact, public investments in rural education, health, and infrastructure directly promote rural wages, nonfarm employment, and migration, thereby reducing rural poverty. For example, improved infrastructure access will help farmers set up small nonfarm businesses in rural areas such as food processing and marketing enterprises, electronic repairs shops, transportation and trade, and restaurant services. A key underlying assumption is that public and private investments are complements (Anderson et al. 2006), so that an increase in public goods and accumulation of capital stock raises the productivity of all factors in agricultural production, which in turn leads to higher farm wages and incomes and poverty reduction.

Investments in the rural sector not only contribute to growth, more employment opportunities, and higher wages in rural areas, but also help the development of the national economy by providing labor, human and physical capital, cheaper food, and markets for urban industrial and service development. This type of growth in the national economy can then help reduce poverty in both rural and urban sectors. Understanding these different effects provides useful policy insights to improve the effectiveness of government poverty reduction strategies. In particular, it provides information on how public investment can be used to strengthen links between poverty reduction channels to increase efficiency in targeting public resources on poverty reduction. More efficient targeting has become increasingly important in an era of macroeconomic reforms in which governments are under pressure to reduce budgets. For examples of tools and approaches to measure the impact of investments, see Appendix A.5 and Benin et al. (2008b).

The question of how resources should be mobilized and allocated across the different economic sectors and geographic regions is essentially answering a range of high-end questions that inform the design and evaluation of a development strategy, such as: (a) What have been the trends of government expenditures by sector, and what have been the reasons for their changes? (b) How has public investment been financed, and how has the burden of financing investment policy been distributed in society? (c) What have been the economic rates of return to various types of government expenditures, including their impact on growth and poverty reduction? (d) What level of effort in public spending is required to achieve targeted goals for agriculture and overall economic growth?

Analyzing these series of questions not only helps identify the kinds of public sector investments which offer the highest economic rate of return (for an example, see Fan et al. 2004 for Uganda), but they also help assess the extent to which past investments have impacted on overall development goals (a topic covered next). It requires sufficient subnational data on the level and distribution of public sector expenditures and investments over time. A public expenditure review is especially useful as a first step in compiling the required data. It will also help determine the extent to which actual resource allocations are consistent with a country's strategy and goals. Combining this information with other data, such as household survey data on consumption, production, and welfare measures, will allow for more sophisticated analyses. For example, using econometric tools, more detailed analysis can be carried out, drawing on the cross-sectional variation of the data, to measure and attribute differences in outcome variables such as growth and poverty to the accumulated stock of past investments and other socioeconomic variables. Where time series data are also available on the same cross-sectional data, the dynamics and lagged effects of public investments can also be analyzed. When combined with independent estimates of the unit costs of different investments, cost/benefit ratios can be calculated.

Results from the econometric analysis can be further translated into unitless elasticity estimates. An elasticity measures the sensitivity or marginal effect of a 1% change in one variable on the percent change in another variable. For example, an expenditure-to-growth elasticity would measure the effect of a 1% change in the stock of investments (or expenditures) on the change in growth outcomes, whether at the sector or economywide level. This becomes useful for estimating future growth requirements in public investments for generating desired sector and economic growth targets. Using estimates of both an expenditure-to-growth elasticity and a growth-to-poverty elasticity, one can then estimate the level of resources required to achieve desired growth and poverty goals (see Fan et al. 2008). A number of country case studies that have estimated resource requirements for meeting the CAADP goal of 6% include Benin et al. (2008a) and Thurlow et al. (2008a, b).

2.3 *How Can Individual Policies and Interventions Be Better Targeted?*

Many of the challenges and opportunities that national development strategies must negotiate are geographic in nature and affect different communities on the ground. For example, economic opportunities can vary widely by location depending on other important factors such as the natural resource base (e.g. agriculture potential), population density, and access to markets and rural services (e.g., education, health, agriculture extension). Development options would be quite different for more remote and food insecure areas versus those areas located in close proximity to large market centers. Thus any interventions should be specifically targeted towards the unique characteristics of the area and depending on the severity of the problem—such as quantifying the extent and distribution of poverty and malnutrition across geographic areas and population groups is an important first step (Babu and Pinstrup-Andersen 1994).

With the increasing availability of spatially disaggregated data and tools to understand those data, it has become increasingly possible to map indicators of biophysical and socioeconomic indicators showing local comparative advantage for different agricultural and rural development options (see example of Uganda in Fig. 2 below). Agroclimatic factors, access to markets, and population density are some of the more important dimensions for assessing agricultural development potential (Pender et al. 2001). By viewing how these conditions correlate and overlap each other spatially with local welfare measures, assumptions can be made about how different development investments will impact the poor and how changing agricultural land uses may have environmental costs. Taken together, these conditions provide an enhanced picture of the costs and benefits of different investments, allowing better targeting towards the goals of sustainable growth, poverty reduction, and environmental sustainability (see Wood and Chamberlin 2003; Wood et al. 1999).

Taking on a spatial perspective helps to seek answers associated with targeting interventions. For example, a range of questions it may help answer include: (a) What are the distribution and extent of income, poverty and malnutrition across

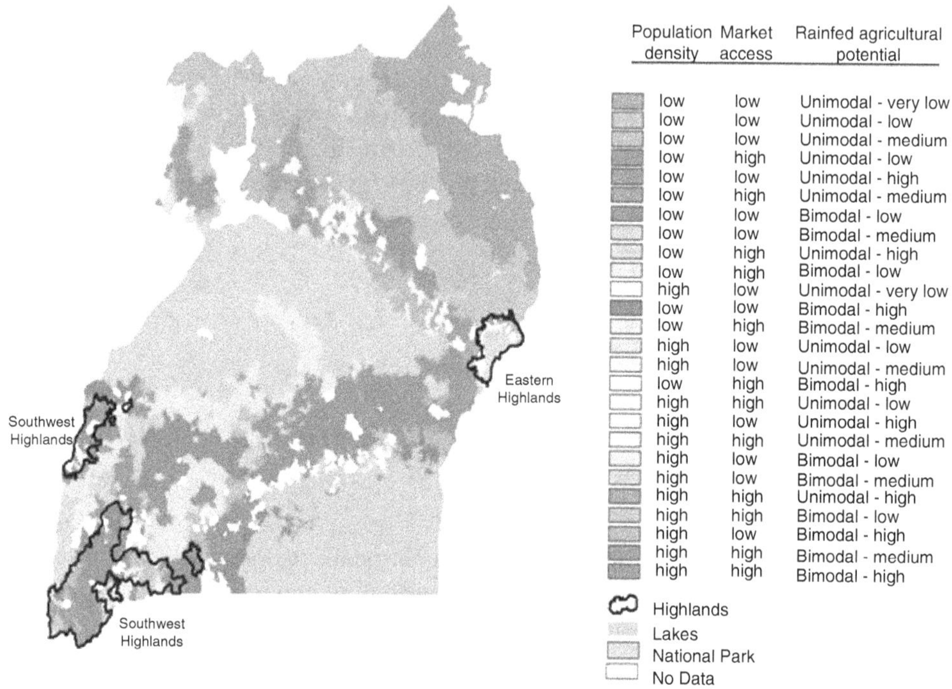

Fig. 2 Mapping out development domains in Uganda. Source: Johnson and Flaherty (2011)

different locations in the country? (b) What kinds of opportunities and challenges affect rural economic livelihoods in different parts of the country? (c) For agriculture, what are the key development domains based on agriculture potential, market access and population density? (d) Which development domains offer the greatest potential for high investment impact among the key subsectors and economic activities identified as key sources of growth in the economywide analysis above? (e) What kinds of interventions (e.g. infrastructure, R&D and extension, institutional) are needed to spur productivity and income growth among select domains? (f) Among the poorest of the domains, in terms of limited resource assets and livelihood options, what are the alternatives for poverty reduction and food security?

Exploring answers to these questions can be answered with tools such as Geographic information Systems (GIS) and remote sensing. Having access to spatially oriented data, including agroclimatic conditions, land-use, production, urban and markets centers, infrastructure, household consumption, and welfare, is particularly critical but often lacking in many African countries. However, with increasing sophistication of computer technologies and satellite imagery, filling in some of the gaps is increasingly possible. For example, You et al. (2007) recently used a cross-entropy approach to make plausible allocations of crop production by small square grids (or pixels) based on available statistics of larger subnational units and satellite imagery.

A number of examples illustrate the usefulness and application of spatial analysis for targeting investments in agriculture. At the country level, useful examples include the work undertaken by Pender et al. (2001) and Bolwig et al. (2002) for mapping out development domains in Uganda. The more recent work by Chamberlin et al. (2006) builds on this concept. At the regional level, the studies by Omamo et al. (2006) and Johnson et al. (2008) are especially noteworthy. Spatial analysis tools were complemented by various economic analyses to assess future agricultural growth options and research priorities in the Eastern and Western regions of sub-Saharan Africa.

2.4 *How Can Lessons Be Monitored and Evaluated During and After Implementation?*

A critical part of any agricultural strategy is to be able to determine at some point whether the strategy is on track to achieving its goals, or whether at the end of its life, people's lives have been positively or negatively impacted on. It helps to justify resource investments and ensure accountability. It also provides the option to adjust the strategy as new evidence becomes available on what has (or has not) been working. From the perspective of the goals of SAKSS, therefore, helping to provide credible and relevant analysis and information related to M&E is a fundamental prerequisite to promoting evidence-based policymaking. And although the importance of M&E systems is well-documented (see for example, Mackay 2007 and Dalal-Clayton and Bass 2002), it is often the most difficult part to set up and maintain. This is because agricultural strategies operate within a broader and complex environment that is inherently dynamic with respect to constantly changing domestic and global economic conditions, social and political trends, climatic shocks, and participatory and political processes associated with designing and implementing policies and investment strategies.

Ultimately, therefore, an M&E system seeks to answer questions that determine whether development objectives are being fulfilled and if there is impact in order to help revise and improve futures strategies, such as: (a) Is the allocation and level of inputs (e.g. spending, investments, policy interventions) of the agricultural strategy (or project) on target? (b) How can the impact of these investments be traced to improvements in outputs (e.g. productivity, viability of production systems, food processors, agro-industries, markets, and trade)? (c) Have these improvements affected outcomes (e.g. incomes and the poverty status of target populations)? (d) What factors have shaped (positively and negatively) the level of impact achieved to date? What needs to be altered? (e) What was the distribution of these intermediate impacts, e.g. on smallholders, on equity, on gender, on other spillover impacts? (f) Are there key ingredients of success or failure based on past experience and lessons learned? What role for public versus private sector?

A desirable M&E system is one that can encompass not only the monitoring of progress among key inputs, outputs and outcome indicators, but evaluates the magnitude and distribution of impact. For the former, simple descriptive narratives of trends among the indicators help to answer the adequacy question: "have expectations in terms of investment flows and achievement of the growth and poverty reduction targets been met so far?" However, it does not answer the key hypotheses on: "how effectively have different types of policies and investments impacted on the goals so far?" and "what factors have shaped the level of impact that has been achieved?" These last two questions are more concerned with the evaluation or impact assessment part of M&E. Addressing all three provides key information that can help guide decisions on what to adjust, as well as the scale and mix of investment priorities needed, in order to keep a country's agricultural strategy on track. In this way, it is a critical component of the strategic analysis agenda of a SAKSS, by coming full circle to helping inform and strengthen future design and implementation of agricultural strategies.

In order to find answers to questions a good M&E system seeks to provide, there are three challenges facing many African countries: the availability and quality of data from national statistical systems from which to gather baseline information and set future targets; having a clear M&E framework in place that describes the interrelationships (or causality) between inputs, outputs and outcomes; and integral to the development of the M&E framework itself, having in place sufficiently robust methods and tools for evaluating impact over time.

2.4.1 Ensuring Availability and Reliability of Underlying Data Systems

The poor availability of reliable data in most African countries makes it particularly challenging for setting up a national M&E system, just as it is for the other types of strategic analyses discussed in this chapter. Especially problematic is the frequency of data collection and quality on agricultural production and marketing. Most African countries have only undertaken a handful of these surveys since the 1970s. In Ghana, for example, the last comprehensive agricultural census was carried out in the early 1970s followed by a smaller sampled survey in 1986. Other socioeconomic surveys, such as the living standards measurement surveys (LSMS), population and housing census, and demographic and health surveys (DHS) have occurred more frequently, but these vary across countries.

Even if there is data available, its quality is often poor due to overall weak technical and managerial capacities of national statistical systems. Explanations for this have included a generally low regard for statistical information by policymakers; poor links between statistical systems and policy processes; inadequate government spending and technical assistance for statistics over long periods of time; and outdated statistical systems and legislation (Kiregyera 2008; Wingfield-Digby 2007). Another weak data area is having timely and sufficient information on the flows of public sector expenditures and investments in agriculture—especially from public expenditure tracking surveys or PETS (Dorotinsky and Floyd 2004). Such information can serve as key input for setting baselines and targets for investment spending and for undertaking impact studies later on, in addition to helping improve accountability and public sector management more generally. Typically, much of this information is found within finance ministries, with details of agricultural expenditures available from the sector ministry.

There are increasing efforts to improve data systems for agriculture in general for many African countries (see Kiregyera 2008). One recent effort being led by the World Bank is the Living Standards Measurement Study and Integrated Surveys on Agriculture (LSMS-ISA) to improve household level panel data on agriculture in sub-Saharan Africa. According to the World Bank's website on this initiative, six African countries will initially benefit from this. In time, and once scaled out to other countries, this should help improve and complement existing data sets for purposes of monitoring performance and impact of ARD strategies in Africa. Another is the introduction of the AU/NEPAD budgetary tracking system for agricultural expenditures to monitor the national compliance of the Maputo declaration. This has begun to make information on total agriculture spending available (AU/NEPAD 2005). However, because it doesn't cover disaggregate flows by subsector and type of investment it is less useful for impact evaluation (see Benin et al. 2010).

2.4.2 Developing an M&E Framework

Simply having sufficient access to data does not guarantee a good M&E system. It also requires having a credible M&E framework in place, as well as the tools to monitor progress and assess impact. As a start, either a logical or theoretical framework can be useful in this regard. Both seek to layout a simple structure which describes the causal relationship between inputs (e.g. investment flows), outputs (e.g. productivity), and outcomes (e.g. growth and poverty), and from which critical corresponding indicators can be identified for the purpose of monitoring and evaluating impact.

The logical framework (or logframe) approach helps describe a simple flow chart of how inputs will achieve intermediate and final outcomes. Performance indicators are selected as part of a results-oriented log frame matrix, measuring performance in terms of input delivery, implementing activities, producing outputs, and achieving targeted outcomes (World Bank 2004; Kusek and Rist 2004; Crawford and Bryce 2003). The measurement of outputs can also include specifying the extent of coverage among target groups, including non-target groups if spillovers are expected and measurable. Performance indicators are then selected at each stage along a simple causality chain, with assumptions about associated risks and other confounding factors which can influence performance and outcomes. Adaptations to improve the basic logframe have occurred over time by seeking to introduce more participatory approaches and/or theory and analytical rigor along the entire length of the causal chain (White 2006; World Bank 2004). The most popular have included the impact chain analysis, outcome mapping, and impact pathway approaches.

Based on the logframe, the impact chain analysis approach essentially maps out the links in the causal chain based on underlying economic theory and evidence. It allows for a more in-depth theoretical understanding of the cause-and-effect relationships or impact pathways between variables and the confounding effects of other potentially influencing factors. And so long as sufficient data exists, empirical evaluations of impact using econometric techniques can also be modeled as discussed further below. Its main disadvantage is that it can easily become unnecessarily complex, data intensive, and costly.

An alternative is the outcome mapping approach, which is more participatory and qualitative in nature, focusing on changes in development processes and outcomes (Earl et al. 2001; Smutylo 2005). Essentially, it identifies expected impacts and outcome indicators based on a map of interrelated factors from intervention to outcomes within a group session. Given the complexity of considering many other noneconomic factors which can influence outcomes, the approach adopts visualization techniques to instill participants to think through the different factors, their direct and indirect effects, as well as causal linkages. This is especially useful for tracing out qualitative changes in development processes which are not easily measurable (e.g. human behavior). A disadvantage of this approach is that it is limited by the complexity of causal relationships that arise as more factors and stakeholders are identified in the process.

More recently, the impact pathway approach was introduced to try and deal with some of the shortcomings of both outcome mapping and impact chain analysis approaches (see Spinger-Heinze et al. 2003 and Douthwaite et al. 2003). The approach recognizes the presence of a number of impact chains and sequences in explaining the overall change process. The analysis of multiple impact pathways can be quite useful for impact evaluation as they avoid the pitfall of assuming a simple linear relationship between an investment and outcome. The analysis of development domains discussed earlier in this chapter, for example, constitutes the existence of multiple but distinct impact pathways. This is because how investments ultimately lead to outcomes depends on the type of combinations among multiple factors—such as agricultural potential, market access and population pressure (Spinger-Heinze et al. 2003; Pender et al. 2001). While it is an improvement, it shares the same drawbacks of outcome mapping and impact chain analysis as it can easily become unnecessarily complex. Additionally, it can quickly become very data intensive and costly when too many other factors and distinct pathways or outcome mappings are introduced.

No matter which approach is adopted, the real challenge from a practical perspective is maintaining sound theory and rigor while at the same time limiting the degree of complexity in drawing out the causality chain and in selecting a minimum set of indicators for which reliable data exists. Depending on the strategy goals and underlying programs, a balance needs to be struck between the need to attribute impact to program interventions and having in place a cost efficient M&E

system, one that has the least likelihood for measurement errors and is simple enough to interpret the information that comes out of it.

Despite various approaches to M&E systems, their basic structure and utility are principally intended to serve as a performance management tool: to help adapt policies and investments during the course of strategy implementation in order to stay on track towards achieving targeted output and outcome goals. An additional advantage of such systems is that they can be developed in a participatory fashion involving broader stakeholder groups. The main drawbacks are that they are less reliable for undertaking a credible impact assessment as they tend to be too static, rigid, and rely only on theoretical assumptions when linking between inputs, outputs and outcomes.

2.4.3 Undertaking Impact Assessment

In order to effectively assess the impact of a strategy (or its underlying projects) after it has been in place for some time requires additional tools, both quantitative and qualitative. A number of quantitative tools exist for analyzing impact at the sector or economywide levels and at the project level. The evaluation of sector or economywide impacts of public sector interventions is particularly useful when the goal is to assess effects on aggregate welfare outcomes (e.g. poverty) and their distribution. Where there is sufficient information on past investments and other key factors which influence outcomes, econometric and statistical methods can help test for the contribution of past changes in investments (e.g. agricultural research, infrastructure, health, and education) on changes in outcome variables. This is very much the same approaches described in the previous section on 'How should resources be mobilized and allocated across the different economic sectors and geographic regions?' emphasizing how ex-post impact evaluation is particularly relevant for informing the design of future strategies.

Given the poor availability and quality of data in many African countries, econometric techniques may not be feasible. Under these conditions, simulation and programming models are useful alternatives. For agricultural R&D, for example, economic surplus models can be used to estimate economic rates of return to investment so long as sufficient information on key technology and behavioral parameters exist (see Alston et al. 1995). Additionally, programming techniques can also be used to estimate changes in agricultural performance (as measured by total factor productivity) that is due to technical change and thus past investments in R&D (see Farrington et al. 1997). For broader categories of investments, it is also possible to apply economywide simulation models as in the earlier section on 'What are the economywide options for reaching high-end agricultural development goals?' if such models already exist. This can be particularly useful for capturing the impact of broader sectorwide investments on overall economic growth.

The application of economic simulation models to the evaluation of impact after the fact (or ex-post) essentially involves simulating how much an actual change in investments or policy may have affected outcomes. A number of indicators that serve as input into the models can be monitored periodically to assess their potential impact on outcomes. As data on outcome variables becomes available, model results can be compared with actual values. If the model predicts an outcome that is below or above the actual observed outcome, it is possible a number of confounding factors could explain the difference, if data and model specification errors are assumed minimal. Results can also be compared against a baseline scenario wherein the intervention is removed to describe a situation 'with and without'—as a type of counterfactual analysis (see example of Bell et al. 1982).

An emerging area is the use of spatial analysis tools for impact assessment. This has become possible as GIS tools, satellite imagery, and computer hardware and software, have advanced over the years. As a result, for example, an increasing number of countries are able to produce high resolution poverty maps. Knowledge of this kind which show disparities in poverty across geographic space, including associated livelihoods and assets, is not only relevant for targeting future investments (as discussed in the section 'How can individual policies and interventions be better targeted?') but can also serve as a monitoring and evaluation tool. Statistical techniques can be applied where there is sufficient data to be able to associate a number of key geographic and socioeconomic factors to changes in welfare over time (e.g. see Minot and Baulch 2005 and Pender et al. 2001).

Impact assessment at the sector or economywide level has its limitations. The effects between investments and outcomes are typically too aggregate to be linked back to any particular intervention (Maredia 2009). The common problem of insufficient data makes econometric and spatial analysis methods difficult and often impractical. While economic simulation models are more feasible under these conditions, their accuracy depends on how well the underlying data, model specification, and behavioral assumptions represent the real world. In many instances, behavioral parameter estimates in a model are drawn from different periods in time and/or different locations.

Impact assessment at the project level, on the other hand, is far more feasible if necessary steps are undertaken from project design to implementation. At this level of analysis, experimental or randomized approaches are more desirable because they can directly test for attribution and causality. This is because randomization allows for measuring impact against some counterfactual or control variable ("before and after," or "with and without," the intervention), while guarding against problems of selection bias in the process. In other words, it can answer questions of how individuals who participated in a program would have fared in the absence of the program, or, how those who were not exposed to the program would have fared in the presence of the program (Duflo et al. 2008; Maredia 2009; White 2006). To ensure sufficient information is collected for randomization, however, early preparations and resources for monitoring and evaluation must be in place when the project is in its design phase—to later provide the "before and after" and/or the "with and without" intervention comparisons.

The experimental or randomization approach is not without its critics. Some question its usefulness at the level of informing policy and strategy design altogether (Ravillion 2009). An obvious limitation is that typically the desire for undertaking an evaluation occurs when a project has already ended which makes the condition for randomization impossible. Another is the ethical question of excluding from treatment a control group when it involves welfare improving interventions. Other problems include: the limitations for scaling up to general equilibrium effects that occur at higher levels of impact but unaccounted for at the project level; the existence of uniquely defined local conditions which affect outcomes but are not always present in other locations; and, the observation that simply identifying 'what' worked from a project is not as useful for policy if it also does not answer 'why' it worked (Deaton 2009). Finally, its high costs may not always be justifiable, especially if they do not contribute much of anything to policy considerations. Weighing in the cost for experimental impact evaluations with the information expected from them should always be considered before undertaking such evaluations.

In most cases, non-experimental and practical alternatives are more suitable when projects are already underway. Among them are commonly accepted statistical and econometric techniques that compare outcomes between project participants and non-participants within a target population, such as controlling for observables, regression discontinuity design estimates, difference-in-differences and fixed effects approaches, as well as the use of instrumental variables (Duflo et al. 2008; Maredia 2009). In other cases, simple economic cost-benefit analysis (or rate of return studies) are just as useful, but only so long as there is sufficient underlying information on costs and behavioral assumptions associated with the project (see Gittinger 1984; Alston et al. 1995, 2000; and Masters et al. 1998).

The choice of economic tools ultimately depends on many factors: whether impact is being evaluated at the project or sector or economywide level; the type of questions being asked to ensure policy relevance; data availability and type; pre-existing models; resources and time available for analysis; and the capacity or skills of the evaluator. Ravillion (2008) offers some useful steps for evaluators to consider in selecting the most appropriate methods and approaches.

Finally, not all impact assessments are amenable to a quantitative set of economic analyses, such as projects that provide services or have a strong social dimension to them. Even when it is, other more qualitative social and political dimensions can also help explain impact. For example, collecting vital information about the social and political context, including the underlying policy landscape and processes, under which impact is being evaluated, can be particularly useful at answering questions about "why" and "how" a strategy or project may have failed or succeeded—rather than simply "what" caused it. In this context, the efficiency and effectiveness of program interventions and projects can also be evaluated.

Some examples of qualitative approaches for impact evaluation include rapid appraisal techniques (e.g. through civil society report cards), surveys of targeted beneficiaries to measure perceptions of impact (Maredia 2009; White 2006); use of impact pathway approaches to better understand processes and behavior; and the application of a sustainable livelihoods framework that considers a broader set of social and political explanations, in addition to the economic ones, in assessing a project's impact on welfare outcomes (Adato and Meinzen-Dick 2007).

Unfortunately, the subjective nature of gathering information, including the lack of good statistical properties in validating results, often implies that the information generated and lessons learned are not always easily transferrable (Maredia 2009).

Given the range of approaches to developing an M&E framework and ultimately assessing impact, the choice of what to use will always depend on: the agricultural strategy and corresponding range of policies and investments underlying it; the questions being asked; level of complexity in the known causal relationships; data availability, frequency, and type; existing tools; the skills of the analysts involved; the budget and costs allocated for M&E; the time horizon for data collection and analysis; and individual country circumstances with regard to the social and political landscape and policy processes. With this knowledge, decisionmakers, technical analysts, and the key stakeholders involved, must together decide on which approach and what tools provide the most robust and cost effective M&E for the particular agricultural strategy in mind. This is where the 'knowledge support system' concept and approach of SAKSS becomes more relevant.

3 The Knowledge Support System Concept and Approach

The 'knowledge support system' component of SAKSS describes a network of individuals and institutions that service the need for strategic analysis and information during the formulation and implementation of agricultural strategies. The network includes a range of individuals (researchers, policymakers, and development practitioners) and organizations (government agencies, research institutes, universities, development organizations, and private and civil society groups). These individuals and organizations are linked through this network under the shared interest of seeking tangible solutions to the challenges facing the agricultural sector.

Three core activities undertaken by the SAKSS network include collaborative strategic analysis, capacity strengthening, and dialogue. Through these activities relevant information from research findings and data analysis is compiled, synthesized, and packaged into evidence that enriches the dialogue on future agricultural priorities in a timely reliable fashion. The collaborative and participatory manner involved is intended to: help validate the relevant questions being asked by policymakers and civil society and the tools of analysis, data sources and assumptions, needed to address such questions; instill confidence in the evidence generated; and ultimately, enrich the capacity to generate and utilize analytical tools and evidence in the process of formulating and implement agricultural strategies.

Applications of this at the country and regional level exist. For example, a number of regional SAKSS nodes (or ReSAKSS) have focused much of their attention in mobilizing networks of individuals and organizations associated with the CAADP agenda at the regional level. Through these networks and a number of workshop forums, the nodes are helping to fill critical knowledge gaps, as well as bringing together a stock of knowledge, expertise, and tools, as countries begin to shape and align their agricultural strategies within the CAADP framework. A website brings together the information being collected to promote peer review across countries and updates on the progress of CAADP implementation (see www.resakss.org). The networks are in turn helping to establish country SAKSS nodes that are intended to strengthen a country's own ability to generate and provide strategic analysis, monitor key indicators, and assess impact of ongoing efforts against the principals and goals of CAADP.

3.1 Linking Evidence with Policymaking

The unknown question within an individual country's own social and political context is whether there is sufficient room to maneuver in order to bring evidence to bear in local policy processes during the formulation and implementation of their agricultural strategy. How research or evidence feeds into the policy process in developing countries is not yet fully understood. Yet, the importance of it so critical given the observation that many developing countries rely very little on scientific-based evidence when making policy decisions (Juma and Clark 1995). While there is a growing body of literature that seeks to explain the research-to-policy gap in Africa, few have come up with a testable hypothesis. Case study narratives are more common. The ongoing work by the International Development Research Centre (IDRC) in Canada and the Overseas Development Institute (ODI) in the UK are particularly noteworthy. Another team of researchers from Harvard University also offer a few African examples (see Cash et al. 2003).

The common accepted viewpoint in the African literature, as elsewhere in the world, is the observation that policymaking in general is a dynamic and complex process, sometimes simply explained as a chaos of purposes and accidents (Clay and Schaffer 1984). This is because the process involves multiple actors (individuals and organizations) which are defined by local political, social (cultural and belief systems), and institutional realities (bureaucratic structures and capacities). And being about people, vested interests among a few powerful elite, corruption, and external influences, can also play a distinctive role, as they still do in many African countries (Juma and Clark 1995). Power relations (people) and ideas (based on both tacit and explicit knowledge) are therefore particularly important. In fact, scientific knowledge often only plays a marginal role in the decisionmaking process (see Sabatier 2007).

Getting a good handle of a country's own policy process, and no matter its shortcomings, is therefore an important first step to understanding how evidence-based information can play any particular role in it. The question is not simply about how to improve the transfer of research into policy and vice versa, but more so about understanding the peculiar conditions under which links between the two can be made more effective.

Although various theoretical explanations of the policymaking process offer useful perspectives and frameworks on how research becomes embedded in the policy process, we do not cover this here but refer the reader to the expanded review in Johnson and Flaherty (2011). Here we focus more is describing how the 'knowledge support system' component of SAKSS is intended to help strengthen the links and capacities for greater evidenced-based dialogue and policymaking, while also ensuring quality in the evidence generated.

Essentially, the 'knowledge support system' component of SAKSS generally describes a network of individuals and organizations that effectively connect those who know with those who need to know. How effectively this helps to bring evidence into the policy process depends on how well the individuals in the network (both the actors who know and those who need to know) and the organizations they represent (e.g. research institutions, nongovernmental organizations, private organizations, and government agencies) are linked to promote dialogue around the knowledge products (i.e. information and results of research) and policy issues.

How the SAKSS network, in particular, can serve as a 'knowledge support system' in the context of an agricultural strategy is best illustrated using the Context Evidence and Links Framework developed by ODI (Crewe and Young 2002; Court and Young 2003). The framework involves four key elements: external influence, political context, evidence and links. It is appropriate for our purpose because it describes the complex interrelationships among a diverse group of actors, given a local political context and external environment, and thus the manner in which evidence can play a role in contributing to policymaking. Nevertheless, it should be underscored that the complexities of the research and policy interface cannot be adequately represented in a single framework as it involves many other dimensions. We only use it here for illustration purposes.

From Fig. 2 below, the processes and outcomes of the planning, implementation, and M&E activities are themselves greatly influenced by the interrelationships among the three spheres in the center, including the external environment surrounding them. Leadership and governance at the top emphasizes the principal role this plays in managing the agricultural strategy process itself, which is inherently influenced directly by the political context and external environment. Usually, the leader and manager of the agricultural strategy sits in the Ministry of Agriculture or other government agency/department charged with this responsibility. The biggest challenge for leadership and governance of the agricultural strategy is to improve the integration across all three activities—planning, implementation and M&E. But also potentially influencing the outcome of this is the evidence that is being generated in the center, the links that influence the national debate, and the emergence of any changing political and socioeconomic realities. In other words, as new evidence becomes available (e.g. lack of progress or impact), or as socioeconomic and political realities change, or as new and emerging issues are brought to the forefront (e.g. via civil society groups, media), the priorities of the agricultural strategy may have to be altered.

Among the inner circles, the political context is the most critical as it describes the environment and process under which policies are made, and thus greatly affects how evidence plays any role in it (if at all). This includes factors such as political culture, extent of civil and political freedoms, vested interests, capacities of government to respond, and attitudes and incentives among officials (Young 2005). Here, the overlap of political context with evidence describes the process of "strategic analysis," drawing ideas and information from both government and the research community, past research, and the experience and knowledge of actors involved. How the two become more closely linked also depends on how well they both overlap with where 'the rubber hits the road'—the beneficiaries and interest groups of agricultural strategies, such as: development practitioners, farmers and trader groups, media, and civil society in general. On the other hand, the intersection between evidence and links can be viewed as one of discourse and dialogue (e.g. through publications, seminars, and media), while the one between the links and political context is more about advocacy (e.g. the world of campaigning and lobbying among local interest groups, media, and the broader electorate or civil society). Finally, the external environment, including the overall socioeconomic environment, as well as the influence of regional and international actors (e.g. donors), can be quite significant in the African context.

Effective linkages between evidence, dialogue, and policymaking are supposed to occur at the intersection of all three spheres, and it is here that evidence is expected to influence a policy change. The assumption is that when such links are established early enough, the evidence generated and discussed at this intersection is likely to be viewed as relevant and salient to the local context (Young 2005; Cash et al. 2003). The big challenge in most African countries is getting all three to intersect, given the poor state of evidence generation (from poor quality data, poor training and incentives, weak peer review systems), poor links (from poor communications, capacities), political context (power play, vested interests, top down bureaucracies, and elitist attitudes among officials), and external environment, especially the exaggerated influence of donors.

This is what the 'knowledge support system' component of a country SAKSS strives to achieve, in setting up an active network of key local actors (individuals and organizations) who intersect from all three spheres. Through extensive consultations and interactions in the network, activities involving strategic analysis, capacity strengthening, and dialogue are laid out. The scope of work under each of these activities draws on the active input of all stakeholders: local research partners and analysts (evidence), key government actors and agencies (political context), and stakeholder groups (links).

3.2 Supporting CAADP Implementation

The SAKSS concept was adopted in 2006 to support CAADP and its principles for promoting progress review at country level, peer review at the regional level, and mutual review at the continental level. This has involved establishing three regional SAKSS nodes (or ReSAKSS) in each of the major regional economic communities (RECs): Common Market for Eastern and Southern Africa (COMESA), Economic Community of West Africa States (ECOWAS), Southern Africa Development

Community (SADC). The ReSAKSS nodes are hosted and led by the International Institute of Tropical Agriculture (IITA) in Ibadan, Nigeria for West Africa; by the International Livestock Research Institute (ILRI) in Nairobi, Kenya for Eastern and Central Africa; and by the International Water Management Institute (IWMI), with the International Crops Research Institute for the Semi-Arid Tropics (ICRISAT), in Pretoria, South Africa for Southern Africa. IFPRI is helping to coordinate a common agenda across the three nodes, providing technical and analytical support, and helping maintain and strengthen links with a broad network of CAADP partners. An Africa-wide steering committee provides overall oversight to ensure the ReSAKSS agenda remains relevant and useful in supporting CAADP implementation.

Generally, the ReSAKSS nodes focus their activities in three main areas: Strategic analysis, Knowledge management and communications, and Capacity strengthening. The strategic analysis activities help fill critical knowledge gaps in assessing progress toward realizing the CAADP goals of allocating 10% of the national budget to agriculture, achieving a 6% annual agricultural growth rate, and meeting the first MDG of halving poverty and hunger by 2015. As part of this, the ReSAKSS helped develop a monitoring and evaluation (M&E) framework for CAADP (see Benin et al. 2010).

Under the knowledge management and communications component, ReSAKSS and its network of partners collect data on key indicators such as public spending; integrating and building upon existing data, analytical tools, and knowledge; and facilitating timely access of the knowledge by African policymakers and development partners to allow for more evidence-based decisionmaking. To this end, ReSAKSS has launched a website to share the information it generates and compiles, on these key indicators and on ARD in general (see www.resakss.org).

A number of country level analyses were also undertaken by ReSAKSS to inform country CAADP Roundtables involving Rwanda, Malawi, Kenya, Uganda, and Zambia in 2006 and 2007, and a number of West Africa countries in 2008. The results served as critical input into the stakeholder dialogue and preparations leading up to the signing of a CAADP Roundtable compact within each country (as Fig. 1 previously illustrated). Further support was also provided in helping inform each country's investment plans during the post-CAADP compact period. By the end of 2011, according to the online ReSAKSS Newsletter (resakss.wordpress.com), 22 countries had signed their country CAADP compacts, 18 have developed national agricultural investment plans, and 15 countries have held their technical reviews, out of which five (Ethiopia, Niger, Rwanda, Sierra Leone and Togo) received a total of $223.5 million from the Global Agriculture and Food Security Program (GAFSP) fund. Other countries continue to sign on to the CAADP framework, including Mozambique, which just formally launched the process on December 13th. Djibouti is the most recent country to sign on in 2012.

In 2010, ReSAKSS began a second phase of its support to CAADP implementation. Much of its activities have been have been focused on consolidating ReSAKSS as a leading knowledge platform for agricultural policy planning and implementation in Africa, more fully operationalizing the CAADP monitoring and

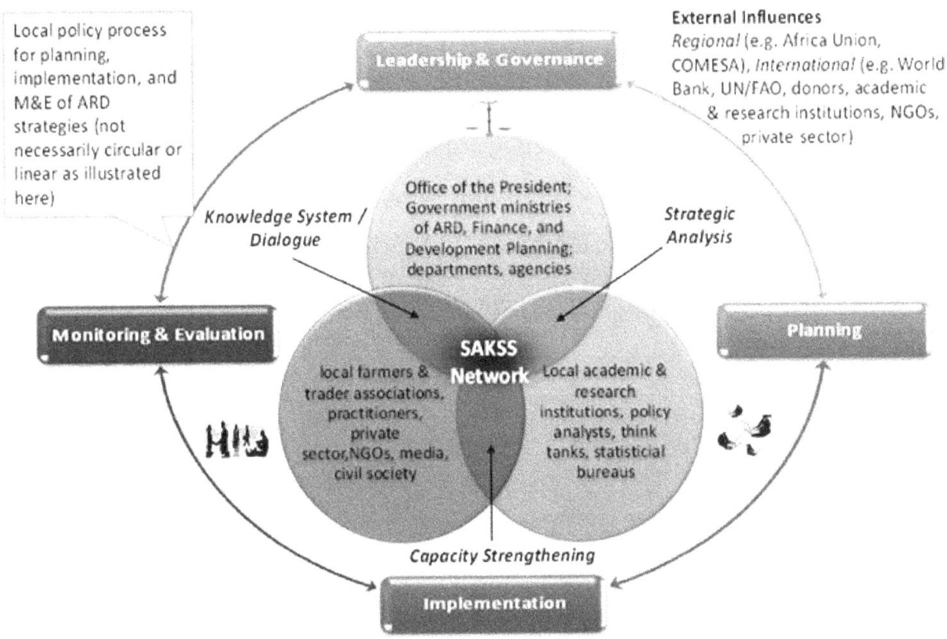

Fig. 3 The 'knowledge support system' framework. Source: Johnson and Flaherty (2011)

evaluation (M&E) system it helped develop at the country level, and providing technical assistance for the establishment of country SAKSS nodes. Because CAADP is meant to be implemented at the country level according to a country's own compacts and investment plans, a goal of the M&E system is to not only help strengthen country capacities for monitoring progress and assessing impact through their SAKSS network of partners, but ensure the adoption of standardized and measurable indicators that are consistent across different countries and regions to facilitate cross-country peer review and mutual learning.

Figure 3 provides a schematic diagram which describes the M&E system of CAADP as set up by the ReSAKSS. Developed around a theoretical framework that is described in more detail in Benin et al. (2010), the system uses a number of indicators to monitor progress of CAADP implementation: inclusive of process, policy, investment and outcome indicators being targeted at all three levels—country, regional and continental. Several important processes associated with CAADP implementation include the signing of CAADP compacts, finalizing investment plans and resource commitments. Other important milestones in the process include tracking and assessing the sorts of policy and strategic issues being raised through stocktaking exercises, reviewing the plans to address them, and assessing the roles of different stakeholders and their capacities to provide and utilize the knowledge.

In many cases, for example, capacity gaps may need to be filled through the provision of appropriate skills training and mentoring for undertaking M&E and policy analysis. These milestones, among others, are represented by the eight circular steps in the country CAADP implementation process at the bottom of the

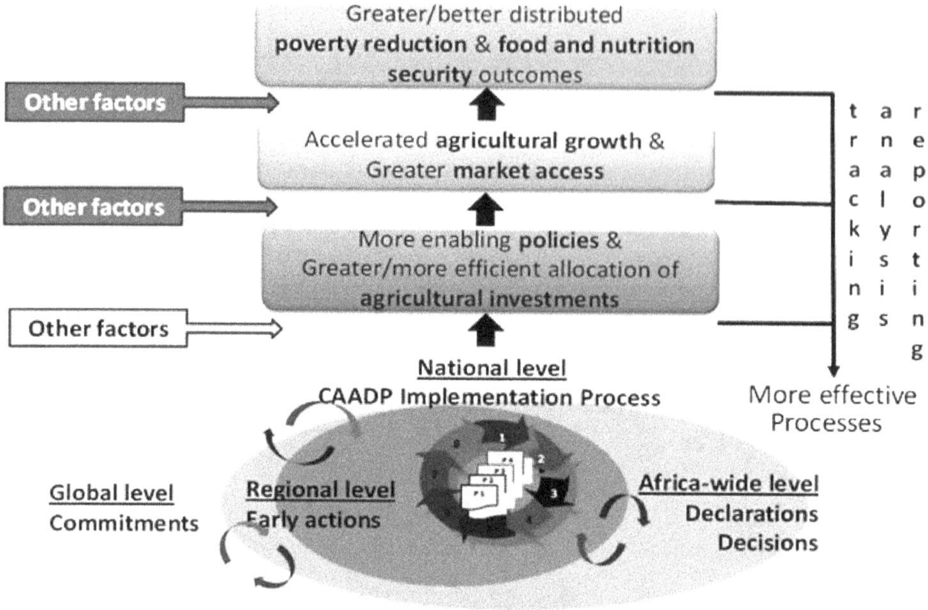

Fig. 4 Supporting the M&E of the CAADP implementation process. Source: Sam Benin, ReSAKSS slide presentation of support to CAADP M&E, 2011

figure. These help lead to increased and more efficient allocation of resources, and in turn, outputs and outcomes (Fig. 4).

The full operationalization of the CAADP M&E system is going to depend a lot on the establishment of country SAKSS nodes, particularly in those countries that have signed their country compacts and validated their investment plans. The generic setup of a country SAKSS node is intended to strengthen the capacities of national knowledge systems to undertake their own strategic analysis, M&E, and in promoting greater evidenced-based decisionmaking. A secretariat is best hosted by a local institution in order to serve the primary function of supporting its country's own need for reviewing progress of CAADP implementation. As a member of the ReSAKSS network of partners, the node is able to draw on a wide range of expertise and knowledge, as well as contribute to the ReSAKSS regional and continental efforts for CAADP M&E. Figure 5 below illustrates the generic structure of a country SAKSS node, showing the relationships between the SAKSS secretariat, in country key stakeholders, funding sources (government and development partners), and links with the broader ReSAKSS network.

3.3 *Ensuring Effective Knowledge Support Systems*

The process of establishing the ReSAKSS and country SAKSS nodes in support of CAADP implementation has relied on a number of practical principles that serve to

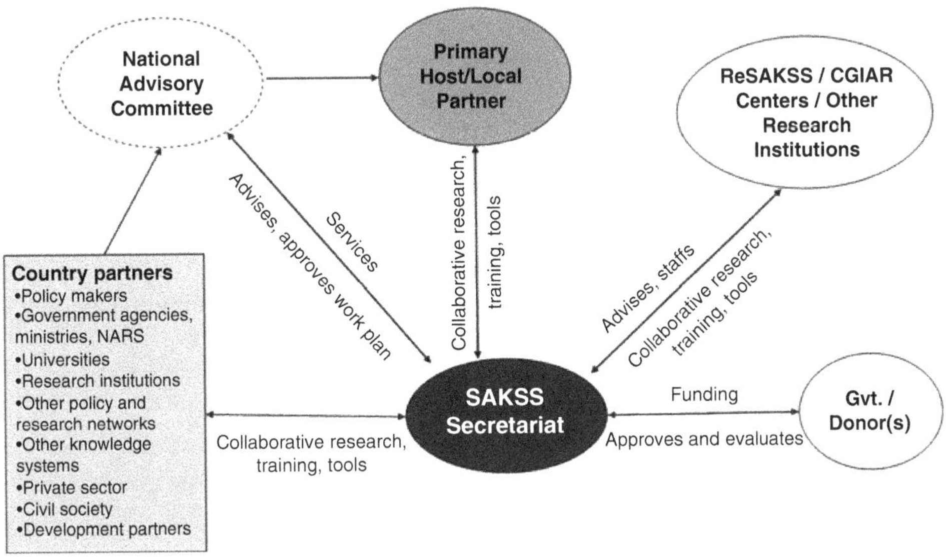

Fig. 5 A generic country SAKSS node. Source: Johnson and Flaherty (2011)

ensure an effective "knowledge support system" among its networks of partners.[2] These have been distilled from both literature surveys and IFPRI's own experiences to date with the setup of several 'country strategy support programs' in Africa; including principles of participation and collaboration, flexibility, high level dialogue and brokering, credibility and legitimacy, sustainability, and capacity strengthening.

3.3.1 Participation and Collaboration

From the beginning, the establishment of a country SAKSS node should be country-owned and driven, and its processes participatory and transparent. For example, any 'strategic analysis' and knowledge management activities should be undertaken in a collaborative manner to promote local involvement and ownership. This ensures that the evidence generated is both relevant and salient to the perspectives, concerns, and issues, of both local researchers as 'suppliers' and policymakers and their stakeholders as 'users,' and thus increasing the chances of policy impact (Cash et al. 2003; Court and Young 2003; Ryan and Garrett 2003; Wangwe 2005).

[2] While we only focus on the principles here, practical steps on how to go about setting up a country SAKSS node are discussed in more detail in Johnson and Flaherty (2011).

3.3.2 Flexibility

Because there is no 'one-size-fits-all' development model, SAKSS should always remain flexible enough to adapt to different country conditions involving institutional capacity and political context, especially as it relates to the ongoing process of strategy design and implementation. The structure of the programs and networks established must also be allowed to vary, depending on existing stock of institutional capacity and knowledge, political context of government and donor relations, level and source of funding, and awareness of the value of scientific evidence for policymaking.

3.3.3 High Level Dialogue and Brokering

Policymakers must be actively involved in helping to review and laying out the scope of work of a SAKSS node in their own country. There should be room for close overlaps between researchers/analysts and policymakers to ensure attention is paid to continuous dialogue by analysts and researchers with key policymakers, executive government officials, as well as parliamentarians. The degree of proximity of outside research institutions to in-house policy analysis units (e.g. within legislative and executive branches of government) has been found to have an important effect on how well research results are communicated and received by policymakers (Ryan 1999). At the same time, the existence of close, personal links between individuals (researchers and policymakers) can also be just as effective (Court and Young 2003; Timmer 1998). A potential disadvantage is when too close a relationship marginalizes the contributions of other researchers and research institutions, limiting the diversity of views to which policymakers have access (Stone et al. 2001).

3.3.4 Credibility and Legitimacy

Knowledge systems and formal knowledge networks should be structured in a way that adheres to the same criteria for credibility and legitimacy that is applied to policy research (Cash et al. 2003). Knowledge networks are credible when the participants represent shared and common institutional mandates rather than personal research interests. The degree of credibility is only enhanced when membership is limited to those institutions with a strong local reputation for their expertise and for their capacity to influence the policy process (Ryan and Garrett 2003).

Depending on the current state of a country's own capacity for policy analysis and research, it may be necessary to rely on foreign experts and institutions, but close links must be established with a local institutions and individuals who have the respect of the domestic policy-making community. They not only offer critical local knowledge, but are more cognizant to domestic policy concerns, and may also be viewed as being less ideologically driven as foreign institutions (Jayne et al.

1999; Wangwe 2005). On the other hand, foreign institutions can provide a basis for enhancing the credibility of the research, bringing in better access to international research resources and standards, as well as on-the-job learning, to strengthen domestic research capacity (Jayne et al. 1999). If sustained over the long term, together with sufficient higher degree training, such efforts can go a long way in promoting and sustaining a think tank culture that effectively influences national dialogue and decisionmaking about future policies and strategies.

3.3.5 Sustainability

Policy research and analysis capacity have to be built incrementally and sustainably, which means ongoing support for key government policy agencies as well as encouragement of a think-tank culture for producing high quality, policy relevant research products. Therefore, countries ultimately need to have ownership of SAKSS from the beginning to enable its principals and tools to become institutionalized within local government agencies and research institutions over time. To accomplish this, both in-country researchers (as suppliers) and stakeholders (as - end-users) need to be actively engaged early on to commit to a long-term institutionalization process that involves knowledge synthesis and generation, compiling lessons from 'learning by doing,' institutional arrangements or platform for linking research to policy, and human and institutional capacity strengthening.

3.3.6 Capacity Strengthening

The SAKSS concept is founded on the recognition that many developing countries lack the capacity to generate reliable research-based information and analysis needed to inform and guide development strategies. Therefore, strengthening the capacity of countries to provide much needed credible information and knowledge systems for strategy development and implementation must be integral to the ongoing activities of a country SAKSS node. The core assumption is that as relevant and timely information is increasingly provided from local sources to the policy dialogue and design of strategies in each region, a greater appreciation and reliance on empirical evidence would emerge and lead to sustained improvements in sector governance and policy impact over time. A SAKSS node, therefore, must play a catalytic role in developing a capacity strengthening strategy that promotes and improves the capacities of local partner institutions best placed to undertake 'strategic analysis' and bring evidence to bear during dialogue and deliberations about future development priorities.

Finally, the success of country SAKSS nodes, especially in their role as 'knowledge support systems' will ultimately depend a lot on how well they are able to establish strong ties across a diverse group of actors in their networks—throughout the process of generating credible evidence, sharing the evidence, and promoting dialogue around the evidence. It will also depend on how well they are able to understand the policy landscape and overall external influences at play within their respective countries and regions, and how they are eventually perceived by their network of partners based on the type of activities it supports and the evidence they generate.

4 Conclusion

The SAKSS concept was developed to provide a framework by which the gaps between evidence and policymaking can be narrowed through the application of 'strategic analysis' and 'knowledge support systems' approaches designed to inform and strengthen the effectiveness of agricultural strategies in Africa, and in particular, CAADP implementation. The chapter has provided a broad overview of the SAKSS concept, a review on the type of 'strategic analyses' it seeks to address, the kind of tools and approaches needed to ensure effective 'knowledge support systems' that promote evidenced-based dialogue and decisionmaking, and a guide on how to go about setting up such systems at country level.

The application of SAKSS in support of CAADP at the country (via country SAKSS nodes) and regional (via the ReSAKSS nodes) is allowing for lessons to be drawn and thus improve our understanding of how such systems can be made more effective in helping to bring evidence to bear during policy dialogue and decisionmaking processes. While it is still too soon to determine the success of these systems without a more detailed comparative analysis, especially if it can be derived from an external and independent evaluation, certain lessons and principles have emerged over time from the experiences of IFPRI in establishing the ReSAKSS and several 'country strategy support programs' in Africa. We summarize some of these here.

- Local partners must shape the relevance of a SAKSS: Key partner organizations (e.g. research institutions, government ministries, universities, and NGOs) must perceive and be engaged to help fashion its relevance and utility. Only through such levels of institutional engagement will SAKSS be able to provide improved and commonly accepted approaches that can foster, enhance, and improve synergies among the varied and multiple development efforts. Dialogue with the local policymakers, analysts, and existing networks is essential at the early stages to determine the local needs and capacity.
- Adapts to local conditions: It must be able to be institutionalized and maintained in ways that enable it to adapt to local conditions and serve as a national and regional public resource.
- Maintains broad representation of stakeholders: Its organizational and governance structure must be established in a way that allows a broad representation of key stakeholders (government, university, think tanks, development practitioners, civil society, farmer organizations, and development partners) to maintain its relevance.
- Establishes strong links with a local partner(s): It must be able to develop strong links with local partner institutions and organizations to help strengthen their

capacities to provide and sustain the SAKSS in the long run. Strong ties with local partner institutions and government bodies help maintain the relevance of a SAKSS program as country-led and owned.

- Produces collaborative quality products: The ability to maintain quality products that have been produced in close collaboration with network partners and institutions raises the credibility of the program while maintaining its relevance and utility among partners and stakeholders.
- Has a local champion: The presence of an active champion within the Steering Committee helps to establish stronger ties among the network data and analysis suppliers, as well as the relevance of its outputs among users (e.g. government agencies, policymakers, development partners).
- Inherits multiple donor support: The existence of multiple donors and a sufficient level of resources strengthen the perception of SAKSS as a general public good in support of local interests and capacity needs.
- Build credibility and trust among competing partners: A SAKSS network is not the only player in providing strategic analysis and information for informing agricultural strategies. It is therefore important to maintain a degree of transparency in reaching out to other experts who may have comparative advantage in a particular area. A SAKSS should utilize this expertise with sufficient incentive structures in place for collaboration. This could also be done in the form of organizing seminars to encourage broader participation by experts outside the network. SAKSS should refrain from giving the impression its network of partners has sufficient expertise in all areas.

Of course there is no single blueprint of a country SAKSS. The experience of existing programs highlights the unique conditions that exist within each country with respect to stakeholder needs, human and institutional capacity, current stock of knowledge, funding levels, data availability and quality, and existing relationships between government, donors, and the research community. We also emphasized the many factors that can influence the effectiveness of a SAKSS for promoting evidence-based dialogue and decisionmaking, including the political context, external influence, and relationships among individual champions and their organizational links. These ultimately shape the SAKSS each country with respect to its governance and institutional structure, relationships with local partners, and analytical agenda, for instance. Despite these differences, however, we laid out some basic principles, definitions, and objectives underlying the SAKSS concept and the process of establishing a country SAKSS. We also offered a step-by-step guideline for setting it up, drawing on the experience of existing efforts and lessons from the literature.

Finally, the operational aspects of SAKSS offer a real world opportunity to test the concept and its principles. For example, certain institutional and political economy issues, including individual and organizational interactions, emerge out of the collaboration and networking inherent in a SAKSS. From this, a number of important questions arise—what drives the interactions in such networks? What factors constrain their ability to function well (such as incentives, institutional affiliations and tensions, transaction costs, competitiveness, different underlying development paradigms, values, and approaches)? Does the type of membership mix in the networks affect the credibility of the analysis? Other challenging questions that can also arise and worth exploring further include—how can a SAKSS balance the supply of credible information (which is limited) with its demand (which is almost endless)? Can those who seek the information most also pay for it? If not, what are the tradeoffs for accepting external donor involvement and influence?

References

Adato, M., and R. Meinzen-Dick, eds. 2007. *Agricultural research, livelihoods and poverty: Studies of economic and social impact in six countries*. Baltimore, MD: Johns Hopkins University Press.

Alston, J.M., G.W. Norton, and P.G. Pardey. 1995. *Science under scarcity*. Ithaca, NY: Cornell University Press.

Alston, J. M., T. J. Wyatt, P. G. Pardey, M. C. Marra, and C. Chan-Kang. 2000. *A meta-analysis of rates of return to agricultural R&D: Ex Pede Herculem?* IFPRI Research Report 113. Washington, DC: International Food Policy Research Institute.

Anderson, E., P. de Renzio, and S. Levy. 2006. *The role of public investment in poverty reduction: Theories, evidence and methods*. ODI Working Paper 263. London, UK: Overseas Development Institute.

AU/NEPAD (Africa Union/New Partnership for Africa's Development). 2005. *Guidance note for agriculture expenditure tracking system in African countries*. Midrand: African Union (AU) and New Partnership for Africa's Development (AU/NEPAD).

Babu, S.C., and P. Pinstrup-Andersen. 1994. Food security and nutrition monitoring: A conceptual framework, issues and challenges. *Food Policy* 19 (6): 218–233.

Bell, C., P.B.R. Hazell, and R. Slade. 1982. *Project evaluation in regional perspective*. Baltimore, MD: Johns Hopkins University Press.

Benin, S., M. Johnson, B. Omilola, and the Technical Working Group (TWG) Members. 2010. *Monitoring and evaluation (M&E) system for the comprehensive Africa agriculture development programme (CAADP)*. ReSAKSS Working Paper 6. Washington, DC, USA: Regional Strategic Analysis and Knowledge Support System, facilitated by the International Food Policy Research Institute.

Benin, S., J. Thurlow, X. Diao, C. Lungren, and F. Simtowe. 2008a. *Agricultural growth and investment options for poverty reduction in Malawi*. IFPRI Discussion Paper 794. Washington, DC: International Food Policy Research Institute.

Benin S., A. Nin Pratt, S. Fan, C. Breisinger, T. Mogues, J. Thurlow, and X. Diao. 2008b. *Growth and poverty reduction impacts of public investments in agriculture and rural areas: Assessment techniques, tools and guide for practitioners*. ReSAKSS Working Paper 7. Washington, DC: Regional Strategic Analysis and Knowledge Support System, facilitated by the International Food Policy Research Institute.

Bolwig, S., P. Hazell, and S. Wood. 2002. *Strategic assessment of land use options for Uganda – Strategic criteria for rural investment in productivity (SCRIP) phase I*. Project document. Washington, DC: International Food Policy Research Institute.

Brinkerhoff, D. 1996. Process perspectives on policy change: Highlighting implementation. *World Development* 24 (9): 1395–1401.

Byerlee, D. 2000. Targeting poverty alleviation in priority setting for agricultural research. *Food Policy* 25: 429–445.

Cash, D.W., W.C. Clark, F. Alcock, N.M. Dickson, N. Eckley, D.H. Guston, J. Jager, and R.B. Mitchell. 2003. Knowledge systems for sustainable development. *Proceedings of the National Academy of Sciences* 100 (14): 8086–8091.

Chamberlin, J., J. Pender and B. Yu. 2006. *Development domains for Ethiopia: Capturing the geographical context of smallholder development options.* DSGD Discussion Paper 43. Washington, DC: International Food Policy Research Institute.

Clay, E., and B. Schaffer, eds. 1984. *Room for maneuver: An exploration of public policy in agriculture and rural development.* London: Heinemann.

Court, J., and J. Young. 2003. *Bridging research and policy: Insights from 50 case studies.* Working Paper 213. London: Overseas Development Institute.

Crawford, P., and P. Bryce. 2003. Project monitoring and evaluation: A method for enhancing the efficiency and effectiveness of aid project implementation. *International Journal of Project Management* 21: 363–373.

Crewe E., and J. Young. 2002. *Bridging research and policy: Context, evidence and links.* ODI Working Paper 173. London: Overseas Development Institute.

Crosby, B. 1996. Policy implementation: The organizational challenge. *World Development* 24 (9): 1403–1415.

Dalal-Clayton, B., and S. Bass. 2002. *Sustainable development strategies: A resource book.* London: Earthscan Publications.

Deaton, A. 2009. *Instruments of development: Randomization in the tropics, and the search for the elusive keys to economic development.* Mimeo. Princeton, NJ: Princeton University, Center for Health and Wellbeing, Research Program in Development Studies.

Dorotinsky, B., and R. Floyd. 2004. Public expenditure accountability in Africa: Progress, lessons and challenges. In *Building state capacity in Africa: New approaches, emerging lessons,* ed. B. Levy and S. Kpundeh, 179–210. Washington, DC: The World Bank.

Dorward, A., J. Kydd, J. Morrison, and I. Urey. 2004. A policy agenda for pro-poor agricultural growth. *World Development* 32 (1): 73–89.

Douthwaite, B., T. Kuby, E. van de Fliert, and S. Schulz. 2003. Impact pathway evaluation: An approach for achieving and attributing impact in complex systems. *Agricultural Systems* 78: 243–265.

Duflo, E., R. Glennerster, and M. Kremer. 2008. Using randomization in development economics research: A toolkit. In *Handbook of development economics,* ed. T.P. Schultz and J. Strauss, vol. 4, 3895–3962. Amsterdam: North Holland.

Earl, S., F. Carden, and T. Smutylo. 2001. *Outcome mapping: Building learning and reflection into development programs.* Ottawa, ON: International Development Research Centre.

Fan, S., M. Johnson, A. Saurkar, and T. Makombe. 2008. *Investing in African agriculture to halve poverty by 2015.* IFPRI Discussion Paper 751. Washington, DC: International Food Policy Research Institute.

Fan, S., X. Zhang, and N. Rao. 2004. *Public expenditure, growth, and poverty reduction in rural Uganda.* DSGD Discussion Paper 4. Washington, DC: International Food Policy Research Institute.

Farrington, J., C. Thirtle, and S. Henderson. 1997. Methodologies for monitoring and evaluating agricultural and natural resources research. *Agricultural Systems* 55 (2): 273–300.

Gittinger, J.P. 1984. *Economic analysis of agricultural projects. EDI series in economic development.* Washington, DC and Baltimore, MD: The World Bank and Johns Hopkins University Press.

Jayne, T.S., M. Mukumbu, M. Chisvo, D. Tschirley, M.T.Weber, B. Zulu, R. Johannson, P. Santos, and D. Soroko. 1999. *Successes and challenges of food market reform: Experiences from Kenya, Mozambique, Zambia, and Zimbabwe.* MSU International Development Working Paper 72. East Lansing, MI: Michigan State University, Department of Agricultural Economics.

Johnson, M., R. Birner, J. Chamberlin, X. Diao, S. Fan, A. Nin-Pratt, D. Resnick, L. You and B. Yu. 2008. *Regional strategic alternatives for agriculture-led growth and poverty reduction in West Africa.* ReSAKSS Working Paper 22. Washington, DC: Regional Strategic Analysis and Knowledge Support System, facilitated by the International Food Policy Research Institute.

Johnson, M. and K. Flaherty. 2011. *Strategic analysis and knowledge support systems for agriculture and rural development in Africa: Translating evidence into action.* Food Security in Practice No.6, Washington, DC: International Food Policy Research Institute.

Juma, C., and N. Clark. 1995. Policy research in sub-Saharan Africa: An exploration. *Public Administration and Development* 15: 121–137.

Killick, T. 1976. The possibilities of development planning. *Oxford Economic Papers* 28 (2): 161–184.

Kiregyera, B. 2008. *Reforming national statistical systems in Africa: A case for making the National Statistics Offices autonomous.* Addis Ababa: United Nations Economic Commission for Africa, African Centre for Statistics.

Kusek, J.Z., and R.C. Rist. 2004. *Ten steps to a results-based monitoring and evaluation system: A handbook for development practitioners.* Washington, DC: The World Bank.

Mackay, K. 2007. *How to build M&E systems to support better government.* Washington, DC: The World Bank.

Maredia, M.K. 2009. *Improving the proof – Evolution of and emerging trends in impact assessment: Methods and approaches in agricultural development.* Background Paper prepared for the 'Millions Fed Project'. Washington, DC: International Food Policy Research Institute.

Masters, W., T. Bedingar, and J. Oehmke. 1998. The impact of agricultural research in Africa: Aggregate and case study evidence. *Agricultural Economics* 19: 81–86.

Minot, N., and B. Baulch. 2005. Poverty mapping with aggregate census data: What is the loss in precision? *Review of Development Economics* 9 (1): 5–24.

Montjoy, R., and L. O'Toole. 1979. Toward a theory of policy implementation: An organizational perspective. *Public Administration Review* 39 (5): 465–476.

Omamo, S.W. 2004. *Bridging research, policy, and practice in African agriculture.* DSGD Discussion Paper 10. Washington, DC: International Food Policy Research Institute.

Omamo, S., X. Diao, S. Wood, J. Chamberlin, L. You, S. Benin, U. Wood-Sichra, and A. Tatwangire. 2006. *Strategic priorities for agricultural development in Eastern and Central Africa.* IFPRI Research Report 150. Washington, DC: International Food Policy Research Institute.

Pender, J., P. Jagger, E. Nkonya, and D. Sserunkuuma. 2001. *Development pathways and land management in Uganda: Causes and implications.* EPTD Discussion Paper 85. Washington, DC: International Food Policy Research Institute.

Ravillion, M. 2008. *Evaluation in the practice of development.* Policy Research Working Paper 4547. Washington, DC: The World Bank.

———. 2009. Should the randomistas rule? *The Economists' Voice* 6 (2): 1–5.

Ryan, J.G. 1999. *Assessing the impact of policy research and capacity building by IFPRI in Malawi.* Impact Assessment Discussion Paper 11. Washington, DC: International Food Policy Research Institute.

Ryan, J.G., and J.L. Garrett. 2003. *The impact of economic policy research: Lessons on attribution and evaluation from IFPRI.* Impact Assessment Discussion Paper 20. Washington, DC: International Food Policy Research Institute.

Sabatier, P., ed. 2007. *Theories of the policy process.* 2nd ed. Boulder, CO: Westview Press.

Smutylo, T. 2005. Outco*me mapping: A method for tracking behavioral changes in development programs.* ILAC Brief 7. Rome: Institutional Learning and Change Initiative.

Springer-Heinze, A., F. Hartwich, J. Henderson, D. Horton, and I. Minde. 2003. Impact pathway analysis: An approach to strengthening the impact orientation of agricultural research. *Agricultural Systems* 78: 267–285.

Stone, D., S. Maxwell, and M. Keating. 2001. *Bridging research and policy*. Sussex, UK: Radcliffe House, Warwick University.

Thurlow, J., S. Benin, X. Diao, A. Kebba, and N. Ofwono. 2008a. *Agricultural growth and investment options for poverty reduction in Uganda*. IFPRI Discussion Paper 790. Washington, DC: International Food Policy Research Institute.

Thurlow, J., S. Benin, X. Diao, H. Kalinda, and T. Kalinda. 2008b. *Agricultural growth and investment options for poverty reduction in Zambia*. IFPRI Discussion Paper 791. Washington, DC: International Food Policy Research Institute.

Timmer, C. P. 1998. *Adding value through policy-oriented research: Reflections of a scholar-practitioner*. Impact Assessment Discussion Paper 4. Washington, DC: International Food Policy Research Institute.

Wangwe, S. 2005. *A review of how external agencies can influence research agendas and research policy links*. Mimeo. Dar-es-Salaam: Economic and Social Research Foundation.

White, H. 2006. *Impact evaluation: The experience of the independent evaluation group of the World Bank*. MPRA Working Paper 1111. Washington, DC: The World Bank

Wildavsky, A. 1973. If planning is everything, maybe it's nothing. *Policy Sciences* 4: 127–153.

Wingfield-Digby, P. 2007. *Towards reforming National Statistical Agencies and Systems: A survey of best practice countries with effective National Statistical Systems in Africa*. Harare: African Capacity Building Foundation.

Wood, S., and J. Chamberlin. 2003. Enhancing the role of spatial analysis in strategic impact assessment: Improving data resolution for regional studies. *Quarterly Journal of International Agriculture* 42 (2): 167–187.

Wood, S., K. Sebastian, F. Nachtergaele, D. Nielsen, and A. Dai. 1999. *Spatial aspects of the design and targeting of agricultural development strategies*. EPTD Discussion Paper 44. Washington, DC: International Food Policy Research Institute.

World Bank. 2004. *Monitoring and evaluation: Some tools, methods and approaches*. Washington, DC: The World Bank.

You, L., S. Wood, U. Wood-Sichra, and J. Chamberlin. 2007. Generating plausible crop distribution maps for sub-Saharan Africa using a spatial allocation model. *Information Development* 23 (2/3): 151–159.

Young, J. 2005. Research, policy and practice: Why developing countries are different. *Journal of International Development* 17: 727–734.

Michael E. Johnson is Director of Research in the Food and Nutrition Security Unit at CARE USA. Previously, he was a Senior Research Fellow in the Development Strategy and Governance Division at IFPRI where he conducted research on various topics including technology adoption and spillovers, knowledge systems and policy process, agro-industry and value chains, and input markets. His contribution to this book is based on the research he undertook while he was at International Food Policy Research Institute (IFPRI).

13

Summary and Future Perspectives

Christian Henning and Ousmane Badiane

> *"Until we understand why our society adopts its policies, we will be poorly equipped to give useful advice on how to change those policies."*
>
> George J. Stigler in "The Citizen and the State." Chicago: University of Chicago Press, p. ix, 1975

This book started with the key challenges for African leaders endorsing the Comprehensive Africa Agriculture Development Programme (CAADP) to make CAADP work. These challenges include at least two aspects. First, to identify, among the programs that do work, those that provide the best value for money. Second, to achieve political feasibility (i.e. to effectively implement identified evidence-based policies). These challenges are not only relevant for political practitioners, but also imply methodological challenges for scientists for at least two reasons. First, linking economic analysis to policy formulation and outcome is a very complex and tedious process. The problem is not just one of applying rigorous economic theory to high-quality data in order to tackle relevant questions. This is difficult enough but may still be the easiest part. A greater challenge is for the knowledge and insights generated from policy research and analysis to find their way into the decision-making process. And even when it does, science-based evidence forms only one part, and often not the most important part, of the understanding that influences the decision-making process, where imperfect political competition often induces biased incentives for politicians, thereby impeding the implementation of available best-practice politics.

In this context this book examines the methodological challenges to analyze and understand simultaneously both which policies work best and why and how these policies can be effectively implemented given the political and economic

C. Henning (✉)
Department of Agricultural Economics, University of Kiel, Kiel, Germany
e-mail: chenning@ae.uni-kiel.de

O. Badiane
International Food Policy Research Institute (IFPRI), Washington, DC, USA

framework conditions in a country. Overall, the following main results can be summarized from the different contributions to this volume.

1 Growth-Poverty Linkages

In line with existing studies (e.g. Diao et al. 2012), the applied CGE modeling approaches highlight the importance of agricultural growth in achieving pro-poor growth in Africa. However, extended linked micro-macro approaches also show that understanding the relative importance of agricultural versus nonagricultural growth also depends on the analysis of economic interlinkages between poor households and the agricultural and nonagricultural sectors. These linkages can be rather complex. In particular, they include household labor market responses to economic shocks as well as nutrition-growth-poverty linkages. Moreover, analyzing public investments that promote technical progress to achieve poverty reduction reveals that agricultural subsectors are key, because investments promoting t.p. in these subsectors are comparatively productive, while vice versa many nonagricultural sectors are characterized by a high potential for achieving pro-poor growth (i.e. assuming exogenous growth for these sectors implies a high impact on poverty reduction) but the investment required to achieve growth is much higher when compared to investments in agriculture. Nevertheless, analyses imply that the classical agriculture-nonagriculture nexus is too simple (i.e. an efficient pro-poor growth [PPG] strategy needs to target specific agricultural and nonagricultural sectors).

2 Policy-Growth Linkages

Promoting pro-poor growth in Africa demands public investment. In particular, to achieve the Millennium Development Goals, public investment in agriculture needs to be significantly increased in almost all African states analyzed in this book, though to different degrees. However, beyond total public investments in agriculture the composition of the agricultural budget is also crucial to guarantee an optimal investment strategy. The latter applies not only to the allocation of budget resources across agricultural and nonagricultural policy programs, but also to the allocation of resources across different CAADP policy programs. For example, microeconometric analyses undertaken for Uganda highlight the importance of agricultural extension services. Furthermore, extended econometric approaches undertaken for Malawi reveal that optimal composition of public investments crucially depend on specific policy-growth and growth-policy linkages, which are country specific. Accordingly, it is impossible to identify a set of key policies that fits all African countries, but rather each country needs to identify its own optimal PPG strategy. Thus, while a focus on investment in agricultural extension may work for Uganda, making CAADP work in Malawi requires major investments in rural infrastructure as well as in water and land management. Beyond the identification of optimal pro-poor growth strategies, the understanding of the political processes involved in formulating and implementing these policies is essential.

3 Incentives Versus Knowledge Gaps

Based on analyses undertaken in this book, political decision-making regarding public investment in agriculture and nonagriculture are determined by three components: first, political incentives of governments to invest and second, political knowledge regarding the impact of different policies on growth and poverty reduction. Thirdly, beyond incentives and knowledge realized, PPG strategies also depend on financial resources available to national governments. Accordingly, the persisting inefficient policies observed in many African countries is the result of a lack of both adequate incentives and political knowledge and also lack of sufficient financial resources. In contrast to existing political economy studies mainly focusing on incentive gaps, e.g. biased incentives in favor of special interests at the expense of the poor, the application of a CGPE approach to the CAADP reform process in Malawi implies that inefficient policies mainly result from knowledge gaps, while biased incentives play only a minor role. In particular, at least in the Malawi case, adequate political knowledge does not presently exist either in the political system or the science sector, but must be generated in a dynamic policy learning process.

4 Stakeholders Play an Important Role in Participatory Policy Processes Determining Governmental Performance

Stakeholders influence governmental incentives to invest in specific programs and sectors via lobbying. Moreover, stakeholders also impact final policy decisions via influencing the political beliefs of politicians (i.e. their applied political knowledge). Politicians apply policy beliefs (i.e. simple mental models) to understand the impact of different policies on poverty and growth, where politicians update their beliefs via communication learning through policy networks. Especially, national research and international donor organizations take a central position in political communication networks and hence exert a strong influence on the final policy beliefs of powerful politicians. In contrast, private interest groups (e.g. farm organizations), which are not as central to political communication networks, influence the political incentives of governments to invest in specific CAADP policy programs mainly via lobbying.

However, given the fact that none of involved stakeholder and governmental organizations cumulates the total political knowledge (i.e. perfectly understands which specific combination of policies works best for Malawi), shifting political power to the research, donor or national stakeholders would not imply more efficient or effective policy outcomes. What is needed to find practical solutions is an institutionalized communication process that allows for a productive combination of individual knowledge among stakeholders via an interactive exchange of ideas especially among political practitioners and scientific researchers.

5 Voter Behavior Is Another Important Determinant of Governmental Performance

Closing the knowledge gap is a necessary but not sufficient condition to make CAADP work. However, given the fact that most African states nowadays are truly democratic, the political feasibility of development policies depends on the electoral responses of the voters. Hence, any comprehensive understanding of the political economy of major policy reforms like CAADP has to take into account the electoral responses of different social groups.

In this book we show that understanding how voter behavior impacts governmental incentives means understanding how voters cast their votes. Analyzing voter behavior (i.e. electoral responses to governmental policies and induced policy outcomes) implies that electoral responses of voters to governmental policies are determined by the relative importance of non-policy oriented voting motives in comparison to policy-oriented voting motives. The more voters base their votes on non-policy issues, the more they can be influenced by campaigning. Hence, elected politicians have high incentives to deliver policies that serve the interests of influential interest groups (i.e., the latter are influential in the sense that they control the voting behavior of their clientele). Hence, governmental policy is highly influenced by the lobbying activities of special interest groups. However, if voters engage in retrospective voting (i.e. base their votes on observed economic performance), the government has a high incentive to deliver good policies (i.e. policies that really work and serve the public interest). As a corollary, retrospective voting implies a high incentive for governments to engage in policy learning. Finally, beyond non-policy oriented voting, voters engage in policy-oriented voting (i.e. they base their evaluation of parties competing in election on party platforms). Policy-oriented voting implies an incentive for elected politicians to deliver policies desired by a majority of voters. However, policy-oriented voting does not necessarily imply efficient policy outcomes. To the contrary, compared to politicians and stakeholders, the average voter is a layman when it comes to development policies like CAADP. Accordingly, policy positions preferred by voters are based on naïve beliefs about how different policies work and therefore can be extremely inefficient. Nevertheless, in political reality the more voters base their votes on non-policy issues, the less is their joint political weight vis-a-vis organized interest groups in determining governmental policy choices. Moreover, to the extent that the relative importance of non-policy voting varies systematically across social groups (e.g. poor versus rich), the relative political weights of social groups also differ. Hence, government capture basically results from the relative importance of non-policy voting.

Empirical analyses of voter behavior undertaken for Malawi implies that the electoral choices of Malawian voters are mainly driven by non-policy issues with an average importance of 66% followed by policy-oriented voting with an average importance of 30%. Very little importance resulted for retrospective voting with an average importance of only 4%. Therefore, governmental incentives are mainly oriented towards interest groups with a total weight of 60% compared to only 40% for the total voter population. However, voter behavior varies systematically across social groups implying different relative political weights across voters. Interestingly, empirical estimations imply that the Malawian government is less captured by rich versus poor or rural versus urban populations, but rather by specific regional and ethnic groups. In particular, the North is significantly underrepresented, while the Chewa and Yao tribes as well as the central region seem to be politically overrepresented.

Nevertheless, based on our empirical results, the political feasibility of CAADP options in Malawi still significantly depends on voters' choices given the fact that policy-oriented voting counts for 40% of voters' electoral responses. Our results clearly imply that the less voters rely on non-policy indicators and the more they base their electoral choices on party policy platforms and evaluate the competence of the government based on observed economic development, the more electoral competition induces incentives for the government to implement policies that correspond to the policy preferences of the majority of the society.

However, our analyses also reveal that a high political representation of voters' policy preferences by the government does not necessarily imply that the government implements the most efficient policies. The latter conclusion results from the fact that voters' policy preferences might be biased. Interestingly, taking biased voter beliefs into account, a high importance of lobbying in combination with governmental leadership that is driven by its own intrinsic political vision might induce more efficient policy choices while simultaneously decreasing governmental performance, as defined in terms of capture and accountability. The highly recognized work of Caplan draws the rather pessimistic conclusion that democratic mechanisms of preference aggregation naturally lead to the choice of inefficient policies. Hence, the analysis of voter beliefs is an important topic of our future research.

6 Donor Funding Can Contribute to Ensuring the Political Feasibility of Efficient Pro-Poor Growth Strategies

Promoting pro-poor economic growth strategies in the future requires investments today. These investment have to be financed. Ensuring there is sufficient funding is a major concern in most African countries (see Benin and Yu 2012). In Malawi, as in most African countries, a large share of financial resources used for project funding is provided by development partners. If donors neglect their commitments, funding by the government only would result in far lower allocation of the total budget to policy programs promoting growth in both agriculture and nonagriculture. In contrast, the large part of the state budget is spent on the provision of public good services such as social and health services. Naturally, the latter has strong political implications. Thus, donors play a key role in determining political feasibility of an optimal PPG strategy, since governmental incentives for public investment are crucially determined by external funds provided by donors.

7 From Political Diagnosis to Therapy

If policy failure is dominated by knowledge gaps, while biased political incentives have only minor importance, formal political institutions (e.g. constitutional rules like electoral rules or legislative procedures) have little impact on political performance. By the same argument, a simple increase in the political influence of any stakeholder organization will also be ineffective. Furthermore, if neither the policy beliefs of policymakers nor the parameter specifications of scientific models correspond to the true political technology, adequate political knowledge does not yet exist neither in the scientific system nor in political praxis and thus must be created in the political process. Designing effective observational policy learning is facilitated by an effective monitoring and evaluation system. However, even with an appropriate M&E system, observational learning often takes a long time and hence is extremely costly. Therefore, beyond observational learning, communication learning is also important. The latter requires an interactive exchange between scientific modelers, politicians and stakeholders. To facilitate this exchange, innovative communication tools, such as computer-based policy toolkits like CAADP-lab, or participatory policy processes including politicians and stakeholders as well as research and donor organizations are required.

8 Innovative Methodological Approaches

The challenge of empirically analyzing and designing participatory and evidence-based policy processes is the development of an applicable model framework that first enables a comprehensive political diagnosis (i.e., the identification of the principal source of low political performance in terms of incentives and knowledge gaps). Such a framework should then enable the derivation of an effective political therapy (i.e., provide tools that allow the identification of adequate strategies for reducing existing political performance gaps). The derivation of a political therapy requires quantitative modeling of the political decision-making and policy learning processes, including the endogenous formation of legislators' political preferences and policy beliefs (i.e., agents' simplified mental models for approximating the complex true relationship between policy instruments and induced policy outcomes).

Facing these methodological challenges this book develops and applies a CGPE model as a new quantitative approach to analyzing the performance of policy processes with respect to the production of efficient policy choices. In contrast to existing political economy models, which highlight the biased incentives of politicians as a principal cause of persisting inefficient policies, the CGPE approach incorporates explicitly the lack of adequate political knowledge as another important source of inefficient policy choices. Within the CGPE approach, a model of political belief formation and updating explains how political agents organized a combination of observational and communication learning processes in networks to improve their political knowledge. According to the CGPE model, the main determinants of the accumulation of political knowledge and the speed of policy learning correspond to policy network structures that reflect the communication and interaction patterns between governmental and nongovernmental organizations. Moreover, in principal a voter module can be incorporated in the CGPE approach allowing the calculation of political feasibility indices for given policy options. Beyond efficiency, political feasibility is another important aspect of evaluating policy options that work in political praxis.

9 Future Outlook and Challenges

Although we think that the work presented in this book makes a significant contribution to the modeling and evaluation of policies and political processes, it clearly has limitations which should be tackled in future work.

First, economic modeling is still rather restrictive, e.g. labor market restrictions as well as price volatility, weather shocks and other exogenous shocks including farmers' risk perception are still excluded from applied economic models. Another important aspects that should be included in future work is the interrelations of agriculture production and sustainability.

Second, although the PIF approach is certainly an improvement in modeling policy-growth linkages, present approaches are still limited. By construction, we assume that budget spending for a specific policy program (γ_i) is homogenously effective in promoting t.p. in different subsectors. However, in reality, it appears more realistic that even within specific policy programs (e.g., investments in infrastructure), different subprograms can be formulated by focusing on specific subsectors. For example, investing in the infrastructure of specific regions or investing in the railroad system versus the road system might be more or less effective for different subsectors. These differences occur because subsectors might be regionally concentrated or dependent on specific infrastructure systems. Thus, including a third stage in our PIF function that allows for sector-specific subprograms within a specific policy program corresponds to a potential extension of the PIF to deal with subsector specific effectiveness of policy programs.

Moreover, the presented PIF function does not explicitly allow the assessment of implementation efficiency. Evaluation of specific budget allocations across different policy programs depends on how programs are finally implemented. For example, investment in rural road infrastructure via building fancy roads to remote villages where no real business exists to take advantage of these roads would not have a real impact on growth. Moreover, buying cars for extension officers who have low capacities to advise farmers would also not make a big contribution to promoting farm productivity. A possible extension of the PIF approach taking implementation efficiency into account would be to incorporate a third or fourth stage corresponding to different implementation mechanisms that determine effective budget uses under various subprograms in the second or third stage.

Regarding political economy modeling, the following aspects are limitations of the current CGPE approach:

First, in its present version, the CGPE does not yet incorporate the voter module (i.e., political support functions are derived exogenously from interview data). Basically, this setup implies that political support is driven by retrospective and non-policy voting only, while policy-oriented voting is neglected. However, as demonstrated in Chapter "Voter Behavior and Government Performance in Malawi: An Application of a Probabilistic Voting Model", policy-oriented voting is an important determinant of voter behavior. Hence, voters' policy beliefs might effectively restrict politicians' policy choices. This aspect is not fully reflected in the presented CGPE analyses. Thus, incorporating the voter module and deriving political support endogenously from estimated voter behavior might imply that observed political performance is actually more restricted by biased political incentives than implied by the presented CGPE analyses. Furthermore, understanding how voters update their policy beliefs within public opinion formation (e.g. what is the role of mass media versus political campaigning and stakeholder communication within this process) is a very important and interesting aspect that needs to be analyzed in future research.

Second, although it has been demonstrated by applying the CGPE approach that interactive communication among politicians, stakeholders and researchers is important for effective policy learning, the concrete institutional organization of such interactive communication has not been analyzed yet. Thus, this is another important aspect we leave for future research.

References

Benin, S., and B.X. Yu. 2012. *Complying the Maputo declaration target: Trends in public agricultural expenditures and implications for pursuit of optimal allocation of public agricultural spending*. ReSAKSS Annual Trends and Outlook Report 2012.

Diao, X., J. Thurlow, S. Benin, and S. Fan, eds. 2012. *Strategies and Priorities for African Agriculture: Economywide Perspectives from Country Studies*. Washington, DC: International Food Policy Research Institute (IFPRI).

Christian Henning is professor and chair of agricultural economics, University of Kiel (Germany). He studied economics, agricultural economics, sociology, political science and mathematics. He earned a PhD in economics, in agricultural economics and in political science. His main areas of specialization are applied political economy and applied economic modelling of agricultural policies. To date he has published five books and various articles in refereed journals including PLoS ONE, American Journal of Agricultural Economics, European Review of Agricultural Economics, Journal of Public Policy, Journal of Mathematical Sociology and Journal of Theoretical Politics.

Ousmane Badiane is the Director for Africa at the International Food Policy Research Institute (IFPRI), based in Washington, D.C. He oversees the Institute's regional offices for West and Central Africa, in Dakar, Senegal, and Eastern and Southern Africa, in Addis Ababa, Ethiopia. He received a Master's Degree and PhD in agricultural economics from the University of Kiel in Germany. His awards include being selcted as a 2015 Yara Prize Laureate, a Doctoral Degree Honoris Causa from the University of KwaZulu Natal in South Africa and induction as Distinguished Fellow of the African Association of Agricultural Economics.

Permissions

All chapters in this book were first published in DPPPAME, by Springer; hereby published with permission under the Creative Commons Attribution License or equivalent. Every chapter published in this book has been scrutinized by our experts. Their significance has been extensively debated. The topics covered herein carry significant information for a comprehensive understanding. They may even be implemented as practical applications or may be referred to as a beginning point for further studies.

The contributors of this book come from diverse backgrounds, making this book a truly international effort. We would like to thank all the contributing authors for lending their expertise to make the book truly unique. They have played a crucial role in the development of this book. Without their invaluable contributions this book wouldn't have been possible. They have made vital efforts to compile up to date information on the varied aspects of this subject to make this book a valuable addition to the collection of many professionals and students.

This book was conceptualized with the vision of imparting up-to-date and integrated information in this field. To ensure the same, a matchless editorial board was set up. Every individual on the board went through rigorous rounds of assessment to prove their worth. After which they invested a large part of their time researching and compiling the most relevant data for our readers.

The editorial board has been involved in producing this book since its inception. They have spent rigorous hours researching and exploring the diverse topics which have resulted in the successful publishing of this book. They have passed on their knowledge of decades through this book. To expedite this challenging task, the publisher supported the team at every step. A small team of assistant editors was also appointed to further simplify the editing procedure and attain best results for the readers.

Apart from the editorial board, the designing team has also invested a significant amount of their time in understanding the subject and creating the most relevant covers. They scrutinized every image to scout for the most suitable representation of the subject and create an appropriate cover for the book.

The publishing team has been an ardent support to the editorial, designing and production team. Their endless efforts to recruit the best for this project, has resulted in the accomplishment of this book. They are a veteran in the field of academics and their pool of knowledge is as vast as their experience in printing. Their expertise and guidance has proved useful at every step. Their uncompromising quality standards have made this book an exceptional effort. Their encouragement from time to time has been an inspiration for everyone.

The publisher and the editorial board hope that this book will prove to be a valuable piece of knowledge for students, practitioners and scholars across the globe.

Index

www.ingramcontent.com/pod-product-compliance
Lightning Source LLC
LaVergne TN
LVHW080643210926
848485LV00003B/312